Map of Sicily

Historical map of Sicily and the Lipari Islands

INSULÆ LIPAREÆ, quæ olim ÆOLIÆ et VULCANIÆ

RUINÆ
Urbium, Oppidorum et Pagorum,
Quæ Anno 1693. die 9, 10 et 11 Ianuary in Regno Siciliæ
horribili Terræ Motu lapsæ
cum centum millibus hominum corruerunt.

Palermo	Spacca furno	la Prage
Messina	S. Croce	Mascalsi
Taurminia	Vittoria	Torre di grillo
Catanea	Chiaramonte	Borello
Augusta	Comite	Pedasa
Lentini	Monte rosso	Nicgrande
Syracusa	Guarratone	Vilcastagne
Ragusa	la Forza	S. Antonio
		la Gadena

The Baroque Architecture of Sicily

The Baroque Architecture of Sicily

Maria Giuffrè

Photographs by
Melo Minnella

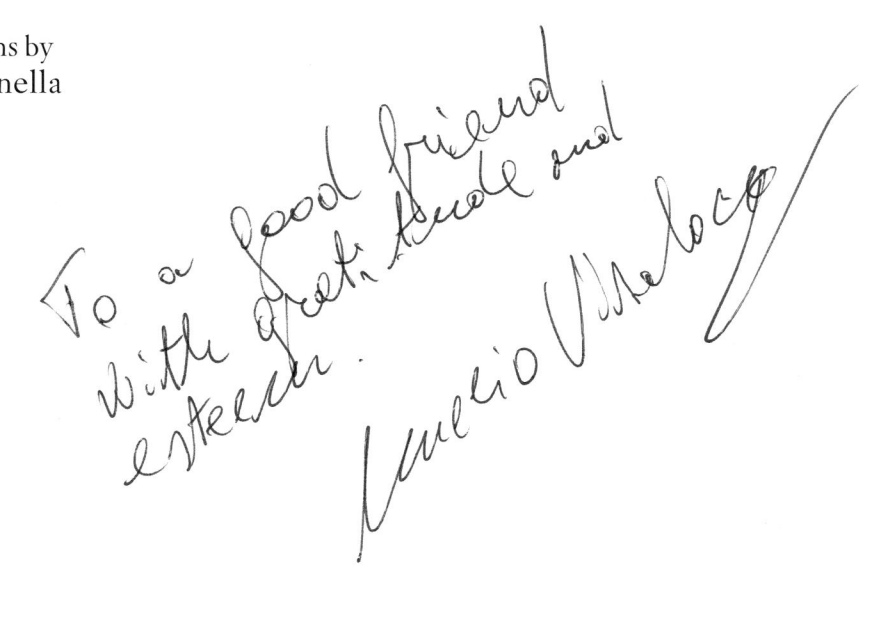

Thames & Hudson

Translated from the Italian *Barocco in Sicilia*

First published in the United Kingdom in 2007 by
Thames & Hudson Ltd,
181A High Holborn,
London WC1V 7QX
www.thamesandhudson.com

First published in 2008 in hardcover in the
United States of America by Thames & Hudson Inc.,
500 Fifth Avenue, New York, New York 10110
thamesandhudsonusa.com

Original edition, *Barocco in Sicilia*, written
by Maria Giuffrè, with photographs by Melo Minnella
© 2006 Arsenale Editrice

This edition © 2007 Thames & Hudson Ltd, London

All Rights Reserved. No part of this publication may
be reproduced or transmitted in any form or by any means,
electronic or mechanical, including photocopy, recording
or any other information storage and retrieval system,
without prior permission in writing from the publisher.

British Library Cataloguing-in-Publication Data
A catalogue record for this book
is available from the British Library

Library of Congress Catalog Card Number: 2007904557
ISBN: 978-0-500-34239-8

Printed and bound in Italy

Contents

A journey through Sicilian Baroque	6
The places: old and new	10
The actors: patrons, architects, and master builders	94
The buildings: tradition and revolution	152
Theory and practice: from the book to the building site	222
One history or many histories: the thousand faces of the Baroque	276
Concise bibliography	281
Index	283

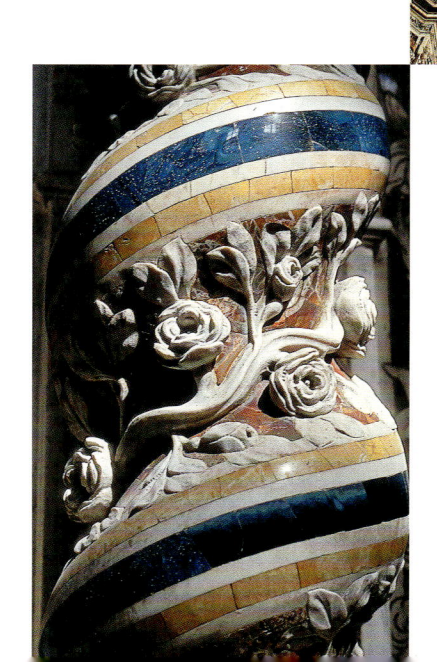

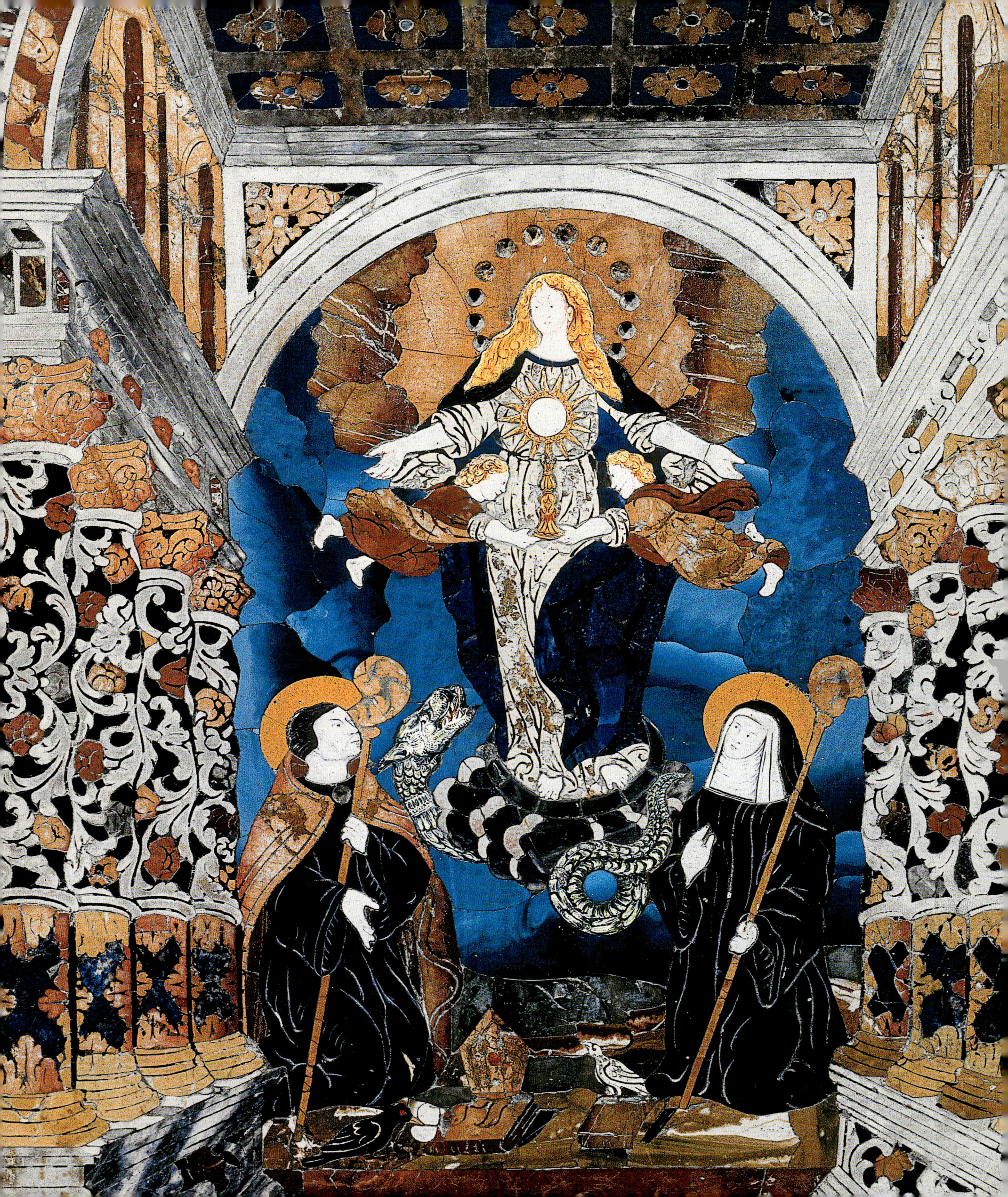

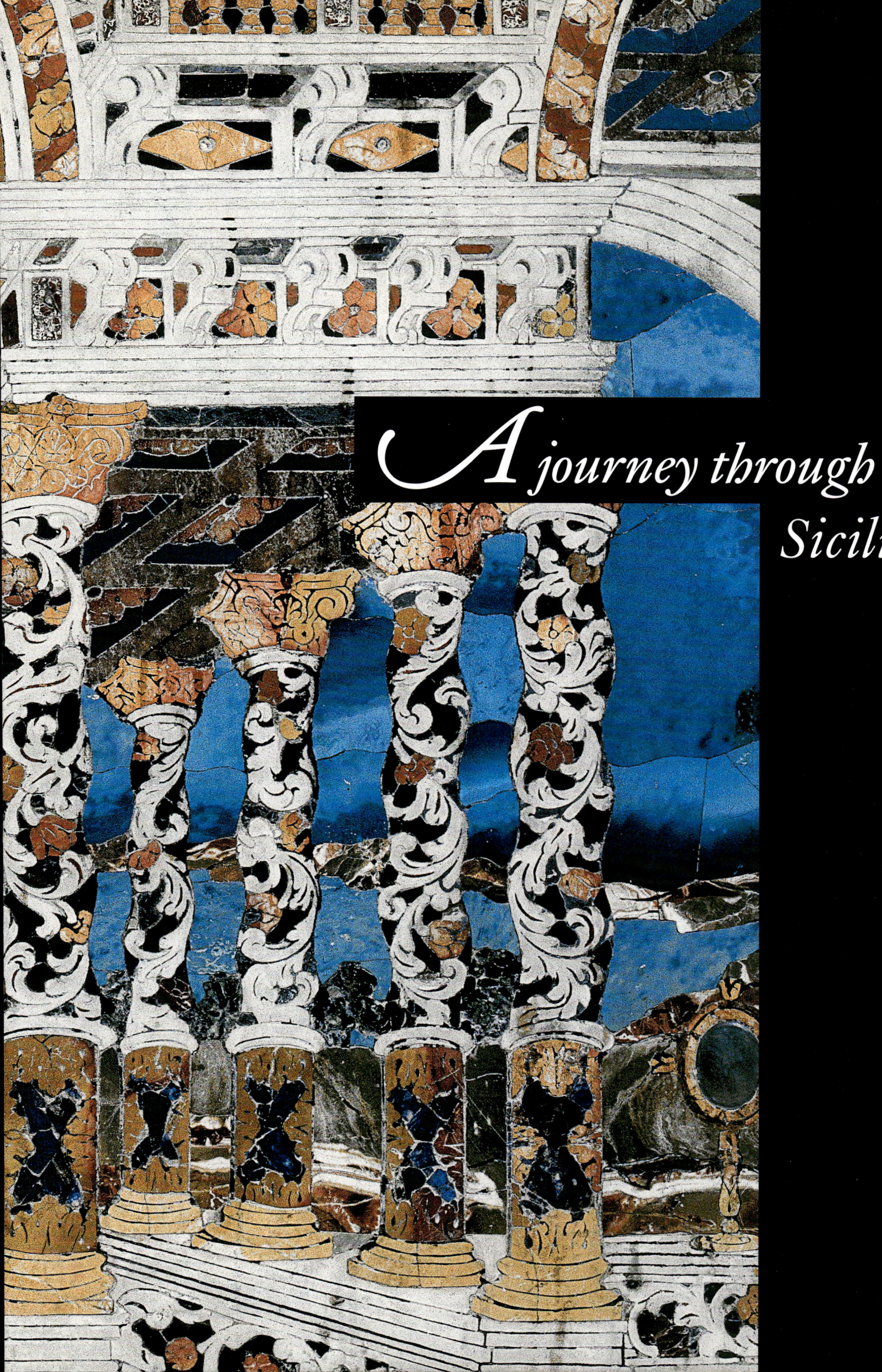

A journey through
            Sicilian Baroque

A new, richly illustrated book on Baroque in Sicily is easier to justify in the English-speaking world than it is in Italy, where the indisputable quality of that architecture is now unchallenged. In Britain and America it is still relatively unknown, with Anthony Blunt's *Sicilian Baroque* and Stephen Tobriner's *Genesis of Noto* honourable but lonely exceptions. In recent years Italian scholars have brilliantly acclaimed the originality and virtuosity of its decorative invention, in carved stone, inlaid hardstone, stucco or fresco, frequently carried out to exuberant excess. The key sites of the Baroque – Palermo, Bagheria, Trapani, Messina, the Val di Noto and the Iblei mountains – have been extensively investigated, as have the principal urban and architectural genres – towns, churches, palaces and villas – and the spatial and compositional inventions expressed in complex plans and façades, and these various themes have been analysed and assigned to distinct chronological phases.

This journey through the Baroque looks at the subject from a slightly different angle: it consists rather of a reflection on the styles and phases of the Baroque in Sicily, with a particular emphasis on the characteristics that distinguish it from parallel regional developments – the way the style was able to impose itself as the prevailing language; the desire to incorporate and experiment with international accents while retaining rich local traditions; the importance of the 'archetypical' cities in the formation of 'schools'; the legacy of the printed word, which was available to the chief actors, whether patron, architect or master builder; the role of earthquakes as occasions of urban and architectural renewal; in short, the identity of Sicily as an island without frontiers, open to all the artistic currents flowing into it from across the seas, and yet stubbornly protective of its own *genius loci*.

The traditions of the two Sicilies, west and east, which throughout ancient history had been distinguished as Punic (Carthaginian) Sicily and Greek Sicily, became substantially unified during the rebuilding of the south-eastern part of the island after the earthquake of 1693. This new unity initiated a period of intense cultural exchange throughout the island, and both large cities and small towns enjoyed the new sense of autonomy and the originality of design that characterized the eighteenth century. There is a great deal yet to be discovered about the architecture of this period, and a great deal of research still to be undertaken, and although over the years important contributions have been made by renowned scholars such as Rudolf Wittkower (1958) and Anna Maria Matteucci (1988), many of their studies are unknown to a wider public.

The writer Gesualdo Bufalino called Sicily 'an island in the plural', and this was particularly true of its multifaceted culture during the Baroque period. Palermo, which had become the undisputed political and cultural capital after the revolt of Messina against the Spanish from 1674 to 1678, is the only city that can trace an unbroken continuity, through which it is still possible to discern the many different elements resulting from foreign intervention throughout its history: Lombard and Romanesque (the latter continued to make its influence felt), Austrian and Neapolitan, depending on the political fortunes of Sicily. Thus Palermo plays a special role in the book, and not only because of the splendour of its architecture.

Everything fell under the direction of the monarchy, the church and the nobility through their cultural authority and their economic power – the monarchy in virtue of its role; the church additionally influential through the presence of architects in religious orders and the vast array of knowledge contained in the valuable libraries of the various orders; and the nobility not only because they owned great estates at home, but because they were enlightened travellers, collecting images which they purchased abroad and sent home. Inventories discovered in private libraries and public institutions all bear witness to these activities. Running parallel to this was practical experience on the building site, which served to form architects and master builders – who were usually trained in family workshops – and revealed itself periodically in decorative and constructional innovation.

According to Giulio Carlo Argan, the Baroque in Sicily 'is evidence of a 'modern' force at work, the most grandiose and audacious that the island has ever produced'. His theory, mostly formulated in the light of the extraordinary abundance of building work in the Val di Noto after the earthquake of 1693, helps to justify a renewed interest in this auspicious period of the island's history, should any justification be required. This era must be preserved in the memory and integrated into present consciousness.

A huge debt of gratitude is owed to the countless scholars, teachers, colleagues, and pupils old and young whose research has inspired many of the ideas in this book, and no acknowledgments or bibliography can do justice to the contributions that they have made. Hopefully, the goodwill between them and the authors will make up for any such omissions; indeed, it highlights the need for a forum in which to discuss one's convictions, and evaluate any conclusions reached thus far, in order to respond faithfully and accurately to the demands of historical research.

The greatest debt of gratitude can sadly only be paid posthumously: it goes to Salvatore Boscarino, for many years Professor of Architectural Restoration at the University of Palermo, who died prematurely in 2001. He dedicated his knowledge, passion and commitment to the topics presented in this book, inspiring in young students, including the authors, an enthusiasm for discovery and research. This book is therefore dedicated to Salvatore Boscarino, a master in the ways of the Baroque and a valued and unforgettable friend.

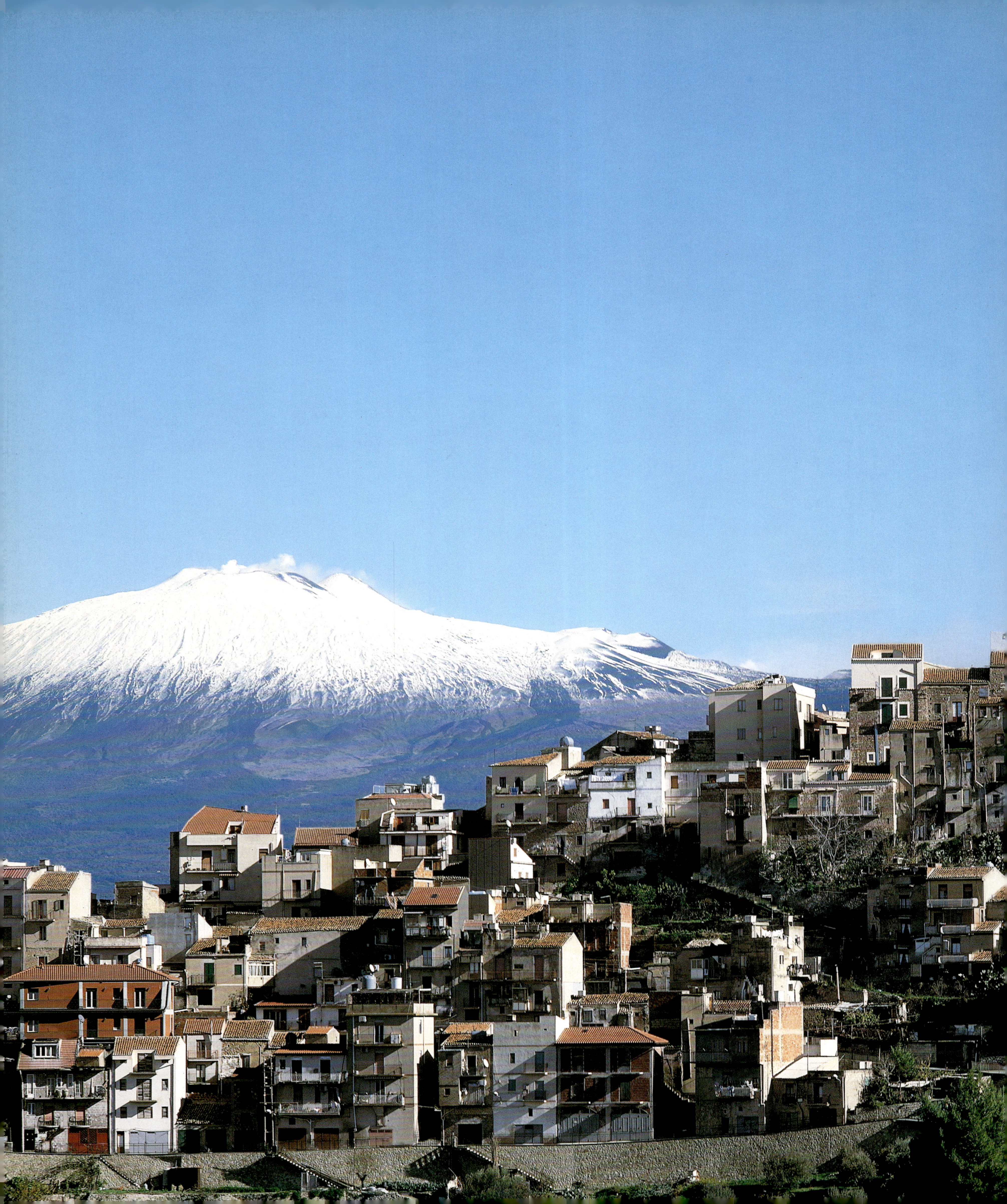

The places: old and new

12 The places: old and new

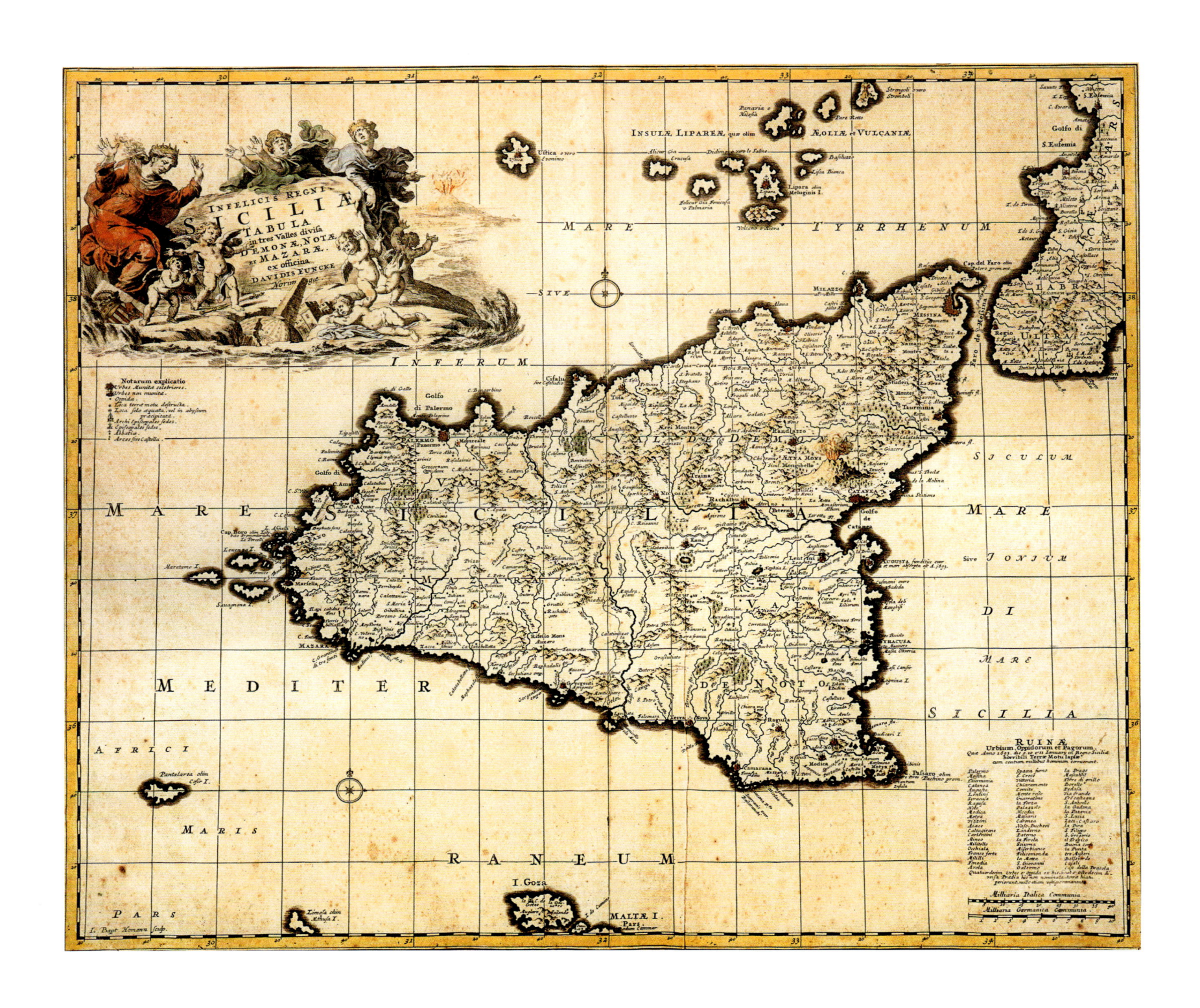

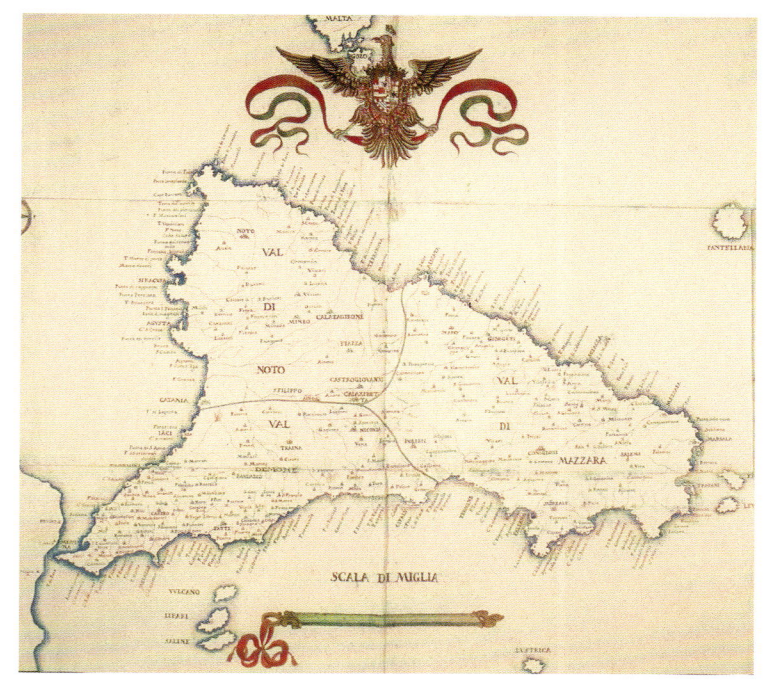

Earthquakes have struck the island throughout the centuries.

opposite A map of Sicily published in 1693. The cartouche shows buildings in ruins and weeping figures, and a list sets out all the cities damaged by the earthquake. (Parodi di Belsito collection, Palermo)

above left A Baroque building in ruins in Gibellina after the earthquake of 1968.

above right A map of Sicily with north at the bottom, from the manuscript *Teatro Geografico Antiguo y Moderno del Reyno de Sicilia*, 1686 (Archives, Ministry of Foreign Affairs, Madrid)

preceding pages The town of Centuripe, with the snow-capped peak of Etna in the background.

Sicily is an island in the Mediterranean, linked to Europe and yet separate from it, open to winds of change from north and south throughout its history. In this respect, the Baroque age was no different from any other. From the late Gothic period onwards currents from the north were stronger and more innovative; the south contributed a long and uninterrupted tradition of construction and decoration. Historical forces from different cultures merged or collided, with varied and remarkable results. These results are visible in the major coastal cities and also in the interior of the island.

The earthquake of 1693 highlighted the division between the two Sicilies, west and east. The latter lost most of its cultural heritage, and reacted by forging a new identity for itself. From that moment on, architecture developed differently in the two halves of the country, with occasional interesting points of intersection.

The two Sicilies: continuity and fragmentation

'The earthquake of 1693 was not like the many earthquakes that have struck Sicily in modern times. It was a disaster that wiped out almost every trace of the existing civilization in the south-east, which had been rooted in stone. According to an official report submitted to the Viceroy, Juan Francisco Pacheco, Duke of Uzeda, twenty cities were destroyed utterly, and fifty-eight suffered substantial damage. After a transitional phase, which relied heavily on the humanitarian and cultural assistance of other areas of the island (particularly Palermo and Messina), south-eastern Sicily set about its own reconstruction, binding up its wounds with the help of a new generation of patrons and artists.

The dominant role played by the Val di Noto in comparison with the Val Demone and Val di Mazara (Sicily's other two valleys), and even in comparison with Palermo, dates from this moment. The area was already important in late medieval times. The reason was perhaps the exceptional quality of its local stone, which stimulated the technical skills and imagination of craftsmen. Why else, in the late 15th century, would the great master Matteo Carnilivari have been summoned from Noto to restore castles and design grand palaces in Palermo? Why else would the new patrons and noble families such as the Abatellis and the Aiutamicristo have chosen not to use local craftsmen from Palermo or Messina to create the prestigious buildings they desired for themselves? Why else would Carnilivari have summoned masters from the eastern side of the island to work at his side, as if Palermo had none of its own to offer, at a time when such work was plentiful? How else to explain the involvement of an architect from Noto in work on the building known as the Steri, a palace that had belonged to the Chiaramonte family until their downfall in the 14th century, and which was subsequently used as a royal seat? And what role did Carnilivari play during his time in Agrigento, a period as yet little documented, before his arrival in Palermo? These questions have interested past and present historians, but have so far received few definite answers.

What is certain is that the phenomenon of Carnilivari, which was probably not unique in the history of the south-east in the late medieval period, helps to explain the standard of artistry displayed in a land robbed of its identity by the earthquake in 1693 – a land whose roots went deep enough for it to survive the tragedy and bear new

The places: old and new 13

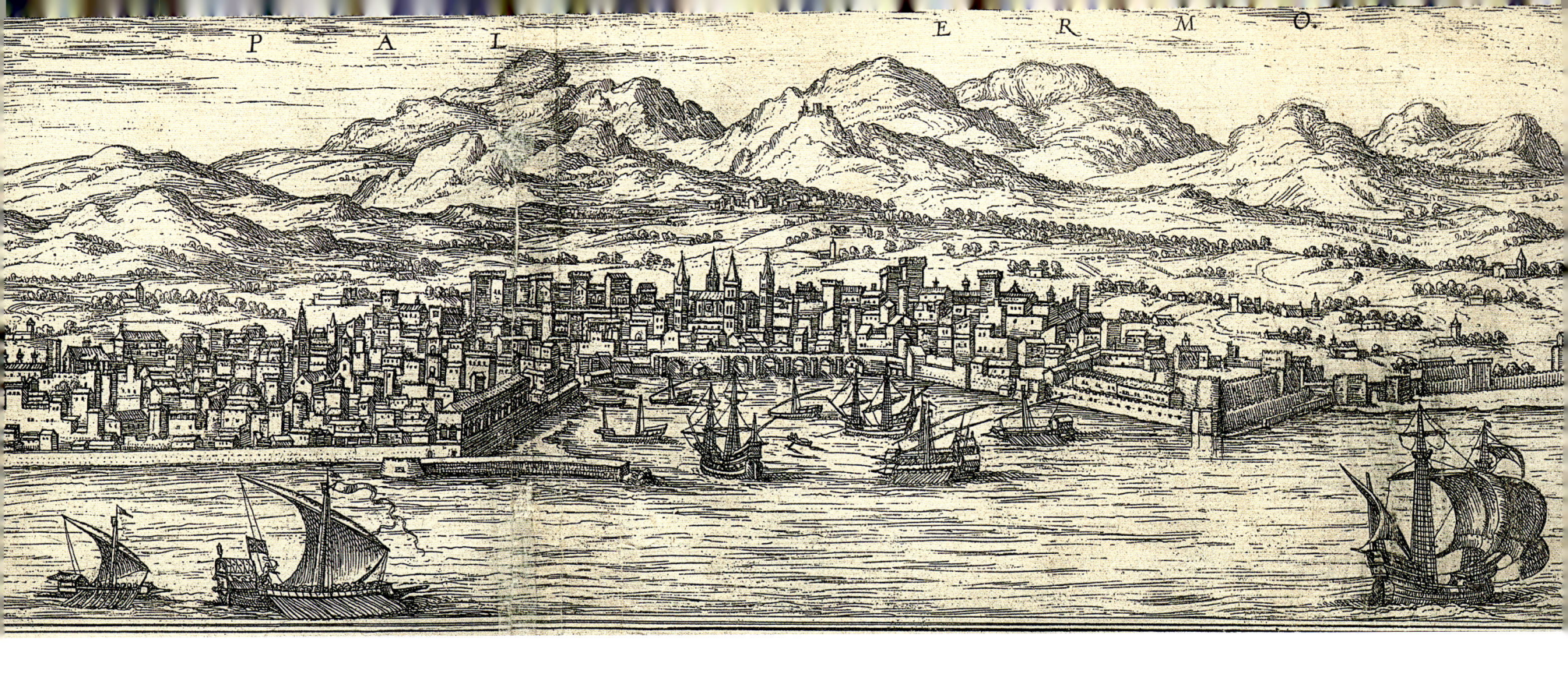

fruit. The myth of the Duke of Camastra, Viceroy of Sicily, visiting the stricken areas riding on his white horse has continued to fire the imagination, but it is only through the meticulous work of researchers in archives and the analyses of historians that the true version of events has been ascertained, and the true nature of the reconstruction process revealed.

The key role played by south-eastern Sicily after 1693, especially from the 1730s, is well documented. Such a total and immense work of reconstruction was bound to produce many ripples, both near and far, extending beyond what is generally regarded as the Baroque period. Throughout the second half of the 18th century and the whole of the 19th, this late Baroque manner marked the difference between the two Sicilies – between Palermo and the south-eastern part of the island which had been stricken by the earthquake.

At the beginning of the 17th century, which is generally seen as the start of the Baroque period, Messina had been dominant. A commercially active and culturally vigorous city, it was separated from the mainland by straits swirling with treacherous currents, yet narrow enough to serve as a link rather than a barrier, each shore being visible from the other side. Sea voyages are a means of union and trade, commerce and culture, and Messina's strength lay in its position as a port. Messina could thus aspire to be the capital of the island, as for brief spells it was the home of the viceroy, and indeed it had aspirations to be the capital of the East, a role for which it made pressing but unanswered appeals to the Spanish crown.

In 1571 Messina received the victorious Don John of Austria after the Battle of Lepanto. A bronze statue in his honour was erected, showing him treading on the head of an enemy, set on a pedestal inscribed with descriptions of the battle and celebrations of victory. It was Messina, not Palermo, which at the end of the 16th century was the first to welcome pupils and colleagues of Michelangelo, such as Giacomo Del Duca, and also sculptors and architects who represented ideas beyond classicism.

At the beginning of the 17th century Messina was in a position to undertake construction on a scale unparalleled in Italy. The magnificent Palazzata, on the waterfront, expressed the civic pride of the city, and in dispensing with its old defensive walls, Messina showed itself to be open to the sea and to new influences.

At the start of the second half of the 17th century, Messina invited the Modenese architect and mathematician Guarino Guarini, a member of the Theatine Order, who was at the beginning of his career, perhaps luring him with the appeal of Norman architecture. This event fixed in Messina's cultural psyche the concepts of modernity associated with the revolutionary ideas of Borromini, which Guarini brought with him. These ideas took root, and later became incorporated in the international language of the early 18th century.

The glorious history of Messina was rudely interrupted, however, not by a natural disaster but by the determination of its inhabitants to break free from the Spanish yoke. They looked to France in 1674, but in 1678 France abandoned them in pursuit of other interests and opportunities. The French caption to a view of Messina had called it 'the capital of Sicily'; now it suffered the vengeance of Spain as punishment for its treason: it was stripped of its privileges, and in order to keep its rebellious people under control, its crescent-shaped harbour was dominated by the most up-to-date defensive system of the

Until the second half of the 17th century, the two most important towns in Sicily were Messina, 'the key to the Kingdom', and Palermo, 'the head of the Kingdom', and as such they featured in many maps and illustrated manuscripts.

above Palermo, depicted in an engraving from *Civitates orbis terrarum* by Braun and Hogenberg, 1575.

right A symbolic representation of the Straits of Messina with Scylla and Charybdis

right, centre The bronze statue of Don Juan of Austria in Messina, set up after his victory at the battle of Lepanto, illustrated in the *Teatro Geografico*, 1686.

right, below The Palazzata in Messina. Engraving from Leanti, *Lo stato presente della Sicilia*, 1761.

time, a pentagonal citadel, designed and built by the Flemish engineer Carlos de Grunenbergh.

The person responsible for the whole operation was the Viceroy, Francisco de Benavides, Count of Santo Stefano, who advisedly balanced military requirements, embodied in the form of the citadel, and civil requirements. At almost exactly the same time, in 1686 he supported the production of an atlas entitled *Teatro Geografico Antiguo y Moderno del Reyno de Sicilia*, with the aim of stressing continuity: in it were depicted the geographical features of the island and also, of particular interest, the major buildings in Palermo and Messina. In addition to its importance as a historical and commemorative document, the *Teatro* is the most extensive and up-to-date source of images of its time. With continued examination, scholars will perhaps eventually be able to establish its authorship, which is as yet unknown.

And what of Palermo? In a notable engraving of the years 1649–51, the historian Agostino Inveges told its story, supplying a particular adjective for each of its three phases: the Carthaginian and Roman ancient city was 'strong',

The places: old and new 15

the Saracen and Norman medieval city was 'large', and the modern Aragonese and Austrian city was 'beautiful'. There was no doubt as to Palermo's political pre-eminence, for all power resided there: the viceroy, the aristocracy, and the church.

Major experiments in urban reordering were carried out, ranging from the straightening and lengthening of the ancient Cassaro, the original axis of the city, to the cutting of the Strada Nuova through the existing fabric – extraordinarily bold operations which required privileges such as those conferred by Viceroys Toledo and Maqueda, after whom two of the finest streets were named. Here in the capital, experimental 'models' were made of designs such as the intersection of roads, using the skills of contemporary cartographers. Attempts were made to emulate Palermo's lavish designs elsewhere – in Messina, in newly founded feudal towns, and in towns reconstructed after the earthquake in 1693 – but they did not have the same meaning. The result for Palermo was a city resplendent with religious houses and aristocratic palaces, not always newly built, but always remodelled with an eye to their public image:

façades, domes, impressive corridors for guests to walk down, decoration using precious coloured marble or smooth, gleaming, white stucco, the formula for which remained a secret. These are but a few of the techniques by means of which the city renewed itself, justified itself, and raised its public profile, in the eyes of its citizens and of its visitors.

Sicily had many visitors in the 18th and 19th centuries, who established a base at Palermo from which to visit the rest of the island, are unanimous in commenting on the city's taste for decoration and magnificence.

In Palermo, earthquakes also provided an occasion for renewal. Two of them, in 1726 and 1751, provided opportunities not only to restore damage but to enhance secular or religious buildings through grand new designs. Evidence comes from a document drawn up by Mongitore in 1727 detailing the damage caused by the earthquake of 1726 (which was concentrated in the area of the original city between the two rivers), in townscapes drawn in the 1750s by Giuseppe Vasi from Corleone, and, a few years later, in *Lo stato presente della Sicilia* by Arcangiolo Leanti, a survey of Baroque architecture in Sicily

published in 1761. It seems that in this period Sicily was establishing a reputation for itself in Europe as a land full of relics of ancient Greece, and equally as an important destination for aspiring architects.

The history of Palermo in the 17th and 18th centuries saw a continuous movement from the Renaissance to the Baroque and late Baroque, from late Baroque classicism to Neoclassicism, and on to historicist styles. In the same period, the history of Messina proceeded in fits and starts, in reaction to revolts and earthquakes. In south-eastern Sicily, especially, most traces of the past were eradicated and a new identity forged after 1693, as the Val di Noto became one enormous, impressive construction site.

Palermo and Messina competed for the best technicians and artists, such as Angelo Italia, the Jesuit architect who worked on the buildings of his own order but also drew up plans for the cities of Avola and Noto, and the various masters responsible for the exuberant decorative style of the earliest building projects, such as the Palazzo Biscari in Catania. Although men travelled far, ideas travelled farther, and one after another they contributed to the variegated identity of the island.

Palermo and its buildings feature in many views.

above left The Stradone Colonna, with the Porta Felice. Designed as an area for strolling, it was also the place for puppet theatres, statues, and decorated floats on festival days. The palaces and churches of the Kalsa appear in the background. Engraving from Thomas Salmon, *Lo stato presente di tutti i paesi e populi del mondo*, XXIV, 1762.

above left Two winged putti hold a scroll with a view of Palermo from the sea. Detail of a painting by Paolo de Matteis in the abbey church of San Martino delle Scale in Palermo, 1727.

above A 19th-century view of the Piazza Pretoria in Palermo. Beyond the marble fountain is the church of San Giuseppe dei Teatini, with a dome by Giuseppe Mariani and campanile by Paolo Amato. (Palazzo Pretorio, Palermo)

Capitals and peripheral regions

If the term 'capital city' can be used in a context other than a purely political one, then certainly in a cultural context there were two capitals in Sicily in the 17th century, Palermo and Messina. Urban cartography, in both engraved and manuscript form, confirmed their roles, and went on to record other coastal cities, giving particular consideration to defensive walls, rebuilt in bastioned form in the first half of the 16th century and continually updated.

A particularly happy time for Palermo, both economically and culturally, was the vice-regency of Marcantonio Colonna (1577–84), which saw the beginning of many enterprises motivated by ideas which were deeply rooted in civil society: the desire to understand the region through descriptions of sites and cities, and the desire to push the city out beyond its walls into the countryside, creating new spaces for business and recreation, with new, bold axes to glorify the city and its history. Thus it was that on separate occasions two people, Tiburzio Spannocchi, an engineer from Siena, and Camillo Camiliani, a Florentine, circumnavigated the island, recording in descriptions and beautiful drawings the locations best suited for the construction of new watchtowers, so that the island was safely enclosed, and identifying the old towns whose defences were in need of modernization, with the intention of creating a unified system of defence.

In Palermo, the ancient street called the Cassaro, which formed the nucleus of the original settlement, had already been widened and extended; it was now extended as far as the coast, and impressive gateways were constructed at either end. In addition, other major streets were built, and although Palermo was still a walled city, it was opened up to fulfil the dual role its geographical location entailed, with the sea on one side, and the curve of the coast – the 'Conca d'Oro' or 'Golden Shell' –, famous for its Norman settlements, on the other.

A map of Palermo of 1580, drawn by Orazio Majocchi and engraved by Natale Bonifazio, was intended both as a record and as a celebration of the new Palermo, a city without boundaries. It was dedicated to the Viceroy Colonna, in recognition of the role he had played in fostering these ideas. The Stradone, the road along the seafront outside the Porta Felice, was named after him. Regarded as a symbol of the 'open' city, it was, according to Domenico Fontana, the architect of Sixtus V, the model for other 16th- and 17th-century seafront roads in Messina (the Via del Molo) and Naples. At the end of the 16th century, Palermo's prestige among Mediterranean capitals was assured, and subsequent developments such as the Strada Nuova, named after the Viceroy Maqueda, refute the idea that the city was looking back to its historical origins, with the sea surrounding the *pan-ormus* ('all-harbour'), the park containing the residences of the Norman kings, and the cathedral at Monreale, founded by William II.

The myth that the Norman era was a particularly 'auspicious' one had been perpetuated through the medieval period. Now it was replaced by a new and pressing desire for display and decoration. All the major institutions – of the viceroy, the municipality, and the church – could use the construction of the Strada Nuova and the octagonal junction known as the Quattro Canti for their own ends. The latter came to be called by contemporaries the 'eye of the city': instead of a main axis, punctuated by gaps and lined with the houses of the great and places of entertainment, a central junction was created that ignored the old

The places: old and new 17

quarters of the city, and power became concentrated around this pivotal point. The first to move in were the Jesuits and the Theatines, who built churches in the immediate vicinity. The Spanish monarchy used it as a theatre to display statues of their kings in the concave corners of the square, but these were forced to share the stage with the four patron saints who protected the four quarters into which the city was divided.

The sense of division was intensified by the intersection of two main roads, the ancient Cassaro, later Via Toledo, and the Strada Nuova, later Via Maqueda, with its central space known as the 'Teatro del Sole' (Theatre of the Sun), an 'eye' from which the entire city was visible and comprehensible. With the backing of the municipality, the Viceroys Toledo and Maqueda initiated substantial building work along new and restored streets, and many grand secular and religious buildings sprang up, the small ones grouped in harmonious units, the large ones standing in splendid isolation.

Existing buildings and open spaces naturally underwent renovation: in the Piazza Marina, for example, the main façade of the 'Steri' – which from being the seat of the monarchy became that of the Inquisition – was given a beautiful Renaissance portal of white marble (which no longer survives) and a Baroque portal. At the other end of the town, site of the first settlement, the palace of the Norman kings had become the seat of the viceroy: links were created between the old medieval structures and the rooms were adapted to new purposes, behind a compact and homogeneous exterior. The decision to enlarge the Piazza Pretoria and add a fountain in the centre – brought from Florence by sea and reassembled on the spot – was made by the Viceroy García de Toledo, desirous of emulating the city's main rival, Messina.

By this time Messina already had monumental sculptures by the Tuscan artist Giovanni Angelo Montorsoli: the Orion Fountain in the Piazza del Duomo, and the Neptune Fountain by the harbour. In addition, the city boasted the Palazzata by Giacomo Del Duca and, later, works by Guarini. Conversely, Messina's attempt to emulate Palermo's Quattro Canti, in the form of a square with four fountains on the Strada Austria, designed by the sculptor and architect Andrea Calamecca from Carrara, was no match in terms of townscape or symbolism. After the revolt of 1674–78, and before the earthquakes of 1783 and 1908, which altered its original appearance, it was only the designs of Filippo Juvarra that conveyed any significance. Juvarra was born and brought up in Messina, but was a citizen of the world by vocation. By the early 18th century he was preparing to leave Messina and Sicily for Piedmont in the footsteps of Victor Amadeus of Savoy, the new King of Sicily, to re-establish the capital of Savoy following the Treaty of Utrecht.

The non-feudal cities could scarcely compete with the likes of Palermo and Messina. In the first half of the 18th century, Agrigento no longer drew any prestige from its temples, and had retreated onto two hills with a river running between them. Drawings of the end of the 16th century (by Spannocchi and Rocca) and the 17th century (Negro and Merelli) show a town crowned with impressive secular and ecclesiastical buildings, including the Cathedral and the 'Steri', now absorbed into the archiepiscopal Seminary. A view from the sea shows only the town, composed of small houses dominated by monumental buildings on the hilltop, and the harbour, omitting anything that was not of immediate

Two views of Agrigento: a drawing from the *Teatro Geografico* of 1686 (*above left*), and an engraving from Leanti, *Lo stato presente della Sicilia*, 1761 (*above*).

opposite Drawings from the *Teatro Geografico* of 1686 showing the areas around Mazara and Trapani, and the walled towns of Marsala and Mazara.

18 The places: old and new

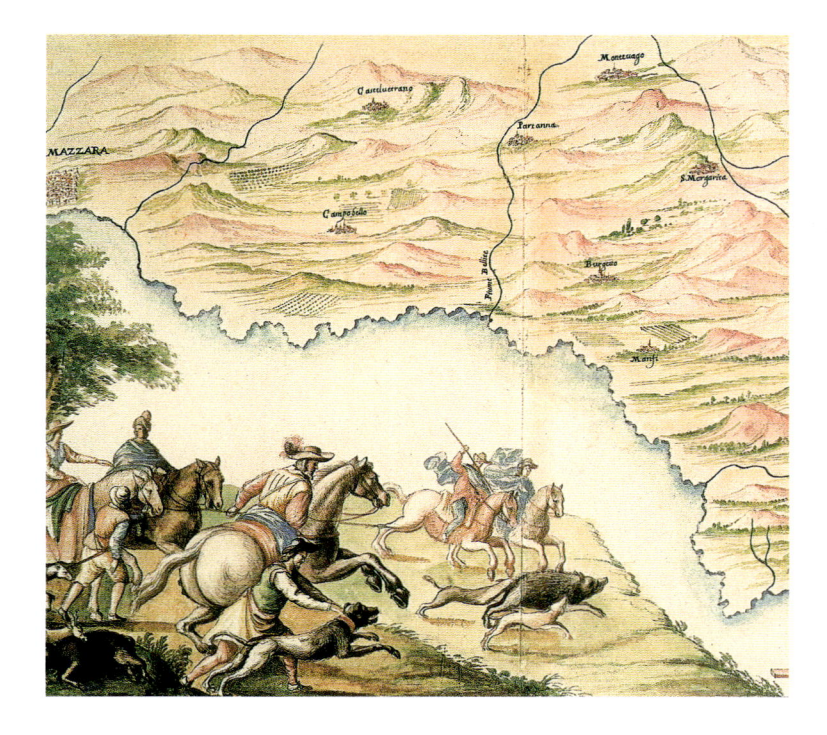

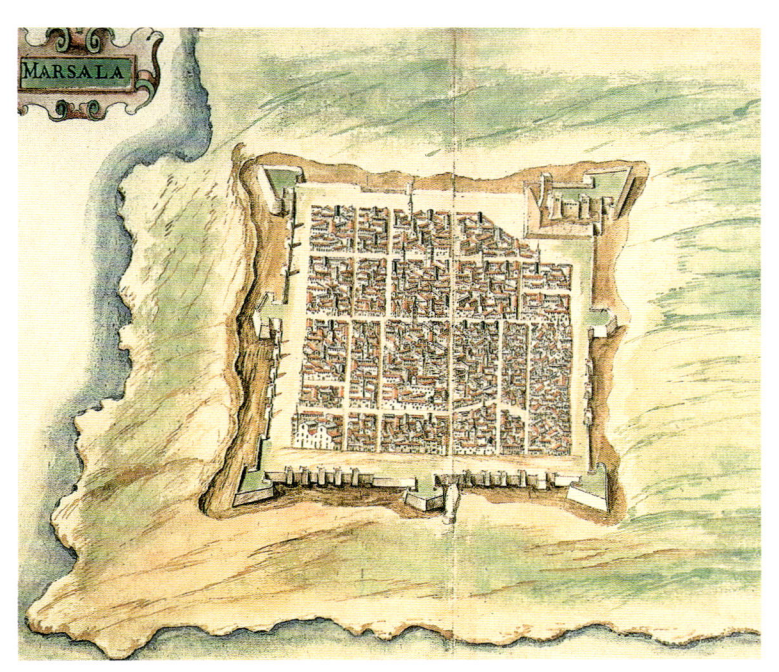

interest. Not until the second half of the 18th century was value attached to the temples of Agrigento and Sicily's other Greek ruins.

Views made in the 17th century of Sciacca, the Greek town which became famous for its waters in Roman times, show the new buildings in the foreground, sited along the southern wall of the lower town. Particularly striking among them is the Jesuit convent, which consisted of two internal courtyards with different functions. It was built slowly over the 17th and 18th centuries, to different designs and by different hands: archives have revealed a sequence of events and names, including those of the architect and mathematician Tommaso Blandino, and the painter and architect Michele Blasco, both hitherto little known. Jesuits had to obtain approval from their central authority in Rome before embarking on any project. This was not to monitor the standard of architecture, or to ensure that it followed prescribed designs (recent research has shown there were none), but to make sure that the building would be suitable for the specific functions of the order. The courtyard surrounded by the living quarters of the fathers was to be separate from the courtyard surrounded by the areas devoted to teaching – which was an integral part of the overall mission of the order, to which it devoted most of its energies. The central authorities also had a say in the choice of location for the new building, which was to be central for reasons both of convenience and of prestige.

Jesuit archives, especially those in Paris, contain fascinating town plans with indications of intended locations, their advantages and disadvantages, any existing buildings, means of access, and any more prestigious buildings with which the convent might be compared. A plan of Trapani was drawn by the Jesuit architect Natale Masuccio from Messina, who was said to have trained in Rome (no evidence for this has so far come to light), and worked all over the island. Documents show the date of the plan to be 1613 and reveal the complex construction along the Rua Grande, a prestigious 13th-century extension of the old medieval centre. On that street at around the same time the cathedral of San Lorenzo was built, which would later receive a façade and portico by one of the greatest artists of the 18th century, the architect and treatise-writer Giovanni Amico from Trapani.

Unlike Trapani, which with its castle and walls formed part of

The places: old and new 19

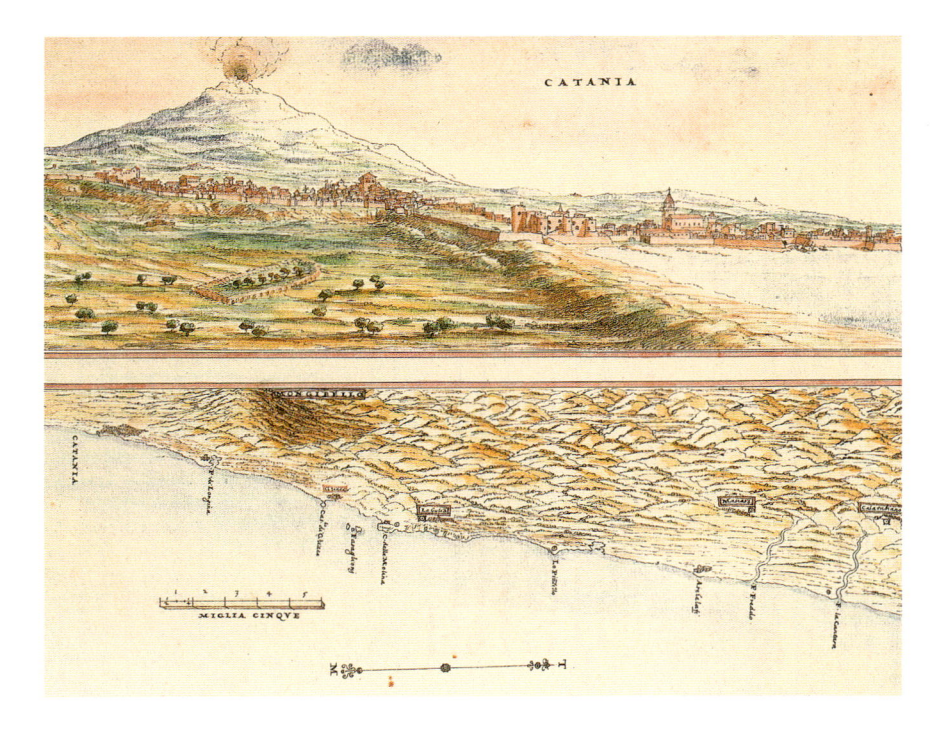

the defences of the island, the neighbouring town of Marsala was deemed in the 16th and 17th centuries to be indefensible, because of technical problems and the onerous costs of constructing and maintaining defences. Therefore during the Baroque period the town was allowed to expand beyond its walls and into the surrounding countryside. Here architecture could be given free rein in terms of expression and execution, and unorthodox designs were welcome, such as the more innovative conceits of Giovanni Amico.

Amico's influence is also seen on the south coast of the province of Trapani, in Mazara. Within its square perimeter, of Arabic origin, in the 18th century new buildings of urban significance were erected. The Seminario dei Chierici, by Amico, looks onto the main square, with porticoes and loggias splayed out at a 45-degree angle, curving into the surrounding space. The theatrical façade of Santa Veneranda follows the line of the street, concealing the centralized scheme of its interior, and is flanked by two belltowers which stand out against the sky. The later campanile of the Benedictine church of San Michele is square in plan, yet seems to fray at the corners.

These and other towns in the west of the island, on the coast and inland, were regarded as 'peripheral' in the 17th and 18th centuries. How the Val di Noto was seen is uncertain, since there is little documentation before the earthquake in 1693. There are a few references, such as those to Carnilivari mentioned above, but these do not permit any judgment of quality, which depended on the superiority of the stone as much as anything else. What is certain is that the earthquake generated energy and stimulated invention to such a degree that the eastern part of the island became the leading actor at the beginning of the 18th century, when the towns were able to erect new religious and civic buildings, either on their original sites, or on new, more favourable sites. The sea remained the enemy and the towns still needed the protection of a wall, and in this instance it was certainly easier to repair an existing one than to construct a new one. Catania, Augusta and Syracuse, the sentinels of the Ionian Sea, thus decided to reinvent themselves using existing structures. These new capitals of the Baroque adapted themselves well to their new roles and circumstances: existing streets were widened and straightened, and long thoroughfares were interspersed with open spaces which could accommodate monumental buildings. In short, they identified themselves as centres of religious and civic power.

As a military engineer, Carlos de Grunenbergh was used to working with expediency in wartime, and the same applied in the case of natural disasters such as an earthquake. He knew how to evaluate situations and dangers, how to harness skills and ensure that work was carried out swiftly on the most urgent issues: clearing away the rubble, creating new roads that would facilitate a swift mass exodus in case of danger, constructing temporary buildings before the final versions.

Reconstruction required both administrative authority, embodied in the Duke of Camastra, and practical skill. Camastra was responsible for the 'modern' plan of Catania, although over the years the rational clarity of his design was obscured by alterations made for ceremonial occasions. On the For a royal marriage in 1768, for instance, a monumental gateway, the Porta Ferdinandea, was built by Stefano Ittar at the end of Via San Filippo (now Garibaldi) opposite the Cathedral, using two different local materials, white limestone and black volcanic lava. Prints and

The cities in the southeastern part of the island flourished after their reconstruction following the earthquake in 1693. These pictures show Catania in its setting and its most important buildings.

left Catania, from Tiburzio Spannocchi, *Descripción de las marinas,* 1578–96. As in all the drawings in the *Descripción* (cf. pp. 24, 25) the lower half of the drawing shows the outline of the coast, with indications of existing fortifications (Catania is at the far left) and locations for new ones to be built, so as to complete the protective circle round the island. (Biblioteca Nacional, Madrid)

The Piazza del Duomo, Catania, with the Cathedral and Elephant Fountain, seen in a rare 18th-century engraving (*below*) and in a 19th-century painting in tempera (private collection).

drawings of Catania record the reconstruction process after the earthquake, against the backdrop of Mount Etna, like a deity to be appeased. Some depict important open spaces such as the Piazza del Duomo, where the prestigious Cathedral, founded in Norman times, was joined by 18th-century buildings designed by the architect Giovanni Battista Vaccarini.

Vaccarini had trained in Rome, and was summoned to Catania from Palermo to give advice on the second phase of reconstruction after the earthquake. His role is now thought to be less significant than once appeared, and new evidence has attributed some buildings to his students and/or contemporaries. The piazza and its immediate vicinity, however, display his most important works, visible as a whole and in detail in an interesting view by Jacob Ignaz Hittorff and Ludwig Zanth. Contemporary sources call the Cathedral in its new form 'a truly remarkable affair', and go on to say that much time and effort was required on the part of Vaccarini and his supporters – the client, Bishop Galletti, and Vaccarini's friend, the architect Luigi Vanvitelli – to secure approval for the design and execution. The Elephant Fountain consists of an elephant supporting an ancient obelisk:

unless another model is discovered, it seems likely that it reflects Vaccarini's time in Rome, when he would have seen Bernini's composition in the Piazza della Minerva. The Palazzo Senatorio is traditionally attributed to Vaccarini on account of the Michelangelesque giant order on its façade, which would suggest knowledge of Rome (though the style was also known, it seems, to other architects such as Francesco Battaglia, through books and prints). Roman influence is also suggested at the nearby Badia di Sant'Agata, in the cruciform plan and certain details of the façade, such as the concave centre, and a fringe motif resembling that of Bernini's famous Baldacchino in St Peter's.

To the south of Catania the town of Augusta, with its large harbour, became the site of many battles against invaders aiming to capture it as a prelude to the island as a whole. Hence it assumed an important political and military role in the course of the 17th century, particularly because of the events in Messina between 1674 and 1678. Its ancient defences, dating back to Swabian times, were rebuilt in an up-to-date style and given sculptural decoration under the supervision

The places: old and new

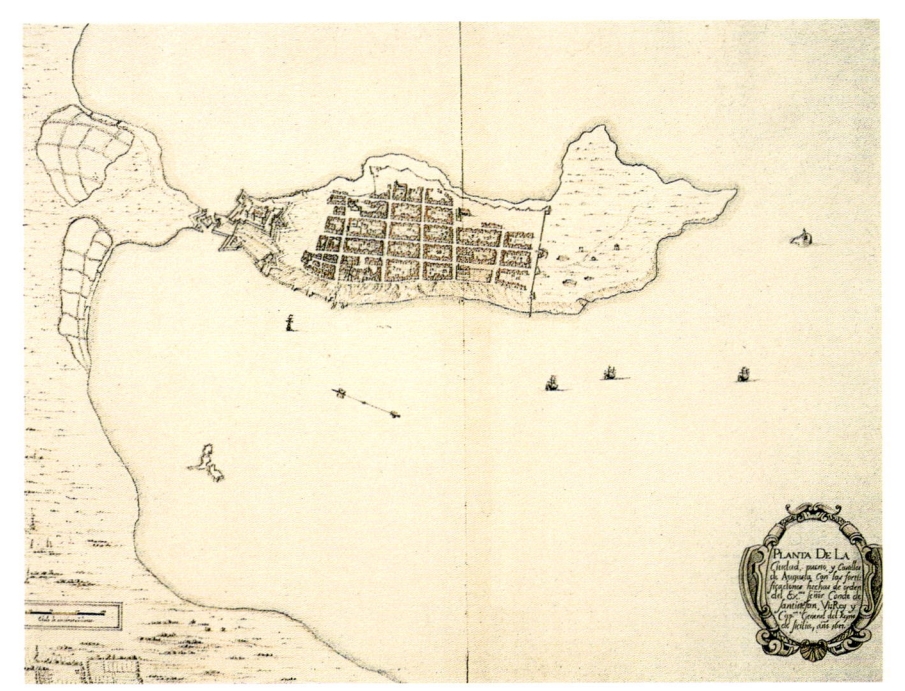

of Carlos de Grunenbergh in the time of the Viceroy Benavides, Count of Santo Stefano. The gate of the city has a Spanish flavour, like the Porta Grazia of the citadel in Messina (now re-erected on another site).

Syracuse at this time occupied the peninsula of Ortigia, site of the ancient Greek city, and was protected by the Castello Maniace, built by Frederick II. The Cathedral was built on the ruins of the Temple of Athena, and its heritage was emphasized by leaving some of the Doric columns exposed. The castle was not so fortunate: it was despoiled of its most important treasures, such as the ancient bronze rams that guarded the entrance, and, inappropriately adapted for different uses, it lost its original geometric harmony and its symbolic significance.

The Cathedral's late 16th-century appearance is recorded in pictures by Tiburzio Spannocchi (1578–96) and Angelo Rocca (1584): its façade was distinguished by a tower which not only housed the bells but created a grand impression commensurate with its status in the city, and the columns of the ancient temple were visible down the side of the building. The Cathedral as rebuilt in the first half of the 18th century, after the earthquake of 1693, is illustrated in Leanti's *Stato presente* of 1761.

The idea of combining façade and campanile or façade and tower is not an 18th-century invention, nor is it due to foreign influences: such façades already existed at the end of the 16th century, for example at Enna, and they probably go back to the Norman fortified cathedrals. The fortunes of the design are difficult to trace because so many buildings have been destroyed, but there are various scattered examples: in Palermo there is the church of San Matteo in the Via Toledo, built by Geronimo Di Bona from 1652; in Messina, the church of the Santissima Annunziata by Guarino Guarini, of 1660–62; and in the south-east, where there was much activity influenced by books, prints, drawings, and renewed contacts with Italy and regions north of the Alps.

Reconstruction work after events such as earthquakes generally involved the re-working of an idea which was already lodged in the collective imagination, as happened in 18th-century Enna and Syracuse. In Syracuse, the idea of the tower-façade, unrelated to the building behind it, was combined with that of the flat façade, articulated and enriched by clusters of columns reaching for the sky. It no longer seems possible to attribute this powerful and coherent design, built over many years, to the architect Andrea Palma, who is mentioned in a document dated 1728 but died only two years later, in 1730, when work had only just begun. Recently a Roman influence has been suggested.

The Baroque rebuilding of the town of Caltagirone, situated in the rich south-eastern hinterland, made use of the characteristic local manner which involved a harmonious blend of majolica tiles and terracotta. Its location on three hills inspired some grandiose architectural solutions, such as the 17th-century flight of steps which leads up from the lower town to the church of Santa Maria del Monte in the upper town. The presence of the architect Rosario Gagliardi from Syracuse, with his designs for the churches of Santa Chiara and San Giuseppe, links the reconstuction of Caltagirone with that of other sites in the south-east where Gagliardi was active. Its position also suggests that Caltagirone might have been on the route for cultural influences travelling in the opposite direction, towards the towns of Petralia Sottana and Petralia Soprana, where the churches of Santa Maria di Loreto

above left Syracuse: detail of a map by Baron Samuel von Schmettau, 1720–21. (Nationalbibliothek, Vienna)

above right Augusta, from the *Teatro Geografico*, 1686. This detailed rendering of its geometric layout may have been copied from drawings by Carlos de Grunenbergh made for Viceroy Benavides, Count of Santo Stefano, in 1682. The town's location, on the east coast, meant that it was the scene of many battles for the conquest of the island.

22   The places: old and new

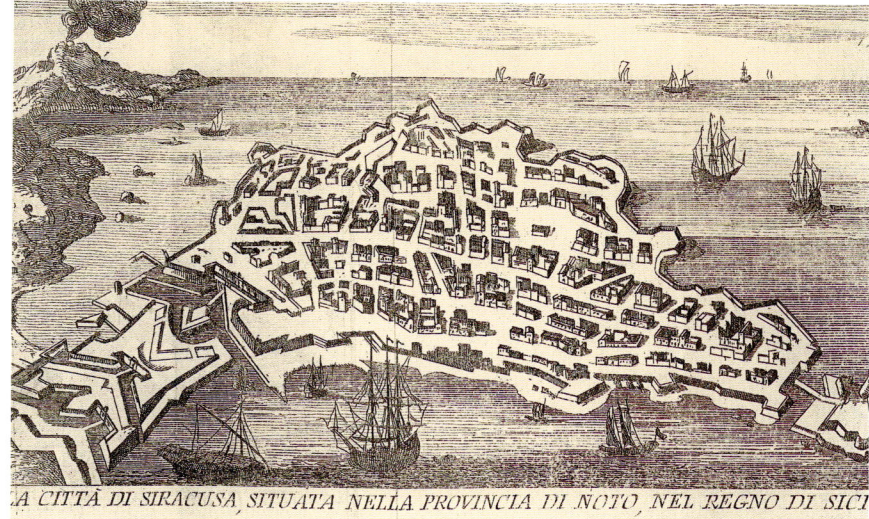

above Syracuse Cathedral, showing along its side the columns of the ancient Temple of Athena. Engraving from Leanti, *Lo stato presente della Sicilia*, 1761.

above right The city of Syracuse. Engraving from Salmon, *Lo stato presente di tutti i paesi e populi del mondo*, XXIV, 1762.

and Santissimo Salvatore display features characteristic of Gagliardi.

A web was being spun between the major cities and places on the periphery, which would envelop a town that was to become a hotbed of new ideas: Noto.

The 'new towns'

In Sicily the use of a grid as the basis of a town plan had its roots in the Swabian era, and in the south-east there is still evidence of this in Terranova – now called Gela – and in Augusta. However it was only later that the grid came into its own as a design for a larger area. Carlentini, a royal town founded in 1551 by the Viceroy Juan de Vega, is the most significant and well documented example. The key words used to describe the new town and its functions were 'refuge' and 'defence'. Surrounded by protective walls, it lay close to the ruins of the ancient city of Lentini, from which it took its name, combined with that of the Emperor Charles V. It was built after the earthquake of 1542, which had damaged the fortifications of neighbouring cities, and its design must have been an important experimental ground for Spanish plans to colonize Latin America.

Carlentini is the only inland settlement included in Tiburzio Spannocchi's *Descripción* of 1578–96. The design followed topography in the construction of its encircling walls, and geometrical rationality in its layout, with orthogonal axes. The only anomaly was the variation in shape of the blocks of houses in relation to the central piazza, which consisted of two intercommunicating spaces with a church. During these years, when the town was still under construction, Spannocchi recorded a population of 360 inhabitants who had come from various parts of the island because of the privileges and exemptions afforded to them there. Many of the features of Carlentini correspond to regulations in the 'Laws of the Indies', promulgated by Philip II of Spain, which reflected what had been achieved so far in Latin America.

In spite of the vast distances between the Spanish colonies, Madrid was still very much in control, and functioned as a centre of communication, transmitting knowledge and experience. A Sicilian diarist of the early 17th century, Valerio Rosso, suggested that the grid system of Palermo was based on the plan of the Chinese city of Canton, brought over by the Jesuits. Perhaps the undoubted continuity in development of the island owed its success to a synthesis of ideas.

After the few Greek and Albanian settlements, which were limited in area, feudal settlements were founded through royal initiatives. At the end of the 16th century, when this was in process, the Spanish crown found itself in severe financial difficulties: wars, and the need to fortify the major coastal cities, which were still subject to Turkish attack even after the victory at Lepanto, forced them to sell everything that it was possible to sell: a document refers to 'qualesquiere rentas, feudos y otro qualquer genre de … Real Patrimonio y qualsquiere Ciutades y lugares de que se puede sacar dinero' (any rents, feus, and any other sort of real estate and any cities and places from which money can be got). Even civil and criminal jurisdiction over feudal territories was for sale, as was the permission to settle such territories, called the *licentia populandi*, which allowed the building of settlements that would enable the land to be cultivated.

The success of the operation exceeded the wildest expectations: in the region to the west of the Val di Mazara, for example, an area of large grain-growing estates belonging to the feudal aristocracy,

The places: old and new 23

from the end of the 16th century to the beginning of the 18th over one hundred new towns were founded, and the number of licensed settlements was even greater. Some enterprises failed in the planning or in the execution; once begun they were interrupted, and many new centres were not completed in their basic structure or in the principal monuments which should have formed their nucleus: the central piazza, the Chiesa Madre, and the feudal palace.

In the same period new centres also sprang up without a licence, as a natural overspill from an older settlement set on high ground, surrounding a feudal castle. An example is Caltavuturo, in the Madonie hills near Palermo, where the original settlement, on a hill dominated by a castle, was gradually enlarged until a new centre was built on a gentler slope, as shown in a rare drawing of 1584. The most fertile period for such enterprises was the first half of the 17th century, during which time a new urban geography emerged in the vast inland areas in the west of the island. The density of the previous medieval settlement there has recently been discovered thanks to the careful studies of medieval archaeologists. Early 20th-century initiatives for developing suburbs were not realized extensively, and where they were, they have not been a success: walking through these areas today, they seem fragmentary and devoid of social vitality.

A new city could not be founded on nothing, so apart from the necessity of choosing a favourable position in a large feudal estate, there were other determining factors, such as the availability of labour, an adequate water supply, and the presence nearby of crown settlements, whose inhabitants would be likely to enjoy better working and living conditions in a new town; and the existence of older structures, such as a cluster of houses, a road junction, the ruins of an ancient centre, a tunny-fishery if on the coast, which might make the place more suited to urbanization.

The old-fashioned scheme outlined in the *licentia*, which involved a town surrounded by walls and standardized towers, was usually ignored in the new inland settlements, which were secure within feudal estates, but it was generally followed on the coast, where there was always the danger of invasion. Although subject to many variants due to existing constructions, the basic plan adopted was that of the grid, ancient in origin but ever practical because of its simplicity and the possibility to extend it in any direction, in accordance with the needs of the settlement. The plan proposed a central piazza, which would accommodate the Chiesa Madre and the palace of the founder (although the latter was not always included, nor did it have to have any particular architectural

left and opposite The cities of Castellammare in the province of Trapani (*left*) and Syracuse (*opposite*), seen in two magnificent drawings from Spannocchi, *Descripción de las marinas*, 1578–96. They are shown in their setting, and in relation to the fortification of the coast. (Biblioteca Nacional, Madrid)

character), and these were the basic architectural entities that would serve the new community. The plan might be elaborated upon, for example with additional religious buildings, or open spaces created by the demolition of blocks of houses, whose square or rectangular dimensions would dictate the shape of the central piazza or side piazzas.

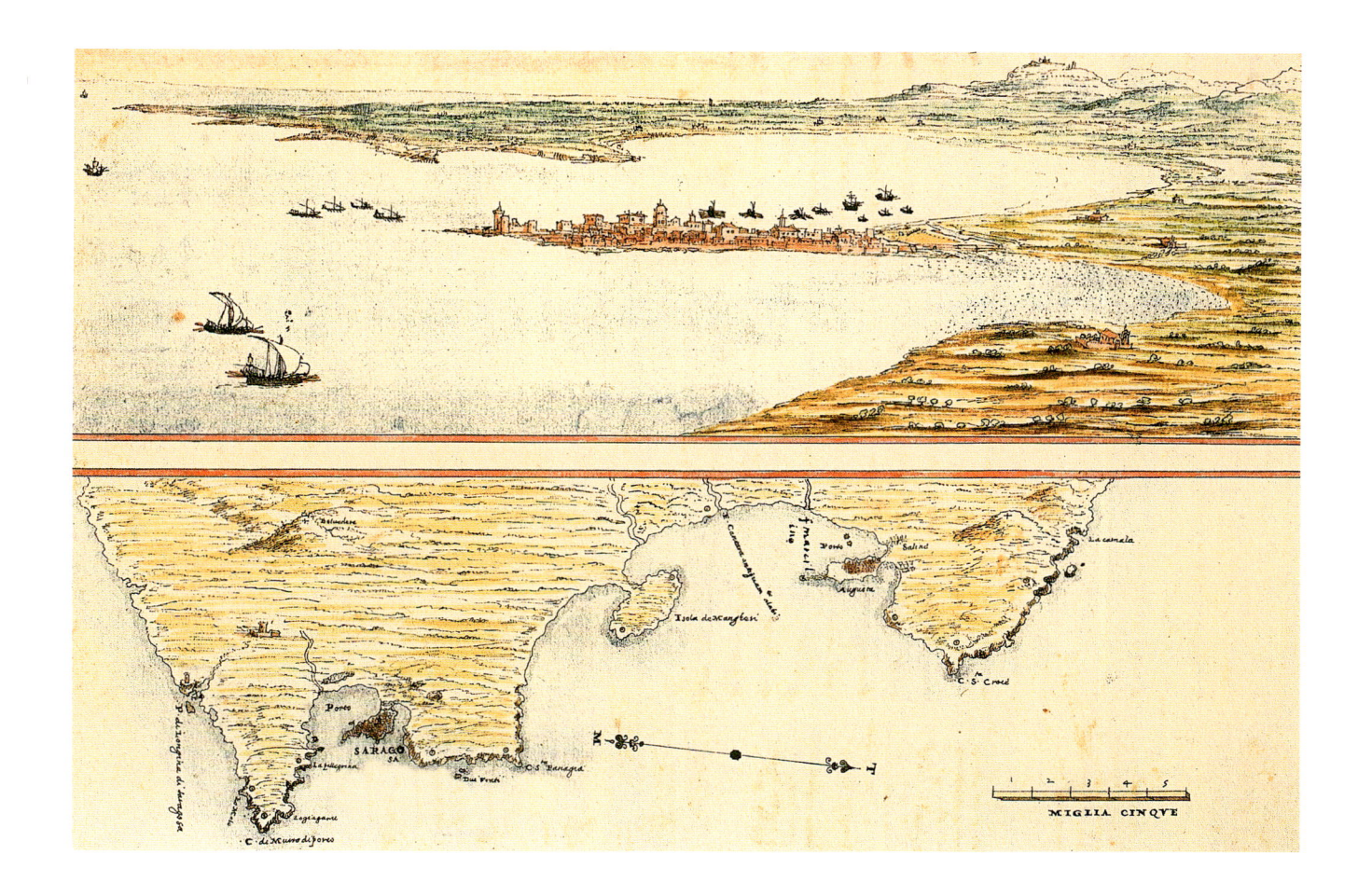

This urban planning and architecture did not usually involve an architect: rather, it was probably executed under the supervision of the founder by trusted masters. But was there a real relationship here between urban design and human settlement? Research carried out in land registers of the time, which were designed to itemize people and property, and thereby identify income, has revealed details of location and property ownership not supplied by ancient maps. The results of the first wave of registration, which was carried out shortly after the foundation of a new settlement, show how the laying out of the urban grid preceded the settlement of the inhabitants and was therefore independent of them: settlement took place gradually through the allocation of housing spaces in the available blocks. At some point maps must have been drawn up with the names of those who had been allocated spaces, like the ones that have been found for several towns in France founded at the end of the 17th century. The only buildings whose locations were determined at the outset of the settlement's foundation were those that were representative of the power of the feudal landlord or of the community, which were the 'monuments' of the new town.

There are many examples of towns that adhered to the old feudal geography, but here we will only consider a few significant examples which are representative of the overall picture. Of the coastal cities, Castellammare and Trabia are illustrated in the manuscript atlas by Francesco Negro and Carlo Maria Ventimiglia dated 1640. The plan of Castellammare was drawn up eighty years after its foundation in 1560, whereas the bird's-eye view of Trabia was drawn only five years after the *licentia populandi* was granted to Ottavio Lanza in 1635 (perhaps it was drawn on the spot: it differs in style from all the others in the manuscript). Both towns were protected by coastal fortresses, and both had an orthogonal street pattern with regular blocks of housing.

Sometimes there seem to have been two distinct phases in the construction of the settlements: an initial phase, which involved reconciling the new plan with existing buildings and constructing houses around the nucleus of the church, and a second phase which saw the construction of more churches, new districts, and above all the feudal residence. That was the case in the town of Aragona, in the province of Agrigento, a province that was largely influenced by the new developments in the west of the island. Aragona originally consisted of a lower nucleus surrounding the church; it was then transformed by the palace of the Naselli princes, counts of Comiso, which was prominently sited and

TRABIA

architecturally distinguished. The palace, built on the new piazza, took the form of a parallelepiped, with loggias on the corners in the style of Messina. Another church was built in this new piazza in the 18th century.

The town of Leonforte, in the province of Enna, which was originally a haphazard and untidy collection of houses, was rebuilt at the beginning of the 17th century, again employing the device of the Quattro Canti (see pp. 17–18): the plan was based on a straight main street which widened at the centre into a space with four diagonal sides. The imposing Palazzo Branciforte and the Granfonte (a fountain with twenty-four jets) symbolized the feudal presence, along with a number of public buildings on a grand scale, which established the character of the new town.

Capaci, in the province of Palermo, rebuilt in the 18th century on the initiative of the Pilo family, who were the local lords, and who owned vast areas of land between Palermo, Marineo and Capaci. The new Chiesa Madre, Sant'Erasmo, is an unusual elongated octagon with an ambulatory and vaulted ceiling and a façade in Rococo style, with two majestic flights of stairs leading up to the main entrance.

Sometimes it happened that the founder of a new town failed to maintain it adequately either economically or culturally. A good example of this is the town of Valguarnera Ragali near Palermo, and its founder Giacomo Paruta: all that remains of what must have been a grandiose plan is a magnificent fountain bearing the date 1609. The fountain is decorated in a style prevalent in Palermo at the time seen in the works of Mariano Smiriglio, the royal architect and painter who designed the Senate. Smiriglio may also have designed the grid plans of Altavilla Milicia and other towns.

In 1682, a landslide destroyed the old centre of Santo Stefano, which had been built on high ground on the north coast, overlooking the Tyrrhenian Sea. In 1683 the town was rebuilt following the granting of a *licentia populandi* to Giuseppe Lanza, Duke of Camastra, and in his honour it was renamed Santo Stefano di Camastra. The new town

The 'new' town of Trabia, near Palermo, founded in 1635, as depicted in the atlas of Francesco Negro and Carlo Maria Ventimiglia, 1640. In the foreground, on the coast, are the 14th-century castle and the tunny-fisheries. (Biblioteca Nacional, Madrid)

26 The places: old and new

Leonforte still displays the imposing religious and civic buildings commissioned by the Branciforte family, founders of the new centre.

was built on a hill, close to the sea, on a rectangular plan, divided into four quarters by two orthogonal axes. Then a grid system of roads was superimposed going in two different directions: one set of parallel roads led down to the sea, along which the houses were aligned, and another set criss-crossed diagonally, connecting the four quarters of the town. This could be seen a forerunner of the many prestigious commissions that were to be undertaken by the Duke following the great earthquake of 1693 in the south-east of the island, when the Viceroy had appointed him Vicar General of the Val di Noto.

As we have seen, some cities, such as Catania and Syracuse, were rebuilt on their ruins. Others were doubled in size, both restoring the old centre and drawing up plans for expansion. This was the case with Ragusa, where the reconstruction work was twofold: in the ancient centre of Ibla, new religious and secular buildings were to be constructed where the existing ones had been destroyed by the earthquake; and in addition a new town was to be built on a small hill to the west, with a new cathedral and an open grid system of roads extending out into the countryside. This enabled existing communities to expand.

Other cities chose to change site completely, abandoning the hills for the plains or gentle slopes, and exploiting the opportunities afforded by the surrounding countryside and any existing roads.

The biggest difference between the old feudal cities in the western part of the island and the new plans for the south-east following the earthquake of 1693 was the amount of space allocated to residential buildings. Despite the depopulation caused by the earthquake, the new plans anticipated a rapid growth in size. The adoption of the grid system allowed for expansion, but whereas the feudal cities had started from scratch and had been able to adopt a standard pattern, schemes for rebuilding existing towns had to accommodate existing social patterns. Grid systems might be doubled in size, with different orientations; more piazzas might be built, each with its church and palace, so as to be almost autonomous districts; and monuments might be erected in front of churches, as in Ispica, Melilli and Sortino. Great attention was paid to the eye-catching effect of striking compositions, whether convex or concave, like the concave façade of the church of Montevergine in Noto.

The intention was to create an impression of wealth and of hope for the future, and such was the effect of the reconstruction of Noto after the earthquake in 1693.

Noto belonged to the state rather than to a feudal landlord, and was the capital of the Val di Noto. It is clear from its design that there were moments of indecision and conflict during its rebuilding, and this has been confirmed by recent archaeological findings during restoration work. In plan it consists of two adjacent towns connected by flights of steps and characterized by a different orientation of streets: one up on the hill, centred on the piazza with the church of the Santissimo Crocifisso, and the other lower down, with one main street widening into monumental piazzas.

The architect of the lower town was Angelo Italia, a Jesuit originally from Licata: he had been summoned to participate in the construction of buildings for his own order, and was then given the commission for the town plan by the Viceroy. The profile of this lower town seen from a distance is still characterized by large and majestic buildings, mostly churches and monasteries, whose construction benefited from the organizational skills and economic stability inherent in the religious orders – so much so that, as a traveller in the late 18th century noted, the population seemed to be composed entirely of priests and monks.

Francesco Paolo Labisi, the learned architect from Noto, active in the town between 1750 and 1760, understood the importance of this, and exploited it to the full. He was aware of mistakes made in Palermo and elsewhere concerning the role of open spaces. His best-known work is the Jesuit church of San Francesco Saverio in Palermo: its plan was conceived from the inside out, as a series of spaces which could be read in different ways, indicating his knowledge of geometry. That knowledge enabled him to design the layout of Noto, starting with the main axes, and playing with regularity and symmetry (as the studies of Stephen Tobriner have shown) to achieve continuity and architectural harmony.

Angelo Italia died in 1700, and various architects, including Rosario Gagliardi and his pupils, were involved in the subsequent development of Noto; however, in working out the overall plan, Italia had also conceived the essentials of the architecture, streamlining his design to maximize order and regularity, and allowing space within it for potential urban development.

Feudal towns destroyed by the earthquake of 1693 were rebuilt much faster than those belonging to the state, partly because they were often smaller, and also because the owner would intervene directly to assist the stricken population. In Occhiolà and Avola, the former dominated by the Branciforte family, princes of Butera, and the latter by the Pignatelli family, dukes of Terranova, the decision to relocate the settlement, abandoning high and inaccessible places, involved bold new projects – and in the case of Occhiolà even involved a change of name: the new town was called Grammichele.

Here and in other towns such as Santo Stefano di Camastra, the rebuilding benefited from the learned character of the feudal landlords, whose libraries contained treatises on architecture and geometry. A contemporary source tells us that Carlo Maria Carafa Branciforte, Prince of Butera, 'excelled in all the arts and sciences, was admired amongst his equals, and revered throughout Italy'. He knew *La Città del Sole* (The City of the Sun) by the Dominican philosopher Tommaso Campanella, and developed a complex plan for Grammichele, with a gnomon as the central focus. The practical work of realizing this idea was entrusted to Michele da Ferla (Ferla is a neighbouring town, now in the province of Syracuse).

The plan of Grammichele is hexagonal, with streets radiating out from the centre and running concentrically around the edge. The original plan, incised in a slab of slate, is preserved in the town. It proclaims the vision of its learned designer, a man of letters and a writer, who founded a printing works at Mazzarino. Carlo Maria Carafa Branciforte took pleasure in geometric regularity as a sure way of achieving beauty, and he was also conscious of his own position: he selected a prime site in the plan for his own palace, and ensured that it was grand enough to project the glory of his name (the Branciforte family were powerful

After the earthquake of 1693 Avola and Noto were moved from their hilltop positions down to the plains, close to the sea, where they were rebuilt on geometric plans designed by architects.

above left A detail from the map drawn by Baron Samuel von Schmettau in 1720–21 shows the old and new locations of both Avola and Noto. (Nationalbibliothek, Vienna)

above Lands of the Branciforte family, princes of Butera, are depicted in 18th-century overdoors with elaborate wooden frames in the entrance hall of their palace in Palermo. Niscemi followed a traditional grid pattern, modified only by the wavy façades of religious buildings.

28 The places: old and new

above Grammichele, founded after the earthquake of 1693, was built on an unusual radiocentric plan. It too is depicted in an overdoor in the Branciforte family palace in Palermo.

right The aristocratic author of the radiocentric plan of Grammichele, Carlo Maria Carafa Branciforte, Prince of Butera.

landowners in the 18th century, and owned vast areas of land in central and eastern Sicily).

The spectacular plan of Grammichele was realized, but its beauty could only truly be appreciated from above. In the realization of the design, with low houses, attempts were made to stress the layout: the obtuse corners of the central space were emphasized by pilasters, and roads opened out from the centre of the sides; the central position of the hexagonal piazza was stressed, with the town hall and Chiesa Madre; the peripheral 'quarters' each had its own piazza and church. Dominating it all was the Branciforte palace.

Paintings of the towns owned by the Branciforte family were displayed in the entrance hall of their palace by the Marina in Palermo. There were towns of medieval origin crowned with castles, such as Mazzarino, and new towns such as Grammichele and Niscemi. The latter had been founded by *licentia populandi* in the first half of the 17th century, but it was rebuilt after 1693 on a regular plan, and many imposing religious buildings were added in the 18th century.

The new plan for the town of Avola, which moved from its old site in the hills down to the plains near the sea, was also based on a hexagon, but here the hexagon enclosed a chessboard of streets, with large, square blocks of buildings, one of which was occupied in the 18th century by the church of the Annunziata (the Badia) with its imposing curved façade. In the central piazza, which was also square, the blocks of buildings were made slightly smaller in order to leave space for the Chiesa Madre. The other piazzas were concentrated around the perimeter of the town, where there were continuous rows of houses, and bastion walls which were begun but never completed.

Sources suggest that the plan of Avola was designed by Angelo Italia: as at Noto it was based on a regular, geometric design, and reflected knowledge of the literature; indeed, one of Italia's contemporaries said that 'he got the plan from a book of town plans'. The practical work on the ground was supervised by Antonio Vella.

The grid was a simple system which could easily be adapted to future needs, and it was the form selected for many of the towns in the south-east that had to be rebuilt after the earthquake. It was never rigid: it could be modified to accommodate buildings of importance to the community, and its two main axes – like the Roman *cardo* and *decumanus* – naturally divided the settlement into four quarters, as in Palermo. The scheme was equally applicable for major cities and small towns, and its widespread usage, even by minor architects, testifies to the existence of direct or indirect channels of communication. The new towns thus differed considerably from their previous incarnations. Fenicia Moncada, now Belpasso, was rebuilt twice, following a lava flow in 1669 and the earthquake of 1693.

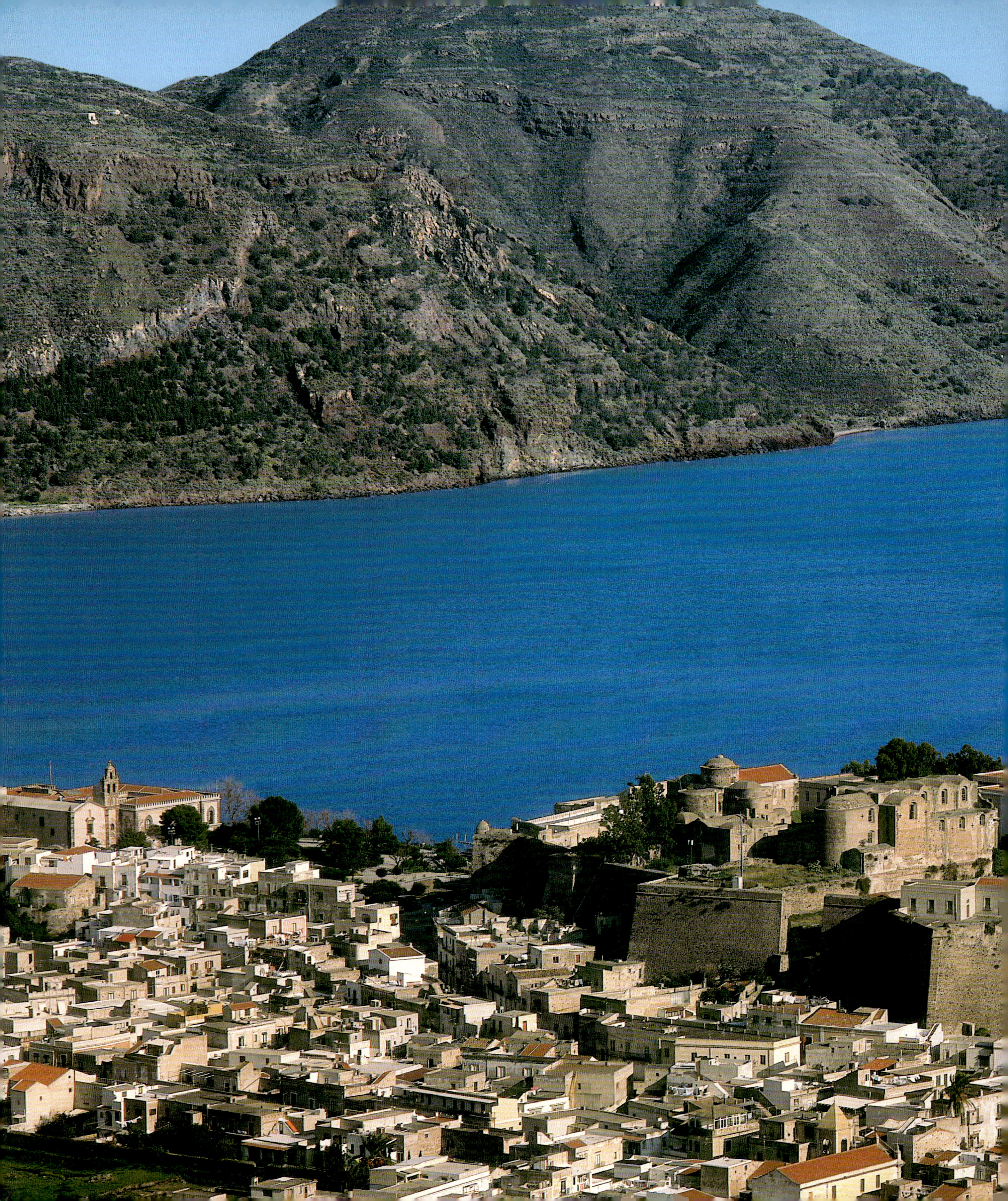

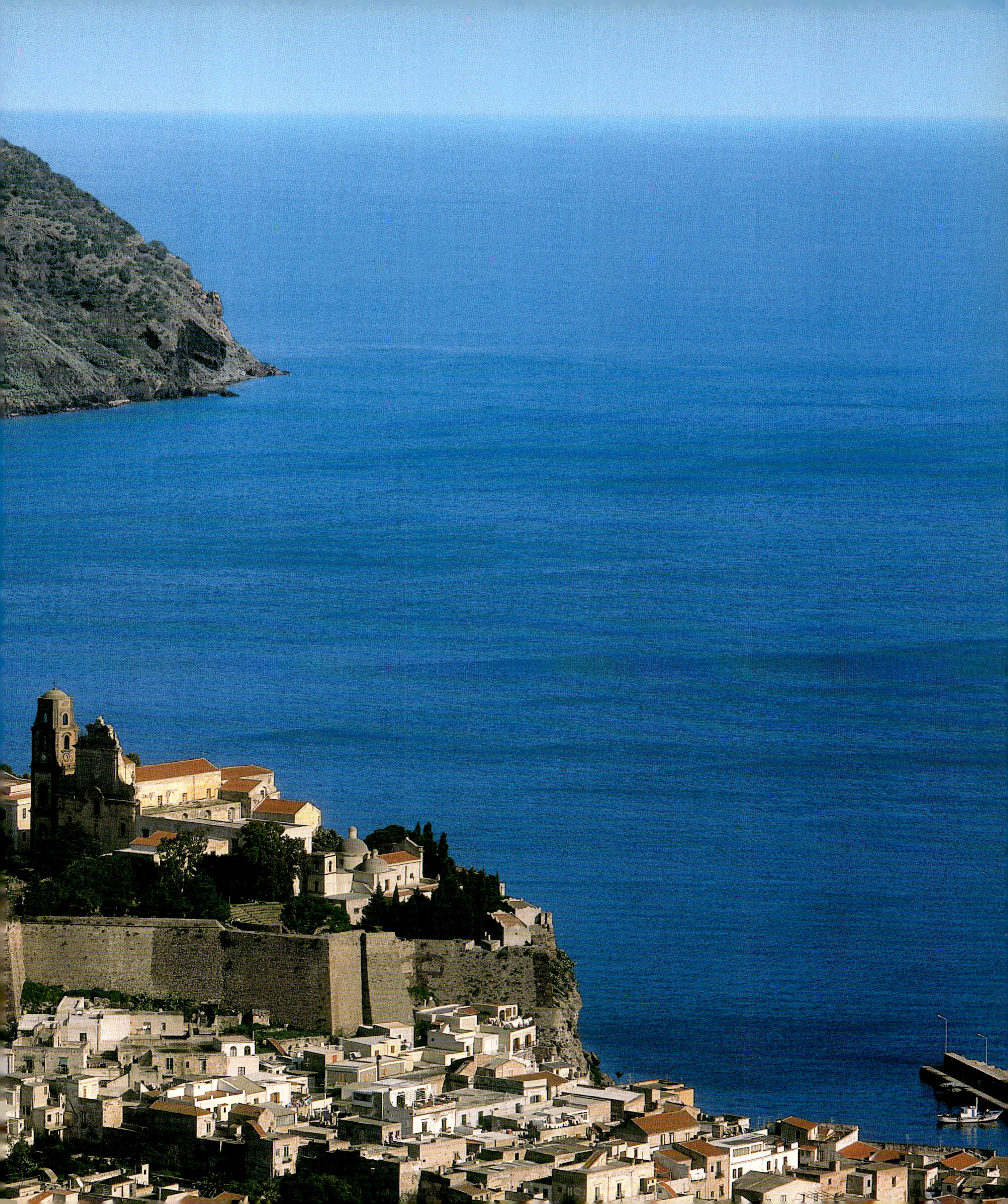

32   *The places: old and new*

left The imposing mass of the cathedral rises above the medieval buildings of Piazza Armerina.

above Mount Etna forms a backdrop to the town of Regalbuto, as to many towns on the plains around Catania.

preceding pages The fortress of Lipari, near Messina, with its five Baroque churches.

The old town of Ragusa Ibla, with the cathedral of San Giorgio.

overleaf Façades of the churches of San Giorgio and San Pietro in Modica.

The places: old and new 35

36 *The places: old and new*

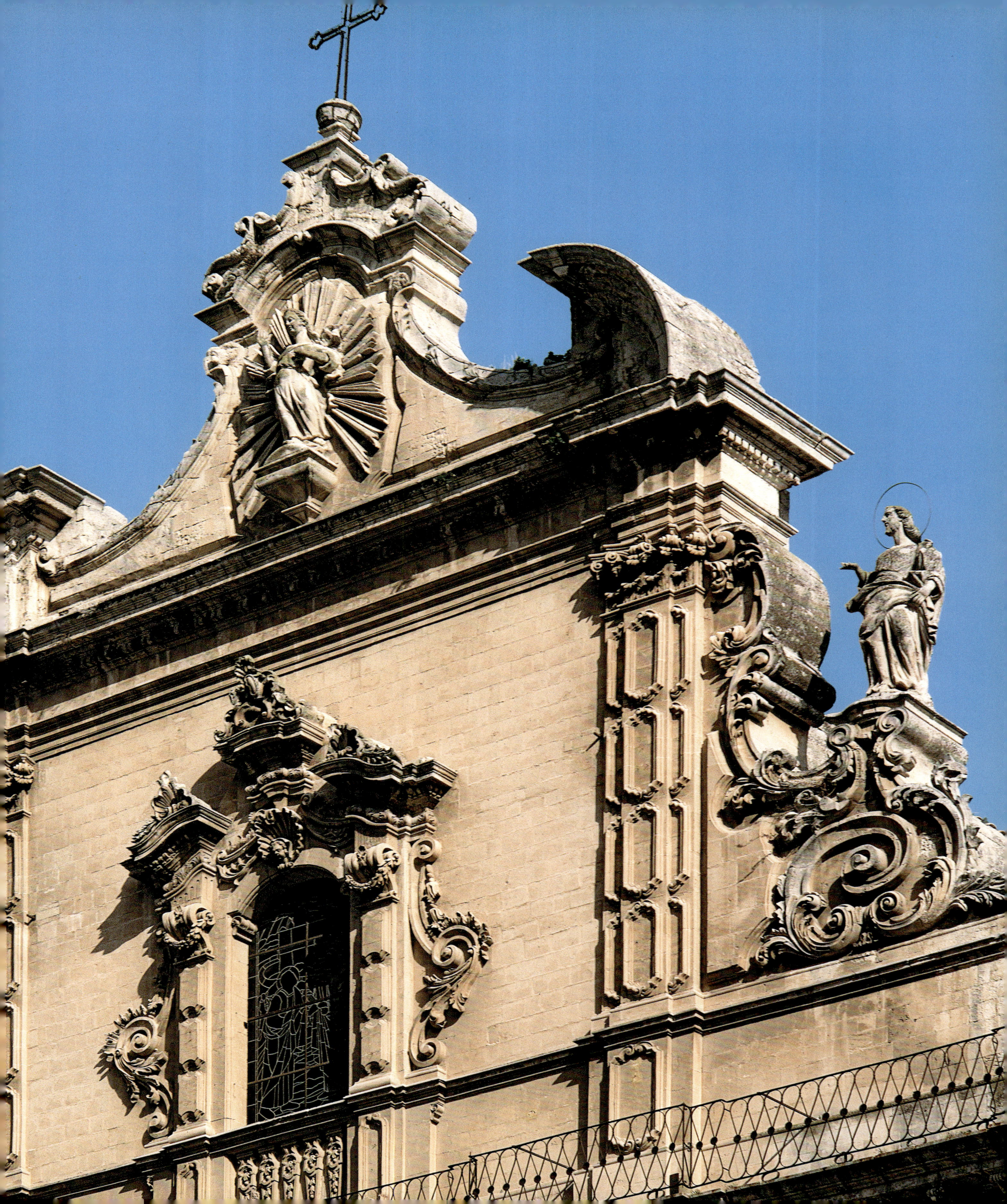

38 *The places: old and new*

The places: old and new 39

preceding pages Scicli lies in a basin dominated by the ruins of castles and churches. The two views show the town seen from a height above the church of Santo Spirito, and the façade of the church of San Bartolomeo.

right In Ragusa Ibla churches and monasteries are crowded together. Here we see the campanile of the Madonna dell'Itria and the church of the Purgatorio.

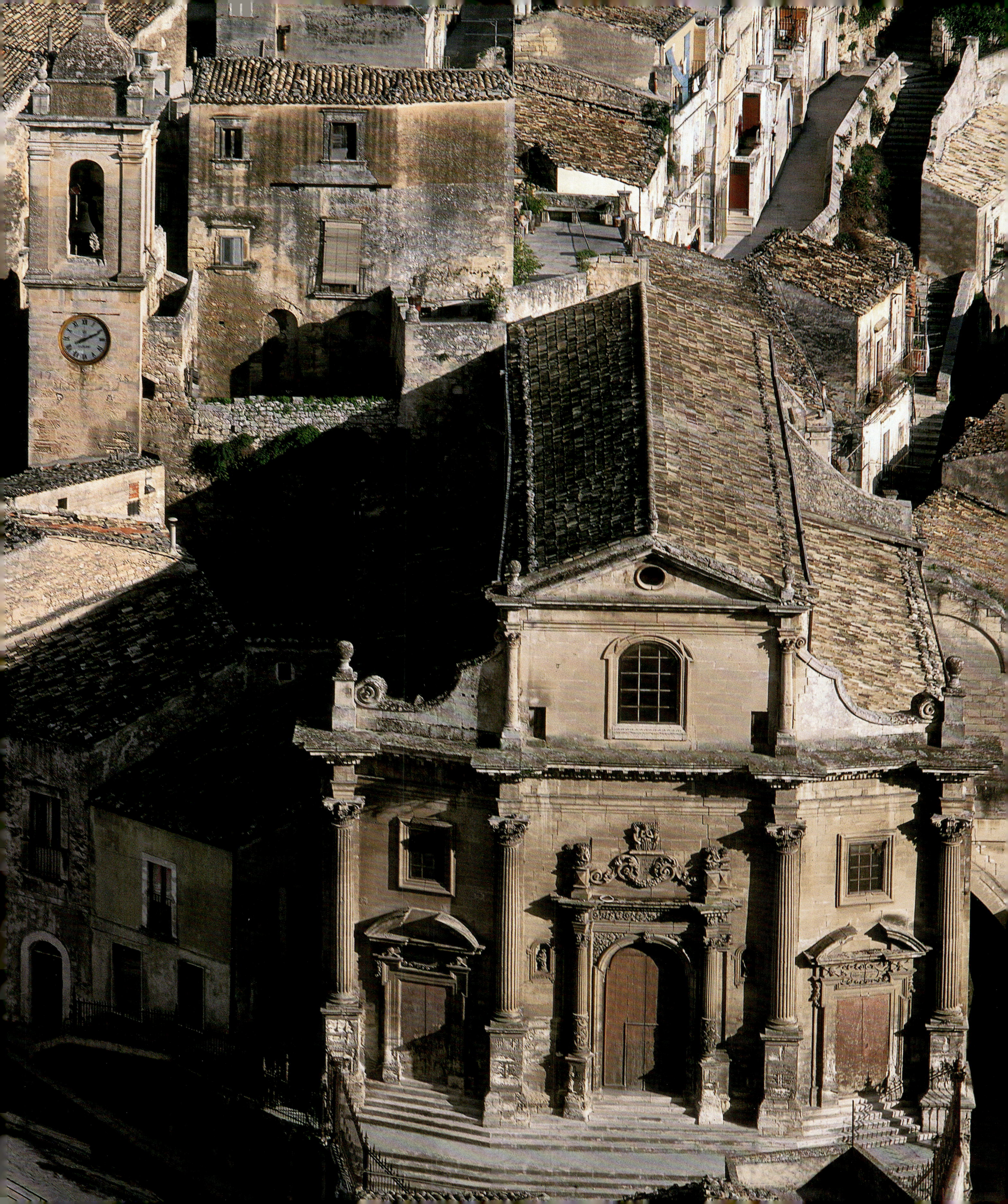

above Noto, looking out from the terrace of the church of San Carlo, towards the Via Nicolaci and the church of Montevergine.

right Palazzo Ducezio, the town hall of Noto. In the background is the Jesuit church of San Carlo.

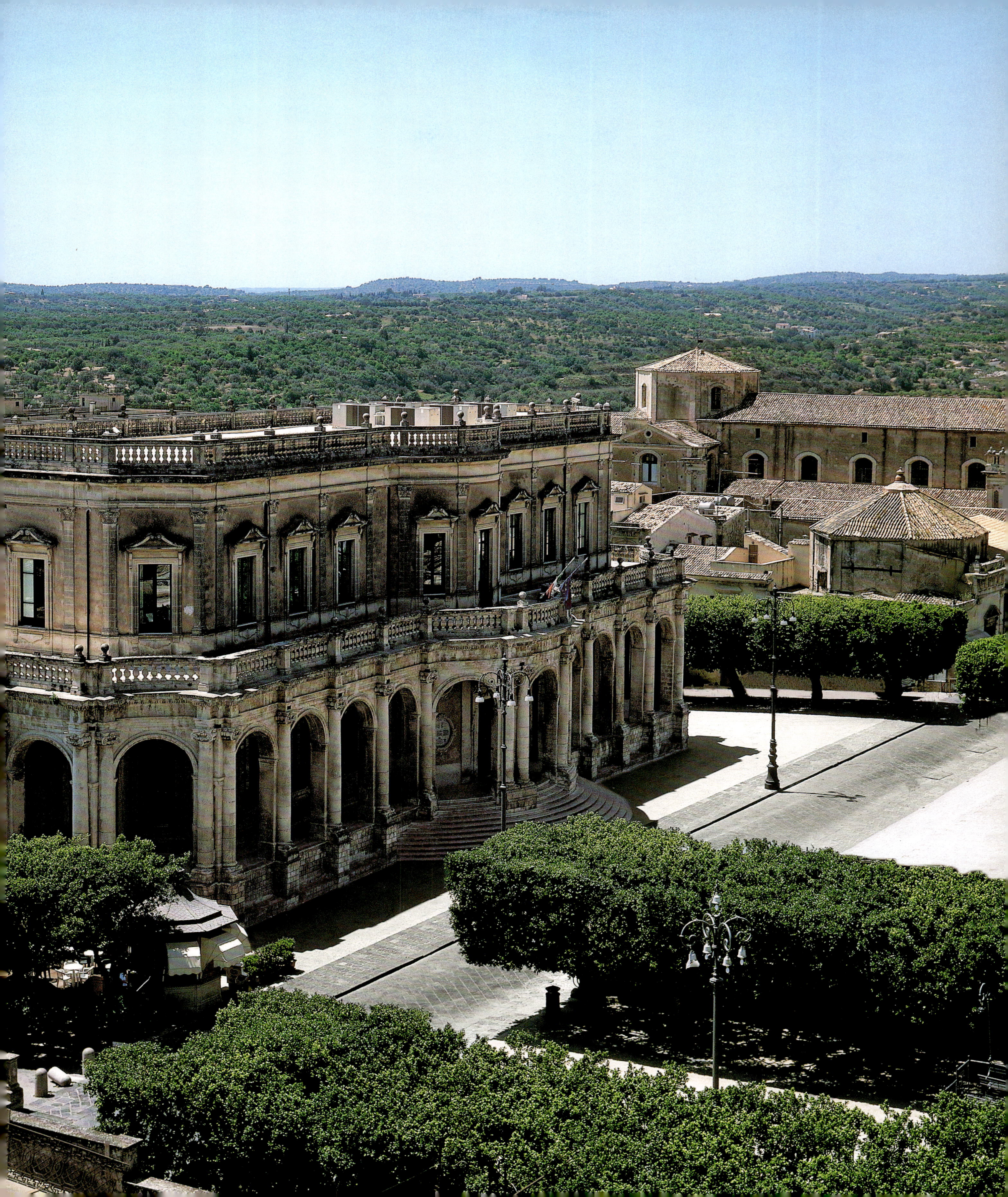

44   *The places: old and new*

left The elegant bridge over the San Leonardo river at Termini Imerese.

above The Alfano bridge at Canicattini Bagni is decorated with statues of figures from folklore.

left The dome of the church of the Carmine, in the busy Ballarò market district of Palermo, is a striking sight with its polychrome majolica tiles and stucco reliefs.

opposite San Francesco Saverio in Palermo.

overleaf Two views of the extraordinary internal spaces of San Francesco Saverio in Palermo.

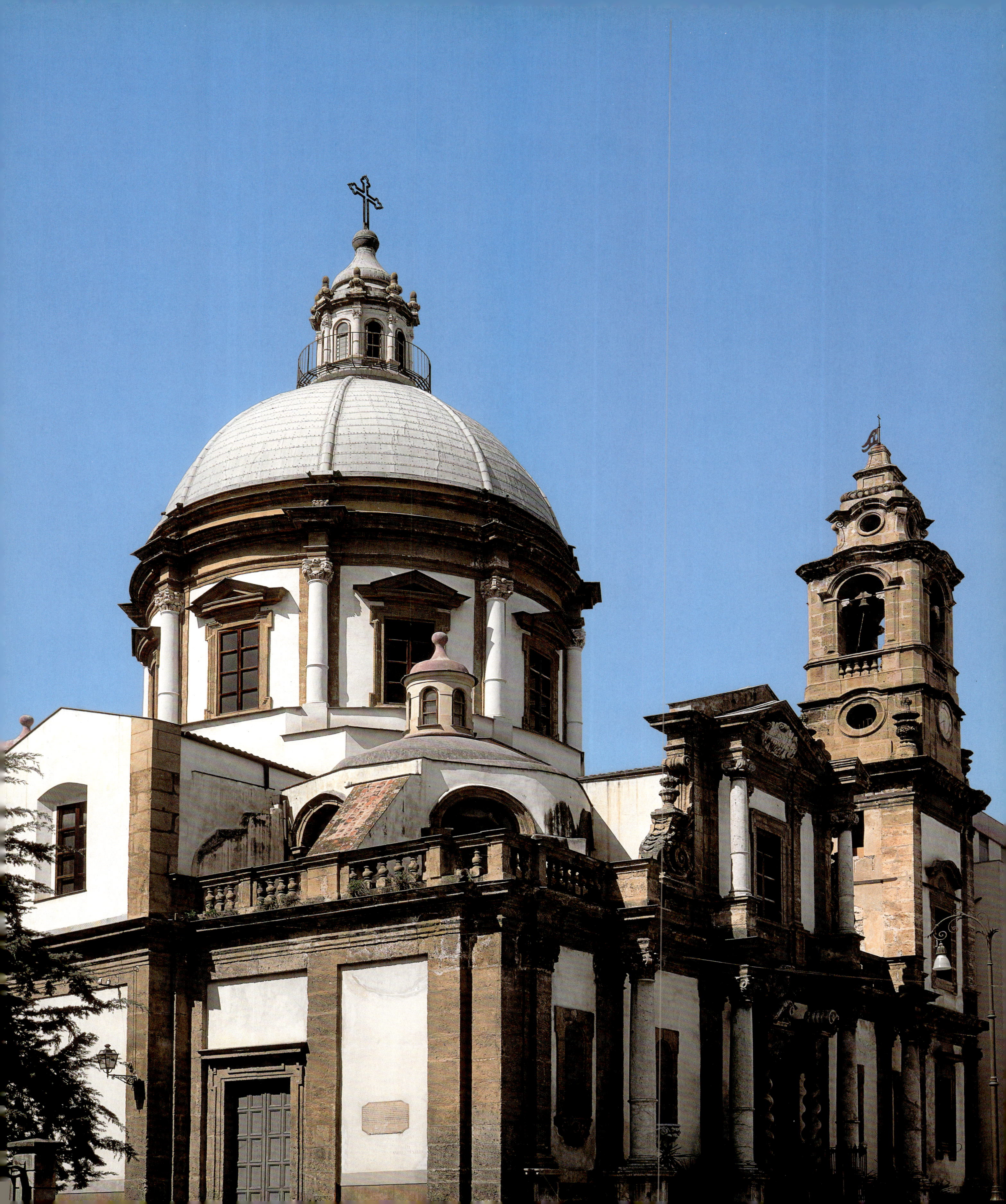

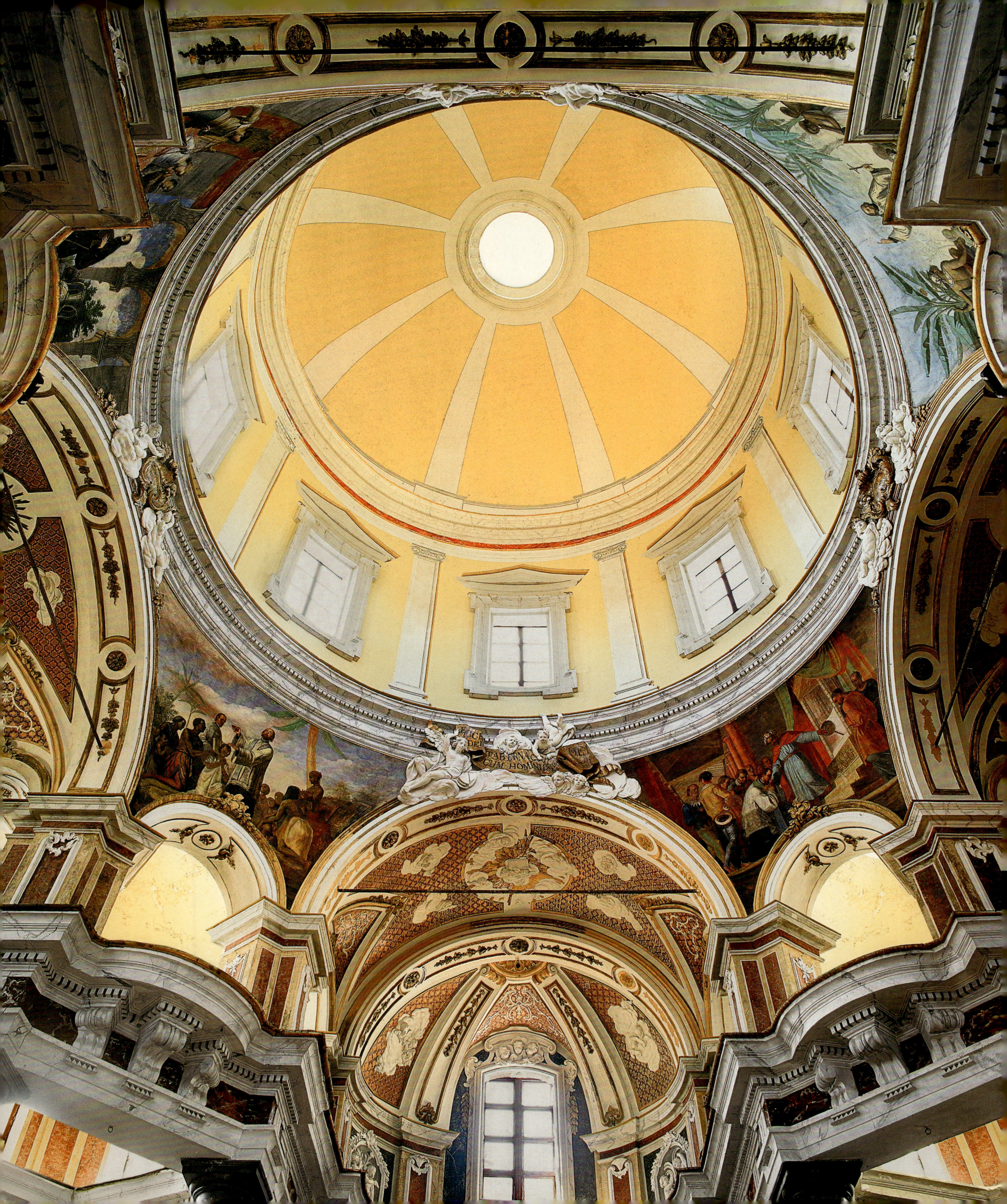

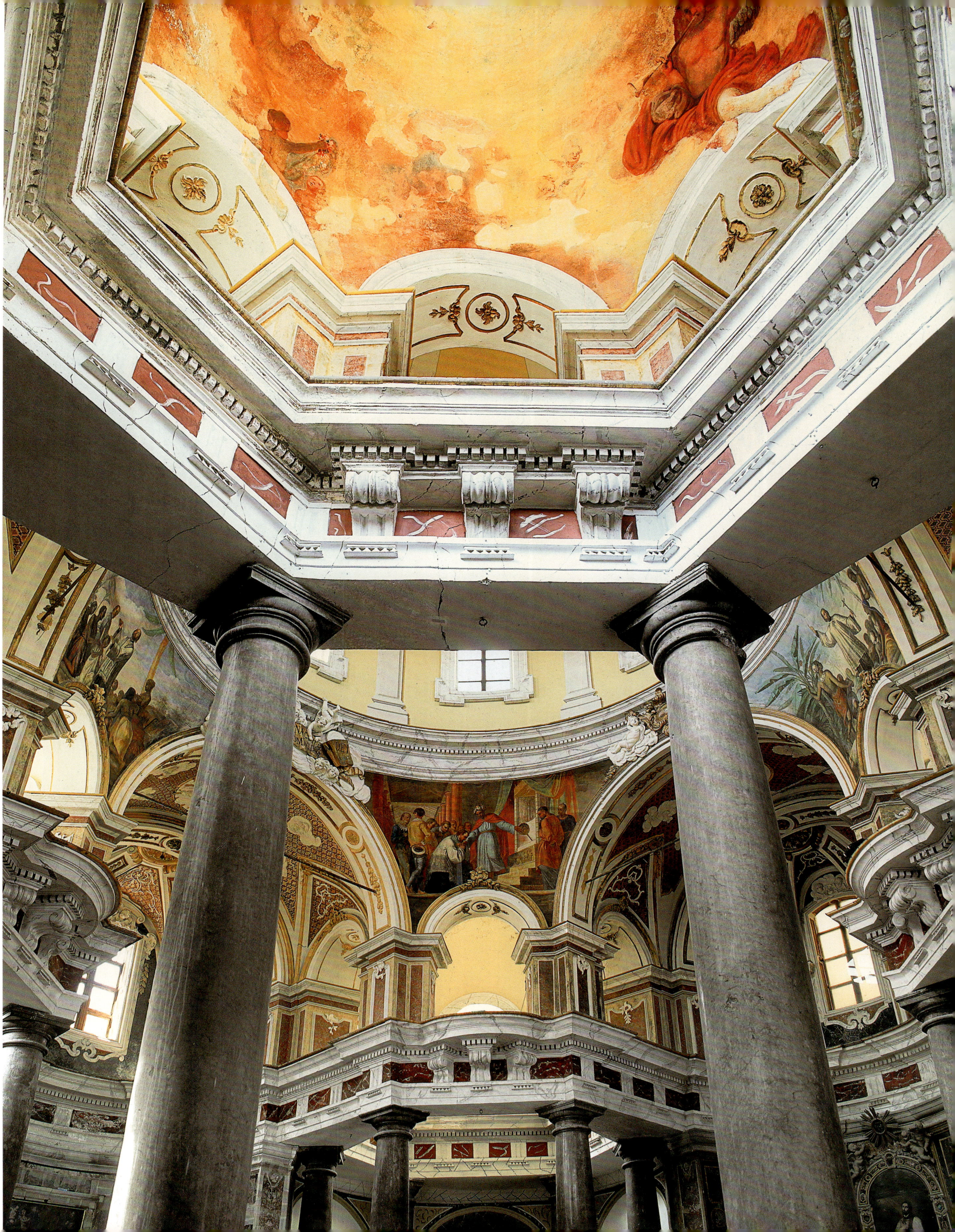

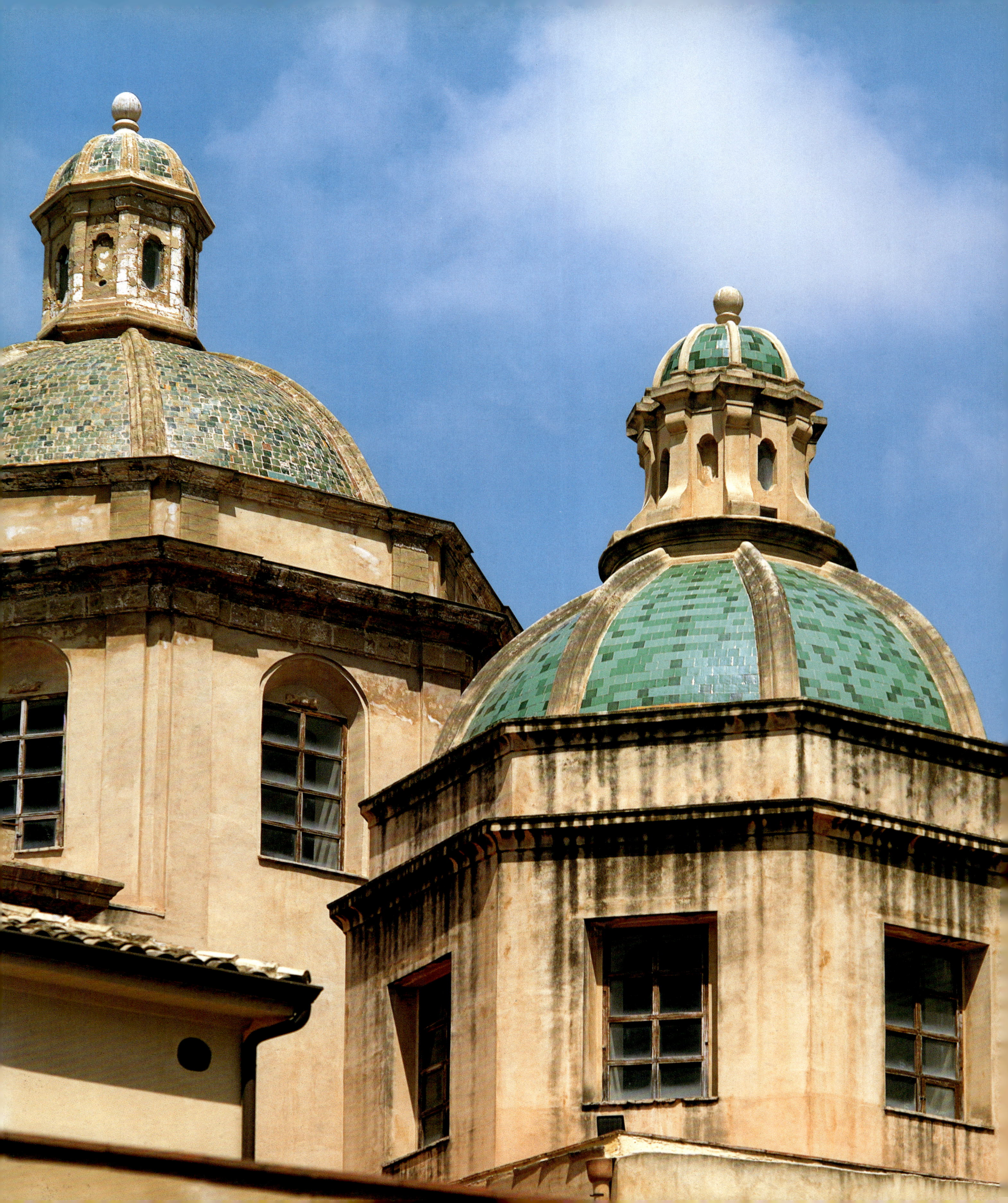

opposite The domes of the cathedral of Mazara del Vallo.

right The dome of the church of the Addolorata in Marsala, covered with majolica tiles.

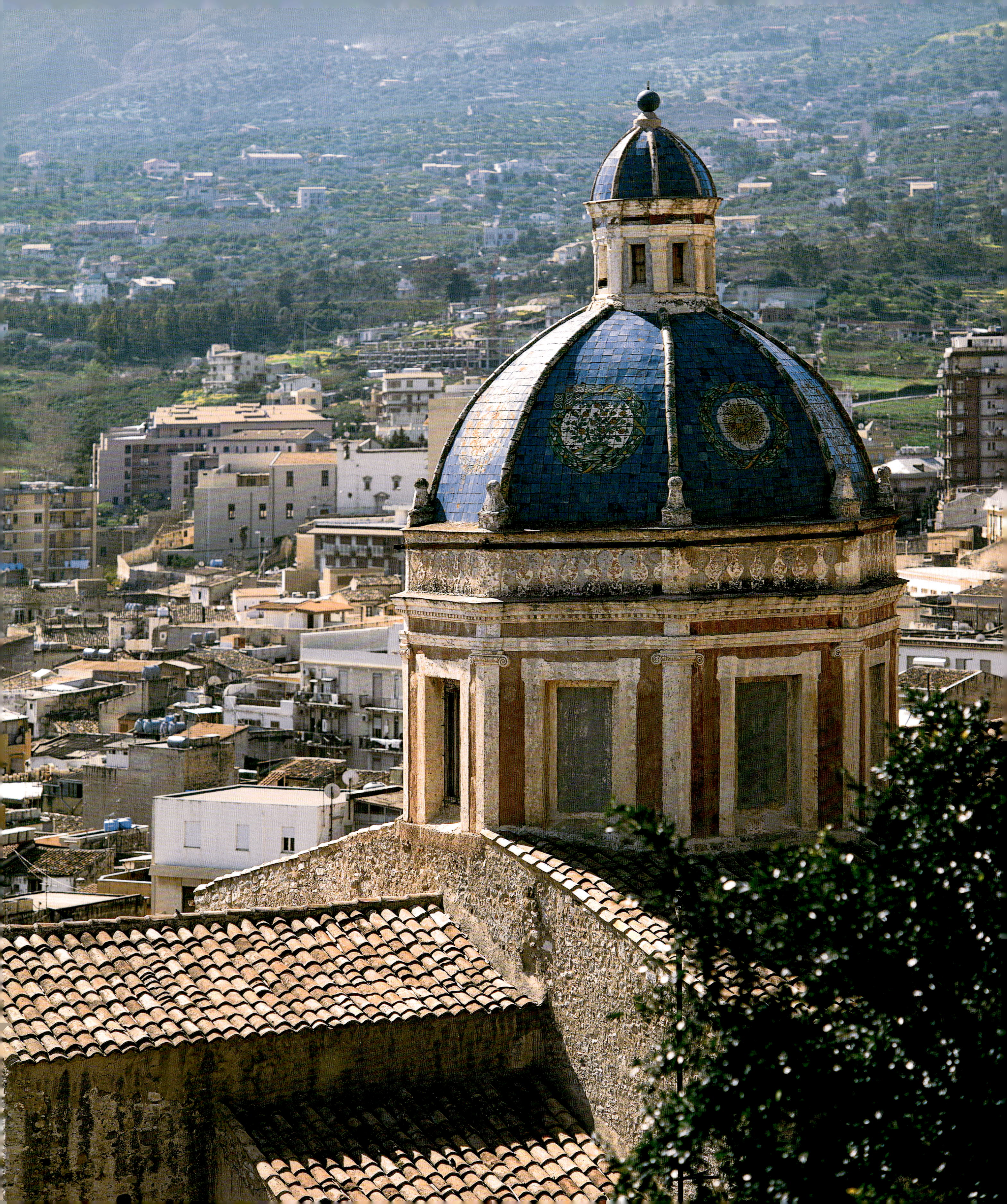

opposite The majolica-covered dome of the church of the Annunziata in Termini Imerese.

above The main dome and small domes of San Giuseppe dei Teatini in Palermo.

overleaf Interior of the church of the Gesù, or Casa Professa, in Palermo.

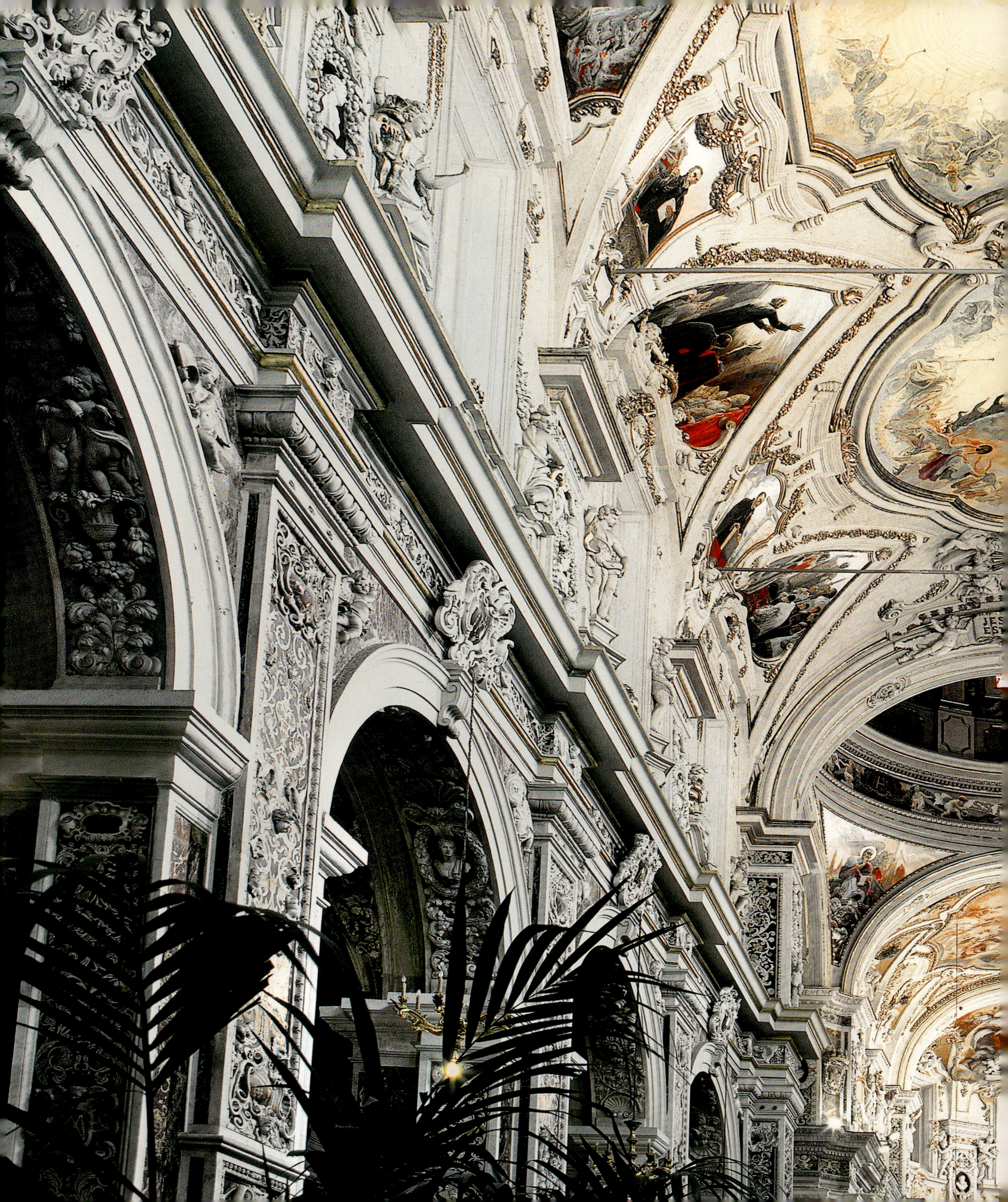

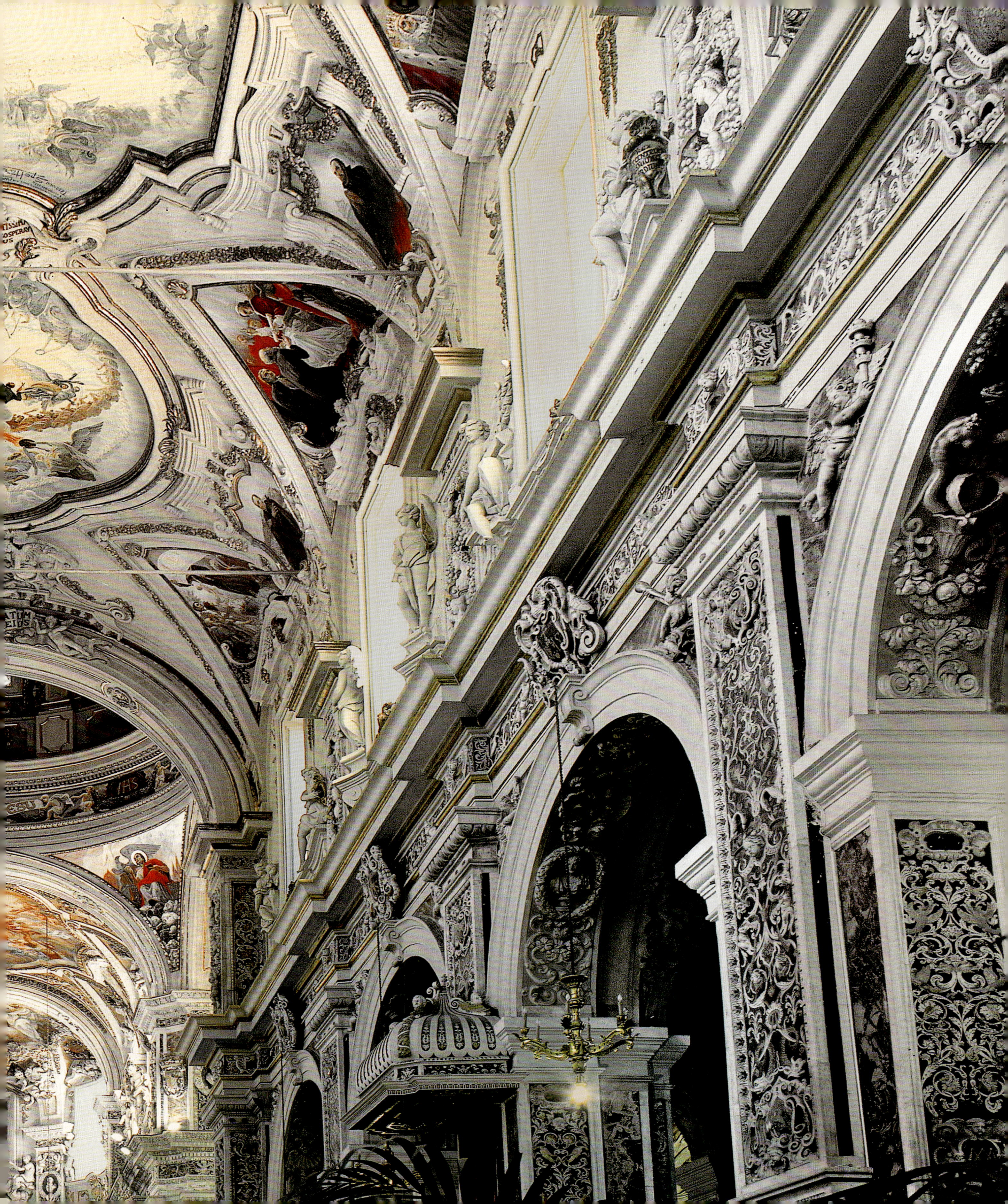

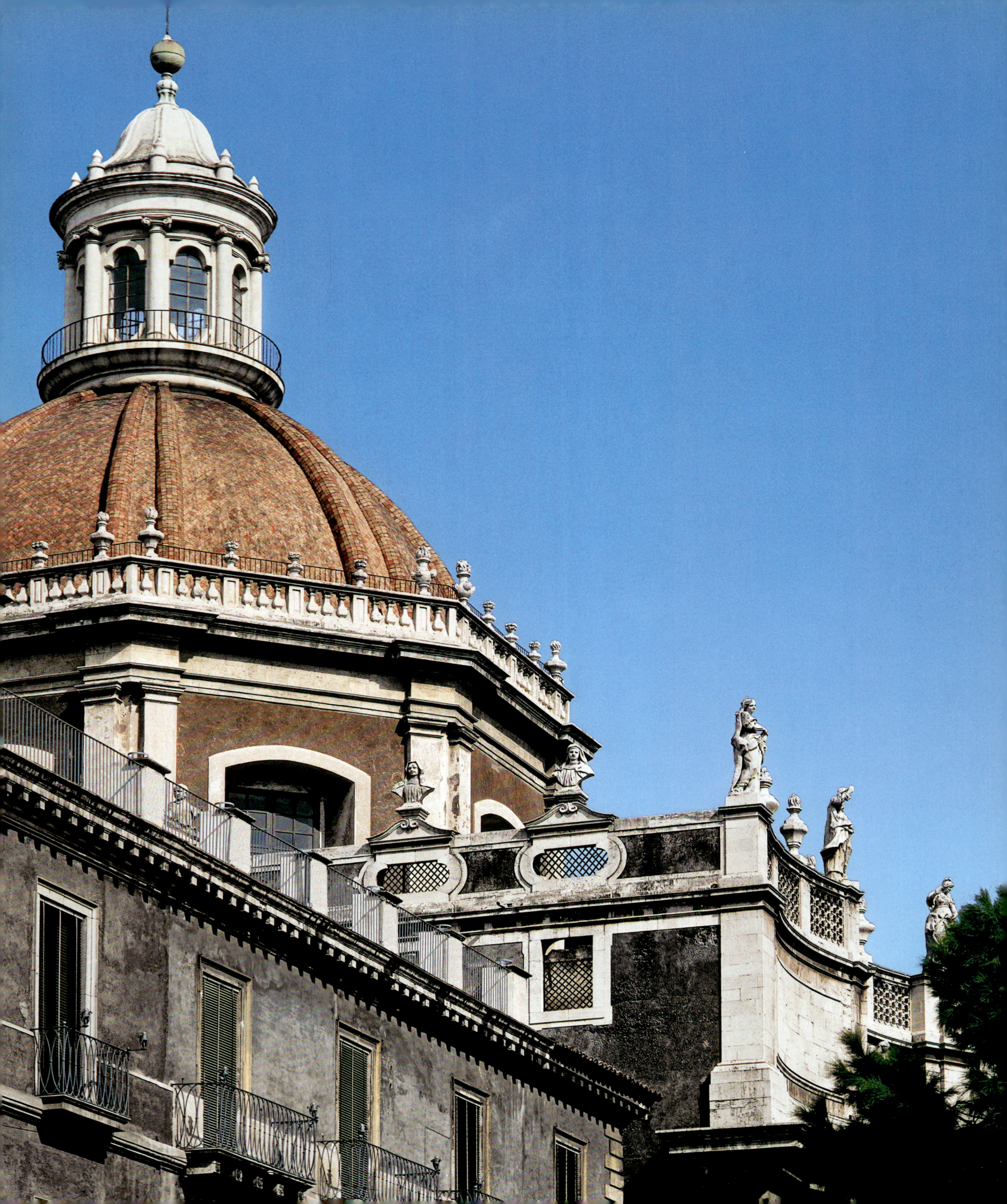

opposite The dome of the church of the Badia di Sant'Agata in Catania.

right The dome of the Chiesa Madre at Acireale. In the foreground is a corner of the Palazzo Municipale, with brackets supporting a balcony.

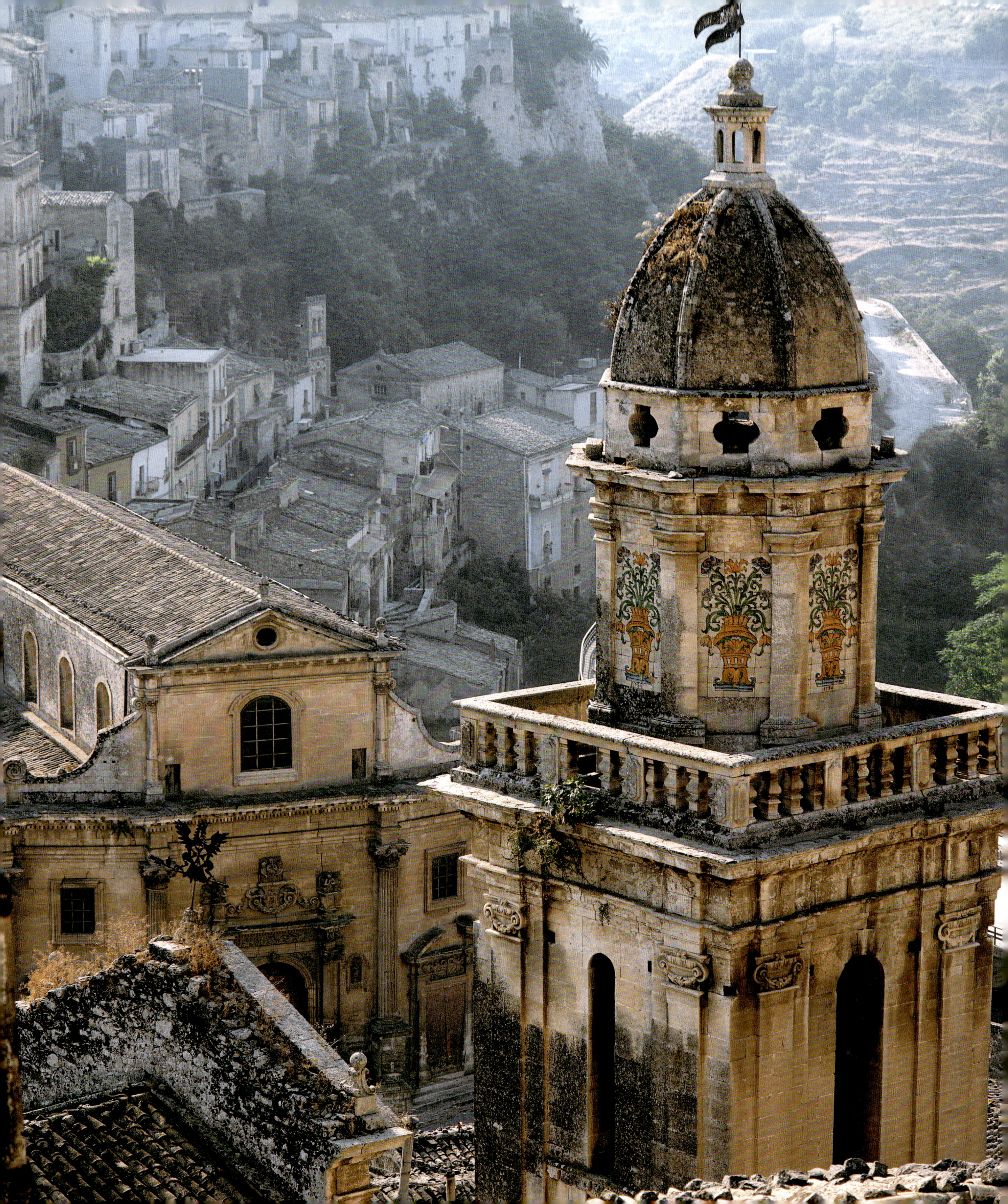

opposite The campanile of the church of the Madonna dell'Itria in Ragusa Ibla, with decorative majolica panels.

right The campanile of the church of Cristo dell'Olmo at Mazzarino, covered with majolica tiles.

left The campanile of San Bartolomeo, Scicli.

opposite The handsome façade of Santa Veneranda in Mazara del Vallo, ornamented with stucco, statues, and wrought iron.

overleaf, left The campanile of the Chiesa Madre, Castiglione di Sicilia.

overleaf, right The towers of the Chiesa Madre of Acireale, added to the façade in the 18th century by G. B. F. Basile.

page 64 The campanile and dome of San Giuliano, Erice.

page 65 The domes of the church of the Madonna delle Grazie in Lipari.

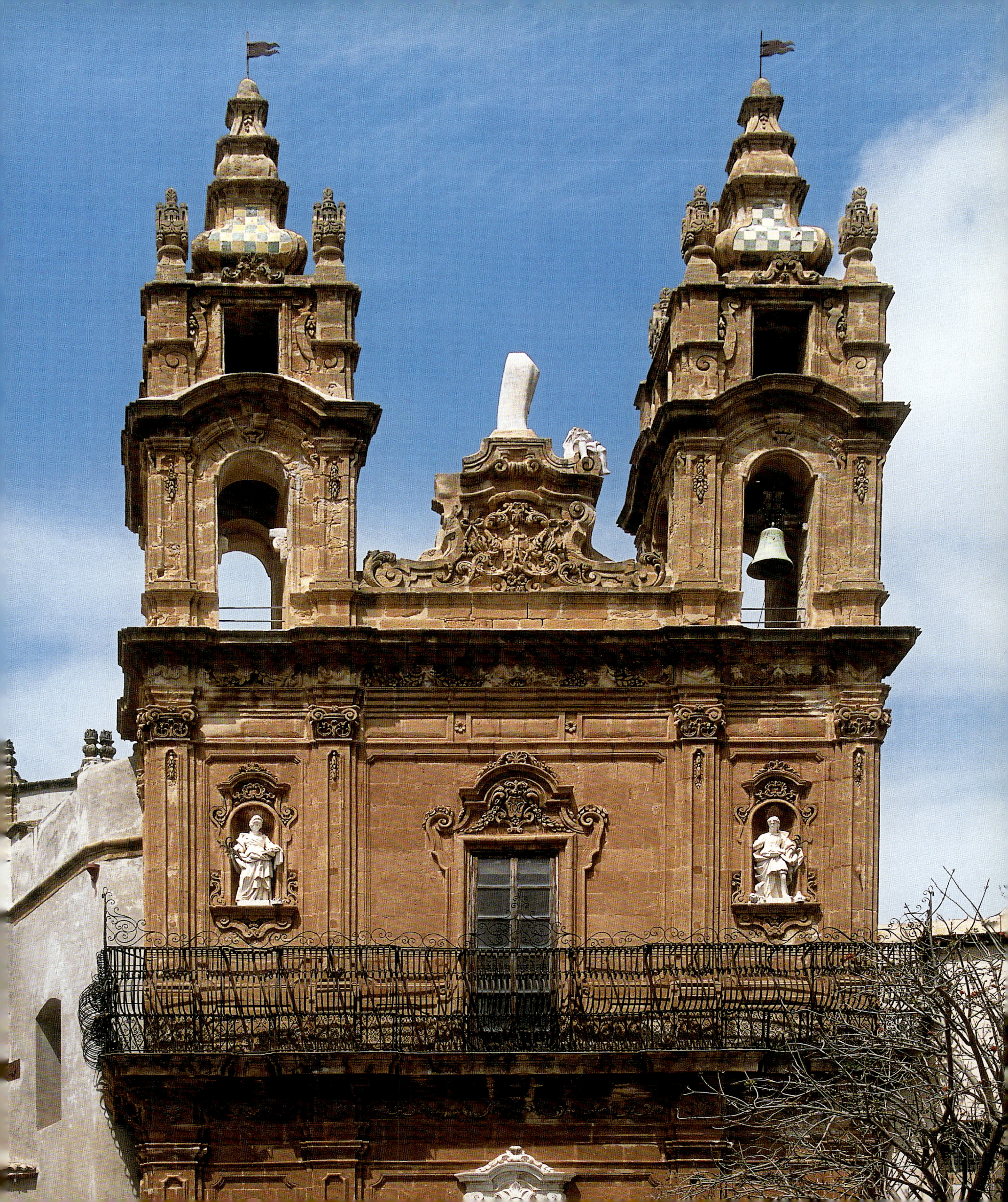

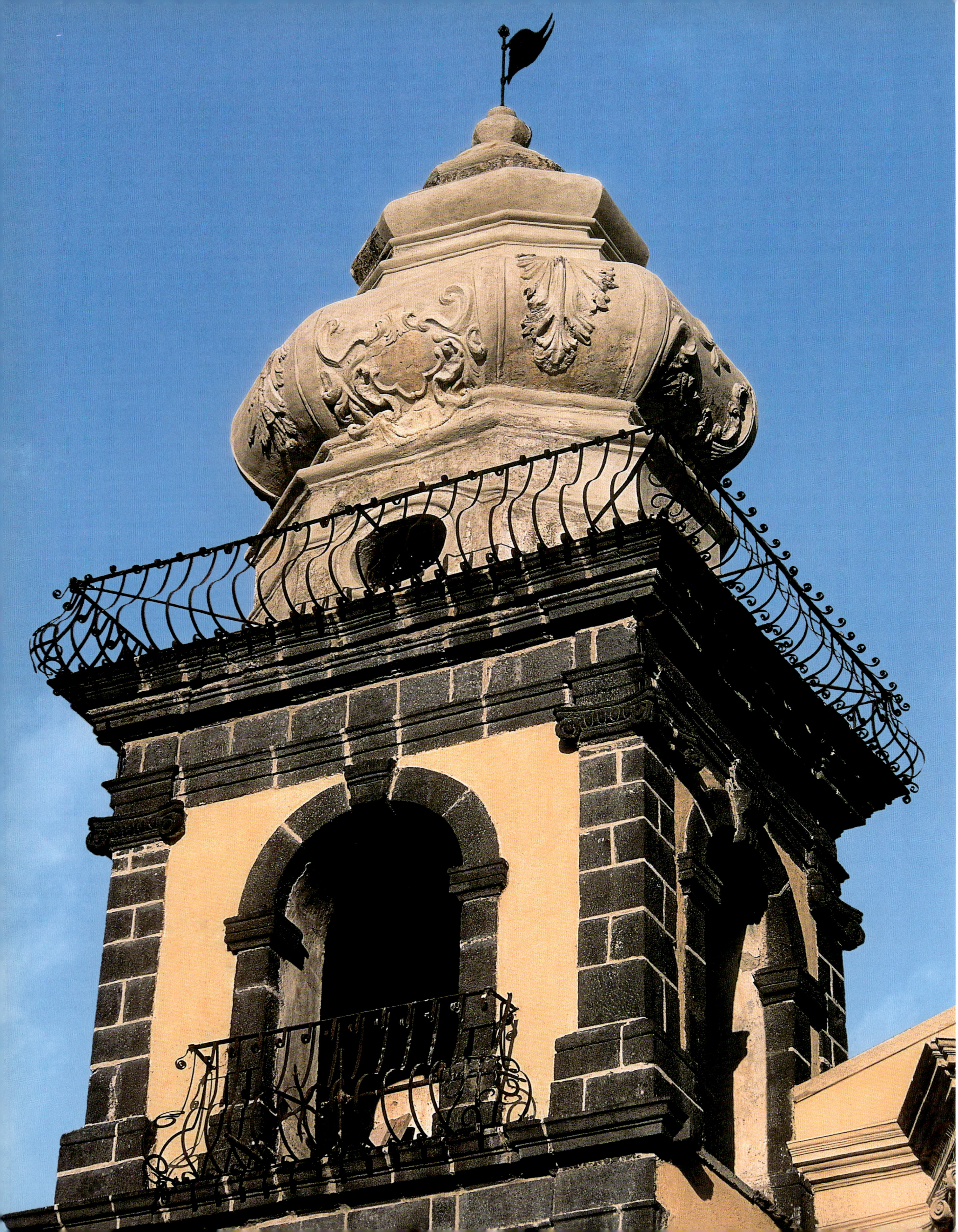

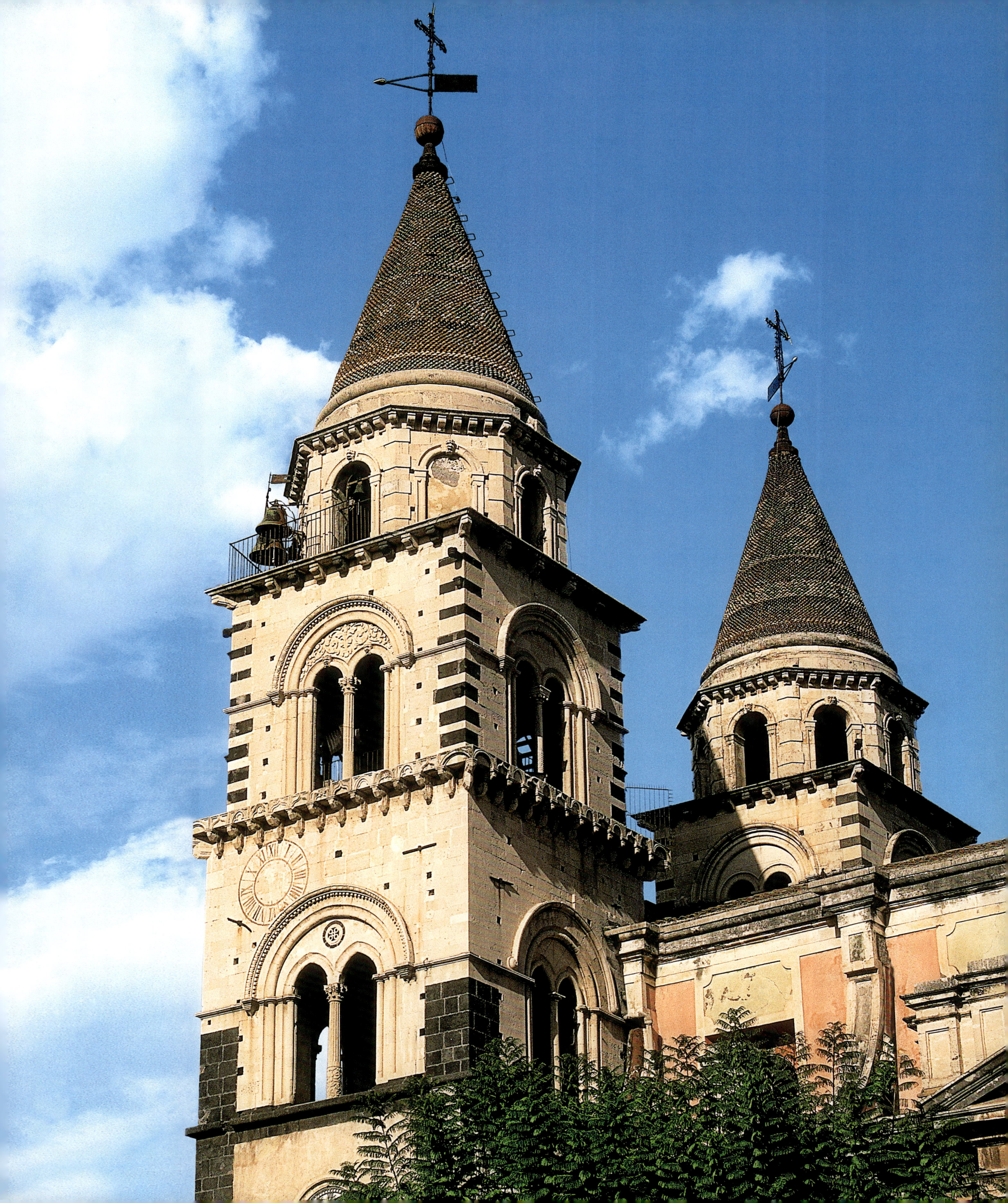

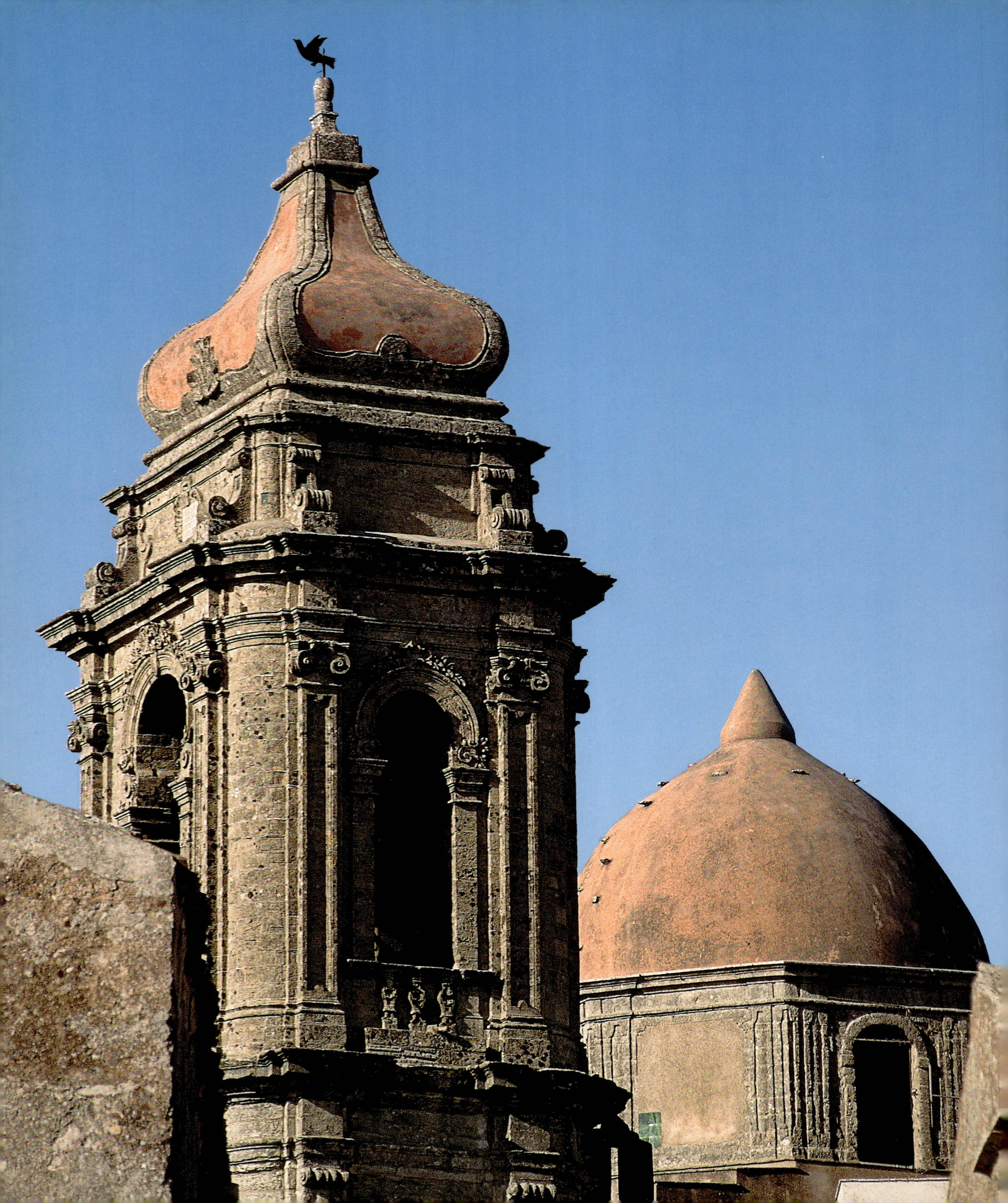

The places: old and new **65**

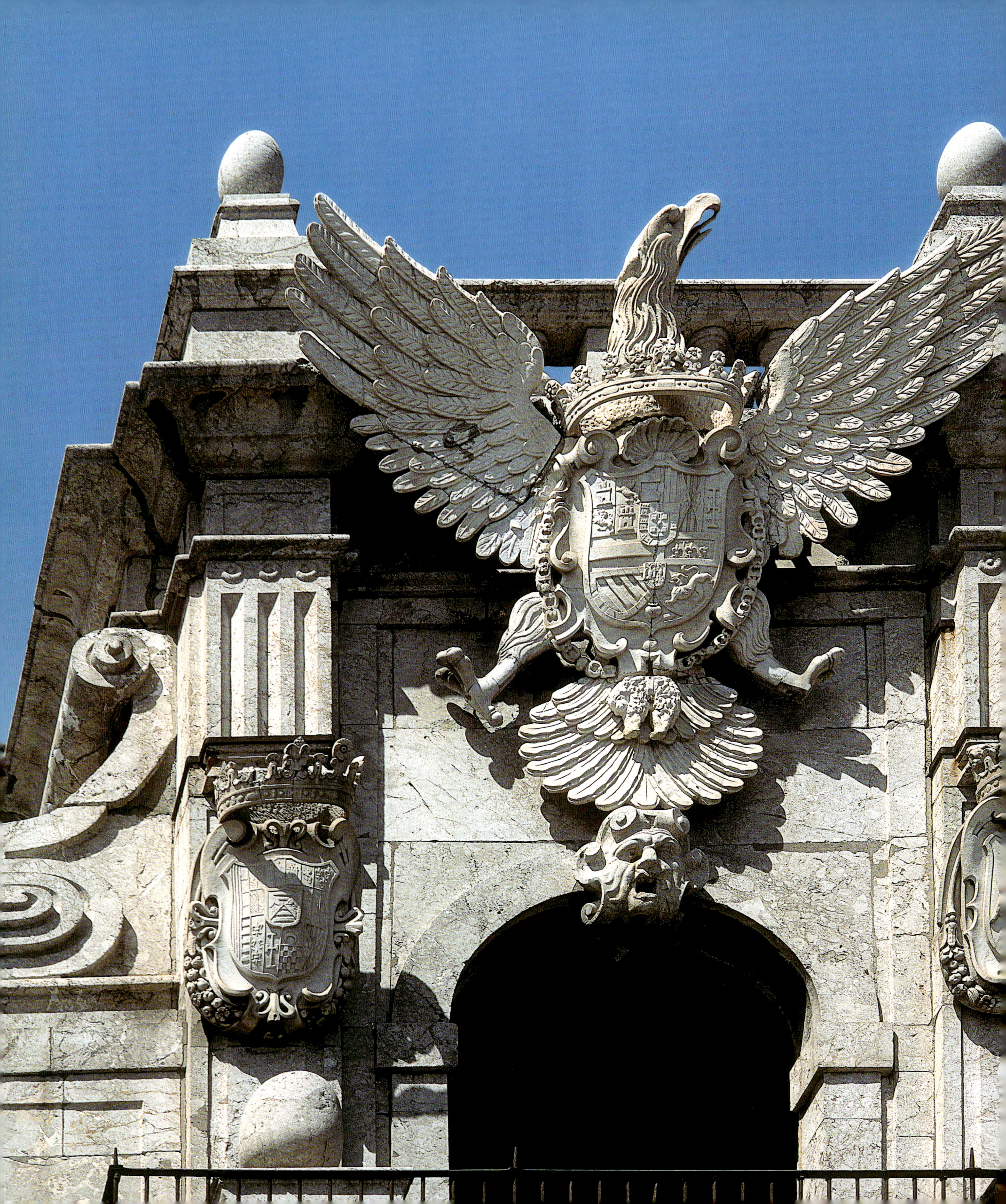

opposite and above The Porta Felice at the end of the Cassaro in Palermo, built in 1582 by Marcantonio Colonna, who dedicated it to his wife.

overleaf Two views of the Porta Grazia in Messina. Few Baroque monuments were left standing after the earthquake of 1908. This gate, part of the citadel designed by Carlos de Grunenbergh, was re-erected on another site.

The places: old and new 67

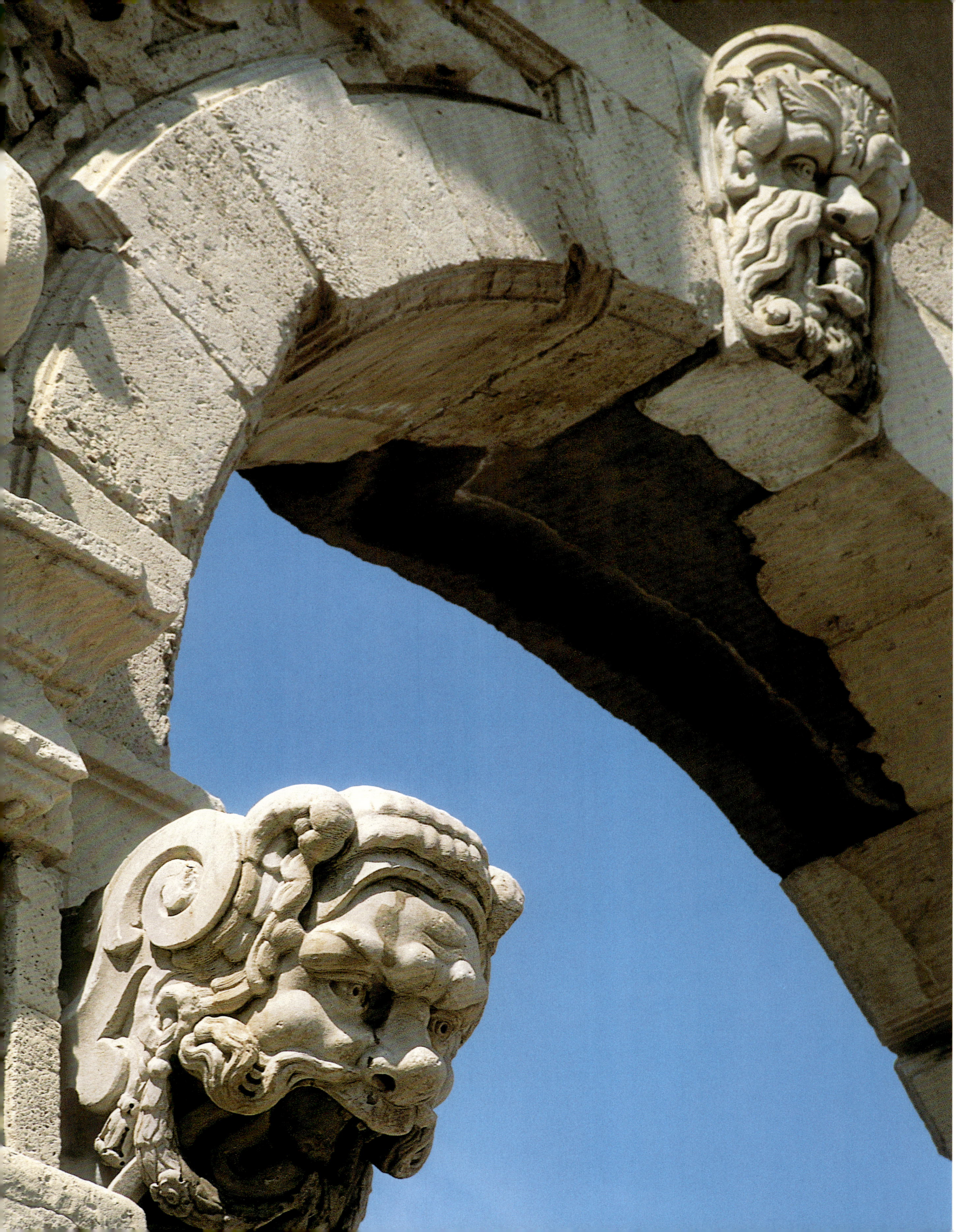

The places: old and new 69

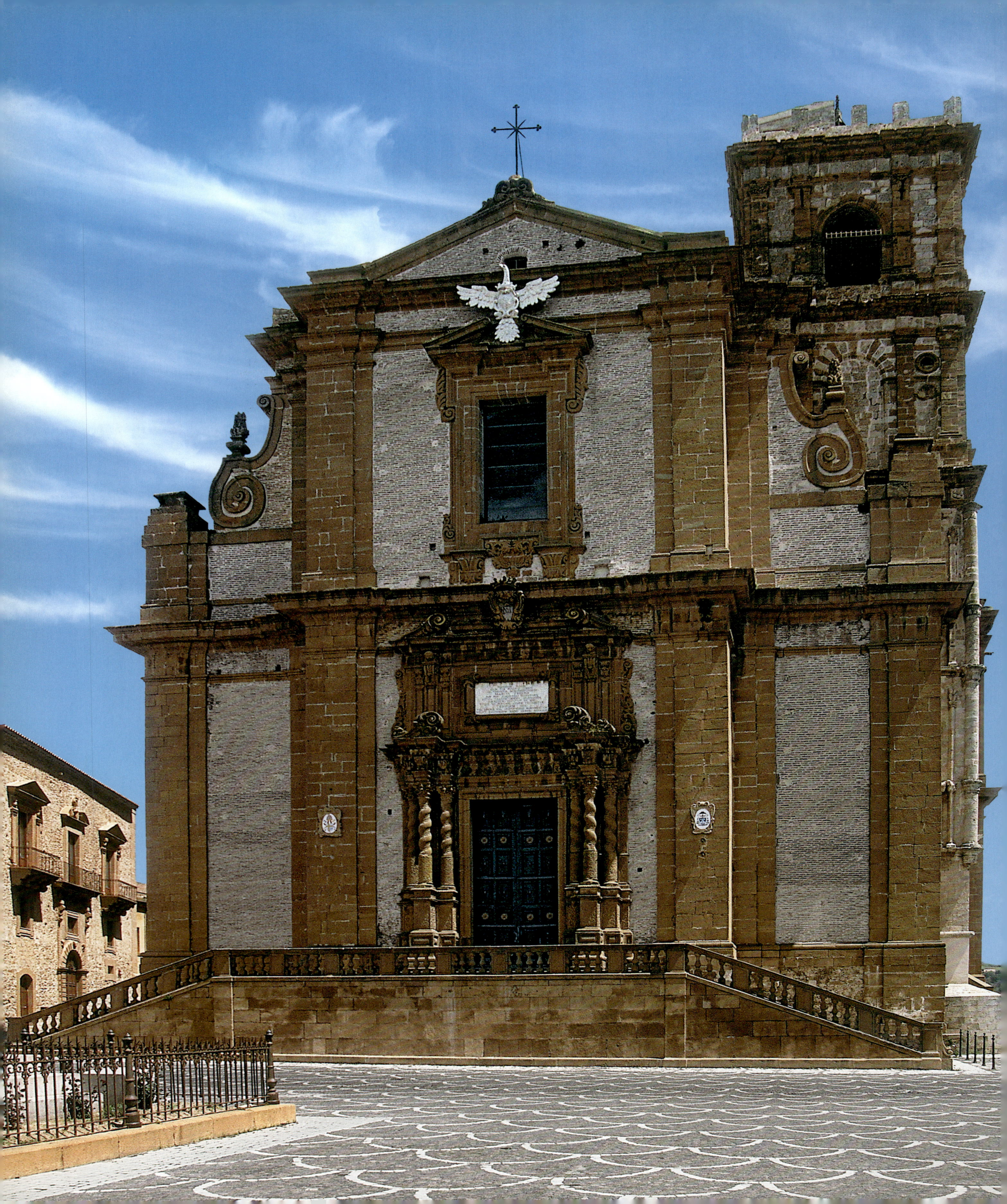

opposite The Chiesa Madre of San Giorgio at Caccamo was founded in Norman times and later rebuilt. It looks out over a beautiful piazza surrounded by Baroque buildings.

right The Chiesa Madre of Piazza Armerina has a Baroque façade and a massive Gothic belltower.

pages 72–73 Detail of the Quattro Canti (Piazza Vigliena) in Palermo, a showcase of the Spanish monarchy and of the saints protecting the city.

pages 74–75 Santa Maria Maggiore in Ispica, and its semicircular courtyard.

The places: old and new 71

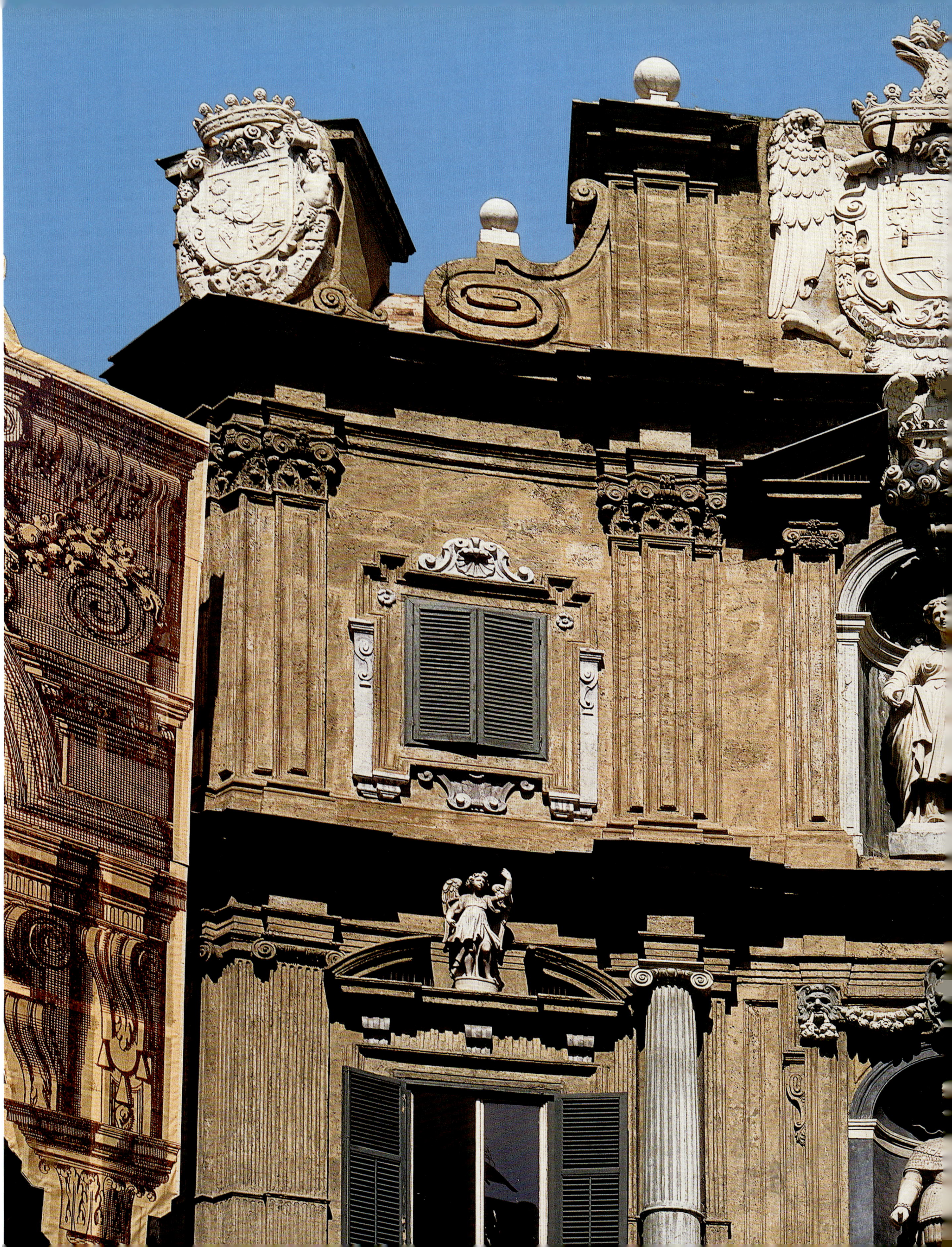

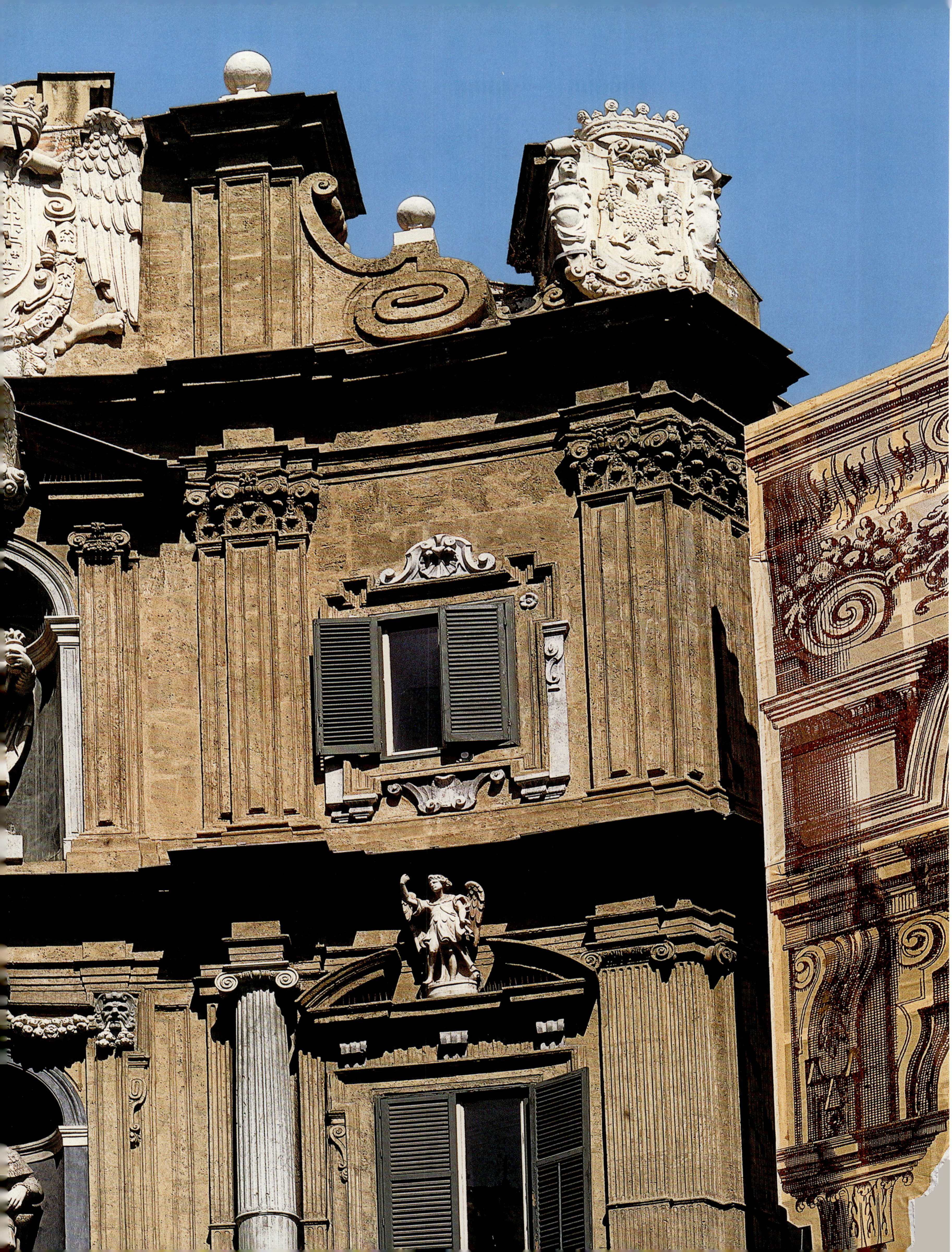

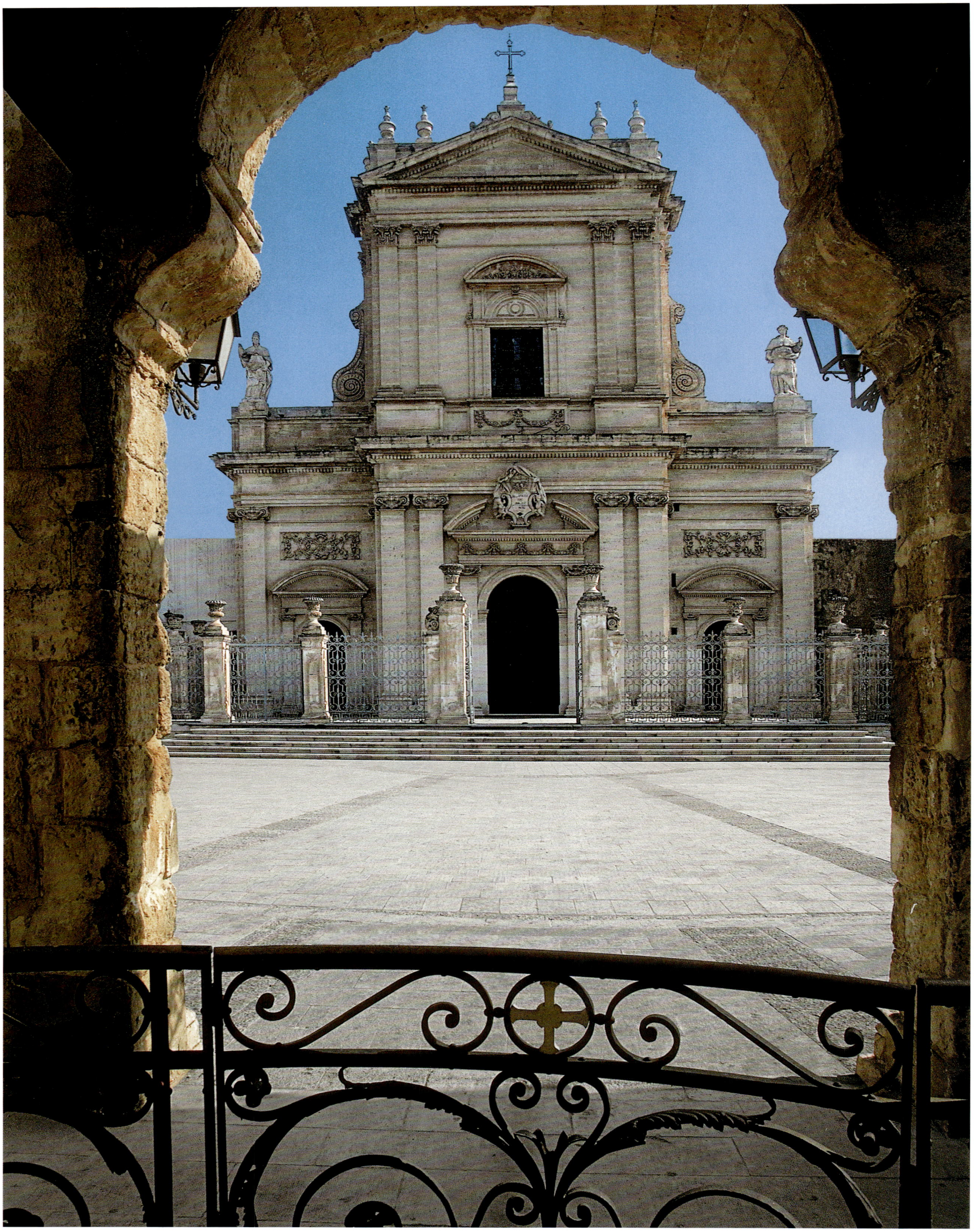

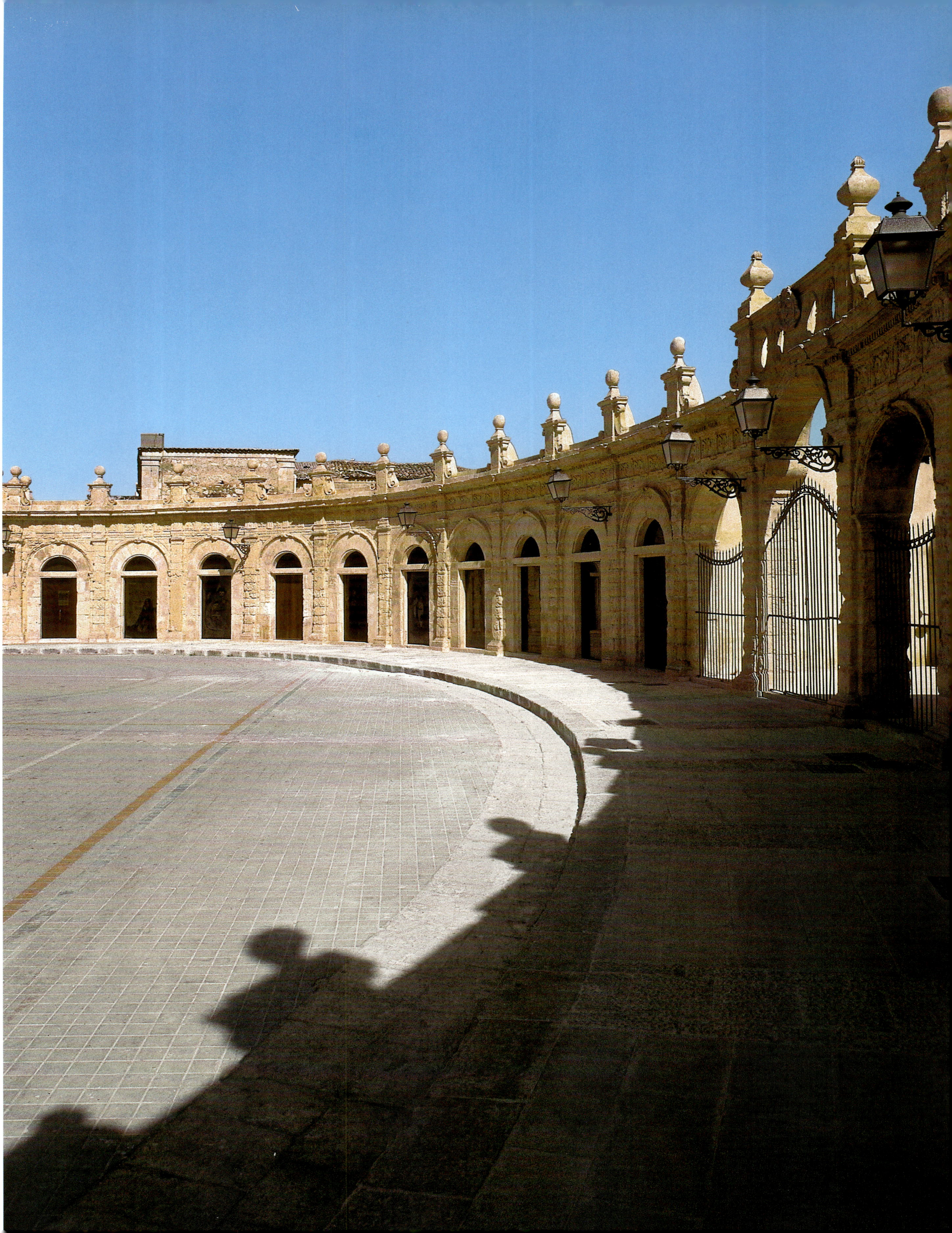

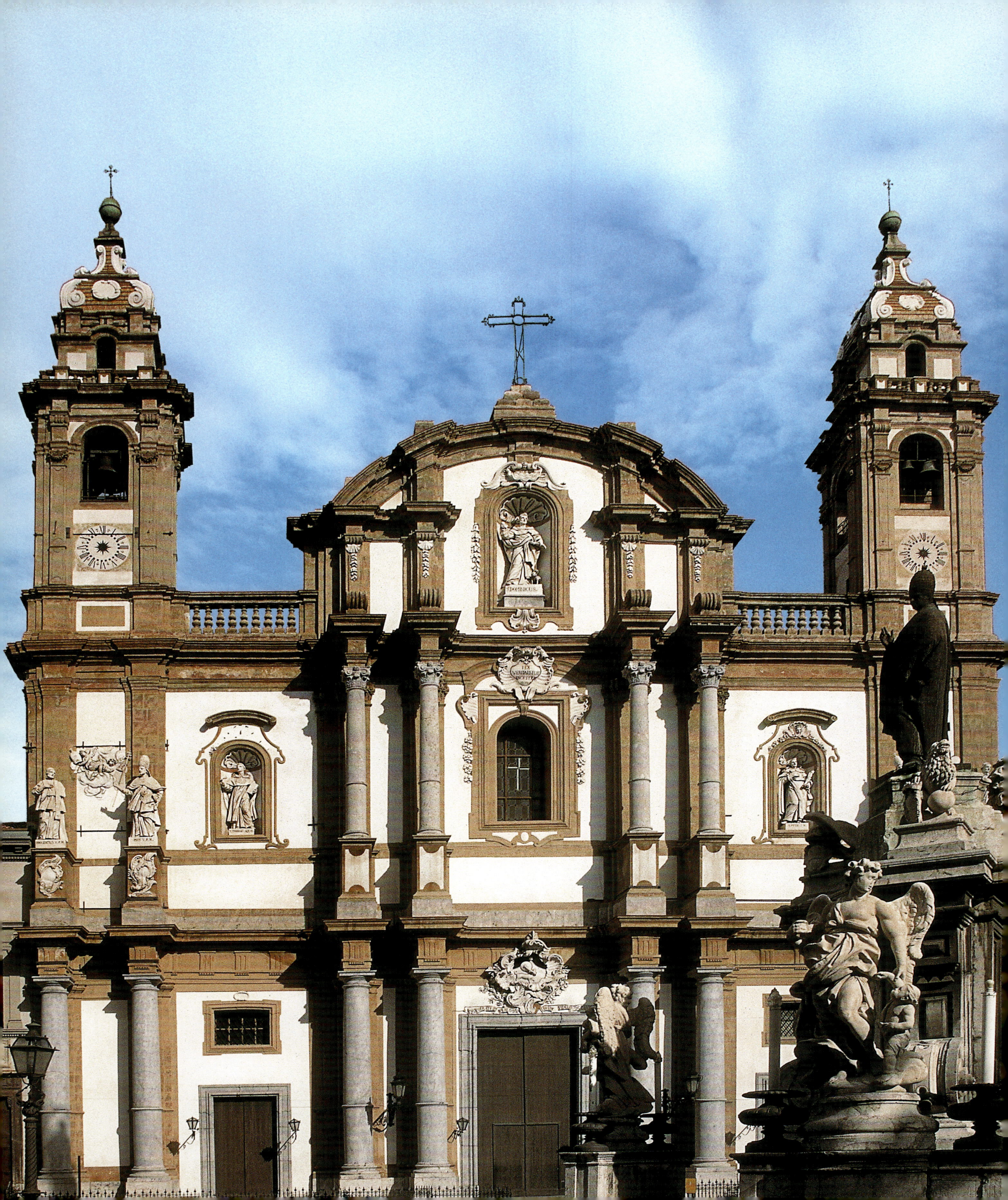

HÆC PORTA DOMINI
IVSTI INTRABVNT IN EAM

preceding pages, left San Domenico, the largest church in Palermo.

preceding pages, right An ornately paved forecourt sets off the church of San Giovanni Battista in Sortino.

left The court in front of San Sebastiano in Melilli.

opposite The façade of the Chiesa Madre in Trecastagni, reached by a flight of steps.

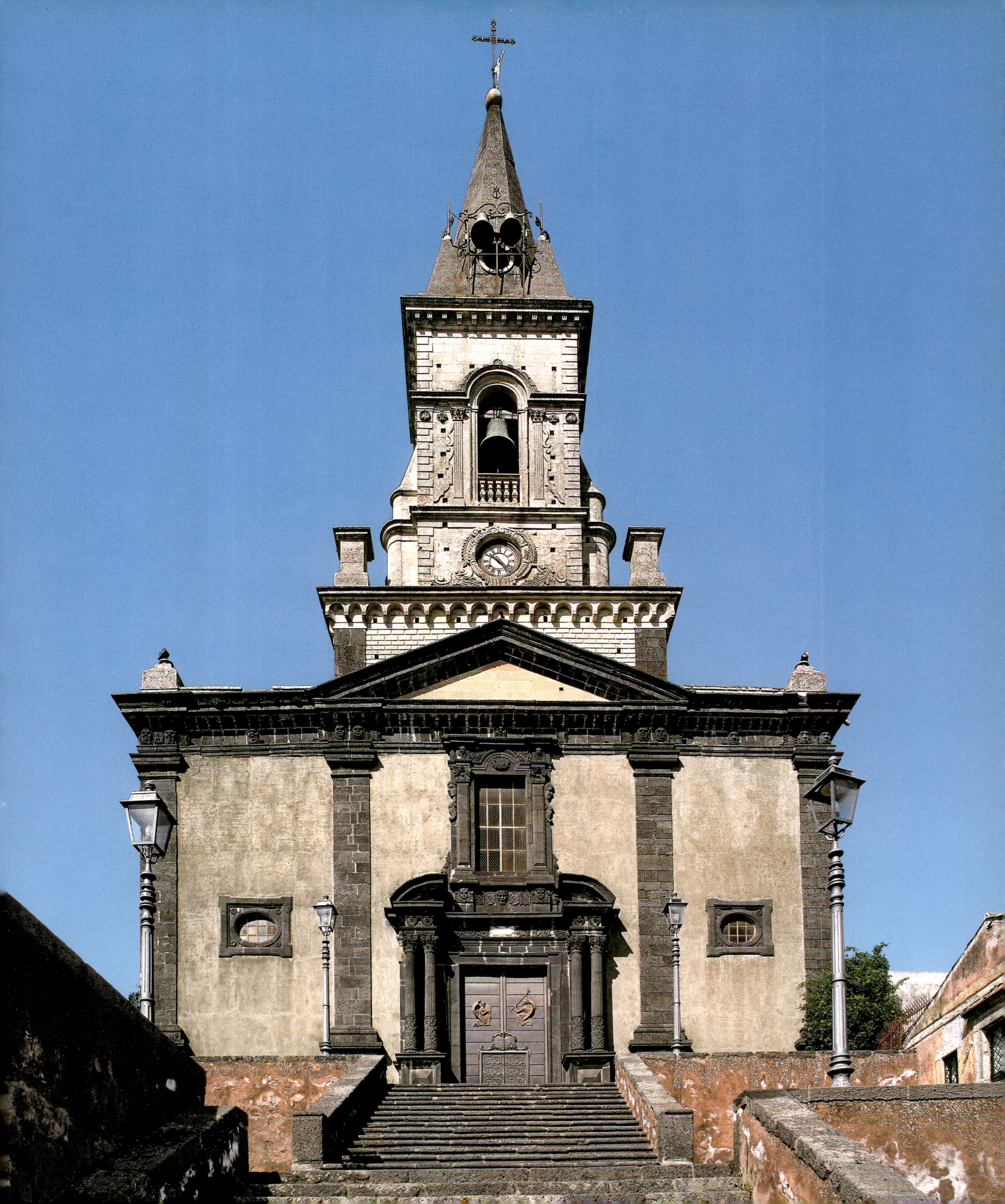

The loggia of the former hospital of San Bartolomeo in Palermo, near the Porta Felice, survived bombing in the Second World War which badly damaged the building.

overleaf The galleries of the Seminario in Mazara del Vallo.

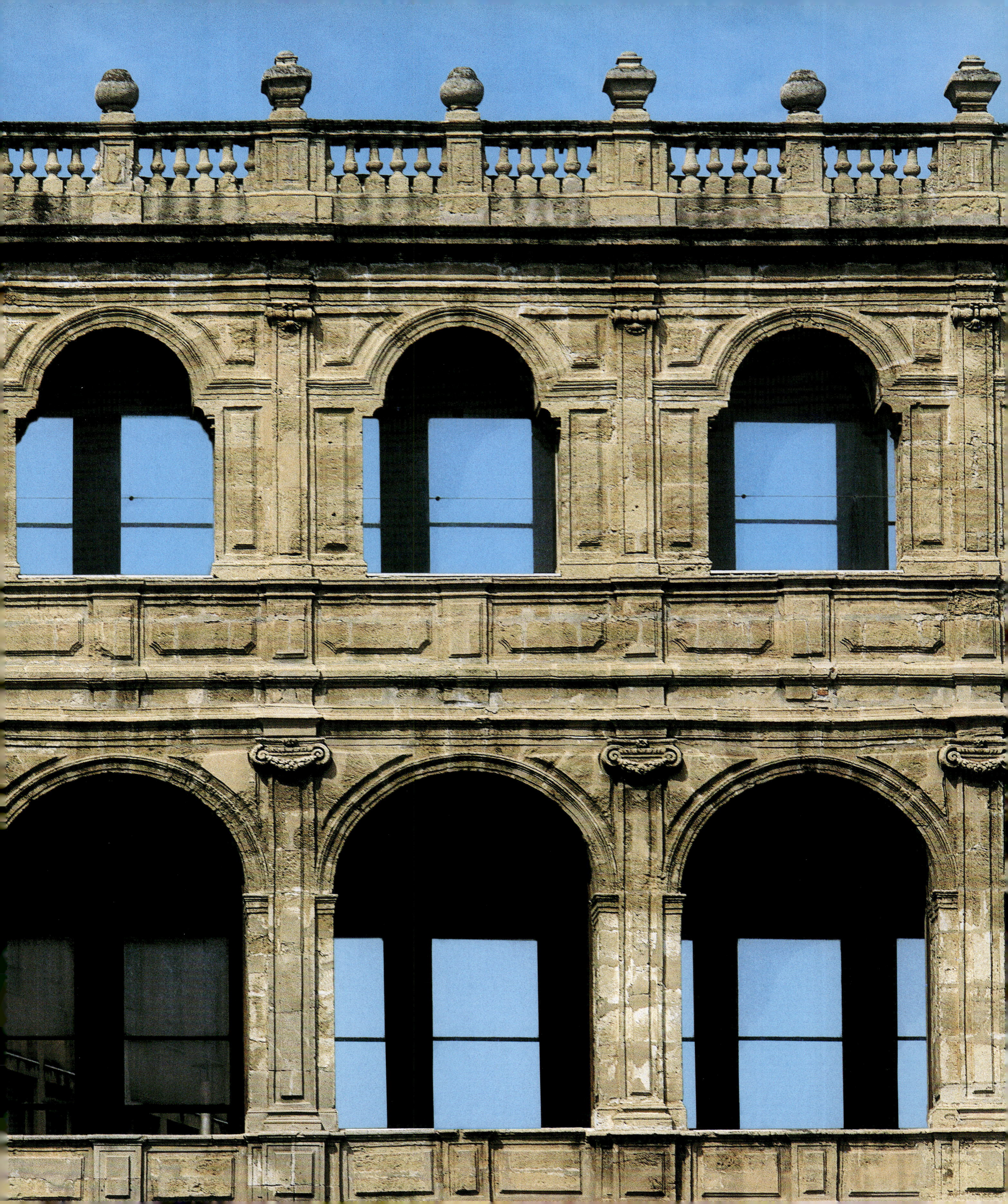

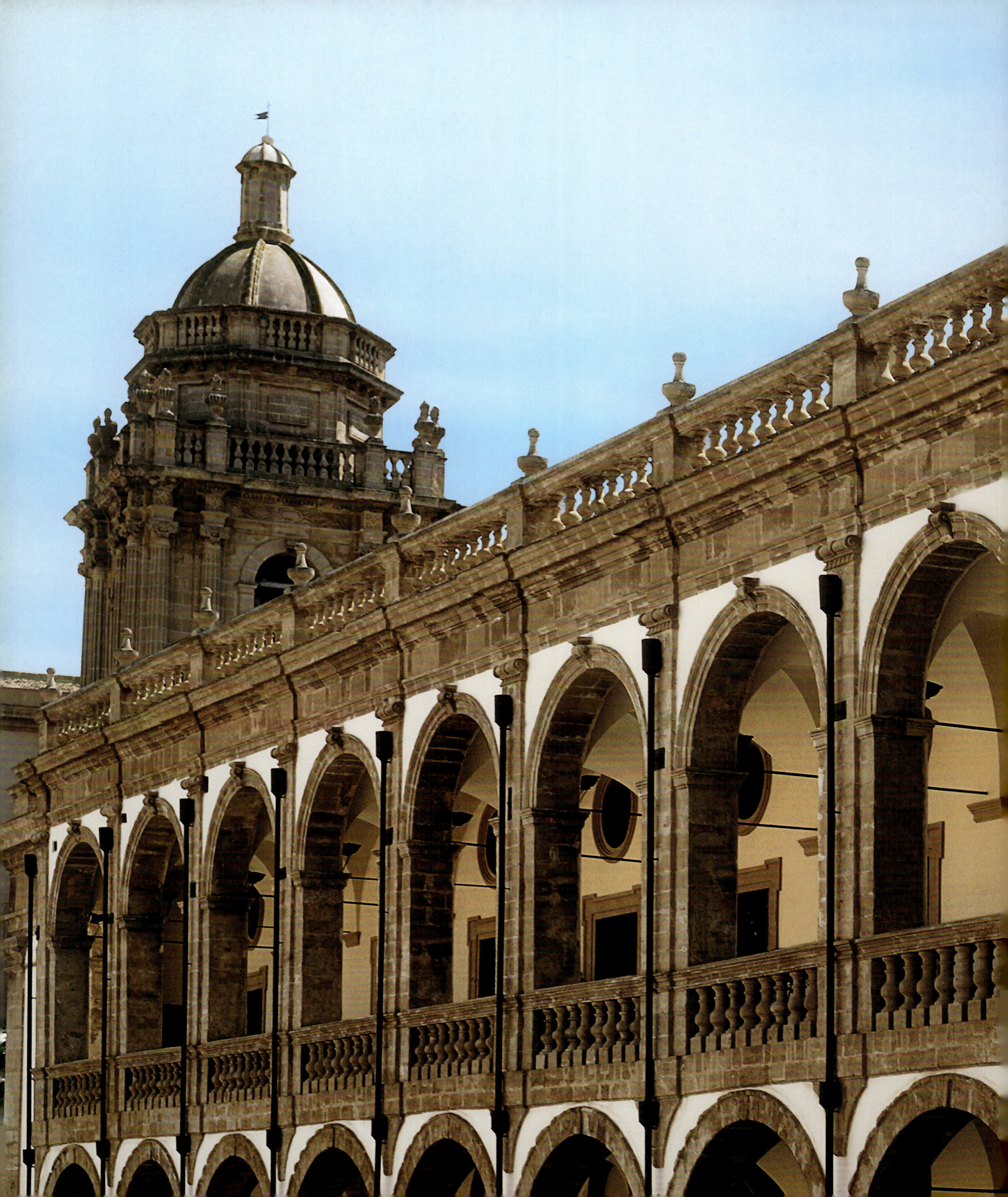

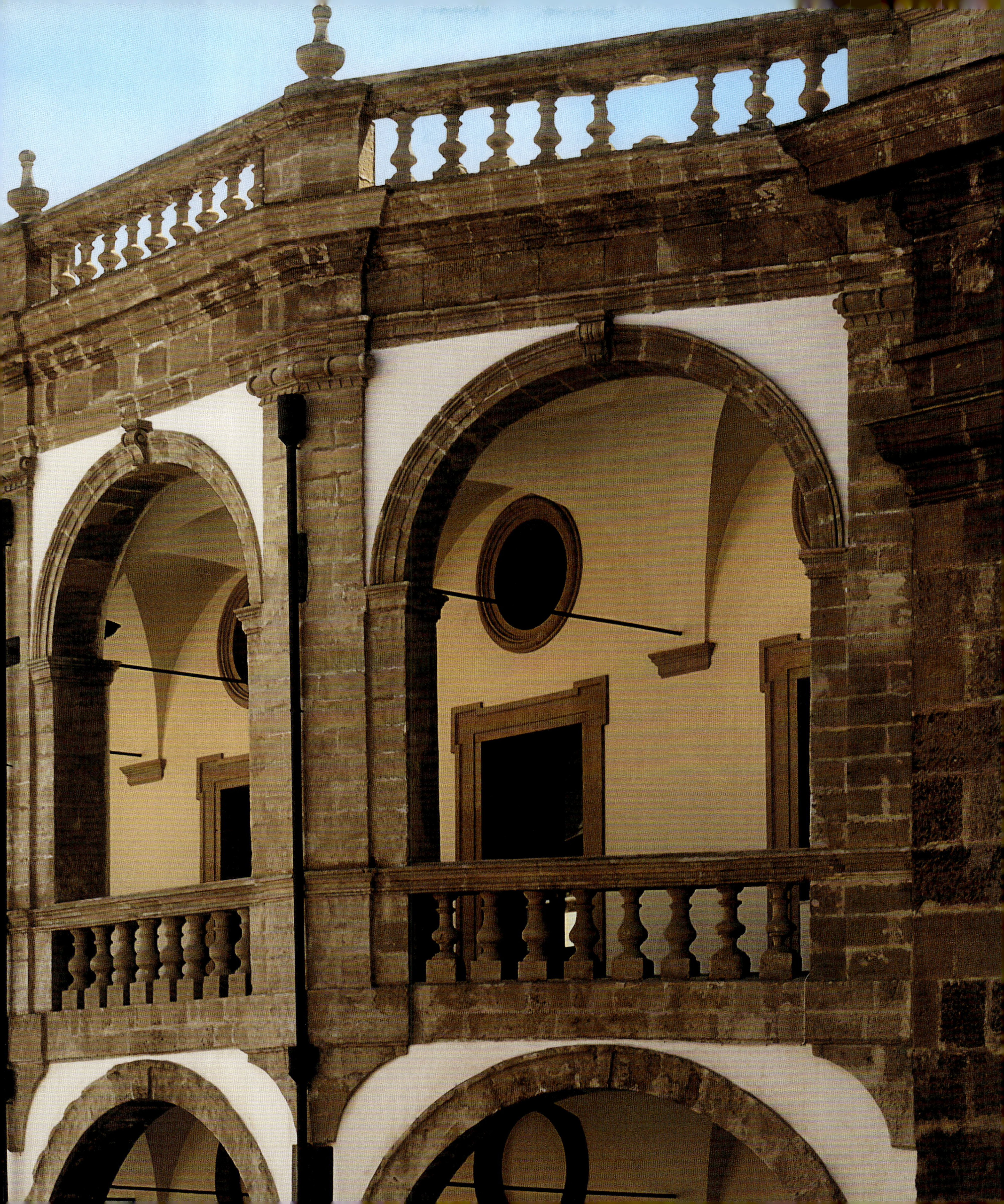

The monumental fountain in Piazza Pretoria, Palermo, designed by the Florentine Francesco Camilliani.

overleaf, left The rocaille nymphaeum of Villa Trabia Campofiorito, Palermo.

overleaf, lright The rocaille fountain of Palazzo Mirto, Palermo.

page 88 The Granfonte at Leonforte, commissioned by the Branciforte family in 1651.

page 89 The Fontana della Ninfa at Castelvetrano, by Orazio Nigrone.

84   *The places: old and new*

The places: old and new 85

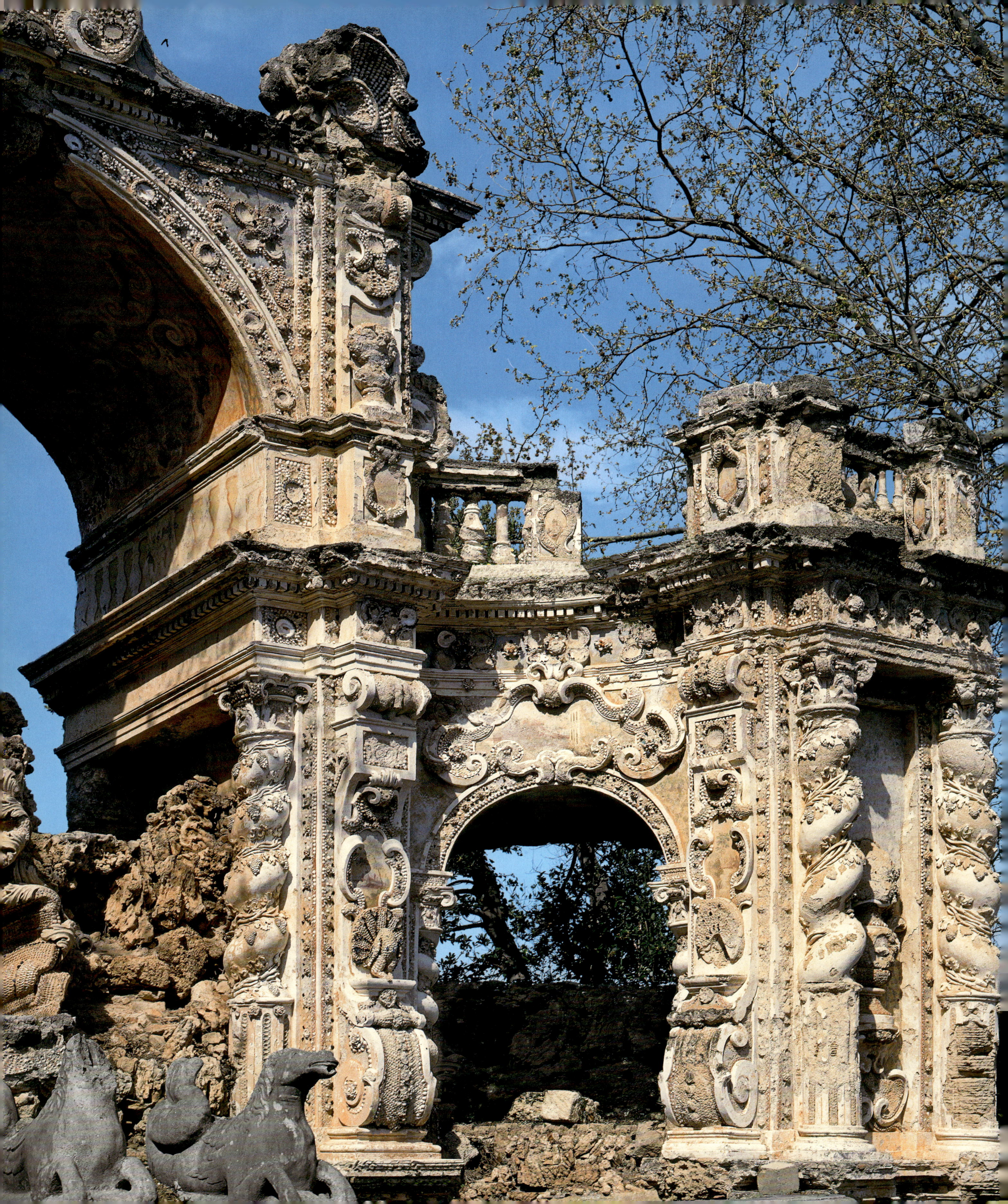

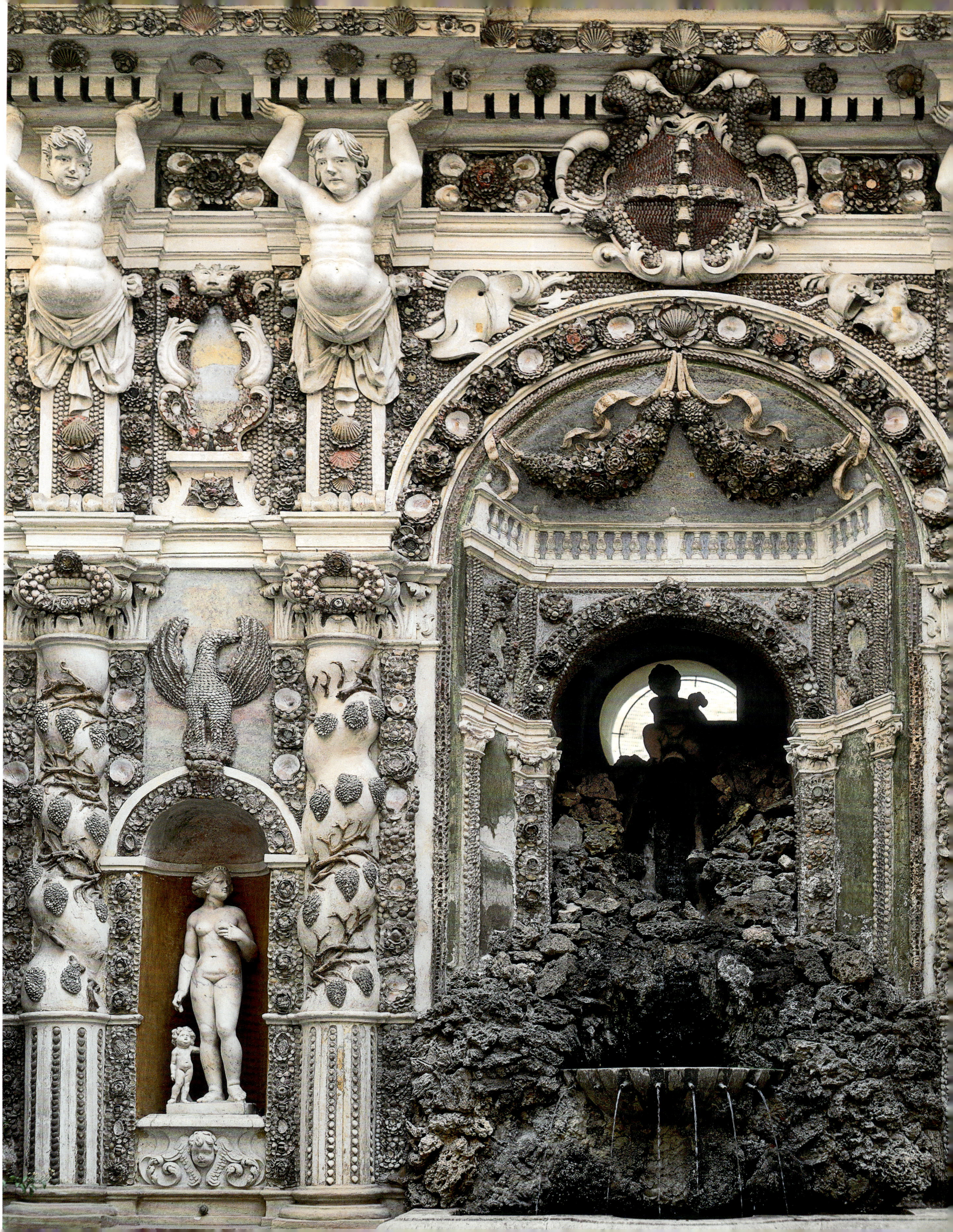

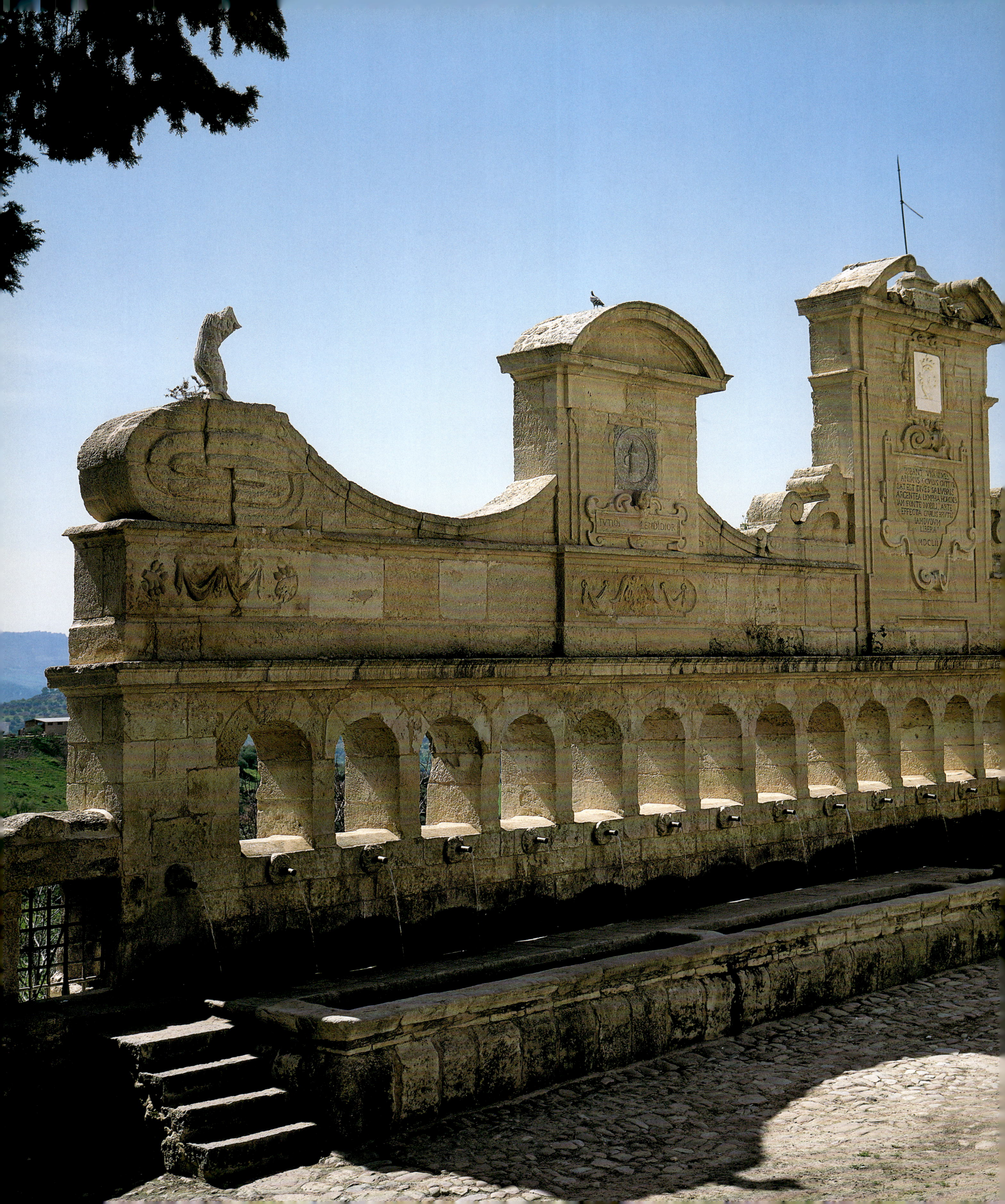

The places: old and new 89

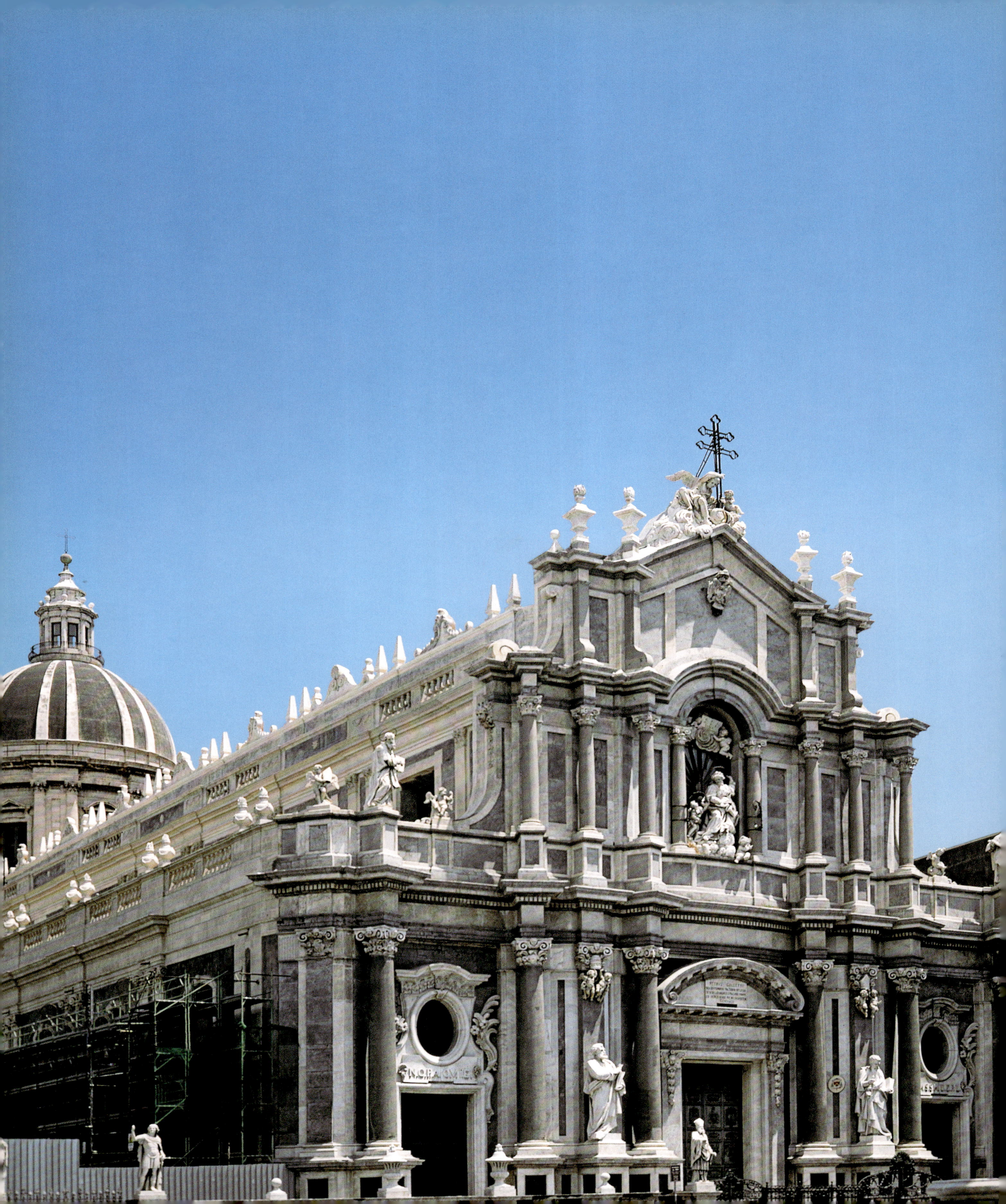

left Piazza del Duomo, Catania, with the Elephant Fountain. The elephant, made of lava, supports an ancient Egyptian obelisk. The design, by the architect Vaccarini, may have been suggested by Bernini's composition in Piazza della Minerva in Rome.

above One of the four fountains adorning the corners of the Quattro Cantoni square in Messina.

The places: old and new

left A detail of the Orion Fountain in Messina, by Montorsoli.

opposite The statue of Neptune vanquishing the monsters Scylla and Charybdis in Messina, also by Montorsoli.

92 *The places: old and new*

The places: old and new 93

D. IOSEPH BRANCIFORTI
PRINCEPS PETREPERCIÆ
ET LEONFORTIS, COMES
RACCVDIÆ, BARO TABARV
EQVES INSIGNIS ORDINIS
VELLERIS AVRI HAS ÆDES
CONSTRVXIT

YA LA ESPERANZA ES PERDIDA
Y VN SOLO BIEN ME CONSVELA
QVE EL TIEMPO QVE PASSA Y BVELA
LLEVARA PRESTO LA VIDA
1658

The actors: patrons, architects, and master builders

As one journeys through the Baroque, the way is crowded with kings and viceroys, Italians and foreigners, politicians who should have been making important decisions but who were out of touch with the problems of the island, and noble dilettantes toying with the study of architecture, a science which they cultivated privately and enriched with collections brought back from foreign travels. Then there were the technical experts, who were sometimes sent away to study abroad but who were mostly trained in Sicily, in workshops which had been honing their skills since medieval times and were given a fresh lease of life by the new culture of ideas. These men were skilled not only in the execution of new works, but also in the invention of new forms and techniques, such as stucco and inlaid stone, which began in isolation and then were taken up for the magnificent projects that became the hallmark of the Baroque in south-eastern Sicily.

During the 17th and 18th centuries, Sicily was the scene of a long struggle for supremacy between foreign powers – Spain, the House of Savoy in Piedmont, Austria, and finally the Bourbon kings of Naples – and so became a stage on which the leading actors played their parts. The stage consisted of the places of power, which were predominantly in Palermo – the Quattro Canti, the Royal Palace, the Cathedral, the Stradone Colonna, the piazzas, and the houses of the most powerful and illustrious nobles. After the defeat of its rebellion in 1678, Messina was constrained to bear the marks of the restoration of the Spanish

preceding pages Detail of the Villa Butera at Bagheria near Palermo, built for the Branciforte family (cf. p. 105).

below Piazza Pretoria in Palermo, with the palace and the marble fountain, which was originally created for a Florentine villa of the Toledo family and then bought by the Senate of Palermo. Engraving from Salmon, *Lo stato presente di tutti i paesi e populi del mondo*, XXIV, 1762.

The actors: patrons, architects, and master builders

GALERIA DE PALACIO DE PALERMO

above A rare view of the old Gallery of the Viceroys in the Royal Palace in Palermo, commissioned by the Count of Santo Stefano, with portraits and, on the left-hand wall, above the door, a map of Sicily. From the *Teatro Geografico Antiguo y Moderno del Reyno de Sicilia*, 1686.

right The most prestigious location for any event was Palermo Cathedral. In the south porch is a relief showing the coronation of Charles III of Bourbon in 1735, flanked by statues of St Luke and St Mark. The statues were moved here from the *tribuna*, which was demolished during the major rebuilding works of the second half of the 18th century.

monarchy, in the form of the citadel on the San Raineri peninsula and the bronze equestrian statue of Charles II, in the centre of the city, which was made by melting down the bells that had summoned the people to rebellion in 1674.

Viceroys, nobility, and clergy

In the 17th century the kings of Spain resided in Madrid, occupied with the difficult role of governing a huge and diverse empire. The viceroys of Sicily divided their lives between Palermo and Messina, and employed the aristocracy of the island as their deputies. The aristocracy gained even more power in Parliament by the acquisition or concession of noble titles, crown-owned or episcopal lands, and the *licentiae populandi* (the licence to found new settlements), thus contributing to the over-stretched coffers of the Spanish crown. The religious orders were peopled mainly by the younger sons of titled families, and thanks to their economic stability and extensive land-ownership they offered the opportunity for an education in the arts and a good career. The reason why Sicily was granted a greater degree of autonomy than other territories under Spanish rule dates back to 1282, the year of the Sicilian Vespers, when the islanders asked the King of Aragon to rule over them. The Sicilians were able to keep the ordinances, rules and prerogatives that had existed under the Normans and the Swabian kings: hence they were subjects, but almost independent. This was very different from the situation in other Spanish territories, where the crown showed itself to be incapable of resolving issues between the central power and the local powers (parliaments, the Inquisition,

The actors: patrons, architects, and master builders 97

feudal privileges, etc.). The only real contact between Sicily and Spain came in the form of 'donations' towards the defence and maintenance of the island, so there were no obvious sources of friction between them. For four centuries, from 1415 to 1812, Sicily was ruled by viceroys who mediated between local authorities and the state, thus achieving a balance of power.

From the 15th century onwards, the Sicilian Parliament consisted of three main components which were socially and politically active: military (barons and aristocracy in general), ecclesiastical (the clergy), and official (the ambassadors of free cities or feudal ones). However, there was not much communication between them: the viceroys were clearly not interested in the island, judging by the reports they submitted on their return to Spain, which were almost identical. The model they followed always gave a greater number of feudal territories than state-owned ones, and described the aristocracy and clergy as being bound by common interests. The barons thus became the key political players.

This would seem to be confirmed by the inclusion of the feudal villa of Giuseppe Branciforte – the first to be built in Bagheria in the second half of the 17th century – in the *Teatro Geografico* compiled by the Viceroy Benavides, Count of Santo Stefano, with the aim of confirming the restoration of the monarchy.

The arrival of Charles V in Sicily, on his way back from Africa in the first half of the 16th century, by then seemed a distant memory. Eventually, after the Treaty of Utrecht under which Sicily was assigned to the House of Savoy, Victor Amadeus was crowned king in Palermo Cathedral on 24 December 1713. There were many celebrations to mark the event, and many temporary constructions, which were documented in a publicly funded commemorative publication.

But the King did not remain in Sicily for long. The capital of the new kingdom was to be Turin, which already had the luminous domes of Guarini and aspired to have splendid architecture worthy of its royal status. The new King discovered the prodigious talent of Filippo Juvarra from Messina, as yet unknown, who was destined to become architect to the courts of Europe. In his book *Controversia Liparitana*, Leonardo Sciascia has a character who is one of the few Sicilians still faithful to Victor Amadeus, but proud of his origins

The Spanish kings made their presence felt in the capital through numerous marble statues set up in prominent positions, beginning with the Quattro Canti, known as the 'Teatro del Sole'. The monument to Philip IV in the courtyard of the Royal Palace is shown here in a 19th-century tempera painting (*above* – private collection) and in an engraving from Leanti, *Lo stato presente della Sicilia*, 1761 (*left*). The statue was destroyed during the 1848 revolt, and later replaced by one of Philip V (see p. 115).

98   The actors: patrons, architects, and master builders

The Quattro Canti in Palermo, seen in a 19th-century engraving.

and of the genius of his compatriots, say: 'Turin is a city which is becoming beautiful. Our Juvarra is seeing to that.' However, the intransigence of the absolutist Piedmontese monarchy sat uncomfortably with Sicilian tradition, and soon came into conflict with the political and administrative system of an island dominated by a feudal aristocracy. The plan for a citadel to force the rebellious people of Palermo into submission was a sign of the tension in the capital.

Between 1718 and 1734 Sicily endured a succession of foreign governments, Austrian and Bourbon, whose grand strategies were alien to the island. On 3 July 1735, however, a Spanish Bourbon, Charles III, was crowned in Palermo Cathedral. The event, celebrated with pomp and ceremony that was recorded on paper at the command of the Senate, marked the dawning of an era of political continuity which lasted until 1860.

The first sixty years of the 18th century, until Charles III was summoned to Madrid in 1759, saw the consolidation of the Baroque style. The streets of Palermo formed the backdrop for the lives of kings and viceroys. There was the ancient Cassaro, which was sumptuously rebuilt; the 'theatre' of the Spanish kings and patron saints in the Quattro Canti; the prestigious palace of the Norman kings, where the Spanish kings had installed themselves in the second half of the 16th century, and which was the seat of Parliament; the Palazzo Pretorio, the seat of the Senate, which had been built in the 15th century on the order of Pietro Speciale and was now embellished by a marble fountain; the Cathedral, where both religious and lay events took place, from funerals to the swearing of oaths of allegiance; the Stradone Colonna; and the other piazzas in the city, where statues of kings sent out a message of regal power.

Drawings and engravings spread knowledge of these developments. The magnificent *Teatro Geografico*, for example, specially featured pictures of the Royal Palace: there was Parliament in session, in the room later known as the Sala d'Ercole (after 18th-century frescoes by the Sicilian painter Giuseppe Velasco), and the Gallery of the Viceroys (now the Yellow Room and the Green Room, on the *piano nobile* of the Maqueda wing), which according to a contemporary source had been 'recently adorned with a series of lifelike portraits of all the viceroys-in-residence who have governed this Kingdom of Sicily, and other paintings commissioned by His Excellency Francisco de Benavides, Count of Santo Stefano'. It is no coincidence that the same person commissioned these works and the *Teatro Geografico*.

Portraits of viceroys, in rich ceremonial costume, also appear in collections and in treatises. The first volume of Giovanni Amico's *L'Architetto Pratico* (The Practical Architect) contains a portrait of the Viceroy Gioacchino Fernandez Portocarrero, to whom the two volumes, published in 1726 and 1750, were dedicated. In 1726 Amico had been commissioned by the Viceroy to complete the Piazza Imperiale (later known as the Piazza San Domenico, from the church that is its main feature).

Pietro La Placa's *Relazione* (1739) illustrates many places decorated for special occasions. The Gallery in the Royal Palace and the chamber of the Senate Court (now the Sala delle Lapidi), designed by the architect of the Senate, Nicolò Palma, are depicted on the occasion of the marriage of Charles III to Maria Amalia of Saxony in July 1738. They are filled with people who are reflected and multiplied in mirrors with golden frames; crystal and velvet adorn the walls; and portraits of sovereigns look down from above. Relative ranks were subject to an immutable protocol, and were sometimes even noted down in the margins of illustrations, as in a view showing the swearing of allegiance to Ferdinand IV of Bourbon in the Cathedral in 1760, before its remodelling in a late Baroque classical style by Ferdinando Fuga.

Patronage was particularly in evidence during the construction or renewal of a building. It might be displayed publicly by the inclusion of a marble bust of the patron on the façade of a palace or villa, perhaps together with a relief of the building. A particularly fine example is the 18th-century remodelling of the palace of the Filangeri Gravina family, princes of Cutò, in the Via Maqueda, Palermo. In the case of churches, patrons were traditionally shown in a way that dates back to the Middle Ages (the subject occurs on a capital in the cloister of Monreale Cathedral), symbolically offering the building to the Virgin, an act usually depicted in a painting or relief. This became less popular in the 18th century, and instead large portraits of the ecclesiastical patrons were hung in the sacristies.

Architects of the 17th century

A wave of architecture strongly influenced by the works of Michelangelo hit Messina in the second half of the 16th century, and in the early years of the 17th century the quantity and quality of architects involved in the new buildings and urban schemes in Palermo created the perfect environment for his influence to flourish there. A dense network of contacts and ideas, particularly between the orders, such as Theatines and Jesuits, facilitated the construction of buildings at home or abroad for the use of their orders. The Spanish crown could rely on royal architects to carry out ambitious projects of urban renewal, such as the Quattro Canti in Palermo, and create new public settings for the display of pomp and splendour. The Senate was left with the task of ensuring the continuity of tradition, both constructional and decorative, in stone, marble, stucco and fresco, in architecture that was permanent or ephemeral.

There were several types of architect. The first comprised architects who were members of the Theatine and Jesuit orders, with a specialized role and affiliation: they include the Theatine Giacomo Besio of Savona, active in Palermo from 1612 to 1645, and the Jesuit Natale Masuccio of Messina (1568–1616), who is said to have studied with his order in Rome. The second type combined the role of architect with that of painter or sculptor: this category includes the Florentine-Roman Giulio Lasso and the Sicilians Mariano Smiriglio, Vincenzo La Barbera, Pietro Novelli and Carlo D'Aprile, chiefly active in Palermo, and Nicolò Francesco Maffei, Giovanni Quagliata and others in Messina. The third type, military architects such as Francesco Negro and Carlos de Grunenbergh, were less in demand as there was no longer such a need for defensive architecture.

Local workshops provided a solid grounding in technical expertise and knowledge, which was perfected with the huge increase in major building projects in the 16th and 17th centuries. Palermo was outstanding, with grandiose churches such as San Giuseppe dei Teatini and the Gesù contending for space in the areas made fashionable by the Quattro Canti and the Strada Nuova.

The employment of foreign architects was already common practice by the second half of the 16th century, and continued well into the 17th. A document dated

Palermo and Messina dominated the Baroque scene in Sicily, with ideas flowing back and forth between the two cities, especially after the construction of the Quattro Canti and the creation of the Via Maqueda, and involving architects including Guarino Guarini and Angelo Italia.

above left A view of Messina with the citadel on the San Raineri peninsula, after the revolt of 1674–78. Engraving from Leanti, *Lo stato presente della Sicilia*, 1761.

above A view of Palermo in 1761 shows the central role of the 'Teatro del Sole' or Quattro Canti, the 'eye' from which the entire city could be seen, as far as the gates.

above The city and port of Palermo, seen in an engraving dating from the first half of the 18th century.

right The extraordinary interior of the church of San Francesco Saverio in Palermo, an experiment in space by Angelo Italia.

1598 relating to the cathedral in Piazza Armerina refers to 'expert architects, highly skilled in their professions, from places all over the world', and indeed that workshop included the Roman architect Orazio Torriani in the first half of the 17th century. For the restoration of Palermo Cathedral in 1651 (a phase of construction that disappeared with the 18th-century alterations), Archbishop Martino de Léon y Cardenas summoned the well-known Neapolitan architect and sculptor Cosimo Fanzago (according to research by Ciro D'Arpa), who also designed the lapis lazuli ciborium for the Chapel of the Holy Sacrament. The architect Francesco Buonamici from Lucca was active on both projects. There is evidence that for many of the new works in Palermo in the 1630s involving a central dome, such as San Mattia dei Padri Crociferi and San Carlo dei Lombardi (originally a Benedictine church), the architects employed were not Sicilian: Francesco Maria Ricchino came from Milan. Significant too were the availability of drawings and prints, and the influence of individual patrons. Spagnolo, who was perhaps from Catalonia, came to Sicily in the suite of the Duke of Maqueda. Diego Sanchez, as yet relatively

The actors: patrons, architects, and master builders 101

unknown to scholars, was active on major sites in the early 17th century, particularly in Milazzo, where he worked on the Chiesa Madre, and in Palermo, where he worked on the Royal Palace and on the interior of the 'Steri', where he created the new prisons of the Inquisition on the most modern principles.

The destruction caused in eastern Sicily by the earthquake of 1693 makes it impossible to form a comprehensive picture of the situation. What is certain, however, is that Messina played a dominant role. It also seems likely that the architecture of Palermo and the eastern part of the island, both ancient and new, influenced another illustrious foreigner, Guarino Guarini from Modena, who trained in Rome and lived in Messina possibly from 1657 and definitely from 1662. It has been suggested that his later designs may reflect journeys to look at Spanish Islamic architecture, but it seems much more likely that during his time in Messina he took the opportunity to travel to parts of Sicily where he saw Islamic and Norman buildings. It also seems likely that he spent time in Palermo, especially as a later source attributes the design of a tabernacle in San Giuseppe dei Teatini to him. Many features of the church and house of Santissima Annunziata dei Teatini in Messina suggest a first-hand knowledge of the architecture of Borromini, which Guarini would have seen during his apprenticeship in Rome. The influence of Borromini is also evident in his designs for the Quattro Canti and the façade of the church of San Matteo in Palermo, where layers are superimposed to create a towering effect, in designs for tabernacles and for temporary architecture built for festive occasions in Palermo and Messina, and in engravings. Guarini's designs for the church of the Padri Stomaschi in Messina, which were formerly thought to have been made during his time in Sicily, have recently been attributed to a later date. They may, however, have been influenced by the unusual central plan with ambulatory of the church of Santa Lucia al Borgo in Palermo, which was begun in the area of the new port in 1601 (and destroyed by bombing in 1943). It would appear that his experiences in Sicily were central to Guarini's architecture.

From the early years of the 17th century, architects assumed overall responsibility for the entire process of construction and decoration, producing significant and lasting results both inland and on the coast, results which were to exert an influence on the reconstruction

A 19th-century portrait of the architect Giacomo Amato, from the collection of 'illustrious Sicilians' in the Biblioteca Comunale, Palermo.

102   The actors: patrons, architects, and master builders

process in the south-east after the earthquake of 1693. During the second half of the century, architect-painters and architect-sculptors were gradually replaced by architects in religious orders, whose affiliation gave them the opportunity to travel throughout Sicily and to Rome, and to visit the great libraries of the time. Their periods of training in Rome are not well documented, and what they could have seen is uncertain (the architecture of Guarini, for instance, was only discovered in the 18th century). There is no doubt that artists from many different countries and backgrounds met as they worked on projects in Palermo and Messina, and exchanged news and views on the latest theories and practices of their profession.

The 'new direction' taken by Sicilian architecture can be traced back to the 1680s, when three ecclesiastical architects from different schools and traditions were in Palermo, along with one sculptor-architect who was a master of stucco work. The architects were the Jesuit Angelo Italia, born in Licata and active in the west of the island; the priest Paolo Amato, born in Cimmina and mainly active in Palermo, where he was architect to the Senate for many years; and Giacomo Amato, a member of the order of the Crociferi, born in Palermo and active there after a well-documented apprenticeship in Rome. The stuccodore was Giacomo Serpotta: he came from a celebrated family of craftsmen who carried on the art of modelling introduced by the Ferraro da Giuliana family in the 16th century. It is certain that the first three met, for they all worked on the church of the Santissimo Salvatore in Palermo. Drawings by Amato show that he knew Serpotta.

The training of Angelo Italia (1628–1700), the son of a stonemason, did not permit him to reach the summit of his profession. His early works, for his native town of Licata and the neighbouring Palma di Montechiaro, have recently been the subject of a study which has found them to be of greater worth than previously thought, but they are not representative of his contribution to the Baroque revolution of the second half of the century. His late entry into the Jesuit Order in 1671 freed him from local constraints and gave him access to international influences, thanks to the presence of the order all over Europe and in Latin America, as well as in its headquarters in Rome. From the 1680s on, as well as working on prestigious projects such as the church of the Santissimo Salvatore in Palermo, Italia was establishing a professional reputation for himself through highly original designs in which he organized space by starting from the interior of the building, a method evidenced by the Jesuit church of San Francesco Saverio in Palermo and the Collegio in Polizzi Generosa. What influences or discoveries lay behind such a sudden change, which thrust him into the avant-garde of Sicilian artistic culture? Who were his teachers, in the absence of any evidence of foreign travels? Was it his contact with other architects in Palermo, such as Giacomo Amato with his experiences in Rome, or Paolo Amato, with whom Italia worked on the hexagonal Cappella del Crocifisso of Monreale Cathedral, commissioned by Archbishop Roano; or was it perhaps his membership of the Jesuit Order? Did he know the church of Santa Lucia al Borgo in Palermo – mentioned above as a possible source of inspiration for Guarini – and could its centralized plan with an ambulatory have served him as a model for the church of the Jesuit College in Mazara? This would seem plausible, but his design may equally depend on a foreign source. And what of the influence of Naples, where the church of Santa Maria Egiziaca in Pizzo Falcone, begun in 1646 and associated with renowned Neapolitan artists such as Cosimo Fanzago and Arcangelo Guglielmelli, might have suggested the plan. These are all questions which cannot yet be answered with any certainty.

Guarini's influence is even more problematical. He died in 1683, after a prodigious career which involved projects not only in Turin and elsewhere in Italy, but also in Paris, Lisbon and Prague. But his treatise entitled *Architettura Civile* (Civil Architecture), in which he discusses his theories about light, and the role of the dome, was not published until after his death, in 1737 (by Bernardo Vittone, an architect from Piedmont). However, it is known that engravings of his designs were in circulation in 1686, probably reaching as far as Messina, where there were existing works by Guarini.

In Angelo Italia's church of San Francesco Saverio in Palermo columns play an important role in articulating the internal space but they do so confusingly, suggesting that he was working to an existing plan but had not got the measure of the vertical dimension. This suggests a design based on theory, as was the case later in his plans for Avola and Noto, where he even quotes a source.

Italia shows a different side in his design for the dome of the church of the Carmine in Palermo, built over the transept of an older building which was being completely remodelled inside. The interior was transformed with carved altars by the brothers Giacomo and Giuseppe Serpotta, in which twisted columns of stucco separate figural scenes. Their dynamism contrasts with the static 17th-century plan and leads the eye upwards to the apex of the dome. The dome was conceived as an integral part of the townscape, and is a magnificent synthesis of the traditional skills that Italia would have learnt during his training: the drum is marked by pairs of columns framing imposing telamones, with a dense exuberance of sculpted decoration around the windows, and the dome itself is covered with a mass of brightly coloured majolica tiles, as in Naples.

During the same period, another architect, Paolo Amato (1634–1714), became well known for his inventiveness in architecture and decoration, both of which are displayed in his most important work, the church of the Santissimo Salvatore in Palermo. It is conceived as an oval structure, with a double-shelled dome and an interior marked by pilasters densely covered with inlaid coloured marble in two and three dimensions, which breaks up the individual architectural shapes. As architect to the Senate, Amato was also responsible for much ephemeral architecture conceived for public festivities, and there tradition triumphed over innovation. Judging by his learned treatise on perspective, and its application in the centralized plans he devised for churches in Palermo such as the Santissimo Salvatore and San Giuliano (demolished for the construction of the Teatro Massimo), he was at the forefront of the avant-garde, a fact which has yet to be fully recognized.

The complexity involved in the realization of these plans was rare in Palermo in the first half of the 17th century. One has to understand the frame of reference, cultural and material, of an architect whose diverse skills enabled him to integrate the vigorous decorative traditions of the island with new ideas coming from abroad, particularly from Lombardy. The result was a distinctively local synthesis of styles, which was open to other influences but where the role of decoration remained the determining factor.

Different problems of interpretation are posed by the third great ecclesiastical architect, Giacomo Amato (1643–1732), who was active well into the 18th century. His story does not begin on a building site, or with a great interest in the arts, as was the case with many of his contemporaries. He was educated in Rome, as a member of the order of the Crociferi, and was surrounded by buildings which were fine examples of classicism. He spent many years in a city marked by the Baroque revolution initiated by the early masters Borromini, Bernini and Pietro della Cortona, and filled with their masterpieces, such as Borromini's San Carlo alle Quattro Fontane and Bernini's Sant'Andrea al Quirinale. But he was also strongly influenced by the styles of Rainaldi and Maderno, and from them he learnt the necessity of establishing a style that was both grand and accessible in order to succeed professionally.

His continual striving to achieve this synthesis led him to experiment with a wide variety of genres. The many volumes of his drawings, preserved in the Galleria Regionale in Palermo, must have served as a kind of visiting card: they include sketches and drafts not only of architectural forms, but also of frames, pedestals and other items of furniture. His late Baroque classicism, nurtured by theoretical treatises in the monastery and by his own personal library (of which an inventory survives), allowed him to work out a style which was well suited to the ideals of splendour so important to the aristocracy in Palermo, but which could also be passed on to numerous pupils throughout the 18th century.

Giuseppe Venanzio Marvuglia perhaps hardly qualifies as a pupil, since he was born in 1729, only three years before Giacomo Amato's death in 1732, but he adopted the 'international' style of Rome, of its academies and

above left The oratories of Palermo are among the most important buildings of the Baroque era, exhibiting a variety of skills. Construction was overseen by Giacomo Amato, but the interiors are dominated by the stucco work of Giacomo Serpotta, the finest of a family of stuccodores. This is the Nativity in the Oratorio del Rosario in Santa Zita.

above The seafront façade of the palace of the Branciforte family, princes of Butera, in the old Kalsa district, decorated for the coronation of Charles of Bourbon, whose portrait appears in the centre, below the crown. Engraving by P. La Placa from *La Reggia in Trionfo*, 1736.

opposite The Branciforte villa in Bagheria, Villa Butera, is the earliest of a series of country residences built outside Palermo. The bust of the founder is displayed on the façade (cf. pp. 94–95). Drawing from the *Teatro Geografico*, 1686.

104 The actors: patrons, architects, and master builders

of the classicizing Baroque that Giacomo had brought to Palermo, building on it during his own well documented apprenticeship in Rome. He ensured the continuity of the style into the second half of the 18th century and into the 19th.

Giacomo Amato's designs for the striking façades of Santa Maria della Pietà and Santa Teresa in Palermo display his consummate skill in inventing a typology which was innovative but easy to replicate, and could therefore serve as a model for smaller towns inland or for churches in the new feudal towns. The design consists of a façade articulated by pilasters, which were already a part of Sicilian tradition in the 16th and early 17th centuries, rendered three-dimensional by the presence of a frame of detached or engaged columns which created a sense of movement towards the centre of the composition.

Giacomo Amato also worked with other painters and sculptors such as Antonino Grano, Pietro Aquila and Giacomo Serpotta, a fact documented by notes in the margins of his drawings.

For Serpotta, the decorative scheme seemed to be more important than the architecture regulated by pilasters (particularly in the Oratorio di San Lorenzo in San Francesco and the Oratorio del Rosario in Santa Zita in Palermo). He excelled in his role as *magister stucchiator, sculptor e architettor*, as he is referred to in contemporary documents which testify to his employment in various contexts. Nonetheless, in the portrait painted of him by Gaspare Serenario he is shown with a pair of compasses on the left, the symbol of architects. The oratories presented a variety of opportunities, leading to a variety of distinctive solutions which share the aim of providing a 'spectacle', in both a religious and non-religious sense, as a means of 'popular persuasion'. In his novel *Retablo* (1987), the Sicilian writer Vicenzo Consolo expresses the sense of amazement felt by one of the characters, Brother Isidoro, when he enters the Oratorio di San Lorenzo, decorated by Serpotta in 1699 (it was already in existence by 1608, when it housed Caravaggio's *Nativity* – stolen in 1969 but later recovered): 'I went in, and thought that I had entered into paradise.' He goes on to describe the narrative scenes: 'I looked at the walls, the ceilings, the altars; they were all of the most exquisite stucco: fascias, panels, statues and cornices, all of milky-white colour; the occasional flash of pure gold, swags, scrolls, flowers, foliage, cornucopias, torches, shells, crosses, haloes, plumes, tassels, cords... There were niches with scenes from the lives of St Laurence and St Francis, joyous angels, roundels, naked children cavorting on clouds, cascades and swirls of drapery. But most imposing were the large statues of dreamy-looking women positioned on brackets, noble women in gracious or imperious poses. I was dazzled by a ray of sunshine which flooded in through the window and was refracted onto my face by a crystal nymph.'

Yet again we are left to ponder the origins and training of the artist. In the case of Serpotta we know that his family were craftsmen, but the quality of his workmanship has led historians to surmise that he may have spent time in Rome, although this cannot as yet be proved. As recent studies have suggested, his repertoire implies a familiarity with temporary architecture and with images that circulated widely, which he might have seen in Giacomo Amato's library; but there is no doubt that he benefited from collaboration with other craftsmen, each contributing his own solutions and theories to the general development of architecture.

The interconnections between projects were thus numerous, if not always apparent; the protagonists were prodigiously skilled and unexpectedly versatile; and the dialectics were continual. According to Father Fedele Tirrito da San Biago, painter, intellectual, poet and art historian, in his *Dialoghi Familiari sopra la Pittura* (On Painting) of 1788, a work of sculpture like the Garraffo Fountain in Palermo was the result of collaboration between several sculptors and architects – Giacomo Serpotta, Giacomo Amato and Paolo Amato.

The architect Giuseppe Venanzio Marvuglia was at the forefront of architectural developments in the late Baroque and Neoclassicism. (Biblioteca Comunale, Palermo)

Architects of the 18th century

Paolo and Giacomo Amato continued their work in Palermo well into the first decades of the 18th century. Paolo Amato continued as architect to the Senate until his death in 1714, though due to failing health he was assisted in his final years by Andrea Palma from Trapani (to whom the mantle then passed), and in this role he designed mausoleums, marble decorations, temporary triumphal arches, and inscribed tablets. During the same period Giacomo Amato, who was some ten years younger, was involved in altering existing buildings, drawing up plans for new ones, such as the church of Santa Rosalia (demolished to make way for the Via Roma), and in constructing flights of steps and decorations to adorn buildings belonging to his own order and to wealthy aristocrats. He was skilled at adapting old buildings: at the Palazzo Branciforte, now Butera, in the Kalsa, where the Tuscan Ferdinando Fuga assisted in the interior, he did not destroy the old structure but rather sought to reorganize the space, as shown by surviving autograph drawings.

In the last years of his life before his death in 1732 (the same year saw the death of Giacomo Serpotta, with whom he had worked on various projects), Giacomo Amato became known as an expert in restoration work. A good example of this is his work consolidating the foundations of the 'Steri', which had been badly damaged by an earthquake in 1726.

Giacomo Amato's method was unusual, based on a 'modern' way of analysing each specific problem and on solid technical knowledge. In his biography of Amato written in the early 19th century, the scholar Agostino Gallo wrote of him: 'He was the first to insist upon the need to restore the foundations of buildings, while supporting the upper part on beams, and he first experimented with this idea at the 'Steri', by now the law courts, in Palermo, which had been damaged

106   The actors: patrons, architects, and master builders

The villa of the princes of Valguarnera at Bagheria. Built on a hill and surrounded by vast gardens, it looks out over the sea and the surrounding countryside.

by the earthquake of 1726.' The technique involved the creation of a wall made of large blocks of stone linked by wooden beams below layers of smaller stones, using technical devices which were to become common on later building sites. They were used, for instance, when quatrefoil piers were replaced by piers with pilasters during the 'restoration' of Palermo Cathedral in the second half of the 18th century under the direction of Giuseppe Venanzio Marvuglia and Salvatore Attinelli.

Two accounts in the first volume of Giacomo Amato's treatise of 1726 point to the widespread use in Sicily of 'walling of stone rubble, roughly squared, the joints filled with tiny pieces of stone and lime mortar well hammered down'. With regard to the insertion of wooden beams in the wall, he writes: 'I have seen in the ruins of old buildings pieces of elm wood and olive wood in the form of a cross in the middle of walls: the patrons thought they had been placed there as a sign of devotion to the Holy Cross, but I suspect they were there in order to strengthen the walls.'

According to research carried out by Rosario La Duca, after the earthquake in 1726 an ordinance was passed which decreed that balconies, particularly where there had been damage – which was widespread, according to Mongitore's plan of 1727 recording the effects of the earthquake – should rest not on stone brackets but on metal supports.

Repair of the domes of large churches was particularly urgent: hence just three months after the earthquake, on 20 December 1726, Giacomo Amato signed a contract to restore the dome of the Santissimo Salvatore, together with the architect Gaetano Lazzara (who had drawn a magnificent map of Palermo in 1703). The following February, the two architects commissioned the expert stonemason Simone Marvuglia to work on the masonry. (Simone was active on many building sites in Palermo in the first half of the 18th century, and was the father of the better-known architect Giuseppe Venanzio.) In a technical report of 1737, a number of unidentified engineers and architects expressed the opinion that the dome should be demolished and rebuilt lower, to reduce its weight. However, Amato and Lazzara proposed a more economical system, involving the use of chains – demonstrating their technical competence – which they entrusted to the capable hands of Marvuglia.

By the time of Amato's death in 1732, the first phase of reconstruction work in the east of the island following the earthquake had been completed: rubble had been cleared away, new town plans drawn up, and work had begun using experts from Messina and Palermo, such as the Flavetta, Blundo and Amato families. The second phase was now entrusted to more 'learned' architects, who were also from Palermo but who had recently returned from apprenticeships in Rome, such as Giovan Battista Vaccarini, or who had studied recent developments in Italy and Europe from books, drawings and prints, such as Francesco Battaglia. In the case of Catania, recent studies have thrown new light on attributions.

In the opinion of Christian Norberg-Schulz, Giulio Carlo Argan and others, Sicily is outstanding for the quality of the work of reconstruction; and the distinction of those involved led to one area, the Val di Noto, and one city, Catania, which up until then had been on the periphery, occupying centre stage.

Palermo, however, remained the political capital of the island, and the schools of Paolo and Giacomo Amato were firmly rooted here, although the complex events of

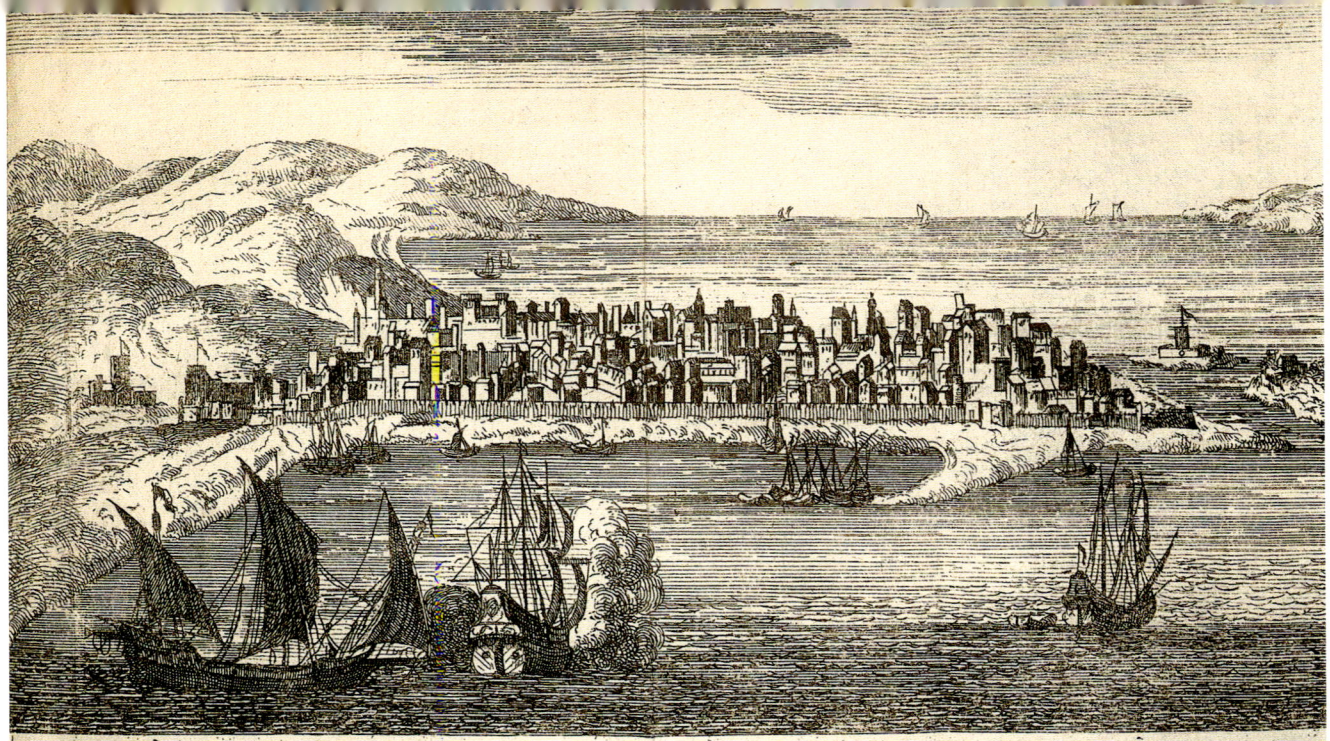

LA CITTÀ DI TRAPANI NELLA PROVINCIA DI MAZARA, NEL REGNO DI SICILIA

history opened the way to new foreign contacts. Among the pupils of Paolo and Giacomo we have already met Gaetano Lazzara (active between 1700 and 1731). Another was Giuseppe Mariani (1681–1731), a member of the order of the Crociferi. Mariani, who had spent a short time in Rome and was supremely familiar with published sources, was responsible for bringing the influence of Borromini's Sant'Ivo alla Sapienza in Rome to bear on the construction of the church of Santi Cosma e Damiano in Alcamo, and his works reflect many other aspects of Roman architecture.

Buildings dependent on Borromini and Sant'Ivo existed in Messina seemingly in the second half of the 17th century, and certainly in the early 18th, but they were lost through subsequent earthquakes. There are references to towers with spiral forms, particularly to the campanile of the church of San Gregorio in Messina, on the interior of which Juvarra worked, which was recorded in photographs before the earthquake in 1908. A young scholar, Fulvio Lenzo, has recently suggested that it was designed by Paolo Filocamo, a painter from Messina, who is known to have spent time in Rome. Borromini's spiral form continued to influence architects later on, such as Stefano Ittar (1724–90), a Pole who came to Catania from Rome in 1765, and used the idea in his façade of the church of the Collegiata.

When Filippo Juvarra finally left Sicily in 1715, to follow Victor Amadeus to Piedmont, the southeast of the island had not yet understood the need to entrust great projects to great architects, and the talents of architects like Juvarra were yet to be discovered. At this time Tomaso Maria Napoli (1659–1725), a Dominican architect and author of a small treatise published in Rome, where he seems to have served an apprenticeship in the studio of Carlo Fontana, returned from his travels, in the course of which he had worked in Austria, Hungary, and in Dubrovnik. On his return he began work on the two most famous villas in Bagheria, those of the princes of Valguarnera and of Palagonia, which have been sought out by visitors to Sicily ever since. Then, as the official architect of the Austrian Habsburgs, he went to Palermo to work on the piazza in front of the church of his own order, which was known as the Piazza Imperiale, with a monument to the Immaculate Conception. As Erik H. Neil has observed, the monument has a Central European character that reflects Napoli's travels: the figures of kings are placed at the foot of the column, and not in the composition as in other piazzas in Palermo. Its style looks to the culture of Austria, which Napoli must have known directly and also through his time in Rome, although as yet there is scant documentary evidence. Might he have met the Austrian court architect, Johann Bernhard Fischer von Erlach? Might he have passed on his international experiences and contacts to his successor, Giovanni Amico from Trapani, who completed the work on the Piazza Imperiale after his death?

Many such cases could be cited, particularly that of Rosario Gagliardi, but that of Giovanni Amico (1684–1754) stands out because of the confidence and authority with which he carried out the tasks entrusted to him, and because of the innovative quality of his architecture. He was trained on the job, with the help of books with which his personal library was well stocked, according to an inventory which has survived. It was Amico who brought the late Baroque era to Palermo and to western Sicily, at the same time as the style of Borromini was being revived in Rome by the Specchi,

In the 18th century many architects, including Andrea and Nicolò Palma and Giovanni Amico, came from Trapani and worked mainly in Palermo.

above Trapani, in an engraving from Salmon, *Lo stato presente di tutti i paesi e populi del mondo*, XXIV, 1762.

108 The actors: patrons, architects, and master builders

above Giovan Battista Vaccarini from Palermo dominated the scene in Catania, building many works from the 1730s onwards. (Biblioteca Comunale, Palermo)

above right The Palazzo del Senato, Palermo, built in two separate campaigns by designers whose identity is uncertain. Engraving from Leanti, *Lo stato presente della Sicilia*, 1761.

Raguzzini, De Sanctis, Gregorini and Passalacqua families. (The revival was scotched by the victory of Alessandro Galilei in the competition for the façade of San Giovanni in Laterano in 1732.) Amico was a religious architect and theorist, certainly well versed in the architecture of Guarino Guarini and Angelo Italia, from which he acquired a particular interest in space and its theatrical handling. In the 1720s he had made his first designs for curved façades in Trapani (the church of the Purgatorio). He exported his ideas to Palermo at the end of the 1720s, simultaneously with the publication of the first volume of his *L'Architetto Pratico*, aiming to secure work in the capital, where reconstruction work after the earthquake of 1726 and the building of new palaces along the Via Maqueda offered glamorous opportunities for employment.

In reality, Amico was always tied to his religious order, and his status as a priest, together with personal circumstances, led him to publish a weighty theological tome in three volumes, entitled *Catechismo storico del Concilio di Trent* (A historic catechism of the Council of Trent), which was dedicated to the Bishop of Mazara, Monsignor Giuseppe Stella. In the second volume of *L'Architetto Pratico* (1750) he lists the religious buildings with which he was concerned, mentioning secular buildings only once, generically, in Palermo: 'many remodellings of private houses and flights of steps for palaces'.

Although Giacomo Amato was officially the architect in charge, Amico worked on the Cathedral after the earthquake of 1726, using the remains of the old tower to create a new campanile, which was called 'borrominesque', disparagingly, in early 19th-century records. He also worked on the façade of Sant'Anna in Palermo. He was chiefly active, however, in Trapani (the cathedral of San Lorenzo and the sanctuary of the Santissima Annunziata) and in the provinces (Alcamo, Marsala, Erice and Mazara). His opinion was valued as a judge of new projects, such as Rosario Gagliardi's design for the church of San Giorgio in Ragusa Ibla, of 1744, and as an adjudicator of competitions, such as that for the Albergo dei Poveri in Palermo in 1746.

After Amato's death in 1754, and after the fruitless attempts of Giovan Battista Vaccarini to obtain commissions for any of the great public projects such as the Albergo dei Poveri and the Cathedral, Palermo succumbed to the Rococo designs of architects employed in the reconstruction of palaces along old and new residential streets after the earthquake of 1751. Two of them came from Trapani: Nicolò Palma (1694–1779), nephew of Andrea, and like him architect to the Senate, who was involved in many major building projects and who designed staircases and temporary structures, and Andrea Gigante (1731–87), a pupil of Amico, whose early works, such as the Palazzo Bonagia and Palazzo Valguarnera-Gangi, reflected the scenographic designs of Giuseppe Galli Bibiena, but who then turned rapidly to Neoclassicism in the 1760s, in reaction to the competition presented by Giuseppe Venanzio Marvuglia on his return to Sicily in 1759 following his apprenticeship in Rome.

Two other architects came from Palermo: Giovanni del Frago (1715–91) and Giovan Battista Cascione Vaccarini (1729–*c.* 1791). Giovanni del Frago designed the staircase of the Palazzo Cutò in Palermo, decorated with extraordinary dynamic volutes, and devised the plan of the Villa Larderia in Bagheria, which drew on international models. Vaccarini was a leading exponent of late Baroque classicism, and was involved in major projects in Palermo and elsewhere. In 1760

The actors: patrons, architects, and master builders 109

he took over from Nicolò Anito on the palace of the marquises of Santa Croce in the Via Maqueda, where he designed the monumental long façade as part of an ambitious restoration project begun in 1756 that incorporated existing structures. With Nicolò and Andrea Palma, Amico and Gigante, Trapani's architectural dominance was assured in the west of the island, and although Amico's approval was secured for a project of Gagliardi's, permission to proceed was probably granted from afar, and with the exception of this one contact which promoted the style of Gagliardi, there was no real relationship with the activities of the south-east and its many original styles, although there does seem to be evidence that both architects were in Palermo during the fateful year of 1726.

The most immediately successful language was that of the 'conservatives' – a term coined by Paolo Portoghesi, which for Sicily meant the Roman language of Giacomo Amato. This language reached the south-east, where it was reinforced by further imports from Rome. In the façade of Syracuse Cathedral the portico form was a radical departure from what lay behind, the remains of the prestigious Temple of Athena. Echoes of Roman churches such as Santi Vincenzo ed Anastasio and Rainaldi's Sant'Andrea della Valle can be perceived in the detached columns. On the basis of documentary evidence, the Cathedral façade is attributed to Andrea Palma (1664–1730), who may have been the winner of the competition announced in 1728. Despite the other well known projects of Palma, many of which were executed during his time as architect to the Senate (between 1714 and his death), there are still doubts as to the validity of the attribution.

Giovan Battista Vaccarini (1702–68) was born in Palermo but spent most of his working life in Catania, and it was he who acted as a channel of Baroque ideas between the two cities. He too was an architect member of a religious order, and he had enjoyed a prestigious training in Rome, which is reflected in his designs more clearly than in any documentary evidence. Both his background and his presence made him the ideal choice to achieve the magnificence to which the authorities in Catania – Bishop Galletti and the municipality – aspired for the reconstruction of their city. Most of the commissions therefore fell into his hands, and his name became associated with the most prestigious projects, beginning with the Cathedral, founded in Norman times, and the adjacent piazza.

below Caltagirone, a town steeped in history, dominated by campaniles and domes. In the foreground is the church of San Francesco d'Assisi.

opposite Drawings of the façade and longitudinal section of San Giorgio in Ragusa, by Rosario Gagliardi, 1744. (Archivo Parrochiale, Ragusa)

Recent studies have shown that some buildings, such as the Collegio dei Nobili, are more likely to be by other architects, especially Francesco Battaglia from Catania.

The Piazza del Duomo is thus the best place to examine the particular characteristics of Vaccarini's architecture, in which he assimilated his recent experiences in Palermo and other influences, such as those of Rome – not just as the capital of the Baroque, but for many different architectural languages – and those derived from his knowledge of Guarini's work,
in particular the façade of the Santissima Annunziata in Messina. The design of the façade of Catania Cathedral is called 'a remarkable affair' in contemporary sources. It took a long time to resolve, with two versions dismissed before final approval was secured. Vaccarini's role was of paramount importance, and he was assisted by his contacts with architects from Rome and Naples, and especially by the relationship of mutual respect that existed between himself and Luigi Vanvitelli, who was then employed in Caserta. These friendships enabled him to see the arduous project through, despite the criticisms of people including Ferdinando Fuga. Professional rivalries lay behind many of the events of the 18th century, events which are only unravelled by a close study of the available documents.

Despite the success of his works in Catania, such as the façade of the Cathedral, the Elephant Fountain, the Badia di Sant'Anna, and the upper part of the Palazzo Senatorio (traditionally attributed to him), all of which were indebted to Rome in their composition and decoration, after 1746 Vaccarini never succeeded in returning in triumph to his native town of Palermo, although in the 1730s many of the earlier architects had disappeared, which should have left him with many professional opportunities. Instead, prestigious projects were given to other architects, some not very well known, such as Orazio Furetto, who received the commission for the imposing Albergo dei Poveri on the road to Monreale.

In comparison with other architects from Catania, such as Francesco Battaglia (1701–88), Vaccarini is superior in his cultural references and originality, but Battaglia's ability to achieve a transformation through a continual study of books and local developments, in which he was not alone, helps to explain the precocious combination of the international language of classicism with an existing love of decoration. A reference to Caltagirone and to the Chiesa Madre, where Battaglia was involved in the second half of the 18th century, reveals his ability to exploit his theoretical knowledge, citing the undisputed authority of Guarini in the course of an argument with Andrea Gigante, who was probably in Noto, making a structural survey of the church of the Santissimo Salvatore. Further research will be needed to provide an overall picture of his cultural background and compositional ideas: it is known that he worked on some of the most important projects of the time, such as the palace-museum of Ignazio Paternò Castello, Prince of Biscari, where certain stylistic elements seem to have been due to the illustrious patron himself, and the Collegio dei Nobili, known as Cutelli after its founder. The remarkable circular courtyard of the Collegio, however, reminiscent of Raphael's Villa Madama, is due to Vaccarini, or based on designs by him that are now lost.

The story of Rosario Gagliardi (1690–c. 1762) reveals a unique figure who operated in isolation in south-eastern Sicily, and yet was part of the international scene.

Many influences seem to have contributed to the formation of this original architect, whose style developed exclusively in and around Syracuse, the city of his birth and formative years: in 1726 he spent some time working on projects in Palermo, when Giacomo Amato was still alive; he may have taken part in the debates concerning Catania and Syracuse Cathedrals; he knew the architecture of Guarini, both at first hand and through circulating treatises, in Messina and perhaps also in Syracuse, if it is true that Guarini was involved in the project to build the house of the Theatines, as has been suggested by Marco Rosario Nobile; and he would have been familiar with engravings of buildings in Rome and Central Europe, with which his work seems to have an affinity. Perhaps his most important architectural contribution is his invention of the tower-façade with a pyramidal form based on the superimposition of layers, and the articulation between the convex centre of the façade and the sides, and the insertion of a frame composed of detached columns at the junctures. An outstanding example of this is the church of San Giorgio in Ragusa Ibla, which was finally approved by the experts Michele Longari from Messina and the better-known Giovanni Amico from Trapani after several attempts.

The true breadth and originality of Gagliardi's architectural designs is only apparent in his numerous drawings, which were probably intended for a didactic treatise, or perhaps as a personal dossier to display his ideas, and which can only rarely be associated with actual constructions.

Gagliardi's significance as an architect can be measured by the quality of his pupils, such as Vincenzo Sinatra (1707–82) and Francesco Paolo Labisi (1720–98?). The buildings by and attributed to them show the existence of a true 'school', particularly in Noto, with the Palazzo Senatorio, the church of Montevergine, the college and church of the Crociferi, and the Villa Eleonora in Falconara.

For the façade of the Cathedral of San Giorgio in Modica, recently discovered documents have ruled out the traditional attribution to Gagliardi, and instead revealed a competition in 1761 which was won by Labisi. He knew the Court Church in Dresden from engravings, as Alexandra Krämer has shown; and one might also suggest a connection with Sinatra's design for the façade of the Chiesa Madre in Floridia.

Competitions were a standard feature of architectural practice at the time, particularly for the most prestigious buildings. There is ample evidence of the competitions for the cathedrals of Syracuse, Modica and Catania, and the Albergo dei Poveri in Palermo. They involved confrontations and encounters between illustrious figures such as Andrea Palma, Vaccarini, Labisi, Furetto and Amico, and sometimes involved new craft workshops. They could be long-drawn-out and controversial affairs, with juries composed of a mixture of well-known names and almost unknown ones, and the decisions were often inconclusive and unrelated to the quality of the submissions. At other times, as for the reconstruction of the Chiesa Madre at Regalbuto, entries were called for in quick succession, causing inevitable disputes between the competitors, who were Francesco Battaglia from Catania and Ferdinando Lombardo from Palermo.

In effect, competitions provided opportunities for architects to display their own particular talents and professional skills. A competition was held in 1722 for a bridge on the San Lorenzo river near Termini Imerese: the competitors were Agatino Daidone, who had already made a design, and three other architects, Gaetano Lazzara, Carlo Infantolino and Filippo del Giudice. Giacomo Amato awarded the job to Daidone. Another competition involved a bridge on the Milicia River near Palermo: Ferdinando Fuga from Tuscany made a design which was criticized in 1730 by Gaetano Lazzara and Giuseppe Mariani. The superior attitude that Fuga displayed over this and other projects sparked off a flurry of controversies and conflicts between Sicilian architects keen to get commissions, and those who came from abroad.

Traces of the influence in south-eastern Sicily of Vaccarini and Gagliardi, the two major actors, are many and varied; in the case of Gagliardi, they also depended on the final completion of the cathedral of San Giorgio in Ragusa Ibla in the second half of the 18th century. The true beneficiaries were, however, the workshops of the Alì, Mazza, Cultraro and Bonaiuto families, who were able to disseminate into smaller towns the language they had learnt from the great masters in the first half of the century, and to apply technical skills with which they were now familiar.

Workshops

The development of architecture in Sicily in the 17th century saw a shift from the role of *caput magister* or master mason to that of architect-designer: from a purely practical trade, architecture became an intellectual one. The Milanese Antonio Muttone, who worked on the Benedictine monastery of San Martino delle Scale near Palermo (from 1590) and the Olivetan monastery of Santa Maria del Bosca near Calatamauro (from 1600) and was involved with many of the workshops in Palermo, is referred to in documents as *caput magister*, and yet he seems to have been an

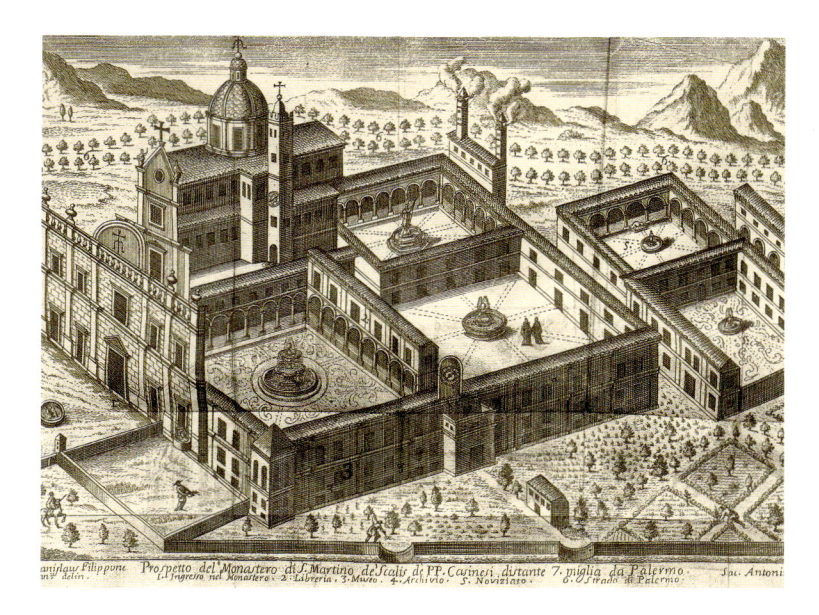

The Benedictine monastery of San Martino delle Scale near Palermo, where the Milanese architect Antonio Muttone worked around 1600. The monastery underwent major alterations by Giuseppe Venanzio Marvuglia in the late 18th century. Engraving from Leanti, *Lo stato presente della Sicilia*, 1761.

architect-designer as well. When he died in 1623 his will listed a large collection of drawings and books (notably the treatise of Vincenzo Scamozzi), showing his desire to move from the purely practical to the theoretical. This is only one of many such cases.

In Syracuse, Giovanni Vermexio, who belonged to a family who had moved to Sicily from Spain at the end of the 16th century, was well known as a *capomastro* and is referred to as *murator* in documents. He was credited with the Palazzo Municipale, under construction from the late 1620s in the piazza in Ortigia, which was given added prestige by the columns of the ancient Greek temple dedicated to Athena, which were visible in the outer wall of the Cathedral. It was a grandiose building, with echoes of older architectural styles and new Baroque flourishes, suggesting that it was the product not only of Vermexio's practical experience in the workshop, but also of a knowledge of contemporary ideas and treatises. In 17th-century Sicily, professional roles were often ambiguous.

In the first volume of his treatise entitled *L'Architetto Pratico* (The Practical Architect), published in 1726, Giovanni Amico addresses himself to a wide range of readership: 'amateurs, desirous of becoming architects', intellectuals, experts, curious youths; but also 'stonemasons, carpenters, and other kinds of craftsmen', who 'can find here solid advice for their professions'. The treatise does not confine itself to theory: it provides the practical advice promised in the title, with comments on materials such as stone, brick, chalk, sand and wood, and illustrations of building methods. In the second volume, published in 1750, Amico added further notes on the materials and techniques particular to Sicily, drawing on his wealth of experience and collecting it together as a legacy.

After the earthquake of 1693 in south-eastern Sicily, the practical aspects of reconstruction were uppermost in the minds of the master builders and decorators of Palermo and Messina. They belonged to a culture rooted in traditional knowledge and experience, a culture which was only superseded in the 1730s with the arrival of intellectual practitioners, glowing with the aura of apprenticeships abroad, men who had been able to cross the barrier of the sea and to explore new horizons in Italy and elsewhere in Europe, learning as they went along. Their workmanship always remained firmly rooted in the Sicilian tradition, to which they added experience gained in the many workshops that persisted in the language of the late Baroque style for far longer than traditional chronology has allowed, with the result that they were able to move away from their humble beginnings and assume new and more prestigious professional roles. The workshops of local craftsmen, strong in their own experience of the building trade, open to new ideas, and able to adapt to the needs of the reconstruction work around them, thus became agents of new, as yet unexplored developments of the late Baroque.

The second half of the 18th century saw artisan-architects come to the fore, such as Luciano Alì, who worked on the Palazzo Beneventano in Syracuse, and also builder-architects such as Pietro and Constantino Cultraro, who were perhaps responsible for the design of the church of Sant'Antonio in Ferla, which is one of the most interesting works of architecture in the hinterland of Syracuse.

left The magnificent bronze statue of Don John of Austria after his victory at the Battle of Lepanto in 1571. The statue, by Calamecca, is in Messina.

opposite The monument beside the Royal Palace or Palazzo dei Normanni in Palermo was erected to Philip IV (see p. 98). His statue was destroyed in 1848, and later replaced by that of Philip V.

114   The actors: patrons, architects, and master builders

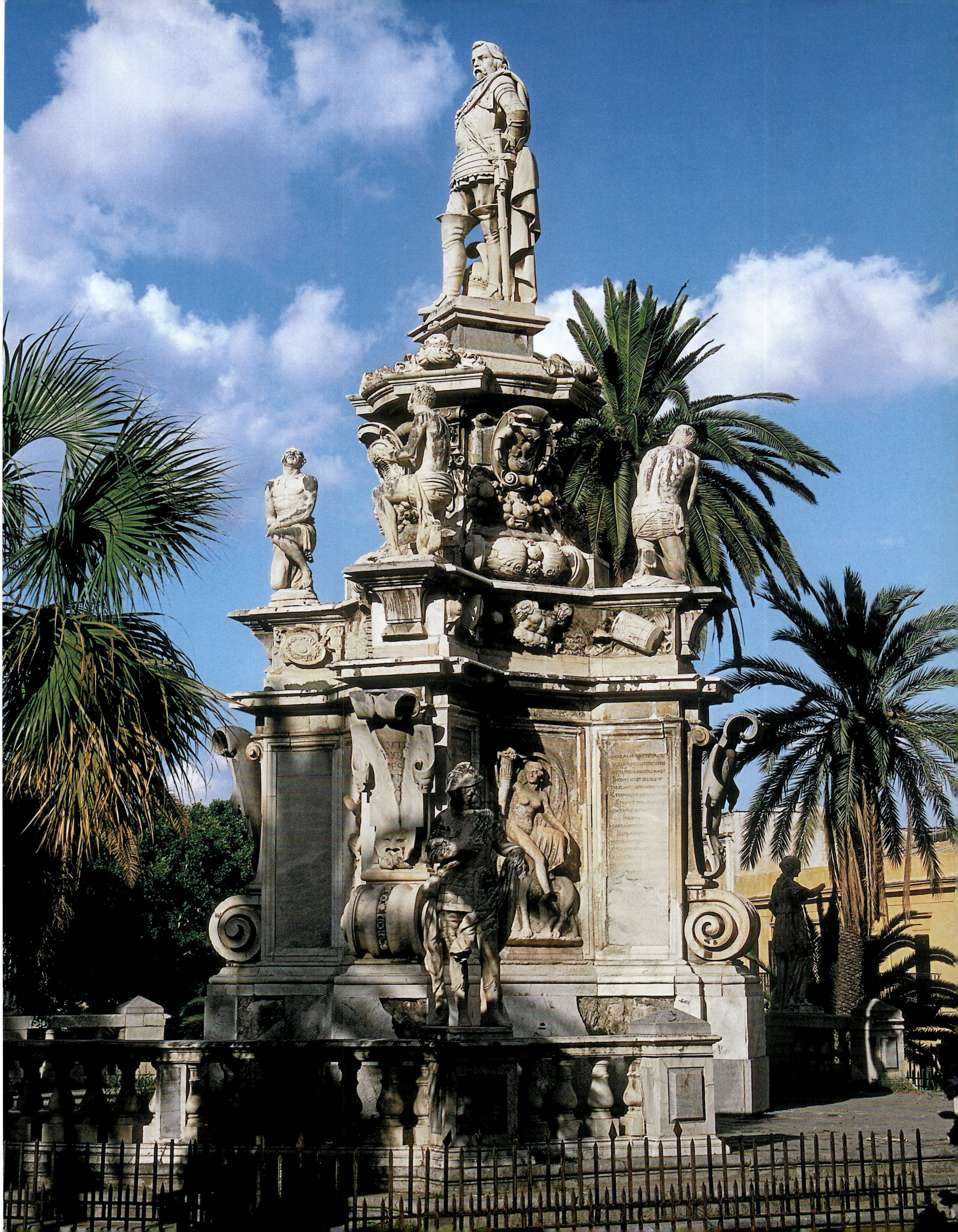

Statues on the façade of the church of San Paolo in Palazzolo Acreide.

The actors: patrons, architects, and master builders 117

below and right Villa Valguarnera, Bagheria.

overleaf The Hall of Mirrors in the Villa Palagonia, Bagheria.

118 *The actors: patrons, architects, and master builders*

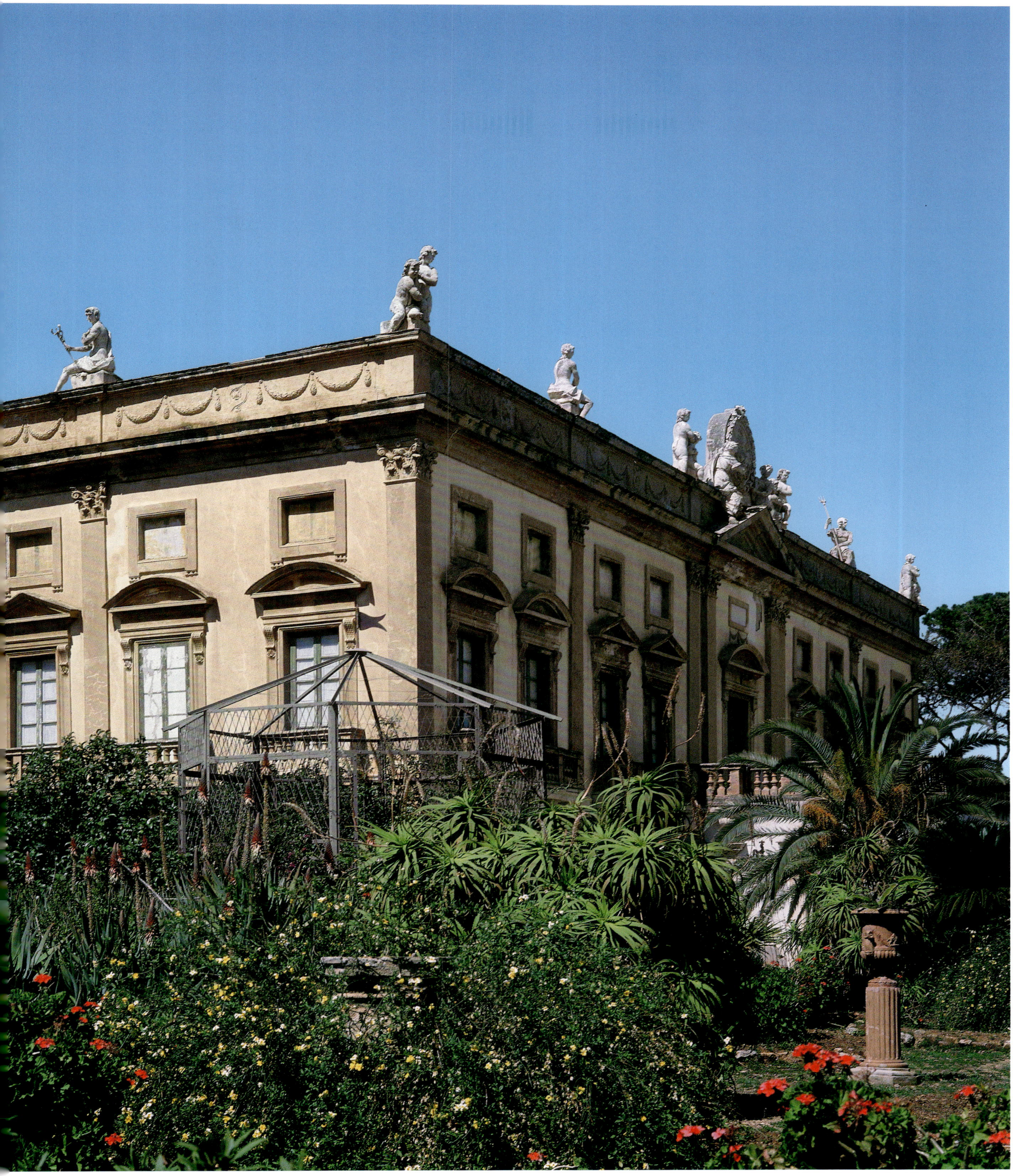

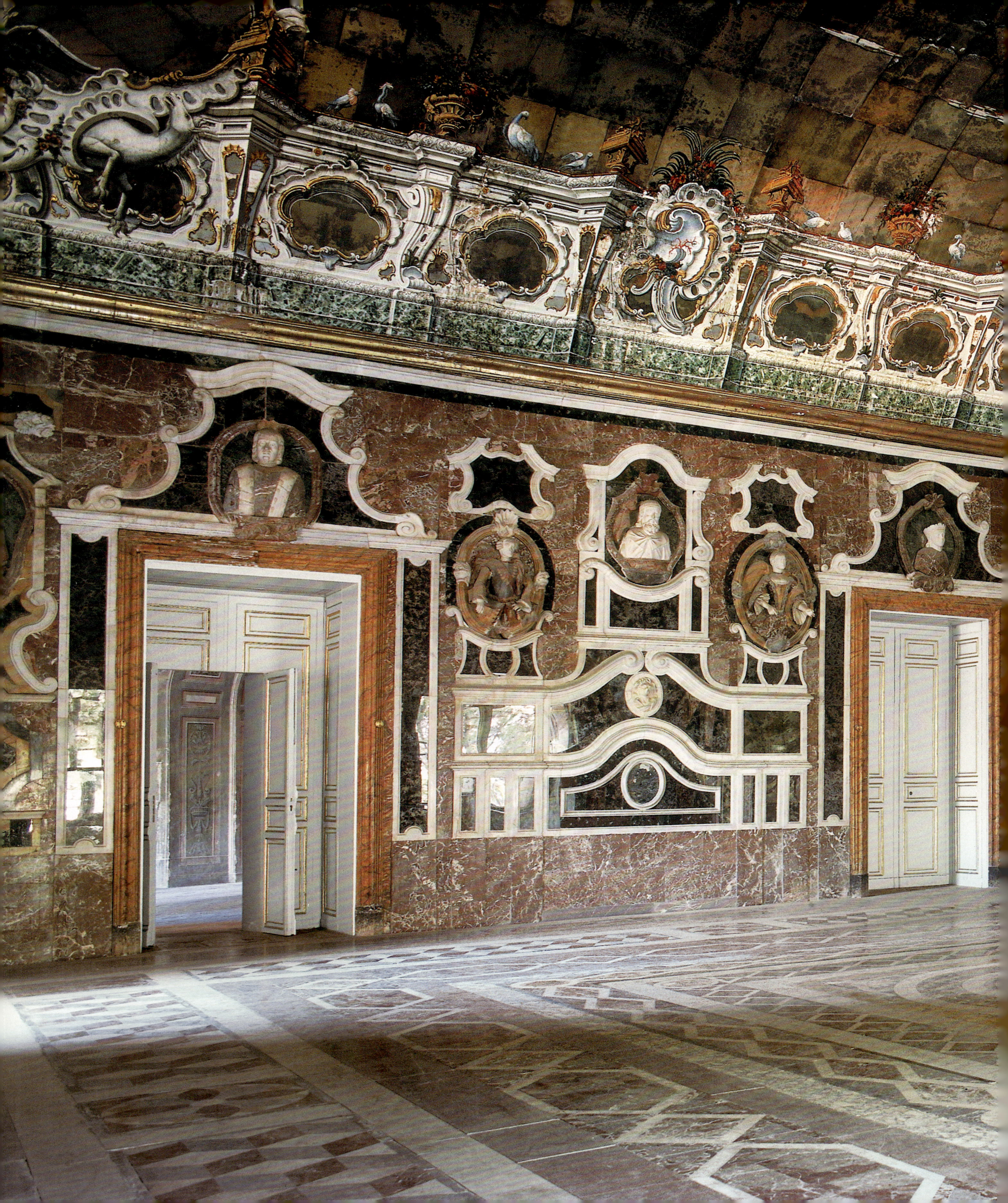

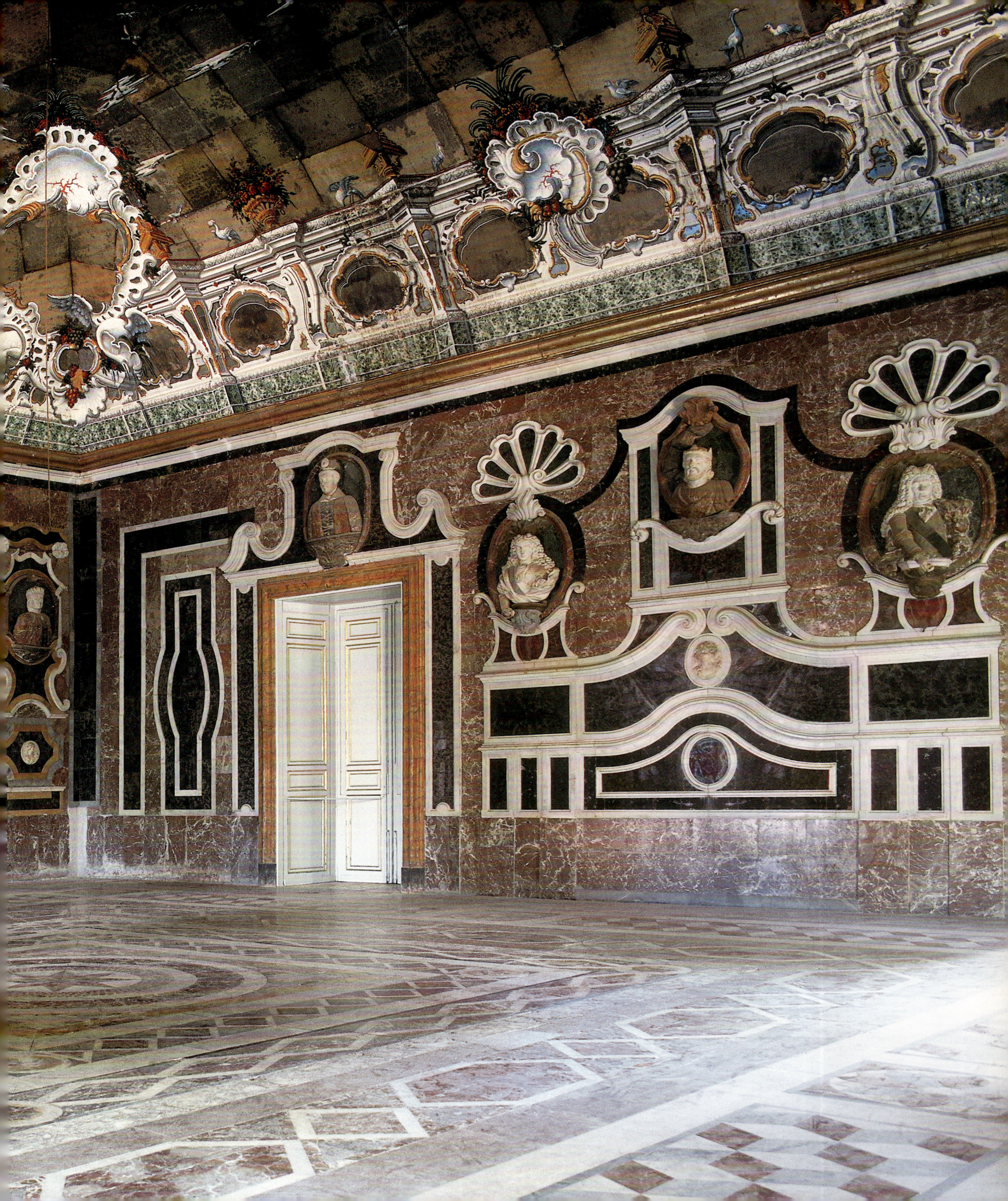

122 *The actors: patrons, architects, and master builders*

The actors: patrons, architects, and master builders 123

preceding pages, left Detail of the Villa Butera at Bagheria.

preceding pages, right Villa San Marco at Santa Flavia near Palermo.

right Villa Filangeri at Santa Flavia.

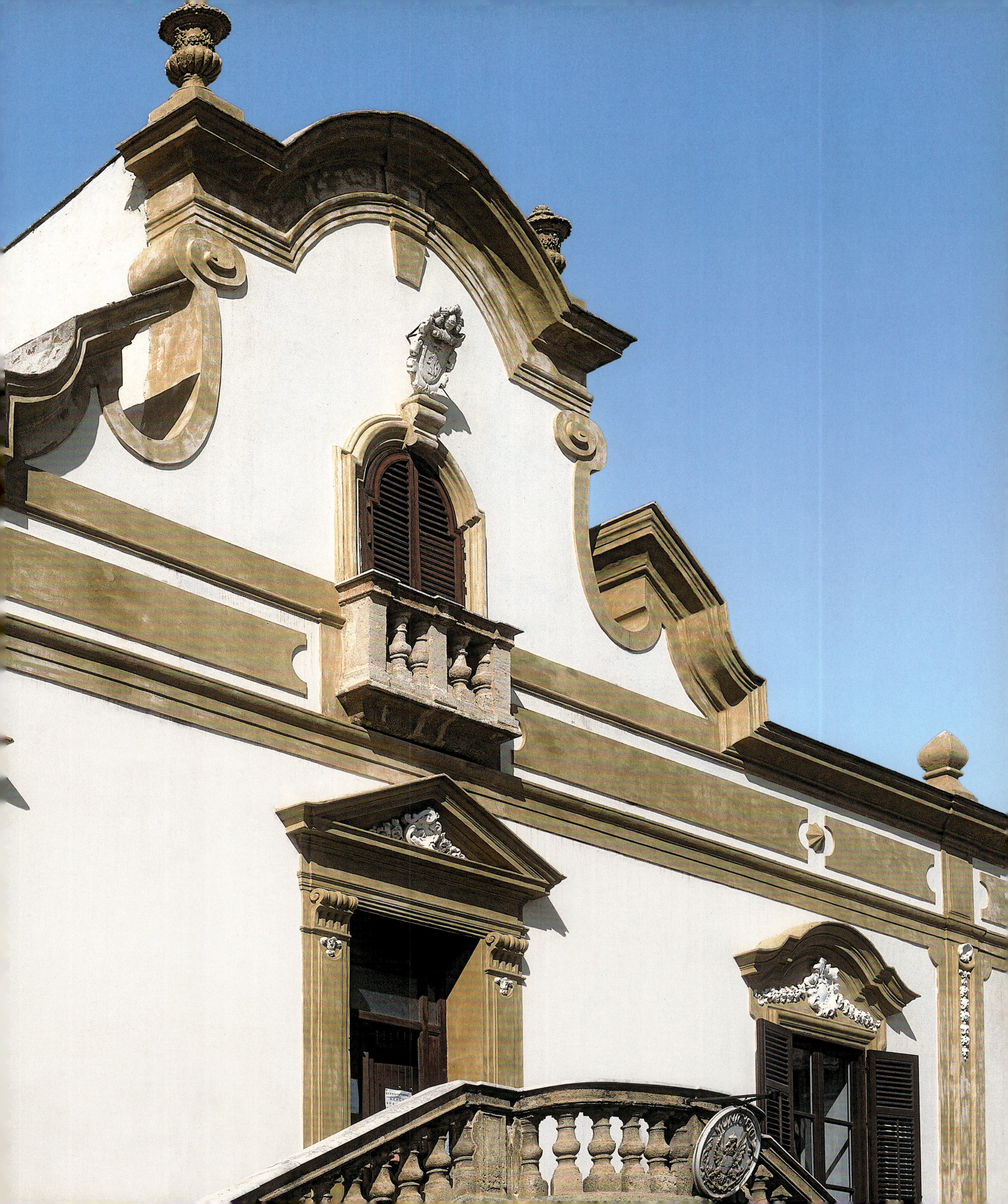

Allegorical frescoes in the feudal palace of the Naselli family in Aragona, in the province of Agrigento. They have recently been attributed to the painter Michele Blasco from Sciacca.

right The undulating façade of the Villa Eleonora near Noto, which belonged to the Nicolaci family, princes of Villadorata. It was probably designed by Francesco Paolo Labisi, a pupil of Rosario Gagliardi.

The actors: patrons, architects, and master builders 127

The terrace of the Palazzo Butera, in the Foro Italico, Palermo, and the entrance hall of the palace; in the overdoors are splendid maps of the feudal cities under the jurisdiction of the Branciforte family.

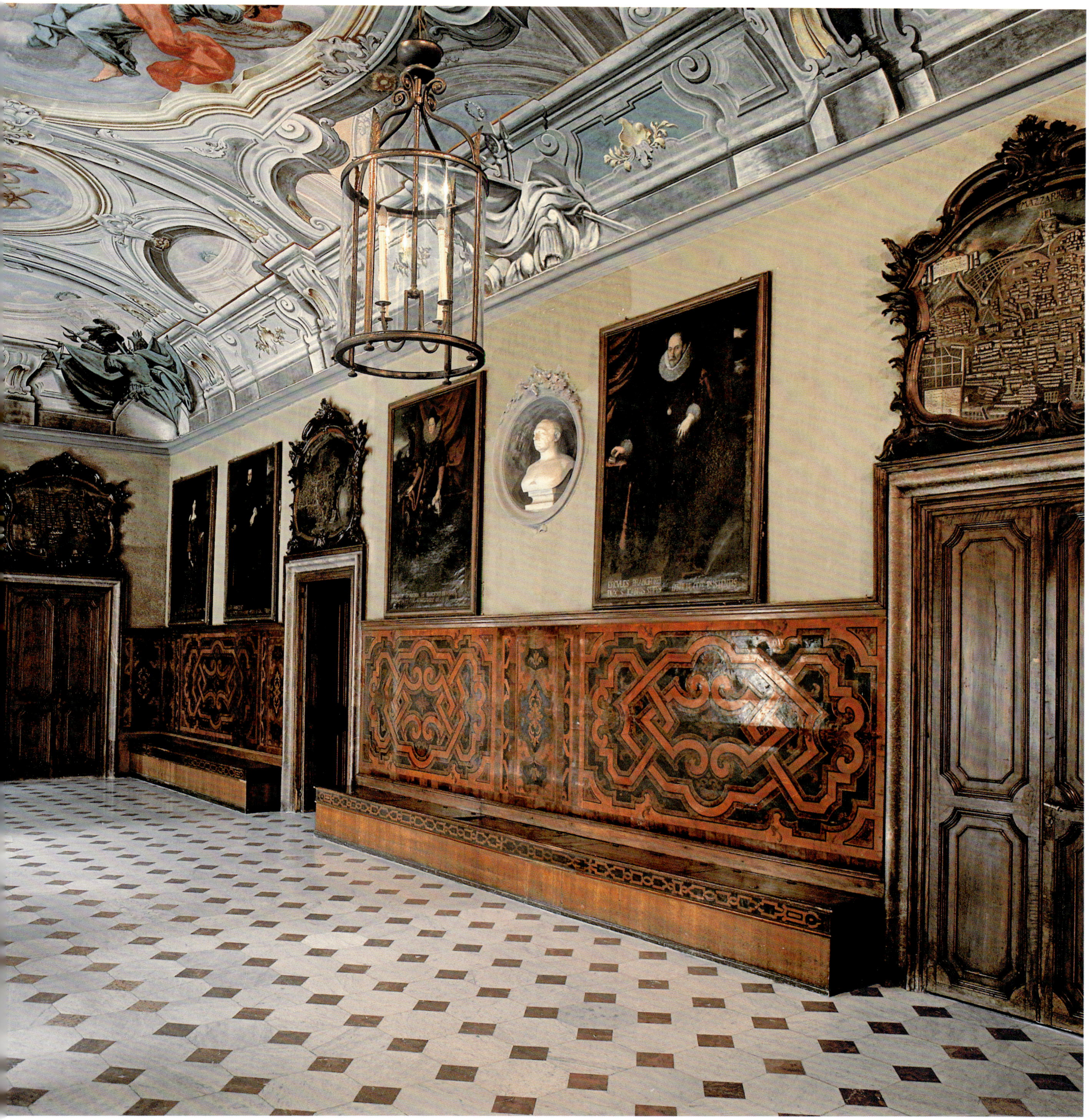

130 *The actors: patrons, architects, and master builders*

opposite The great staircase in the Palazzo Cutò, Palermo.

right The staircase leading up to the Villa De Cordova, Palermo.

overleaf, left The great staircase in the Palazzo Gangi, Palermo.

overleaf, right A room in the Palazzo Sant'Elia, Palermo.

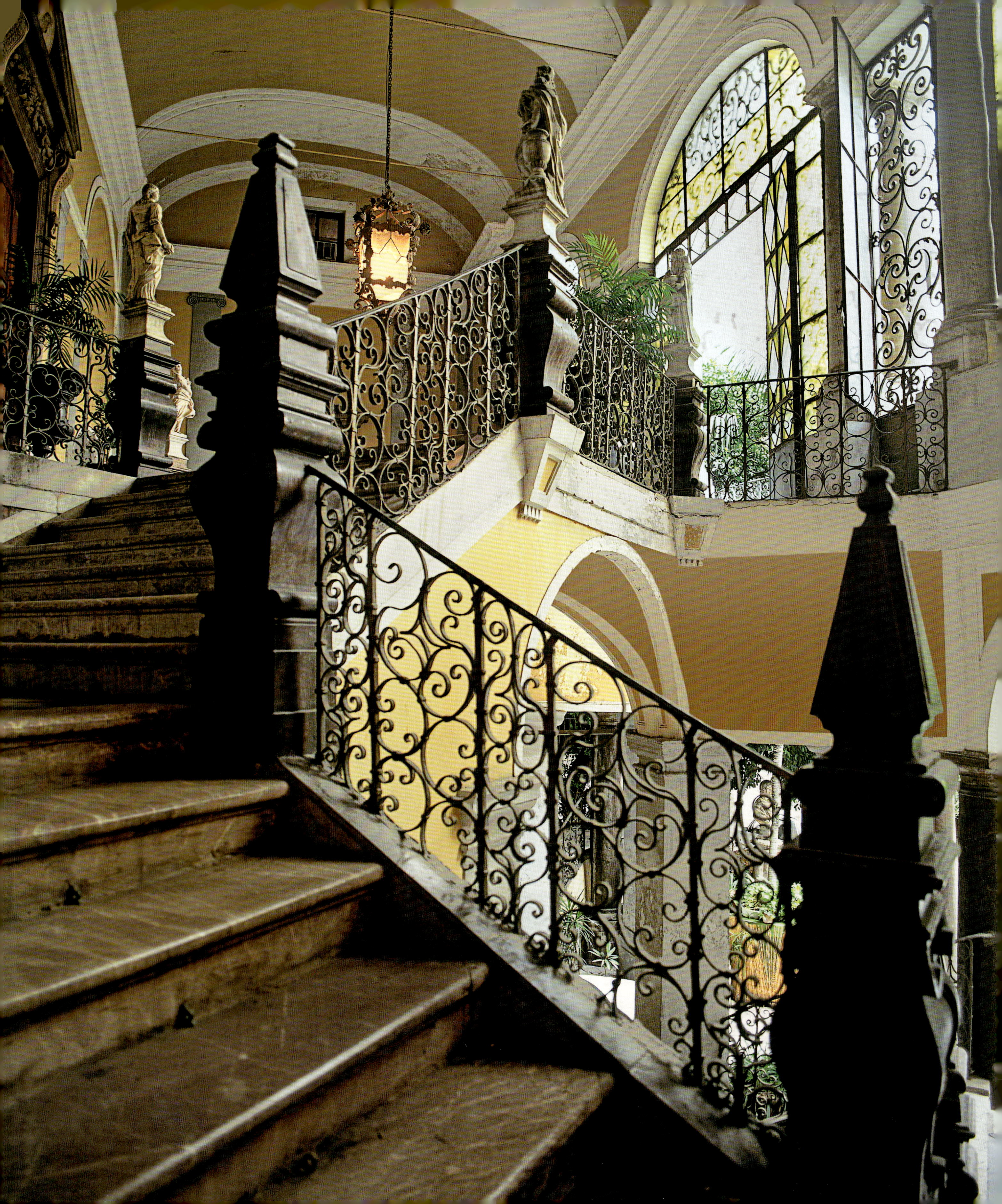

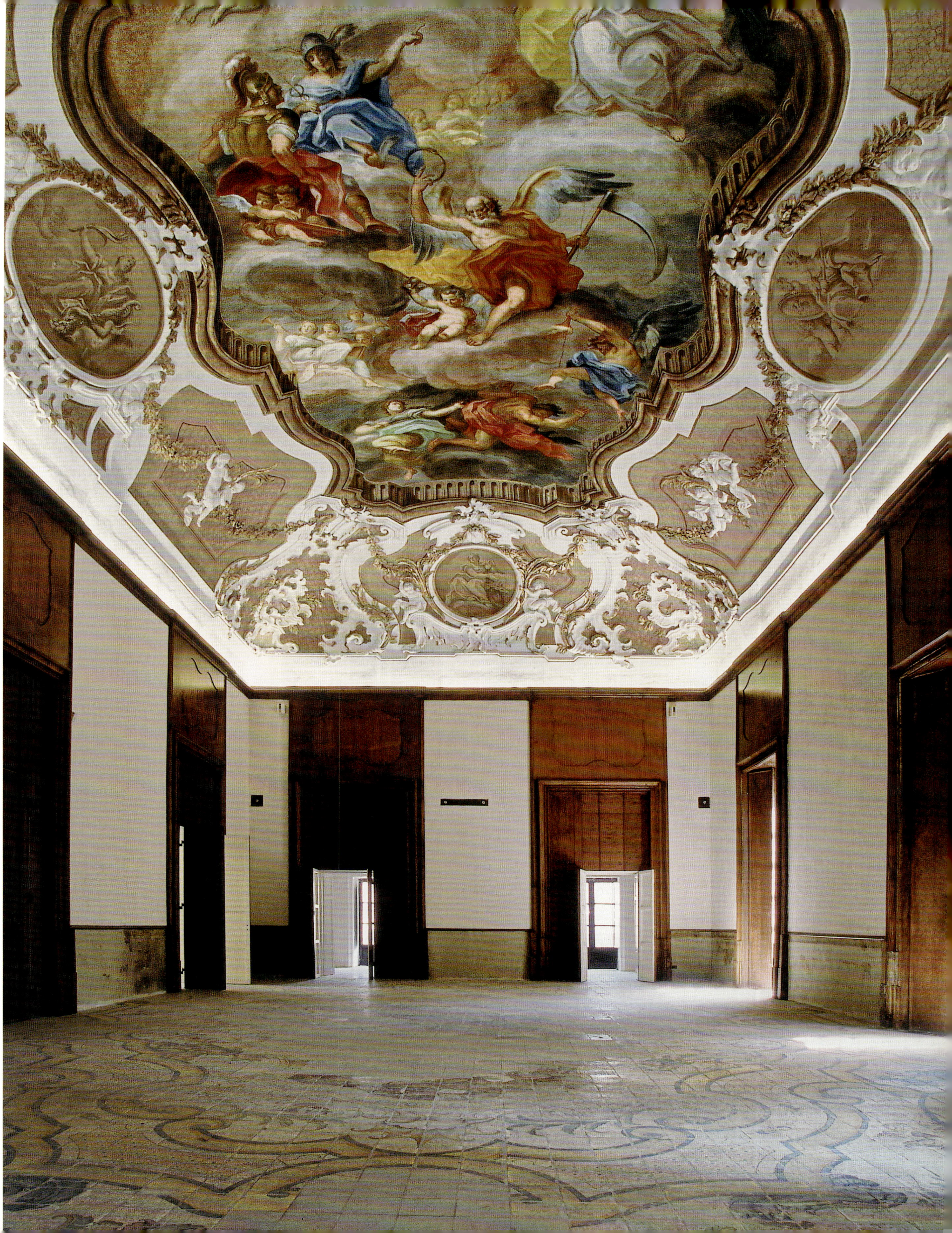

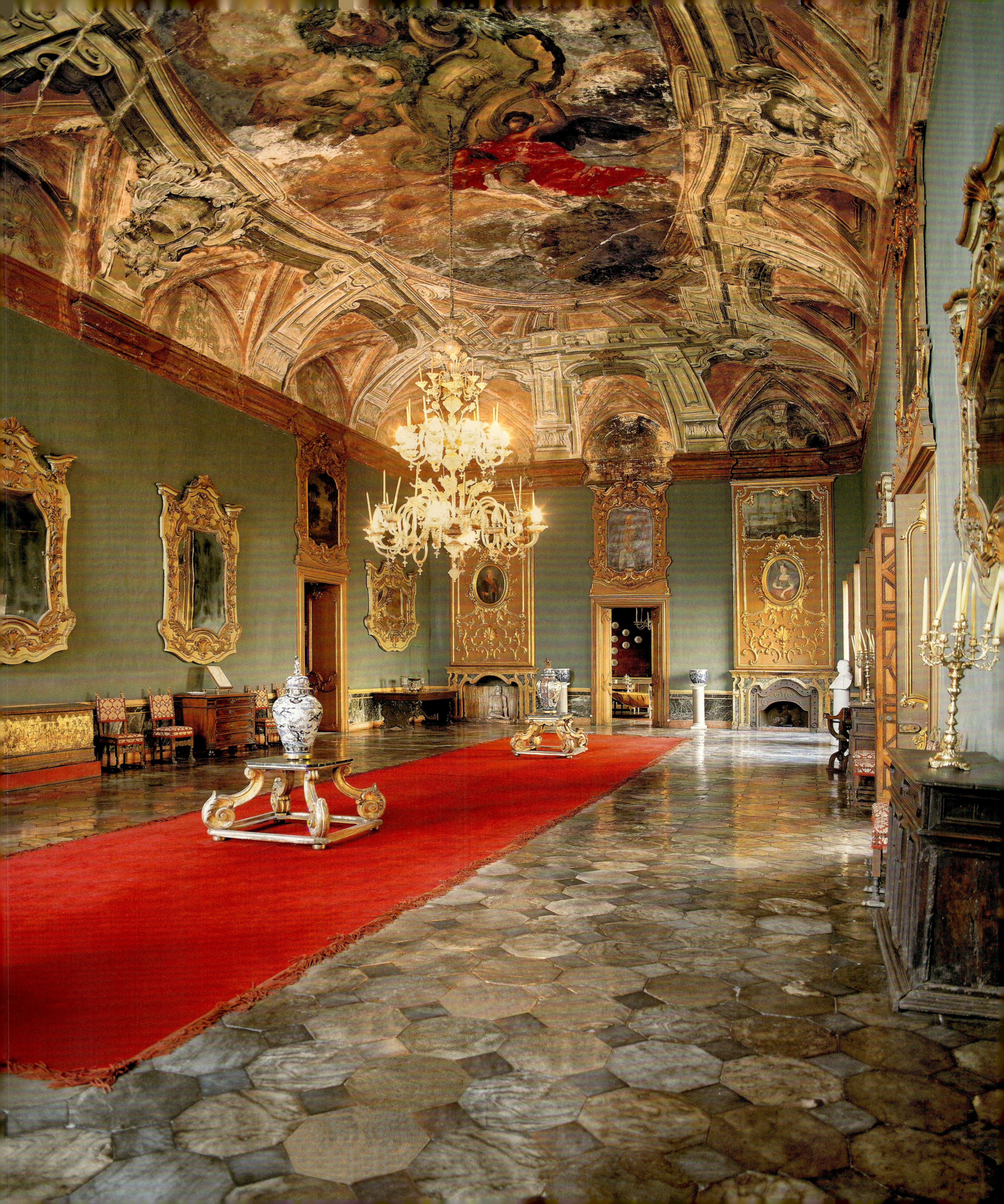

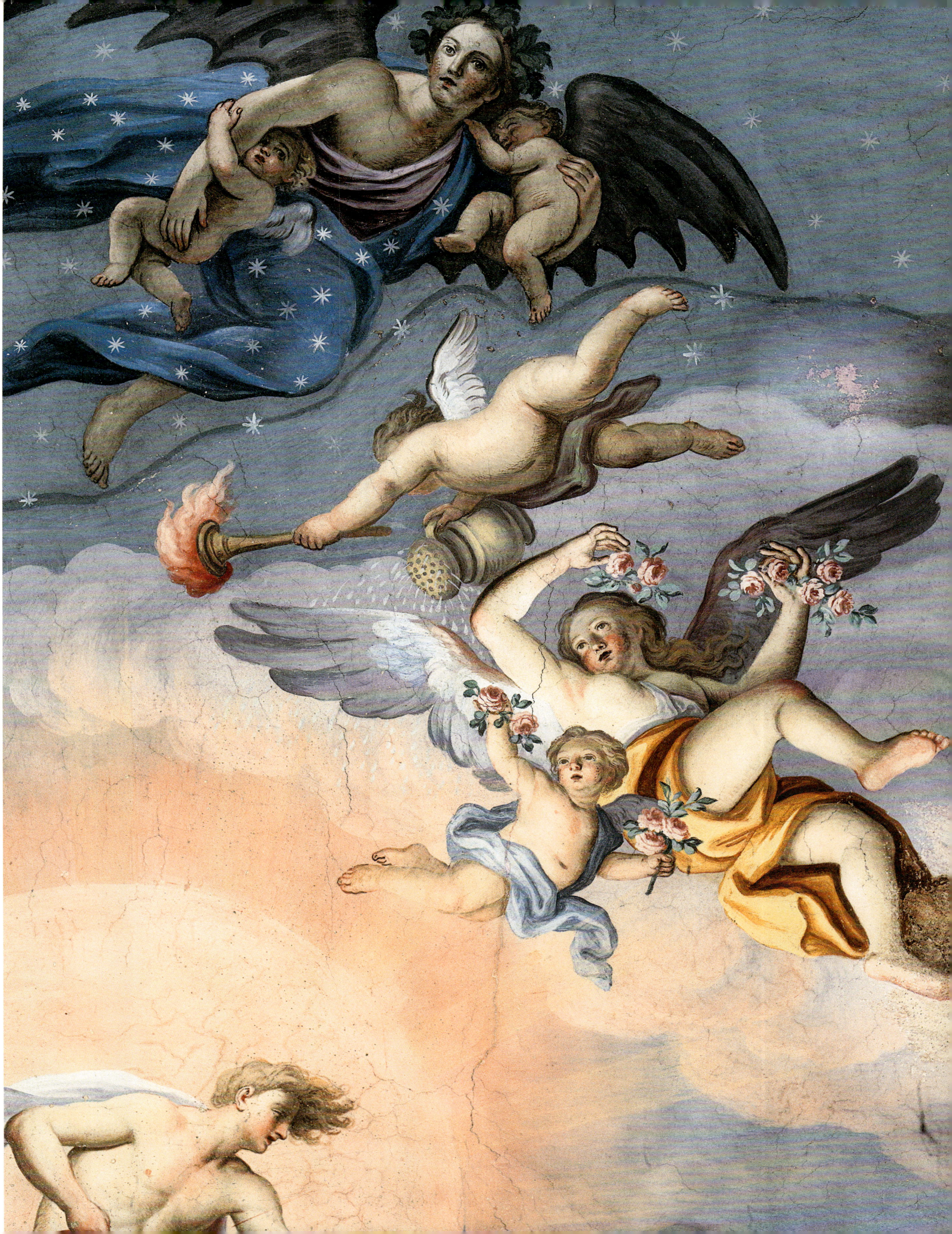

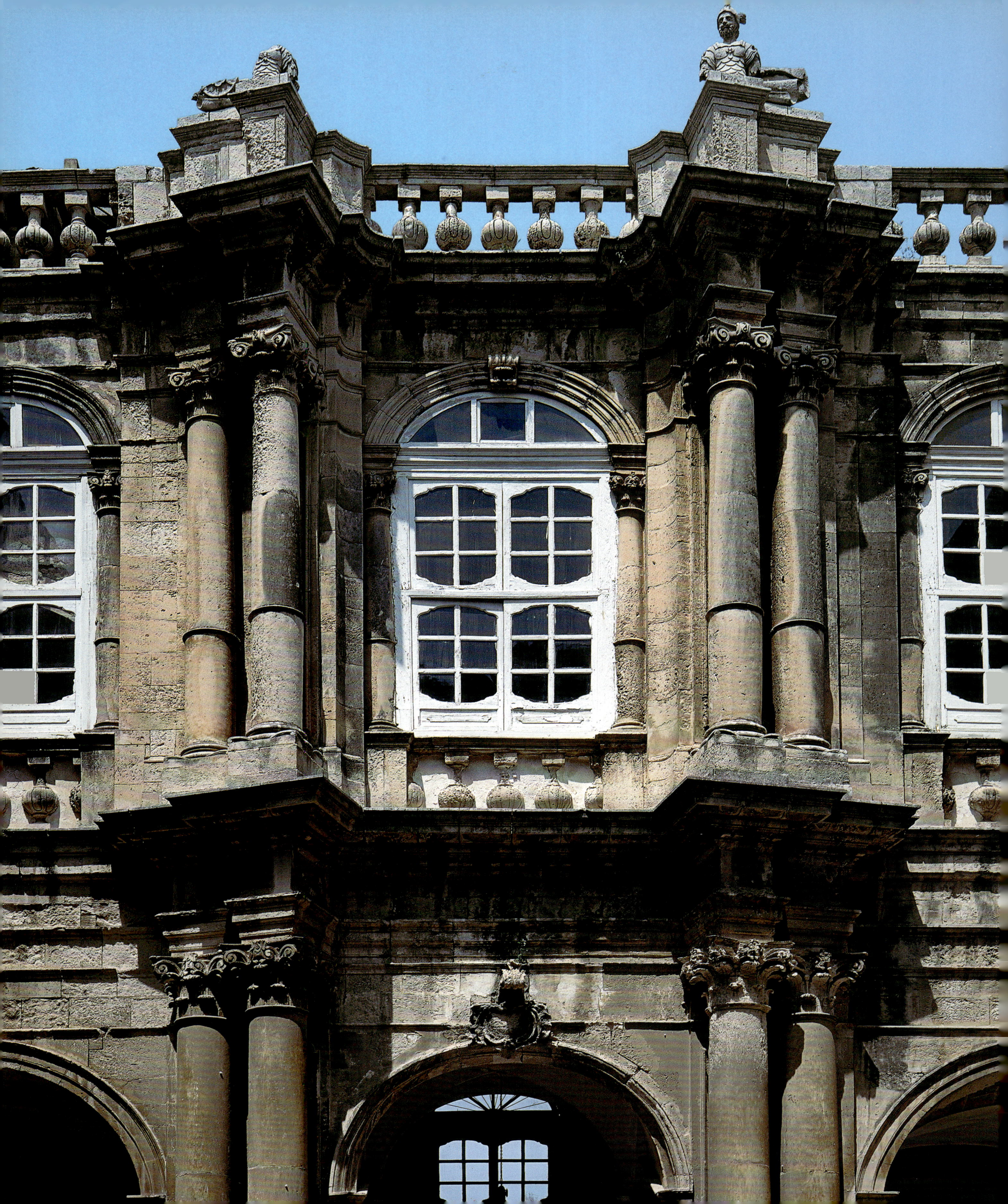

preceding pages, left The *salone* of the Palazzo Mazzarino in the Via Maqueda, Palermo.

preceding pages, right A fresco by the Roman artist Gaspare Fumagalli in the Palazzo Bongiorno in Gangi, in the province of Palermo.

opposite Detail of the Palazzo Beneventano del Bosco in Syracuse.

above The church of Montevergine in Noto has one of the most extreme examples of a concave façade.

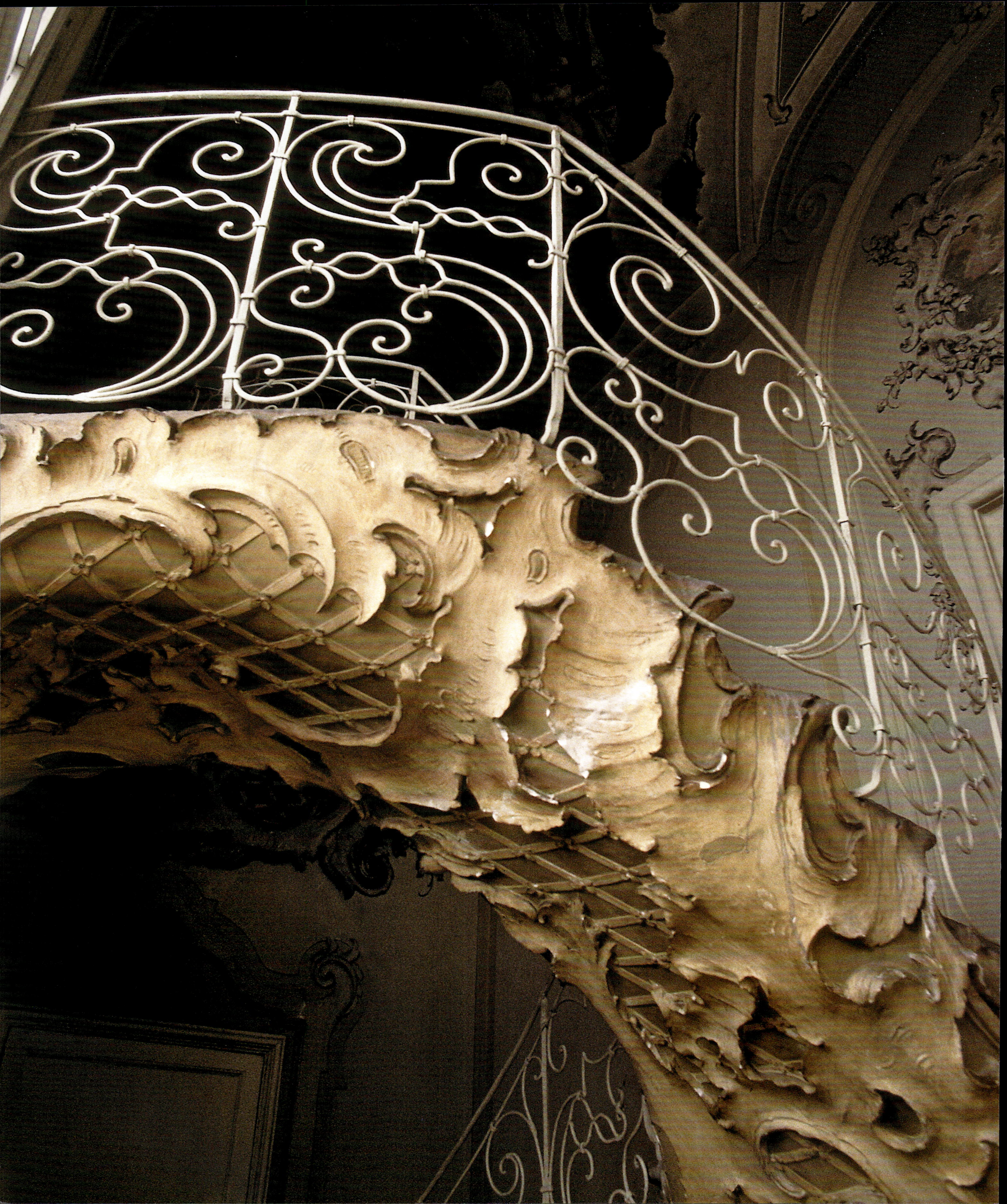

opposite The musicians' staircase in the Palazzo Biscari, Catania.

right Courtyard of the Palazzo Sant'Elia, Palermo.

The actors: patrons, architects, and master builders 139

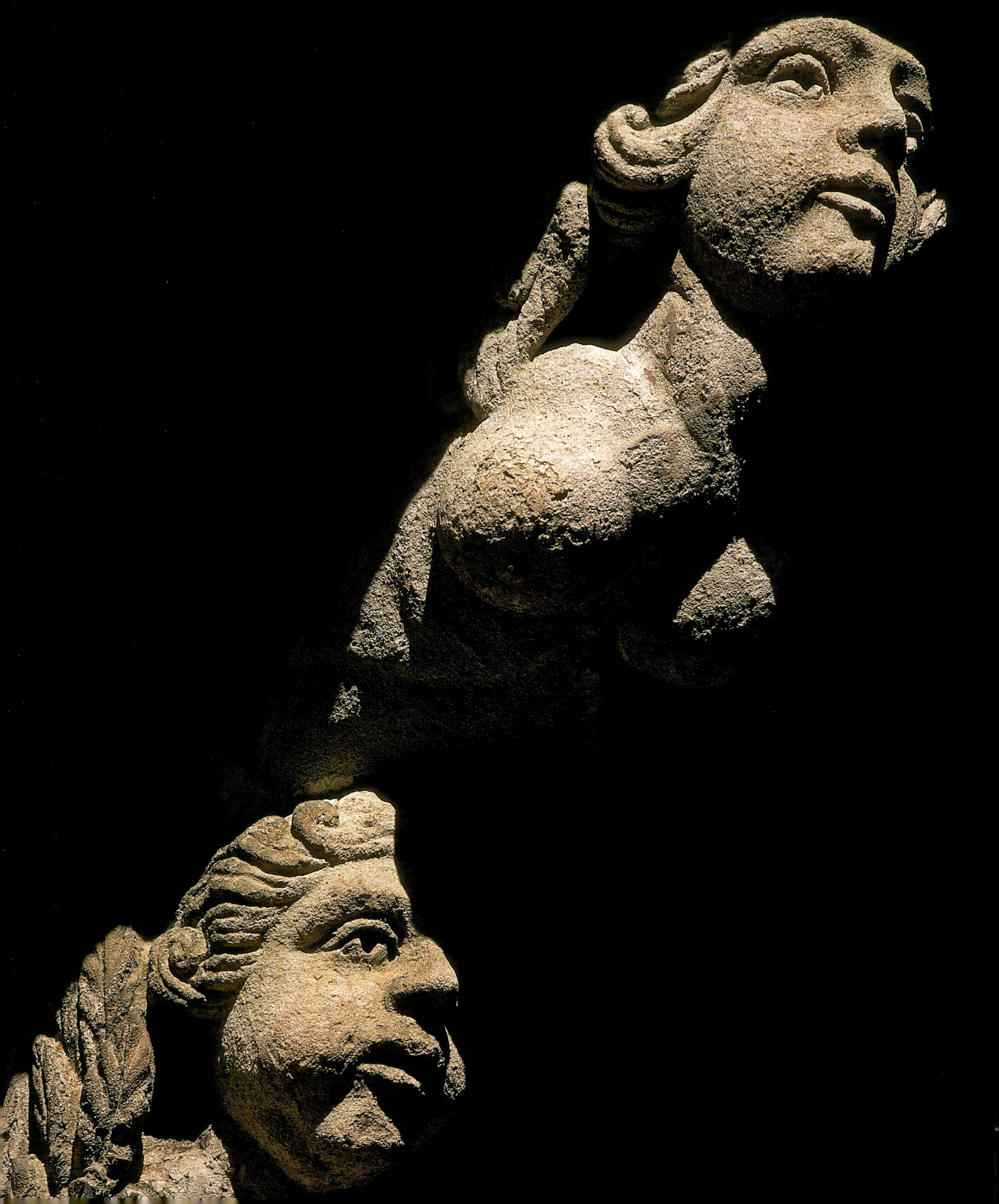

Many Baroque balconies, particularly in eastern Sicily, have intricately carved brackets.

opposite Detail of a balcony in Modica.

right A balcony of the Palazzo Cosentini in Ragusa Ibla.

overleaf, left A balcony of the Palazzo Beneventano in Scicli.

overleaf, right The extraordinary cresting of the Palazzo Impellizzeri in Syracuse.

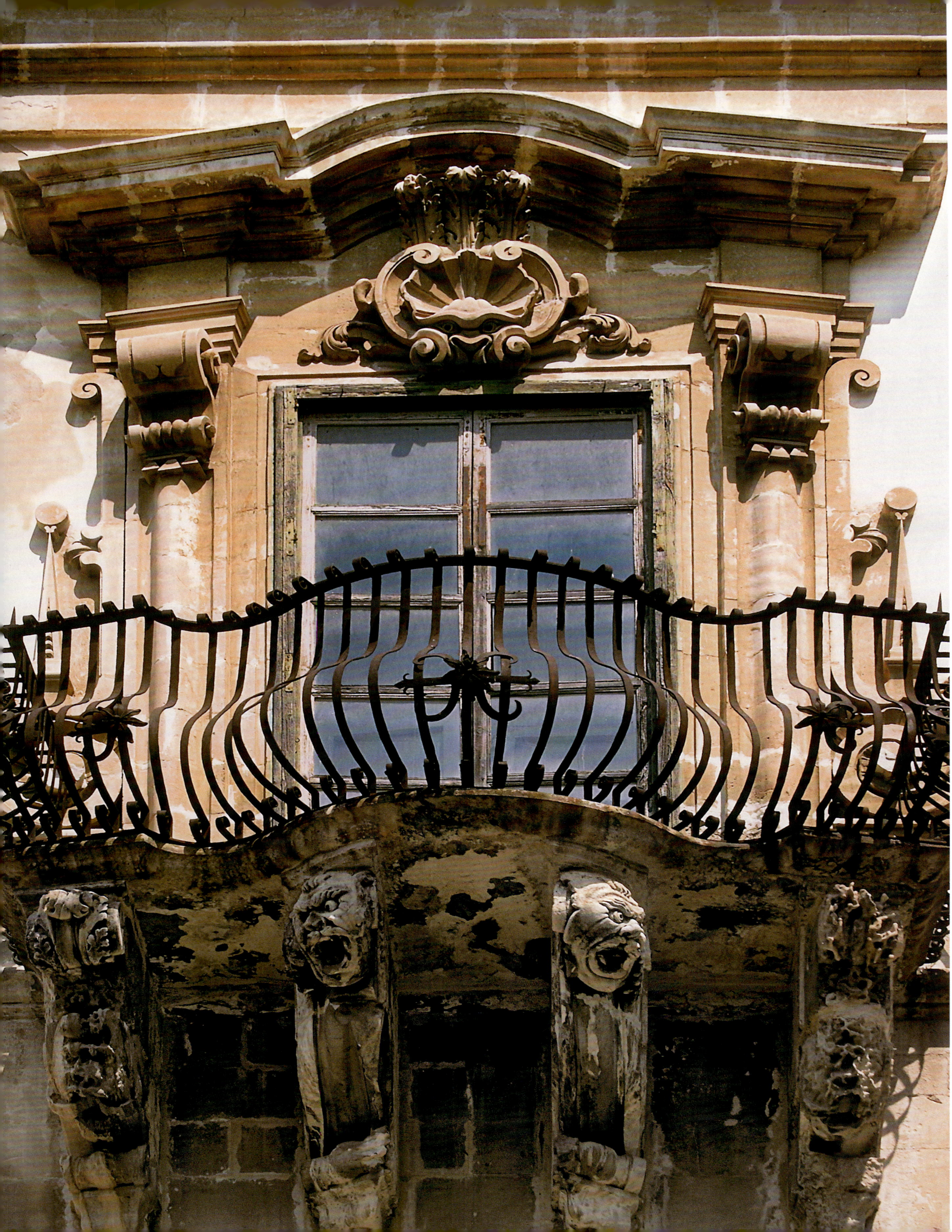

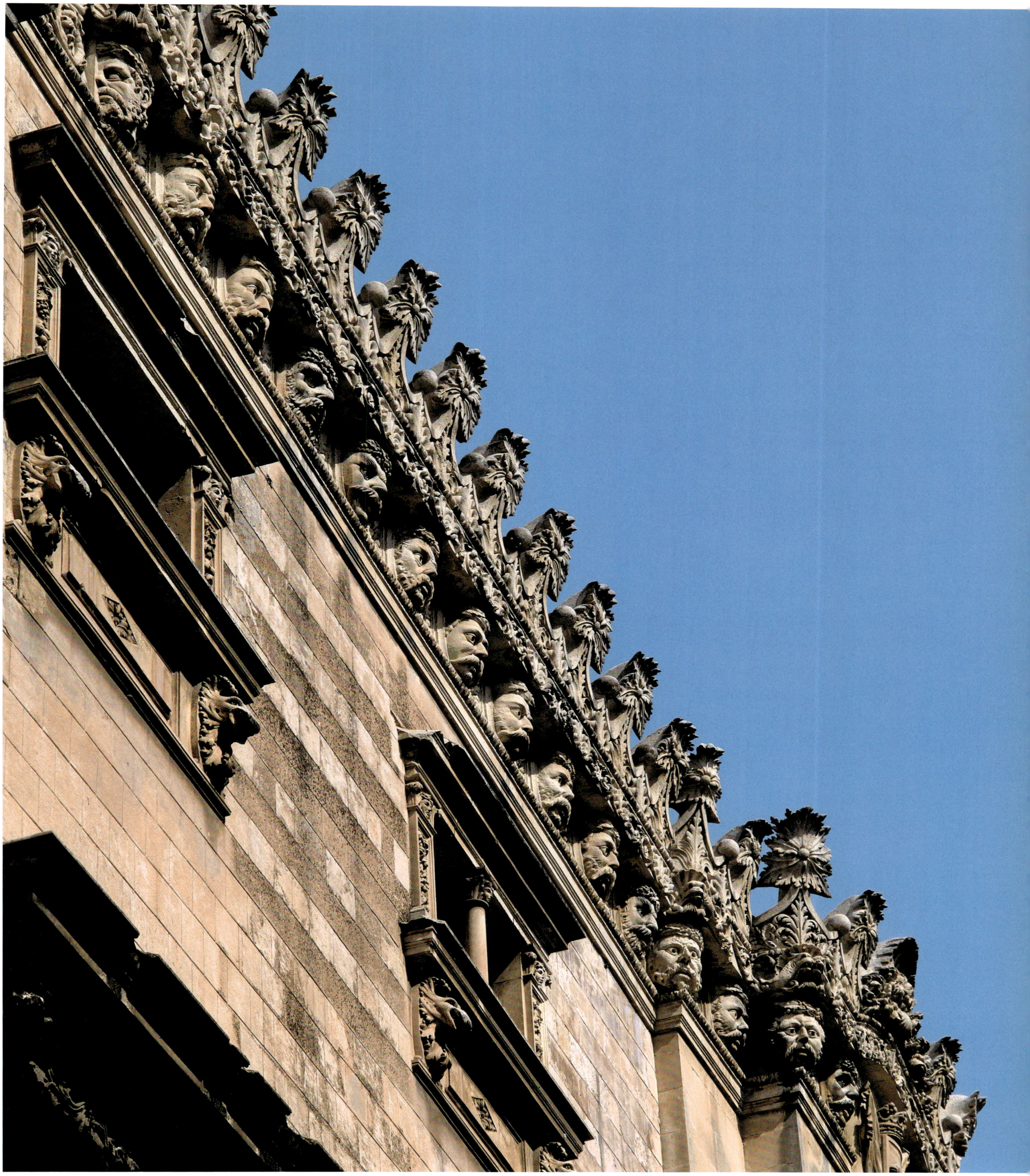

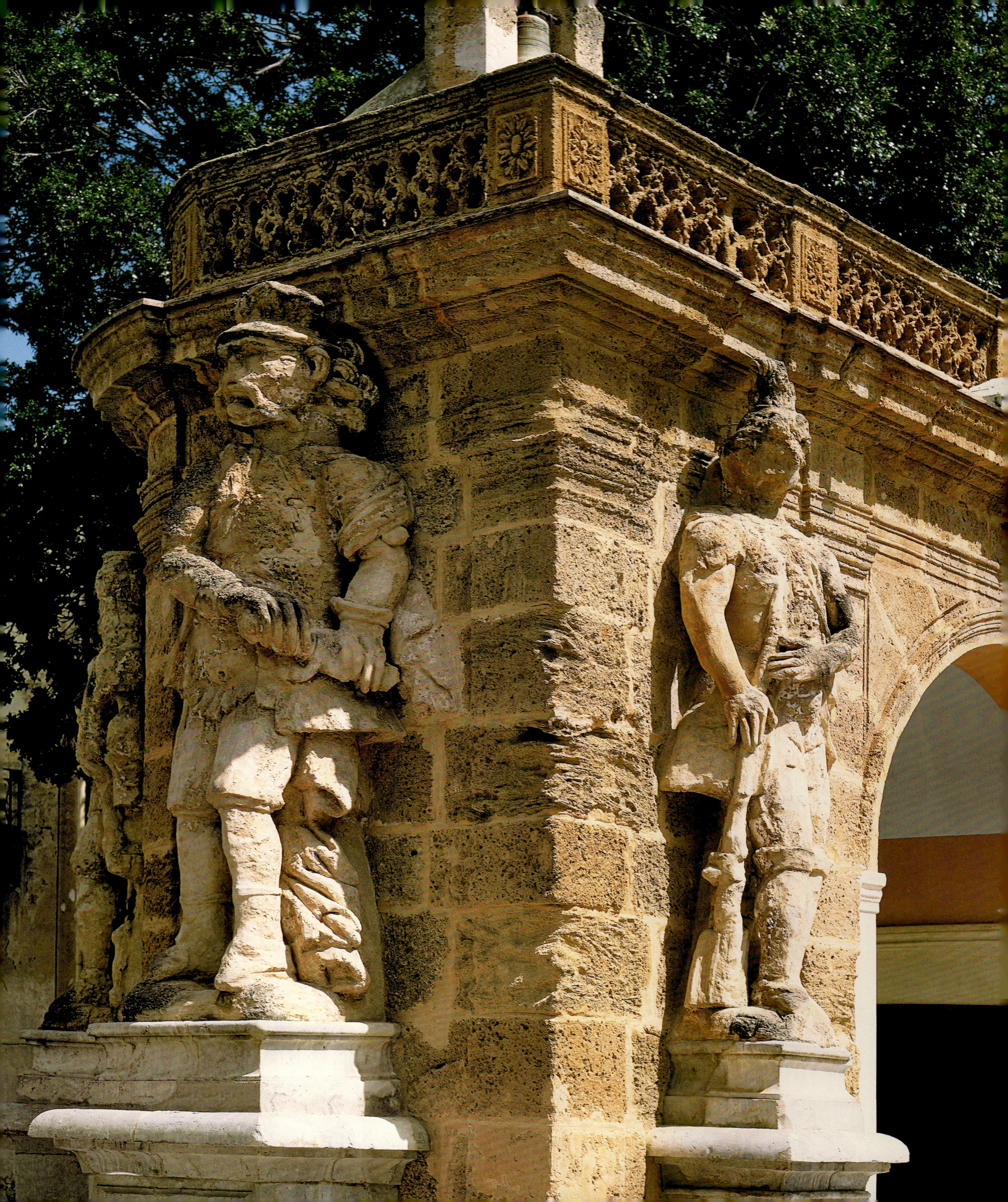

left The gateway that formerly led in to the Villa Palagonia in Bagheria.

above Telamones on the Porta Nuova, Palermo.

overleaf The entrance to the Jesuit college in Mazara del Vallo, in the province of Trapani.

The actors: patrons, architects, and master builders 145

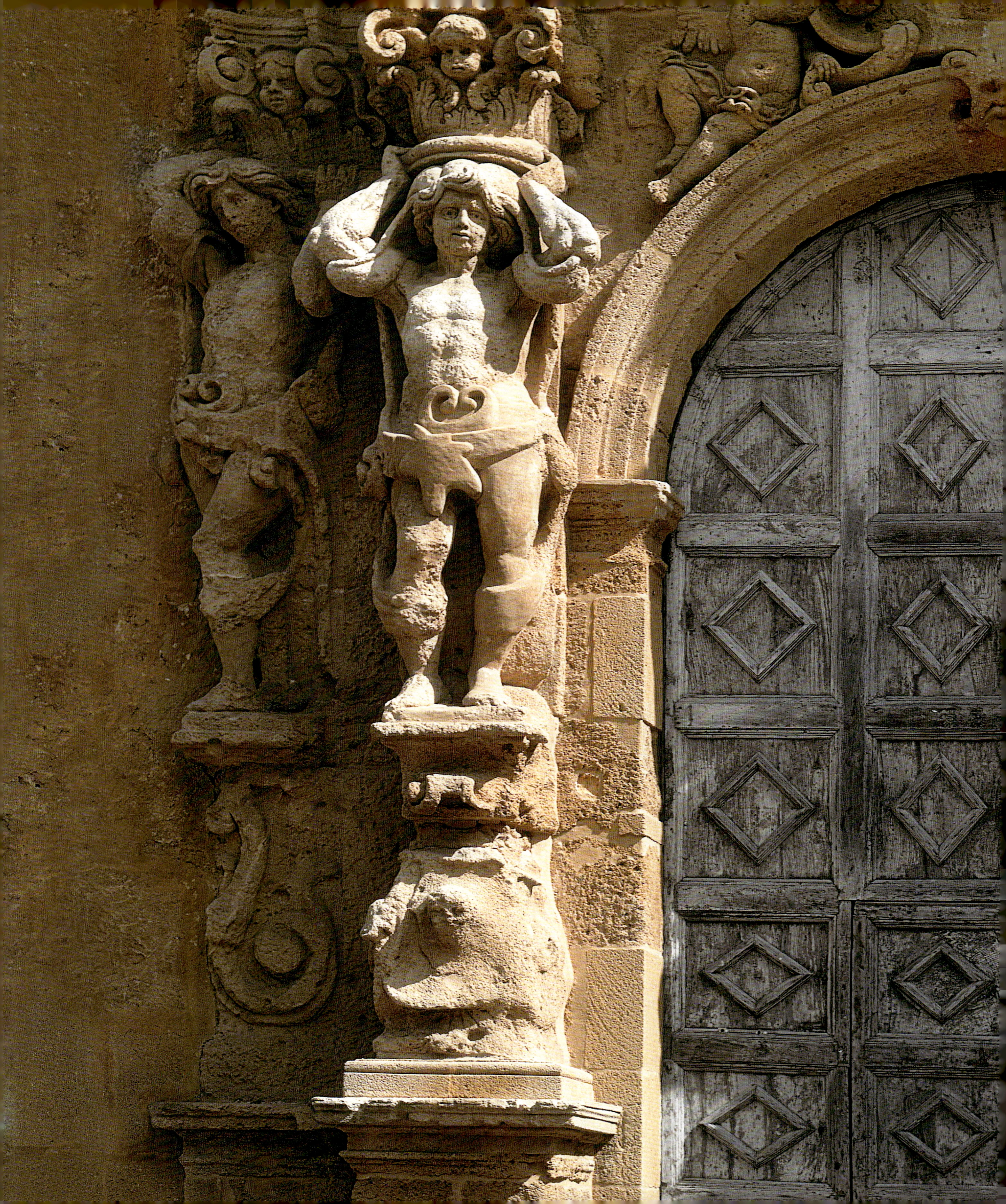

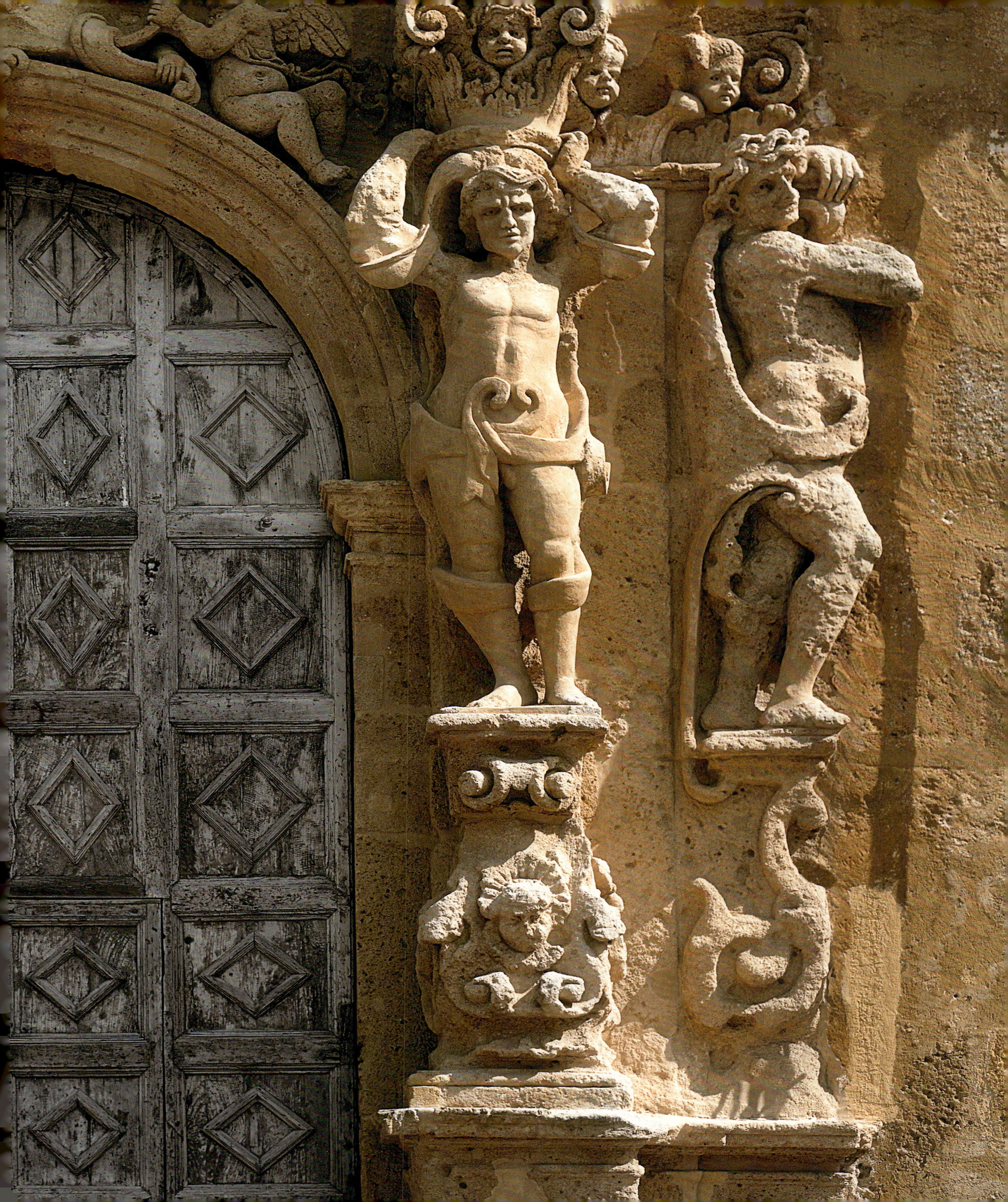

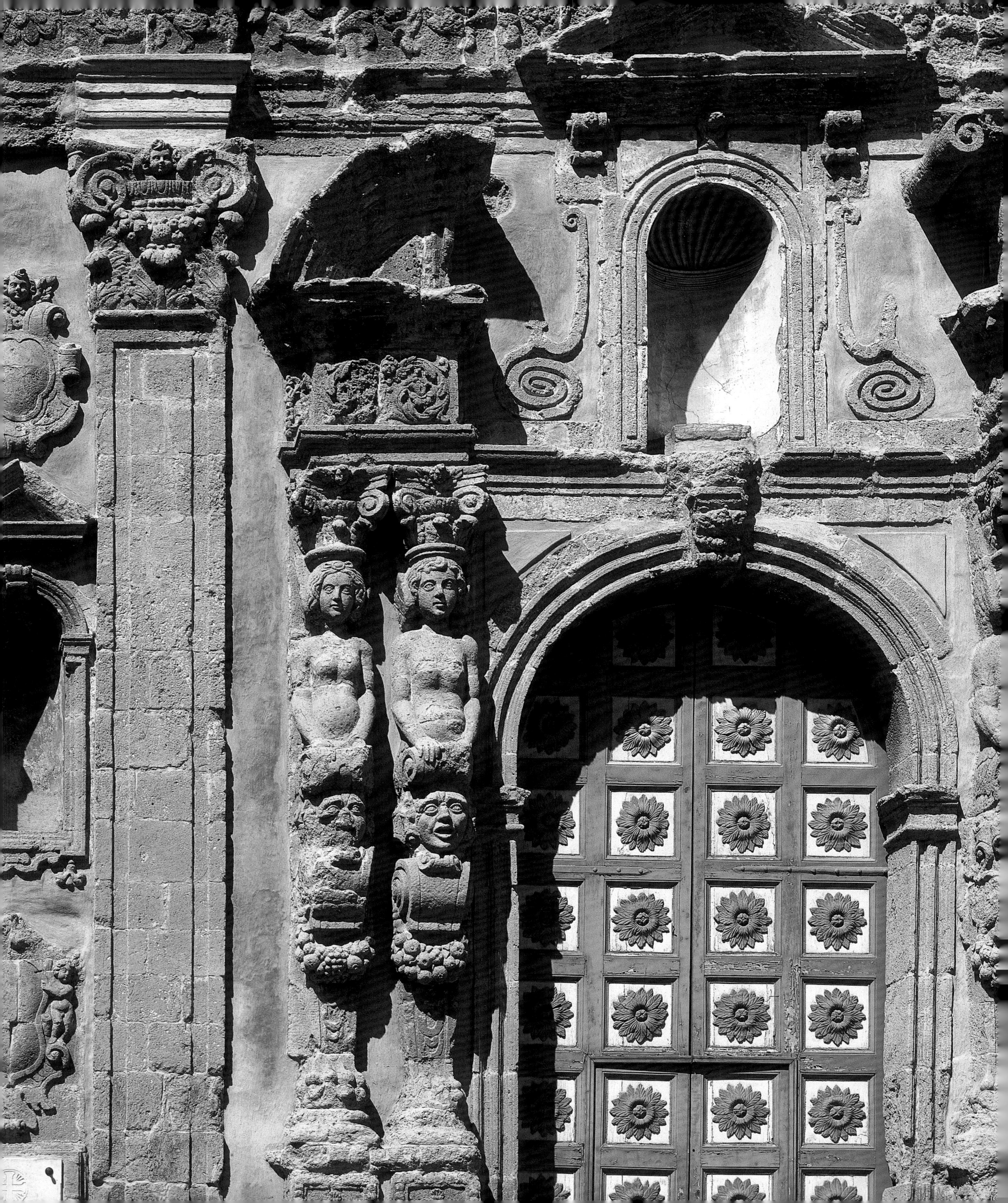

left Entrance to the church of San Francesco at Naro, in the province of Agrigento.

right Detail of the Palazzo La Motta at Nicosia, in the province of Enna.

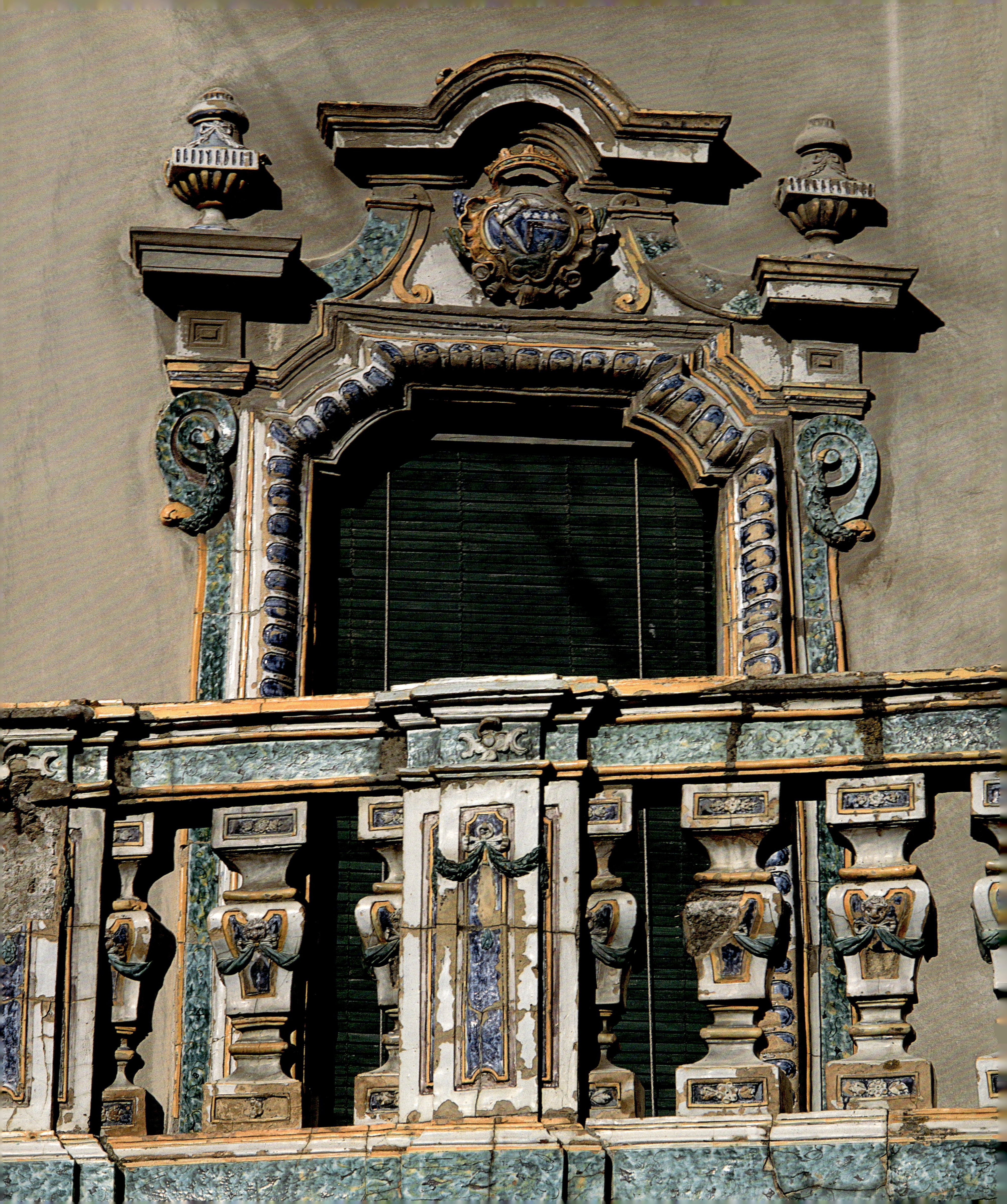

opposite Majolica decoration on the Palazzo Ventimiglia in Caltagirone.

right Detail of the entrance to the Chiesa Madre in Mistretta, in the province of Messina.

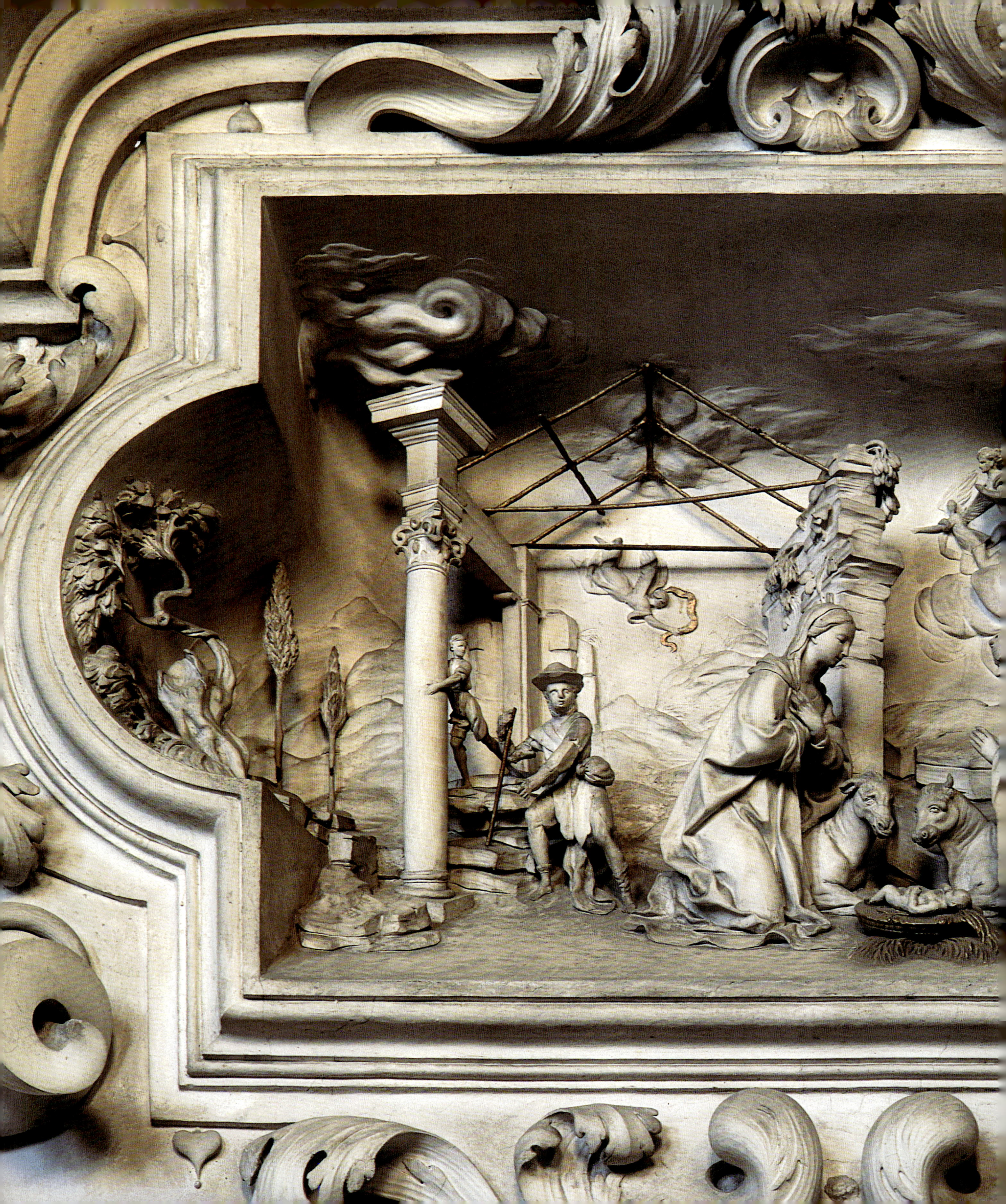

The buildings: tradition and revolution

As we have seen, in the major coastal cities the Baroque era, which lasted from the early 17th to the mid-18th century, can be divided into three phases, characterized by continuity and fragmentation. Apart from the south-eastern region, which was struck by the earthquake in 1693, it is clear that inland areas in the centre and west were slow to absorb any new ideas, and tended to build on ideas from the past. This was not due to geographical isolation, for the existence of vast feudal estates meant that there was communication and circulation of information. Rather, it was due to the desire of patrons to favour centres of power, and the desire of workers to maintain tradition. Hence this long period was marked by ususual parallels and contrasts: the simultaneous existence of great projects and great actors; the increased contact with foreign cultures; the impact of the earthquake of 1693 and the subsequent influx of architects and master builders; and the sheer vitality and richness of the decorative schemes which were expressed in different materials, techniques and styles over the years.

The long 'Renaissance'

The term 'Renaissance' when applied to Sicily can give rise to confusion, something historians have recently been eager to dispel. The styles which, variously interpreted, defined architecture during the 15th and 16th centuries were affected in Sicily by deep roots going back to Norman and Swabian times, and by the desire to maintain continuity, resisting attempts to graft new ideas onto the solid trunk of a still vigorous tradition. In the 16th century, architecture on the island had been influenced by mainland Italy, particularly Lombardy, Tuscany and Rome, and by the arrival of the founder of the Gagini dynasty, bringing with him a style substantially derived from Michelangelo.

At first, judging by contemporary sources, it was seen as appropriate and convenient to go on building in the existing style, but by the end of the 16th century the severity of classicism began to be undermined by the use of decorative details which, although Italian in style, were inextricably linked to the vigorous local craft tradition.

By the beginning of the 17th century, Palermo and Messina had been remodelled: buildings had been demolished to make way for new developments, new roads and impressive junctions had been created, and it was appropriate to use architecture and decoration as a means of creating an atmosphere of splendour. The city was the main locale of such developments, calling for an abundance of surface ornamentation to consolidate its traditional image. Thus the architecture of the early 17th century was characterized by continuity with the past, both recent and distant, in its geometric layouts and in its façades.

The grand churches belonging to the new orders like the Jesuits, Theatines and Oratorians generally kept to the established tradition of a longitudinal structure with nave and aisles separated by columns, and façades articulated by pilasters as already seen in the 16th century.

In the new town layouts the palaces, often dating from the 16th century, were reconfigured in relatively small, freestanding square blocks, with a single inner court

preceding pages Stucco work by Giacomo Serpotta in the Oratorio del Rosario in Santa Zita, Palermo

opposite After the Council of Trent, the architecture of the new orders spread across the island. The Jesuit complex in Trapani, comprising a church and college, was built in the Rua Grande, now Corso Vittorio Emmanuele. Engraving from Leanti, *Lo stato presente della Sicilia*, 1761.

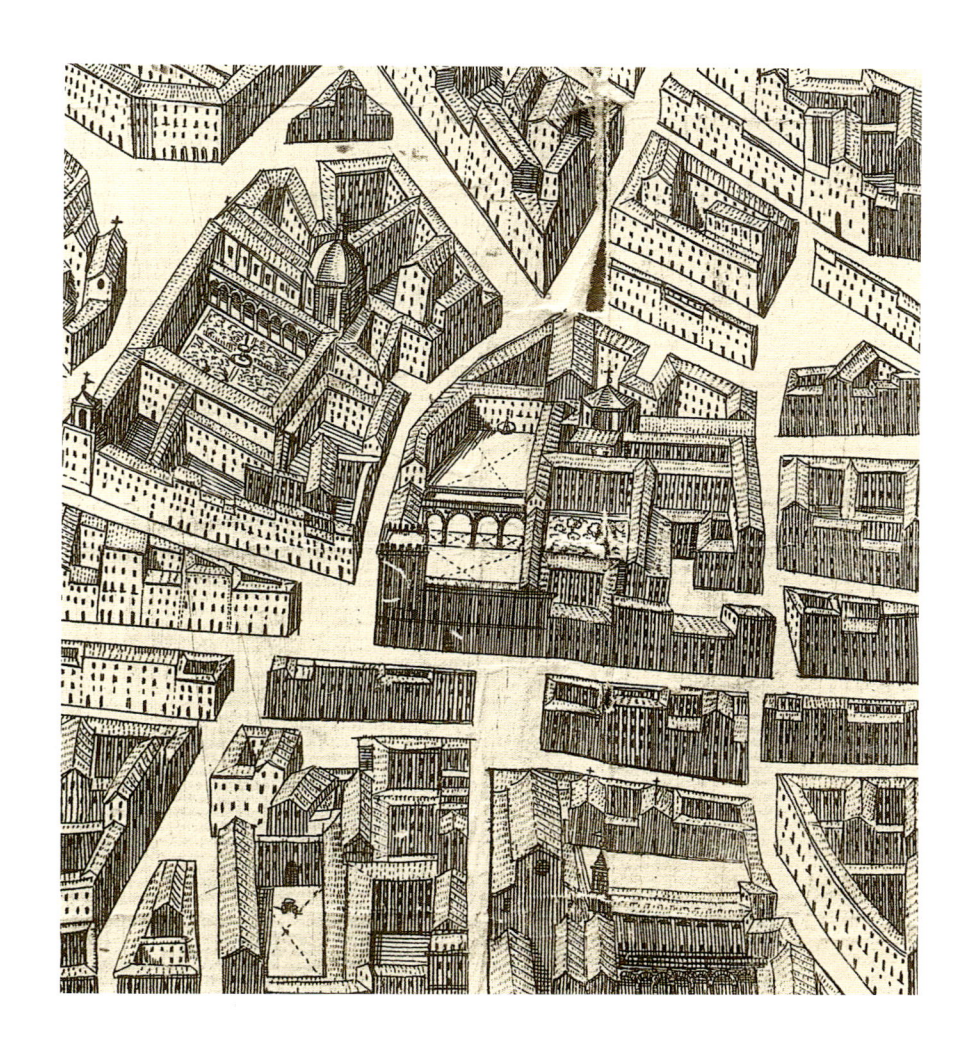

above right For their palaces, aristocrats sought the most prestigious locations in the cities, especially in Palermo. The palace of the princes of Cattolica, built in several stages in the 17th and 18th centuries, faced onto the old Via dei Pisani (now Via Alessandro Paternostro). This detail from an annotated copy of Gaetano Lazzara's city plan of 1703 shows the 17th-century phase, with the first *passetta*. (Archive, Servicio Geografico del Ejercito, Madrid)

which gave access to and illuminated the surrounding inward-facing rooms. There were a few exceptions, such as the Palazzo Moncada in Caltanissetta: here the design, drawn up in the early 17th century, maintained the same typology, but was to have been on a scale that rivalled the Palazzo Farnese in Rome. It was left unfinished, probably because of the departure of the client, Luis de Moncada, Duke of Montalto. At the Palazzo Raccuja in Palermo, the Branciforte, princes of Pietraperzia and Leonforte and counts of Raccuja, proposed to double the size of the existing building, adding a large riding school with a gallery above it to house a collection of paintings, and linking the two blocks by a courtyard with doors ornamented with sculptures of lions that would give access to all other parts of the building.

Also in Palermo, the palace of the princes of Cattolica was the grandiose result of several phases of building, due to the presence or absence of the patron. It has recently been suggested, however, that the innovative attitude established here in the first half of the 17th century determined the direction of successive developments, such as the opening up of the house towards the garden by means of an arcaded *passetta* or raised walkway linking the two sections of the building. The master in charge from 1624 to 1636 was the Lombard Giovanni acolino.

There is no doubt as to the Genoese origin of the *passetta*, possibly stimulated by the presence of the Genoese Cardinal Giannettino Doria, Viceroy of Sicily from 1610 to 1626. Nor is there any doubt as to the technical skill of Macolino, who later worked on the church of Santa Ninfa dei Crociferi, and later still, in 1643, became *Capomastro* of the city of Palermo. However, in the absence of precise documentation, two factors cast doubt on the attribution of the *passetta* to Macolino: the early date of the work (1623), and research conducted in the 19th century by Jacob Ignaz Hittorff during a visit to Sicily, which led him to attribute it to Giacomo Amato. That the *passetta* was in place in the 17th century is demonstrated by its depiction in Gaetano Lazzara's plan of Palermo, dated 1703. A further *passetta* was added in the first half of the 18th century, along with other structures, after the earthquake of 1726, which linked the palace to adjacent buildings; but for this work Giacomo Amato's name does not appear in any documents. Andrea Palma, who was by then a very old man, is mentioned as being carried there to inspect the work, along with the Genoese Michelangelo Cannepa. Such arcades were to become a standard feature of old and new palaces in Palermo in the course of the 18th century, as the nobility, now settled in their town residences, sought ways to enhance their prestige through architectural display.

In the early 17th century, the façades of both religious and

The buildings: tradition and revolution 155

secular buildings began to be adorned with a style of decoration that originated in Lombardy. Three examples among many are the church of the Jesuit college in Trapani, the Palazzo Scaduto in Mistretta, whose entrance portal bears the date 1660, and the villa in Bagheria which Giuseppe Branciforte, count of Raccuja, began in 1654, initiating a wave of construction of country residences.

For the traditional Sicilian technique of stone carving we should look at the region of Enna, and in particular at the church of San Domenico in Aidone, with its early 17th-century façade using diamond rustication. The style was taken up by architects from Catania immediately after the earthquake.

It seemed that there was still a need to maintain adequate defences against enemy attack: the new atlases compiled by Francesco Negro in 1640 and Carlo Maria Ventimiglia in 1677, echoing those of Tiburzio Spannocchi and Camillo Camiliani in the 1570s and 1580s (see p. 17), contain copious references to castles and fortifications on the coast. It was also important to maintain defences against internal rebellions, by constructing ramparts and citadels to protect the seat of power, as around the Royal Palace in Palermo after 1648, and on the San Raineri peninsula in Messina after 1678.

The desire to maintain continuity, which was common to both religious and lay commissions, did not preclude the desire to create an impression of grandeur and magnificence. Tall and imposing columns of Billiemi marble divide the internal space of San Giuseppe dei Teatini in Palermo into nave and aisles, and the church of the Gesù or Casa Professa has a framework of robust and decorative piers which survived Masuccio's addition of an outer row of interconnecting chapels.

A decorative frenzy, which concealed the strictly architectural articulation of the structure, continued uninterrupted throughout the early Baroque period and into its 18th-century epilogue. In Palermo particularly it took the form of dense patterns of inlaid coloured marble and hardstones (*marmi mischi*) in the Gesù and in the Dominican church of Santa Caterina. Streetlines were not always respected: the church of San Matteo in the old Cassaro boasted a façade that was inordinately tall in proportion to the narrow street in front of it, and consisted of a succession of layers, decreasing in size, connected by volutes. If the building was completed in 1652 (as suggested by the research of Maria Sofia Di Fede), it might have served as a model for Guarini's façade for the church of the Santissima Annunziata in Messina, where the concave movement reflects Guarini's education in Rome.

Examination of the different phases of the Baroque in Sicily shows a constant concern for the relationship between a building and its setting, resulting in new and original solutions. In Palermo around 1600 detached columns were used on the outer façade of the Porta Felice, and that may have served as a model for the central loggia of the Palazzo Senatorio in Trapani, when first conceived as a major link between two parts of the city. It may also have influenced the design of the four concave elements in the new urban centre cut into the Strada Nuova (Via Maqueda), known at the time as the 'Teatro del Sole' and now called the 'Quattro Canti'.

The innovative themes claimed by Sicily in the late 17th and 18th centuries in fact involve references to the prestige of antiquity (Rome, in the case of the Porta Felice) and of modern rulers (Spain, in the case of the Teatro del Sole, which showcased the Spanish monarchy

Detached columns were already in use in Sicily at the end of the 16th century, as in the Porta Felice in Palermo (*above left*: drawing from the *Teatro Geografico*, 1686). That probably served as a model for the loggia of the Palazzo Senatorio in Trapani (*above*: engraving from Leanti, *Lo stato presente della Sicilia*, 1761).

A rare drawing of the interior of the church of the Gesù or Casa Professa in Palermo, with its decoration of coloured stone inlay. Drawing from the *Teatro Geografico*, 1686.

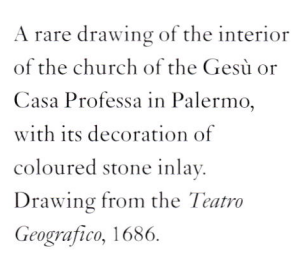

and also the municipality of the city). References to antiquity as a source of local identity also characterize the Palazzo del Senato in Syracuse, situated opposite the cathedral in Ortigia– the historic core of the city, a site with celebrated memories of ancient Greece.

Naturally there are exceptions to the picture of continuity presented here. Most significant of these is the adoption of the centralized plan for churches, which is found chiefly in Palermo, owing both to the complexity of its construction and to the absence of significant earthquake damage, compared with other parts of the island. Santa Lucia al Borgo (destroyed by bombing in 1943) had a centralized plan with an ambulatory. The early date which has been attributed to it by the research of the architect Anna Giordano – 1601 – suggests that historians need to explore new ways in which cultural influences arrived from mainland Italy.

Marco Rosario Nobile has investigated the origins of the plans of two churches, San Mattia dei Padri Crociferi and San Carlo dei Lombardi, both of which are elongated octagons covered by imposing domes, a formula generally attributed to the Jesuits in the 17th century, and suggests that they may have been influenced by typological schemes from Lombardy. In the case of the church dedicated to St Charles Borromeo this was not due to any direct patronal action: the building, which was probably originally covered by a Lombard *tiburio*, was built for Benedictine nuns, and only later became known as the church of the Lombards.

At San Mattia, it seems that the influence of the Lombard *capomastro*-cum-architect Giovanni Macolino was theoretical rather than practical, for he was working at the same time on the church of Santa Ninfa and the Casa Professa dei Crociferi in the Via Maqueda. The church may have been intended as a mausoleum for its patron, Donna Francesca Aragona, Princess of Roccafiorita. What is important is that both buildings were to remain the subject of discussion and imitation by major figures in years to come.

The role of Guarino Guarini is still very much an open question. His travels in the island and his influence there are still mysterious, as is the possible influence of his Sicilian experience on his later work. However, a mystery always has the power to fascinate, and historians are particularly susceptible.

The buildings: tradition and revolution 157

The birth of a new architecture

The influence of Guarini was not felt in Sicily in the second half of the 17th century. After the failed revolt, Messina became inward-looking and dominated by Spain, and it was not until the time of Juvarra that it succeeded in creating a new role for itself, and in regaining its importance as a port city. Now the single, undisputed capital of the island, Palermo was able to foster more prestigious talents and accommodate new projects which would herald the advent of a new architectural culture. On the one hand, it still tended to favour traditional solutions, albeit the more innovative ones such as elongated centralized plans for churches; on the other, it embraced the styles of Baroque classicism which were becoming well established, especially in Rome, in the second half of the 17th century. (Again, the picture is incomplete: the situation was different in the south-eastern areas affected by the earthquake.)

The real turning-point came in the 1680s, with the simultaneous presence in Palermo of Angelo Italia, Paolo Amato and Giacomo Amato: the works they realized there made a radical change to the direction taken by architecture, which was no longer subservient to the dictates of the city, but became master of its own destiny. This was not true of every work carried out by these three architects, who were involved with many different projects at the same time, and faced with a variety of tasks. The church of the Santissimo Salvatore was fortunate in having all three working together on its interior; the design of the elongated central space and the two- and three-dimensional decoration in coloured stone was due to Paolo Amato alone, however, according to an unsigned drawing in the church, which Stefano Piazza believes to be in Amato's hand.

Other buildings that were instrumental in bringing about the change include San Francesco Saverio in Palermo, which was immediately echoed in the church of the Jesuit college in Polizzi, both by Angelo Italia, and the churches of Santa Maria della Pietà and Santa Teresa alla Kalsa by Giacomo Amato.

Although the concave façade of the Santissima Annunziata in Messina did not have immediate imitators, later works by Guarini, designed and executed after his time in Sicily, do seem – together with other sources – to have influenced the two works by Angelo Italia mentioned above: in San Francesco Saverio, the cruciform interior space is generated internally by the juxtaposition of a series of hexagonal cells (these become octagonal in the church in Polizzi) in the central space below the dome. Christian Norberg-Schulz calls this a 'mechanical' space, in contrast to a Borrominian 'organic' space, a term he coined to explain the characteristics of the synthesis of styles employed by the Modenese master Guarini: there is no integration between the different spaces, despite the use of a framework of Palladian windows and the circular form of the columns, which draw the eye

The column assumed a new importance in the 'Roman' works of Giacomo Amato, giving church façades a new grandeur, as in two churches in the Kalsa district of Palermo – Santa Teresa (*left*) and Santa Maria della Pietà (*opposite*).

in a circular direction, thus creating a continuous effect. The design of the exterior was generally one of the most important considerations of Sicilian Baroque (particularly in the reconstruction work in the south-east following the earthquake of 1693), but here it was not especially inventive in comparison to the interior, and focused on the role of the columns. These were detached, in the manner of Giacomo Amato, and twisted, a common feature of temporary architecture and of *marmi mischi* decoration, two areas in which Paolo Amato excelled (for example in the entrance to the church of Santi Pietro e Paolo in Palermo).

In Santa Maria della Pietà and Santa Teresa alla Kalsa Giacomo Amato's innovative drive was focused on the design of the façade. The churches were situated in the area of the ancient citadel, La Kalsa, along a road running parallel to the sea where many of Amato's other creations stood. Some of those were constructed *de novo*, such as the Novitiate of the Crociferi, which was attached to the existing church of San Mattia (the façade of which may have been remodelled by Amato, who supplied a design dated 1689); others were remodellings of previous structures, such as the palace of the dukes of Branciforte, princes of Butera, which today bears little resemblance to his original design.

Such a concentration of works, which date from the early 1680s–1690s, might suggest that there had been a coherent plan for the whole axis, from the Cassaro to the piazza where the church of Santa Teresa is situated, designed to show off individual skills. It seems, however, to have been no more than a fortunate coincidence, but it enabled Giacomo Amato to demonstrate his talents, including his sensitivity to the local environment, as evidenced by a watercolour of the Piazza Marina, found among his drawings.

Santa Maria della Pietà, where Amato worked from 1689 onwards, was already under construction, with a single nave and side altars set into the walls, an apsidal presbytery, and a choir gallery over the entrance: Amato continued the decoration of the interior. He was entirely responsible, however, for the earlier church of Santa Teresa in 1686, which followed the same overall plan. His drawings of the plan and constructional and decorative details are contained in a volume now in the Galleria Regionale in Palermo, which is recorded in the itemized inventory made after his death.

It is the façades of these two churches that are particularly worthy of attention, both for their quality and for the clear intention behind them of establishing a common language – a language that was traditional and recognizable, being based on classical forms, and yet innovative through new forms based on an interplay of Roman and local features.

Two designs for the façade of the Pietà are preserved among Amato's drawings. They differ in that one has a circular window (reminiscent of a medieval rose window) in the upper level, and in the treatment of their sculptural decoration (skilfully executed by Pietro Aquila). Both are more complex than what was finally built, which was a synthesis of the two: there, in a desire to establish continuity between the two levels of the façade, Amato emphasized the absolute primacy of architecture.

Columns played a purely decorative role, which was in accordance with the prescriptions for church façades laid down by Charles Borromeo in his *Instructiones* after the Council of Trent. They conferring movement and fluidity on an otherwise rigid system, without complicating it by the introduction of curvilinear forms in the actual structure of the wall. The latter technique was far from straightforward, and could certainly not have been mastered by all those working on a project. Nonetheless, it was used by Amico and by the architects working in south-eastern Sicily in the first half of the 18th century. Over time, such 'unusual' designs were also used in smaller places in western Sicily: in the façades of churches in Cerda, Casteltermini, and San Cataldo, the 'new' towns of the western inland areas, flat surfaces and curves are combined in a provincial version of an alien figurative language. But, as can be seen in the Chiesa Madre of San Cataldo, tradition coloured the new ideas from outside: the undulating movement of the heavy stone façade is scarcely perceptible, and the emphasis is on the horizontal dimension. The possibility of Vaccarini's involvement in the design, suggested by the scholar Eugenio Magnano di San Lio, makes the story all the more intriguing.

The use of columns – detached or engaged, single or paired – or ornamental pilasters was a simple way of decorating a façade, and it was used in areas on the periphery to give a building importance and symbolic significance. However, the idea was taken up only slowly (with a few exceptions), and local stonemasons favoured the more traditional modes with which they were familiar. Exceptions in the late 17th century are the façades of the Chiesa Madre of Cattolica Eraclea, that of Santa Caterina Villarmosa, and that of Comitini, if research confirms their dating. All three are independent of the internal space behind them, and are given greater width to make a show in their urban setting.

Also in the 1680s, the order of the Padri Crociferi in Palermo turned their back on their ideal of poverty and embarked upon grandiose plans for their Casa Professa in Via Maqueda and their Novitiate in the Kalsa, the latter completing the project that had begun with the church of San Mattia. The order counted among its number the architect Giacomo Amato, fresh from his sojourn in Rome and flushed with his first successes in Palermo. Both projects were blighted by problems of funding, expropriation, and acquisition of private properties – problems frequently encountered in the schemes for religious houses – and there was a real risk that the whole enterprise would remain unfinished, as did happen in the case of the Casa Professa.

Giacomo Amato's successful ploy for the Novitiate was to provide two alternative designs, one more elaborate and one simpler, both complete schemes based on an additive method in plan and elevation. What was internal in the greater scheme could become external in the lesser one; the solemn façade facing the sea could be reduced in size; the grand courtyard which had been envisaged as an oasis of air and light could be omitted; communication between floors might involve a grand staircase, or in the more modest scheme an oval staircase with an open well – a staircase that appeared to an 18th-century observer 'as though it was built upon air'. It is a mark of the calibre of the architect that even his minor design, which was eventually realized, was worthy of the architecture of Rome and its Baroque classicism.

A similar strategy was adopted in the late 18th century by the architect Francesco Battaglia from Catania, who was commissioned to consolidate the structures of the Chiesa Madre in Ragusa and that in Caltagirone. He drafted two schemes, one minimal and the other more ambitious, either of which could be realized, depending on the means and preferences of the

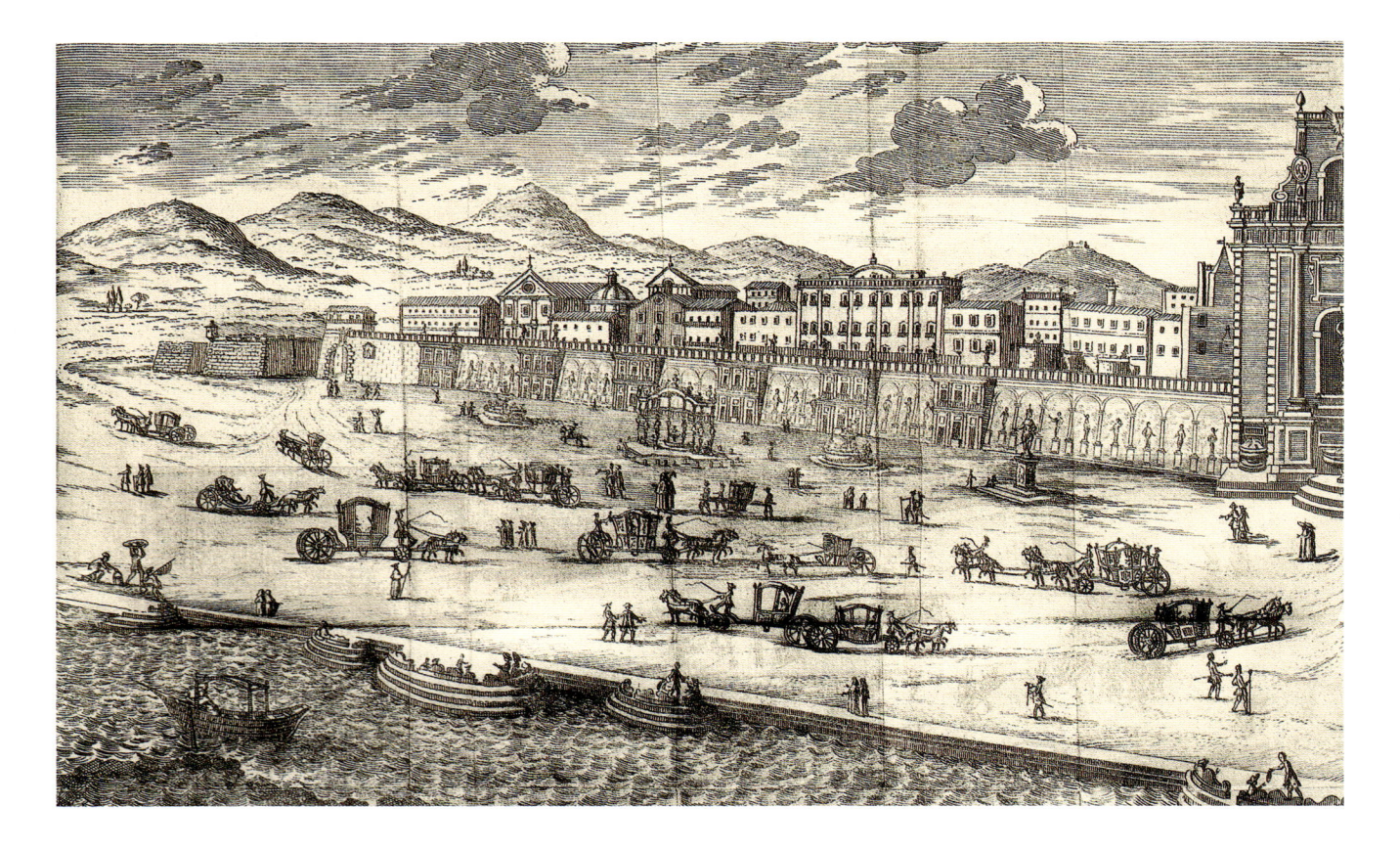

The area of the Kalsa in Palermo, with the ancient Arab citadel (which archaeologists are in the process of excavating and restoring), was the scene of major activity by Giacomo Amato, who may have made a design for the area as a whole. Here we see the Stradone Colonna on the seafront outside the Porta Felice, thronged with people, carriages and sedan chairs. Engraving from Leanti, *Lo stato presente della Sicilia*, 1761.

patrons. That way, the possibility of losing the commission, as had happened on previous occasions, was drastically reduced.

The palace of the dukes of Branciforte, princes of Butera, stood in the same street as the Novitiate of the Crociferi in Palermo. Amato was given the commission to remodel a vast 17th-century *tenimento di case* (the term used in documents in the archives). Comparison of his drawings of the existing buildings and his new design shows his intention to regularize the internal spaces, linking them in enfilades, and to adorn the courts with fountains on the show sides. These scenic devices negated the key role usually played by the staircase up to the *piano nobile*, which was here relegated to one side. A series of fires, together with alterations and extensions made as the family prospered, have so changed the 17th-century appearance of the palace that it is now very hard to find any trace of Amato's original design.

The plan of Palermo drawn and engraved by Gaetano Lazzara and published in 1703 (see p. 155) gives a comprehensive view of the city's architecture at the end of the 17th century, on the eve of further great transformations which would substantially alter its architectural character. It was an up-to-date record which included work in progress, in an attempt to give it it a long life. But other earthquakes, in 1726 and 1751, were just around the corner, and further rebuilding soon altered the 17th-century appearance of the capital through the prestigious character of the new commissions.

Baroque internationalism

Consideration of architecture in the first half of the 18th century involves looking at a much wider geographical picture than the one which has been sketched in the preceding pages. Palermo remained the political capital of the island under the foreign domination of Piedmont, Austria, and the Bourbons of Naples, and Messina was intent on recovering its lost prestige, but other cities emerged in search of the limelight, leading to local autonomies that have lasted to this day. This was the case with Catania, which had rationally and magnificently reinvented itself after the earthquake – rationally through the influence of the Flemish architect Carlos de Grunenbergh, and magnificently through the influence of Giovan Battista Vaccarini from Palermo.

Given the power of this unusual alliance, which gained in strength with the addition of new players, the fact of being a political capital no longer seemed to count for much: Palermo might, of course, welcome kings and viceroys; celebrate coronations, weddings, births, visits, funerals; receive the new feudal aristocracy, ever keener to demonstrate the power they had gained over the countryside by building or rebuilding imposing palaces; and host a proliferation of churches and convents, whose

After the earthquake of 1693, the rebuilding of both large and small towns in the Val di Noto – from Catania to Syracuse, Palazzolo Acreide, Noto and Scicli – brought these formerly 'peripheral' areas up to the same cultural level as the new capitals. Catania overcame its fear of earthquakes and was rebuilt with impressive domes, as shown in this engraving of 1785 by Saint-Non.

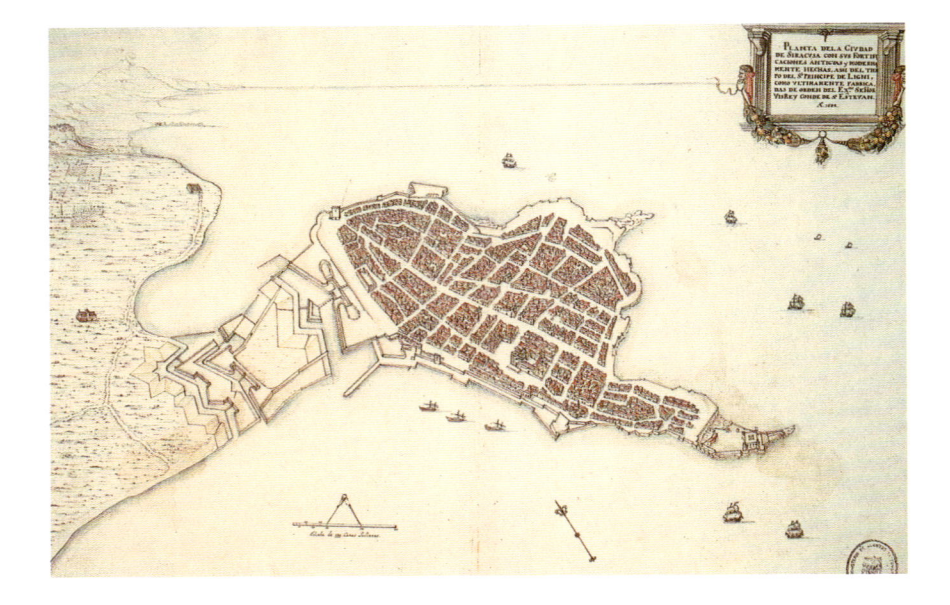

construction was financed by the coffers of the religious orders and facilitated by the many architects belonging to those orders.

But other 'capitals' were developing, often in small, peripheral places that rose to positions of cultural preeminence through a particular work or a particular personality that brought them into contact with the 'international' languages emanating from the centres of the Baroque. They were the signs of something new, especially in the south-east, within a vast cultural context which remained rooted in tradition but was adapted for new expressive functions, for example in buildings of particular public significance, such as church façades with their entrance portals; in palaces and villas with their desire for display; and in the three-dimensional decoration that took over the exteriors of religious and secular buildings, providing a whole new range of subjects for the skills of dynasties of craftsmen.

In terms of the quality and quantity of buildings all across the island, religious architecture occupies the prime position. There are many façades of churches, convents and colleges which are regarded as 'Baroque' because of the quality and exuberance of their decoration, but which are actually a timeless and universal form of architecture current all over Sicily, bearing traces of previous styles as well as of those of the early 18th century.

Among examples of this in the western part of the island, the Jesuit college in Mazara stands out, with its smooth façade interrupted by a sculpted entrance topped by a balcony. The figurative themes, although executed with much greater elegance, are similar to those on the 17th-century church of San Francesco in Naro, which has an entrance flanked by pairs of telamones, a scheme that may go back to the church of the Jesuit college in Trapani.

In the area around Syracuse, there is the church of San Sebastiano in Ferla, where above the entrance flanked by columns there is small aedicule containing a statue of the saint, protected on either side by other saints and soldiers. The portal is imposing not only for its size, but for its decorative impact in a façade which is otherwise plain and articulated only by pilasters.

Other examples include churches in the Nebrodi mountains, in particular the Badia di San Salvatore and the church of Sant'Antonio in San Marco d'Alunzio, a town whose ancient origins were manifest in the Hellenistic Temple of Hercules, which was later turned into the church of San Marco. The town's decorative tradition is conditioned by the use of the local red and pink chalcedony.

In the eastern part of the island, which was substantially rebuilt after the earthquake in 1693, there was naturally a strong relationship between architecture and decoration as 17th-century themes were carried on into the 18th century. One example that stands out among many is the great Benedictine monastery at Militello, in the Val di Catania, which was founded at the beginning of the 17th century by the Branciforte family, and rebuilt after the earthquake. (It is now the town hall.) Its impressive façade has a giant order of pilasters and an abundance of decoration.

Another sign of the continuity between the two centuries is the creation of many imitations of the portals designed by Paolo Amato, characterized by twisted columns wreathed with garlands, in various places around 1700 – in the Jesuit church in Salemi, in the Santissimo Salvatore in Naso, and in the cathedral of Piazza Armerina. Particularly striking is the church

above left Syracuse before the earthquake. The drawing is from the *Teatro Geografico* of 1686, but its style, and the date '1682' in the cartouche, suggest that it is by Carlos de Grunenbergh.

above Palazzolo Acreide chose for its rebuilding a highly decorative style which blurs the architectural forms.

In the 'peripheral' Val di Mazara, the small town of Alessandria della Rocca claims attention for this sophisticated portal with detached columns, turned outward at an angle of 45 degrees, which is worthy of Giovanni Amico.

of the Annunziata in Palazzolo Acreide, which is characterized by *horror vacui* both outside and in; the local stone, as is common around Syracuse, is a fine white limestone which is particularly suited to intricate carving, as displayed in the twisted columns and dense decoration that flows over the entrance portal and onto the altars placed on the side walls.

A further sign of continuity, but with an openness to the international currents of the Baroque, can be seen in church façades making use of detached columns, something that had started with Giacomo Amato's grand Dominican church in Palermo, and passed through Catania, Acireale, Syracuse, Regalbuto, Marsala and elsewhere before eventually reaching the façade of the Chiesa Madre of Palma di Montechiaro.

The subject is much broader than this brief summary can cover, for the style transformed, updated and modified itself constantly, establishing a long genealogy in south-eastern Sicily. The role played by the column underwent a succession of variations, in tower-façades and campaniles; flat, concave and convex façades; and major and minor locations.

There is a lack of documentary evidence of the activities of architects and master builders, and of books, drawings and engravings. Nonetheless, there seems to be a thread that connects many different types of architecture. Starting in Palermo with the 'Roman' façades of Giacomo Amato, undergoing modifications at every stage, it leads on to Syracuse and its cathedral, influenced by Andrea Palma or by Rome (the church of Santi Vincenzo ed Anastasio?), then on to Catania Cathedral where

Vaccarini fans out the granite columns in groups on either side of the centre, preparing the way for the articulation of the columns of San Giorgio in Ragusa and for the device of turning them outward at an angle of 45 degrees, so that they project from the façade, as in the Chiesa Madre in Buscemi and in the church at Regalbuto, which the architect Francesca Randazzo recently argued may be by Francesco Battaglia from Catania, whose presence is recorded on the site in successive years.

century at the time when Borromini's style was being revived: the oscillation between convex and concave eventually led to the undulating façades of Giovanni Amico, seen in the churches of the Purgatorio and San Lorenzo in Trapani, and Sant'Anna in Palermo. The style spread to south-eastern Sicily after 1726, the year when many different key figures were present in Palermo, possibly including Rosario Gagliardi. Here, the thread became interwoven with other direct or indirect influences, local and foreign, national and international, and produced the late Baroque works of Giovan Battista Vaccarini (the Badia di Sant'Agata in Catania), Rosario Gagliardi (San Giorgio in Ragusa; the Jesuit church in Modica; San Domenico, and according to recent research, San Carlo and the tower of the monastery of the Santissimo Salvatore in Noto; and Sant'Anna in Piazza Armerina).

Gagliardi's pupils and followers, many as yet unidentified, drew on his designs: this is visible in San Giuliano, the Collegiata and San Placido in Catania; in Santa Maria di Montevergine and the Carmine in Noto; in San Giorgio in Modica; Sant'Antonio in Ferla; Sant'Antonio in Buscemi; the Chiesa della Natività in Sortino; San Giovanni in Scicli; the Madonna delle Grazie in Vittoria; the Addolorata in Niscemi; Santa Maria di Loreto in Petralia Soprana, and elsewhere, up to the late, coarse work on San Giuseppe in Casteltermini. It is difficult to trace these threads when the evidence is so scanty. In reality, each building existed in isolation and was a law unto itself, as is the case with Gagliardi's façades, which consist of a convex centre and two straight wings linked by groups of engaged columns turned at an angle.

Domes were rarely used in south-eastern Sicily because of the danger of earthquakes, but they were common in the west, where

left In Noto, the undulating façade of the tower of the monastery of the Santissimo Salvatore interrupts the geometric regularity of Angelo Italia's plan.

opposite, left Design for the church of San Camillo and the house of the Crociferi in Noto, by Francesco Paolo Labisi, 1750. Incorporating a partial plan, section and elevation, it demonstrates both his graphic skills and the refinement of his compositional ideas, inherited from Rosario Gagliardi. The work was entrusted to another pupil of Gagliardi's, Vincenzo Sinatra, who introduced changes to the original design. (Biblioteca Comunale, Noto)

opposite, right Aerial view of Scicli, showing the Baroque 'acropolis' created when the town was rebuilt.

Other threads run from the campanile-façade of San Matteo in Palermo, which was based on older designs (in Enna and Syracuse), to the celebrated church of the Santissima Annunziata in Messina, by Guarini; that, together with other influences, underlies the self-contained and compact tower-façade of San Giorgio in Ragusa; and that in turn exerted an influence in other places in the south-est. Tower-façades and campanile-façades existed in neighbouring Modica, in Noto, Floridia, Sortino, Avola, Ferla, Buccheri, Buscemi, Scicli, Palazzolo Acreide, Giarratana, Grammichele, and Vittoria; and also in western Sicily, in the Chiesa Madre of Salaparuta (now destroyed), which is attributed to the architect Antonino Gugliotta and the mid-18th century.

Yet another thread starts with the concave façade of the Santissima Annunziata in Messina, which was rediscovered in the 18th

there was a long tradition. Architects such as Angelo Italia, at the church of the Carmine in Palermo, drew on a decorative repertoire that involved styles and materials from other regions. This makes it difficult to accept the attribution to Italia of the dome of Sant'Angelo in Licata, which has turrets on the canted corners of its drum; yet the attribution is backed by a document dated 1696, discovered by Liliane Dufour and Henri Raymond. The model would certainly have been familiar to Giovanni Amico, who was active on various sites in the town, possibly including that for the new façade of Sant'Angelo. Amico drew up a scheme for the completion of the façade of the cathedral of San Lorenzo in Trapani and the construction of its dome, with circular turrets set on the diagonals of the square plan – as if, Salvatore Boscarino observed, expressing on the exterior the centrifugal force of the internal space.

By the first half of the 18th century, following the pioneering experiments of the 17th century, the centralized plan was widely in use, and existed in a variety of forms: an elongated octagon, an oval, a cross with apsidal arms, a square, a hexagonal with concave chapels, a polygon, and many other combinations of centralized and longitudinal schemes, which usually involved placing the chapels on the diagonal, to give movement to the interior and to direct the gaze of the beholder.

There are many reasons for the success of these plans: some architects could look back on their training in Rome, as Vaccarini did for the Badia di Sant'Anna in Catania; for others, there was a great deal of second-hand knowledge to be gleaned from books, as reflected for example in Mariani's Borrominesque plan for Santi Cosma e Damiano in Alcamo. Then there were the 'inventions' of local artisan-architects, as seen in Sant'Antonio in Ferla, with its indefinable plan based on a synthesis of spaces.

Giovanni Amico, who is generally considered to have been influenced only by Borromini and Guarini, must have been familiar through engravings with Borromini's remodelling of San Giovanni in Laterano and Rainaldi's Santa Maria in Campitelli in Rome, and also with buildings in places farther away, such as Guarini's Our Lady of Altötting in Prague. How else could he have produced the compositions of spatial cells found in the designs for Sant'Oliva

The buildings: tradition and revolution 165

in Alcamo, Santa Caterina in Calatafimi, and above all in the new design for the Santissima Annunziata in Trapani, where he used attached piers of trapezoidal plan, fronted by columns, as Michelangelo had done in the Sforza Chapel?

The Chiesa Madre in Regalbuto, San Basilio (already mentioned in connection with its façade), reflects a knowledge of the centralized and longitudinal schemes of Carlo Rainaldi, and possibly also Juvarra's ideas for San Filippo Neri in Turin. It has been attributed to Ferdinando Lombardo from Palermo, a pupil of Giacomo Amato.

Amico was also responsible for the idea of breaking up the solidity of the wall by means of portals whose lateral supports are turned outward at an angle of 45 degrees. This is particularly striking on the façade of the church of the Carmine in Alessandria della Rocca (p. 163), a refined design by a master whose identity is still unknown.

While religious architecture took precedence over secular architecture, the latter gradually came into its own, particularly in Palermo and its environs, but also, to a lesser extent, in Catania, which had grown to rival the capital in the 18th century, due to the illustrious presence of Giovan Battista Vaccarini, Francesco Battaglia and Stefano Ittar.

Other, smaller cities remained on the periphery, having less need for grand public buildings, and only boasted a few private ones, which were, however, often extremely significant. This was certainly the case in Trapani, but also in many of the towns in the south-east, such as Caltagirone, Militello, Acireale, Palazzolo Acreide, Noto, Ragusa, Modica and Scicli. In these places, innovations in planning and in the configuration of external or internal space were less important than the decorative effect of a building in its urban position, and the establishment of an individual character. This was ensured by the work of the stone carvers, given a new lease of life by the huge need for reconstruction, who adorned palaces both large and small with extraordinarily inventive devices such as the decorated brackets used to support balconies. These were the happy products of a unique period in which 'fantasy triumphed over the power of architecture', in the words of Carlo Cresti, who produced a monograph on the topic, based on a study of 12 locations, 67 buildings, 270 balconies, and a total of 1,210 decorated brackets.

Other decorative schemes contributed to the development of an original and widespread culture of stone decoration that turned the Val di Noto into a Baroque wonderland. They include the fan-shaped wall decoration on the façade of the Palazzo Judica in Palazzolo Acreide, the fantastical ear-shaped carving by an unknown master around a window of the Palazzo Borgia in Syracuse, and the decoration of the Palazzo Beneventano in Scicli, which draws the gaze of the passer-by to the corner of the building.

Syracuse was an exception in the late Baroque era. Here, the rebuilding of the Palazzo Beneventano del Bosco, which incorporated existing buildings in the Piazza del Duomo in Ortigia, envisaged a grand façade with a monumental portal flanked by columns and connected to a gallery above. It led in to the building, where one crossed a courtyard with a beautiful patterned floor, similar to those of Catania, created by the alternating use of white stone and black lava, and reached the grand staircase, which was signalled by columns turned at an angle to

The palaces of the nobility in Palermo and Catania were designed to display the wealth and culture of their owners, and were covered with magnificent decoration.

opposite, left The frescoed ceiling of the Salone di Apollo in the Palazzo Butera, Palermo.

opposite, right In its decoration the Palazzo Biscari in Catania, with its private museum (seen in an engraving of 1786), looked forward to Neoclassicism. (Biscari Collection, Catania)

In Regalbuto, near Enna, the monumental Chiesa Madre towers over the surrounding buildings, affirming its central role in the community.

the wall. The scheme was designed by a local architect with a craft background, Luciano Alì, who demonstrated his ability to handle space, making use of some of the devices invented by Gagliardi.

Secular architecture was more subject to change than religious architecture, due not only to catastrophic events, but also to the wishes of ambitious patrons, who, Stefano Piazza has shown, seized every opportunity, such as those provided by the earthquakes in Palermo in 1726 and 1751, to 'restore' their property. Hittorff in 1835 wrote of many great palaces in Palermo which 'would have compared favourably with most of the palaces in the great cities of Italy, as much for the beautiful distribution of space in their design as for the style and character of their architecture'. Many of them were created on the site of existing buildings in the most prestigious streets, with unusually extensive façades, and occupied an entire block. The residence of the marquises of Santa Croce in the Strada Nuova was remodelled from the mid-18th century onward around two courts, one grand, the other a service area accommodating the passage of carriages. At more or less the same time, on the same alignment, the palaces belonging to the Filangeri family, princes of Cutò, and the Gravina family, princes of Comitini, were remodelled on ambitious lines (only partially realized in the case of the Palazzo Cutò). In both cases the original entrance in the Via del Bosco was given up. For the Palazzo Comitini, a new block was built fronting on the Strada Nuova; for the Palazzo Cutò, property was bought along that street and within the block. The courts were doubled and connected by a *passetta*, and monumental staircases were inserted leading up to the state rooms on the *piano nobile*.

The 1750s was a decade of intense activity along the residential streets. Giovan Battista Vaccarini was working on plans for the palace of the princes of Villafranca, in the Piazza Bologni, and for the palace of the princes of Larderia in the Via Toledo (now the Corso Vittorio Emmanuele), and thereby trying to re-establish himself professionally in Palermo. Works were in progress along the Via Alloro for the enlargement and remodelling of the Palazzo Bonagia (largely destroyed by bombing in 1943 and currently undergoing restoration) and for the palace of the princes of Valguarnera, Gangi and Gravina. Both of these palaces had inventive staircases, and the

The buildings: tradition and revolution 167

latter had a large gallery with a majolica floor and a vault pierced with openings (it was used for the ballroom scene in Visconti's film of the Prince of Lampedusa's novel *The Leopard*). It now seems certain that the idea for the staircases and the vault of the gallery was due to Andrea Gigante, from Trapani: a pupil of Giacomo Amico, he was then at the beginning of a promising career which would see him at the forefront in the final years of the Rococo and the initial stages of Neoclassicism.

Before beginning work on their palace in the city, in the 1720s, the princes of Valguarnera had commissioned a villa in Bagheria, situated on a hill within a park. Inspired by the example of Giuseppe Branciforte in the second half of the 17th century, the nobility of Palermo hastened to build themselves grand country residences, competing in a display of wealth and magnificence. All around Palermo – in Bagheria, Mezzo Monreale and the Colli – villas sprang up, sometimes incorporating existing towers or other structures, surrounded by low walls or, as in the case of the Villa Valguarnera, by gardens. The gardens were in different styles, and some included artificial hills from which to admire the view. In the 1780s the Villa Valguarnera was altered in Neoclassical style by Giovan Battista Cascione Vaccarini, and at the beginning of the 19th century the German architect Karl Friedrich Schinkel recorded on paper the splendid setting of this then magical and unspoilt place (now sadly much decayed).

Also in the early 18th century, the neighbouring villa of the princes of Palagonia was under construction, supervised by its designer, Tomaso Maria Napoli. Later, after the mid-century, it was enlarged and its *piano nobile* enriched by the famous hall of mirrors, which reflected and multiplied the images of the owners

Architects and masters were constantly updating their work with new decorative details and with convex, concave and undulating architectural forms. Country villas, from Bagheria to Noto, provided the opportunity for architects like Tomaso Maria Napoli and Francesco Paolo Labisi to display their skills.

left An ear-shaped opening ornaments the Palazzo Borgia in Syracuse, near the Piazza del Duomo.

left, below The Villa Palagonia, Bagheria.

opposite, left The Villa Eleonora, built for the princes of Villadorata near Noto.

above right The monumental Albergo dei Poveri in Palermo, built in the first half of the 18th century outside the Porta Nuova. Engraving from Salmon, *Lo stato presente di tutti i paesi e populi del mondo*, XXIV, 1762.

and their guests, and also by the grotesque carved figures of monsters, dwarfs and animals on the garden walls. Goethe's description of the latter in his *Italian Journey*, following his trip to Sicily in 1787, made them unjustly more famous than the architecture, which was important for its connections with the culture of Rome and the rest of Europe.

Other villas were built at Bagheria, always with grand staircases: the most interesting design was one with three separate flights, by Giovanni del Frago, in the villa of the princes of Larderia, begun in 1749 but never completed. Once again, echoes of foreign works, by architects such as Carlo Fontana and Filippo Juvarra, show how Sicily was open to the international language of architecture.

One building in Piana dei Colli could rival the villas of Bagheria: that of the princes of Resuttano. Its importance in the contemporary architectural scene is clear from its inclusion, along with the Villa Valguarnera, among Leanti's views published in 1761. The villa was the work of two architects, Paolo Corso and Carlo Infantolino, from 1728 onwards. In the same area, in 1722, Agatino Daidone designed a villa for the princes of Partanna (after whom the village was later named), on a complex trapezoidal plan similar to those seen in sketches made by Juvarra during his time in Rome.

Eastern Sicily had no equivalent of the complex of villas outside Palermo, but there are individual examples of great interest, enhanced by the skills of their builders, who were masters in the handling of stone. There are obvious connections with the circle of Gagliardi, for instance in the Villa Eleonora, built by Francesco Paolo Labisi for the Nicolaci family, princes of Villadorata, in the countryside near Noto, where the family flaunted its status in its town palace. Another example is the Villa Gargallo, on the feudal estate of Priolo in the province of Syracuse, which is mentioned by Francesco Fichera in his book on Vaccarini. The Villa Eleonora has an undulating façade, and wings in which triangular openings are pierced with consummate skill. In a drawing in the archives of Casa Gargallo, the Villa Gargallo is shown with a symmetrical layout hinging on an oval church with convex forms both to the exterior and to the inner court, preceded by a portico, and leading on the opposite side to a staircase with two flights which followed the contours, in a manner seen in Guarini's palaces in Turin and Fischer von Erlach's in Vienna.

The porticoed Palazzo Senatorio in Noto, opposite the cathedral, is due to Labisi's rival Vincenzo Sinatra, with references to Gagliardi in some of the external features. It has a convex centre and corner elements set at an angle of 45 degrees to stress its freestanding character. (The upper storey dates from the 19th century.)

Palermo can claim another outstanding work: the vast Albergo dei Poveri, begun *c.* 1746. It was to be built outside the Porta Nuova on the road to Monreale, and the design was to be chosen by competition. The building was ambitious not only in its size – it was almost as big as the Royal Palace nearby – but also in the determination, on the part of the royal authorities and aristocrats who were supporting its construction, to refer to authoritative models such as the Escorial in Spain. Their desire was not shared by the little-known designer of the project.

Catania was jealous of Palermo and hoped to emulate its magnificence with palaces of its own. One such was the celebrated palace of Ignazio Paternò Castello, Prince of Biscari, the enlightened custodian of antiquities of the Val di Noto and the Val di Demone, and patron of projects including the bridge that bears his name, which is mentioned by Milizia and which appears in contemporary maps. His palace as remodelled in the late 18th century by Francesco Battaglia centred on a sumptuous frescoed ballroom, with a musicians' staircase leading up to a gallery in the vault: both are remarkable examples of Sicilian Rococo, inspired by books and prints with which the prince's library must have been well supplied. It was also intended that the palace should have a museum, a theatre, and a Chinese pagoda, reflecting the cosmopolitan tastes of its patron.

If the plans drawn up in 1714 by Juvarra for the Royal Palace in Messina had been carried out, the city might have regained the cultural prestige it had sought since 1678, the year when the Spanish monarchy resumed control after the revolt. In the early 18th century Messina was governed by the House of Savoy, and the project was one of many conceived by Juvarra which would have expressed the character of a port city with a unique role. The plan envisaged an enlargement of the harbour as far as Grotte, and made the new palace, and above all its gardens, which were overlaid on land already built up, the key element in a system which was on a scale that was not merely urban but territorial: a city within a city, which would stress Messina's civic character, as opposed to the military character of the neighbouring citadel, which faced out towards the boundless horizon of the sea. However, the palace conceived by Victor Amadeus and Juvarra was never completed, since both men soon departed, and the old Royal Palace was further damaged by earthquakes until it was finally destroyed in 1853. Juvarra was able to drawn on his experience years later, in 1735, when as a famous architect he was summoned by Philip V of Spain to build a new royal palace in Madrid. He died a year later, and the great project fell to other architects.

Decorative schemes: materials, techniques, languages

Anthony Blunt and other eminent historians of the Baroque have always stressed the unique role played by decoration in Sicily at the time, producing something that was almost like a trademark – a style that was instantly recognizable; a necessary finishing touch to any building; an innate

The numerous prints showing the Straits of Messina and the cities on either side were designed to counter the idea of Sicily as an island cut off both geographically and culturally. This engraving is from Salmon, *Lo stato presente di tutti i paesi e populi del mondo,* XXIV, 1762.

Details of three church interiors in Palermo decorated with inlaid coloured stone and stucco: the Gesù or Casa Professa (*above*), the Concezione al Capo (*above right*), and the Carmine (*below*).

quality based on a long craft tradition. The arts of stonework, of inlaid marble and of stucco were an integral part of architecture and its history, in which they often played a leading role.

Fantastical brackets on secular buildings, elegant volutes connecting the lower and upper levels of church façades, minute carving around openings: these are but a few of the types of decoration characteristic of the period. All showcase the quality of the local stone and the continuity of skills passed down from father to son, updated to meet new requirements.

All the buildings considered in these pages, built of stone suitable for carving, are expressions of this culture, which blended old and new.

Sicily has always been rich in coloured marble, especially reds, yellows and greys, and in polychrome marble breccia, as well as in hardstones, all of which were also exported. The technique required to exploit these stones to the full involved the use of slabs 4–8 cm thick of dense white Tuscan marble, imported by sea, into which indentations were carved to house the precious hardstones, which were cut from thin sheets and held in place by an adhesive made from a hot mixture of Greek rosin and marble dust. That is how the decorative technique of coloured stone inlay began – with a little help from Tuscany and especially from Naples (the technique of inlay itself went back to antiquity). The technique on flat surfaces was called *a mischio*, on three-dimensional surfaces it was *a tramischio*. Coloured stucco was used to fill any empty spaces. First came chapels inserted in churches of an earlier date, such as the Cappella di Santa Rosalia in Palermo Cathedral, built in 1626 (no longer in existence). Then came the more general decoration of church interiors, as in the Gesù or Casa Professa, Santa Maria di Valverde, Santa Caterina, the Immacolata al Capo, and Santissimo Salvatore in Palermo. And then there are sophisticated architectural perspectives on altar frontals, frequently designed by architects, who could experiment in such fictive compositions with ideas that they would later realize in practice.

The hexagonal Cappella del Crocifisso in Monreale Cathedral, commissioned by Archbishop Giovanni Roano and built in the last twenty years of the 17th century, is one of the most significant examples. It involved

The buildings: tradition and revolution 171

three artists – Giovanni da Monreale, Angelo Italia and Paolo Amato – as well as the craftsmen who actually executed the inlay, but the patron appears to have had the final say.

Given the expense of the materials, inlaid stone decoration was widespread only in Palermo and Messina. There is one exception in Naso, in a wonderful 17th-century chapel that served as the crypt of the church dedicated to San Cono, with twisted columns above the altar.

In inland areas, the favoured technique involved stucco, a humble material which was readily available in Sicily because of the presence of rocks made of calcium sulphate. Ground into a powder and mixed with water, they produce gesso (frequently used in Sicily for vaults, partition walls, etc.). Gesso, mixed with the correct proportions of chalk and marble dust, produces stucco. The outermost surface as then covered with a patina known as *allustratura*, which was mixed according to a secret formula handed down from father to son. This patina gave the stucco a luminous quality, almost like alabaster, and made it translucent.

Decorative virtuosity reached its peak in designs such as that of the crypt of the church of San Cono in Naso (*above*), and the nymphaeum of the Villa Trabia Campofiorito in Palermo (*opposite*), where diverse materials come together to create an exceptional work of art.

The buildings: tradition and revolution

Compositions in stucco work were executed for older churches (as in the altars of the church of the Carmine in Palermo) and for new ones, such as Santi Cosma e Damiano in Alcamo. But the most significant works in this genre are three oratories in Palermo: the Oratorio del Rosario in Santa Zita, the Oratorio di San Lorenzo in San Francesco, and the Oratorio del Rosario in San Domenico. These austere, rectangular spaces dating from the late 16th century were redecorated in the Baroque period with dense schemes designed and executed by Giacomo Serpotta (1652–1732), who was the most celebrated and skilled of a family of stucco workers in Palermo. The Oratorio del Rosario in Santa Zita has a stucco relief of the Battle of Lepanto on the back wall; the side walls are articulated by an architectural order, perhaps designed by Giacomo Amato, but it seems to be overwhelmed by the decoration, with echoes of Michelangelo's figures on the Medici tombs in the sacristy of San Lorenzo in Florence, and of Gagini in the tribune of Antonello in Palermo Cathedral. It is not easy to attribute authorship for these and other works, but drawings by Amato sometimes provide help.

In both inlay work and stucco Sicily could compete with the finest in Europe. The effect was of a complete visual spectacle, which could employ other arts in its pursuit of even more ambitious effects. One last example must be mentioned, again from Palermo: the nymphaeum of the Villa Trabia Campofiorito, which still exists. Generally attributed to Paolo Amato, it is decorated with twisted columns, stuccowork, and shells – a triumph of all the arts.

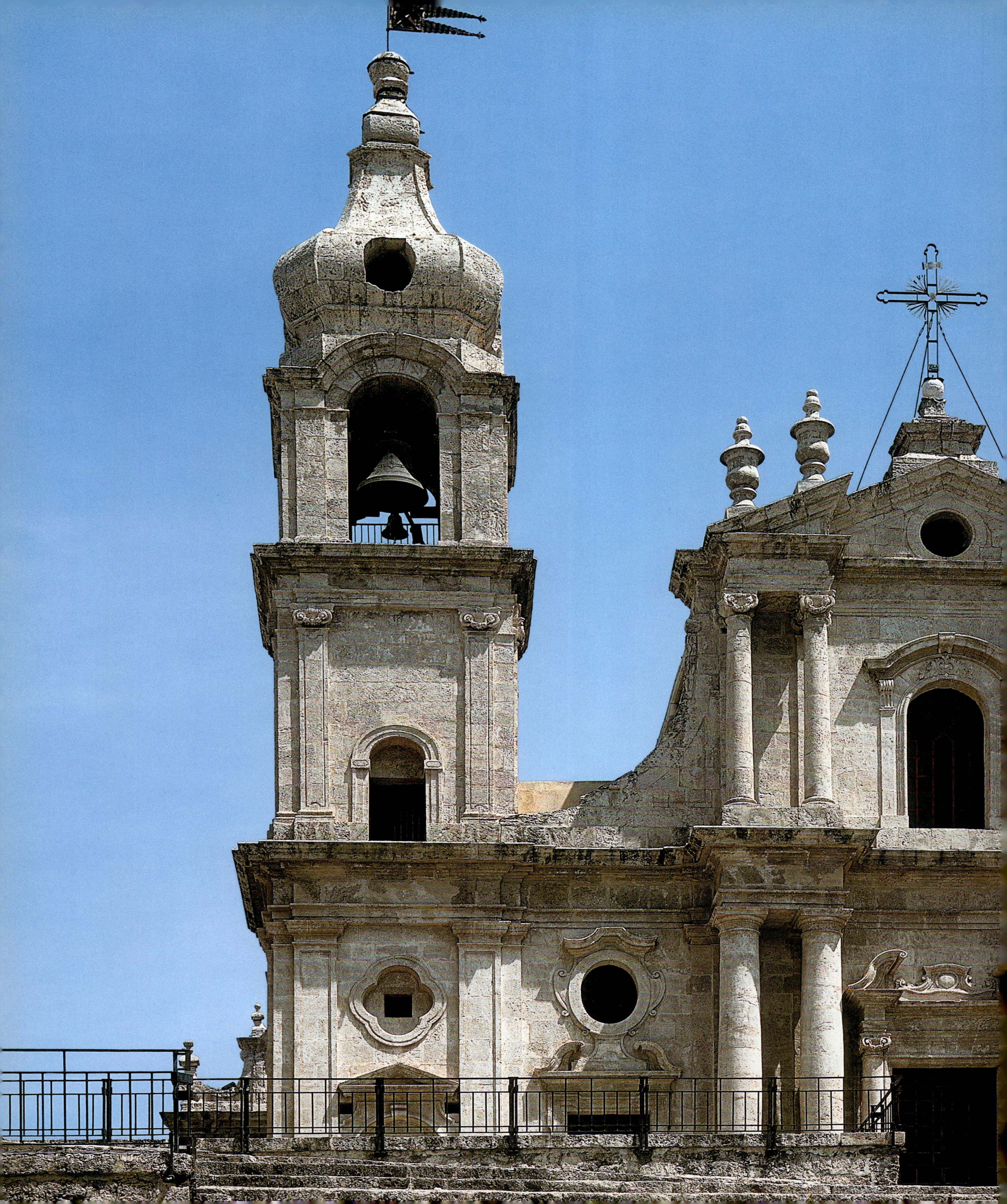

The belltowers of the Chiesa Madre of Palma di Montechiaro tower above the flight of steps leading up to the church.

overleaf, left The church of Sant'Antonio in Ferla, with its undulating façade of convex and concave forms.

overleaf, right The unusual church of Sant'Agostino in Naro.

page 178 The church of the Purgatorio, Marsala.

page 179 Noto Cathedral, before the collapse of its dome.

page 180 The Chiesa Madre, Buscemi.

page 181 The portal of Santa Maria Maggiore in Nicosia.

page 182 The Badia del Santissimo Salvatore or Badia Grande in San Marco d'Alunzio. The church goes back to Norman times, but its portal with twisted columns dates from 1713.

page 183 San Giovanni Battista, Vizzini.

176 *The buildings: tradition and revolution*

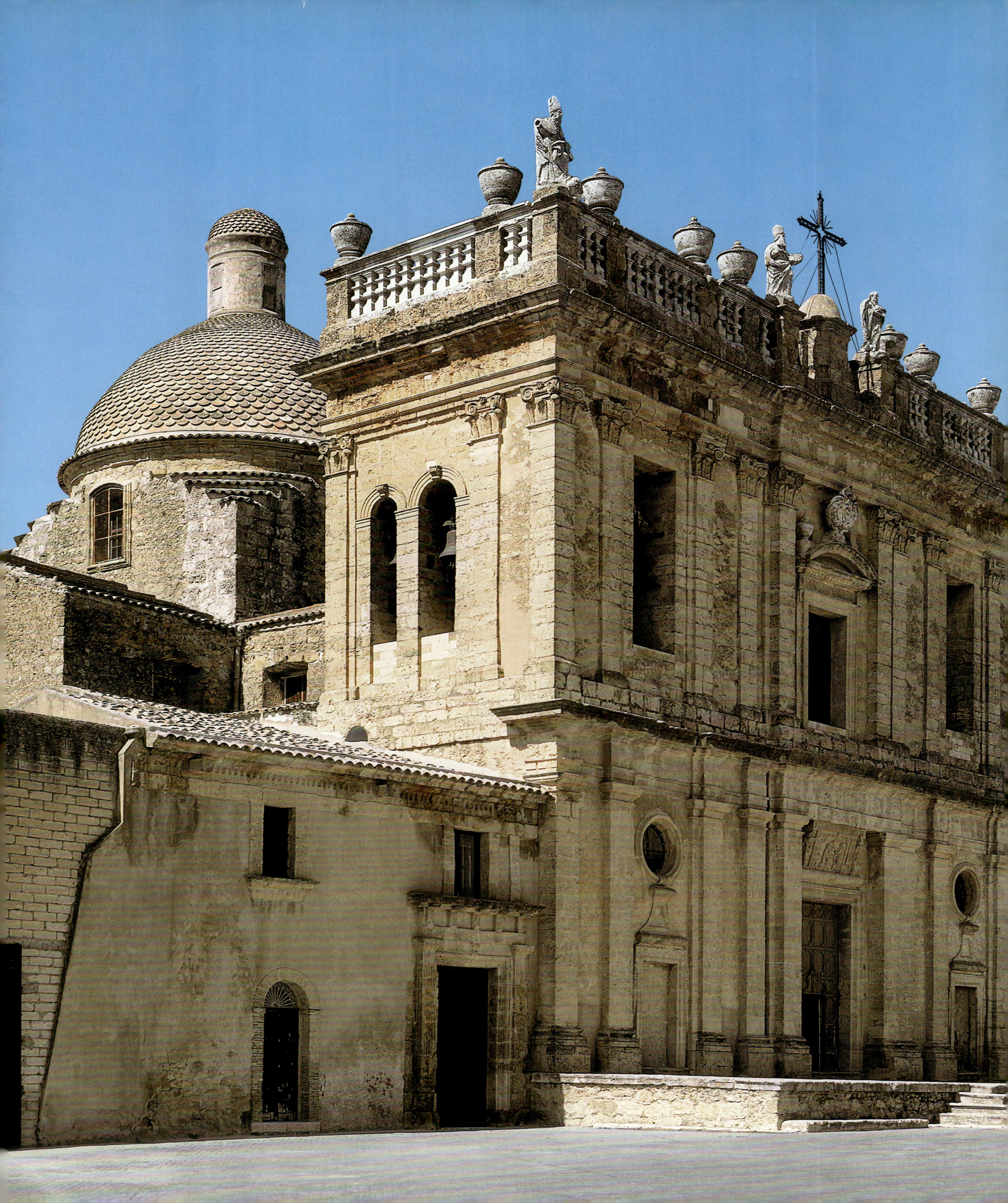

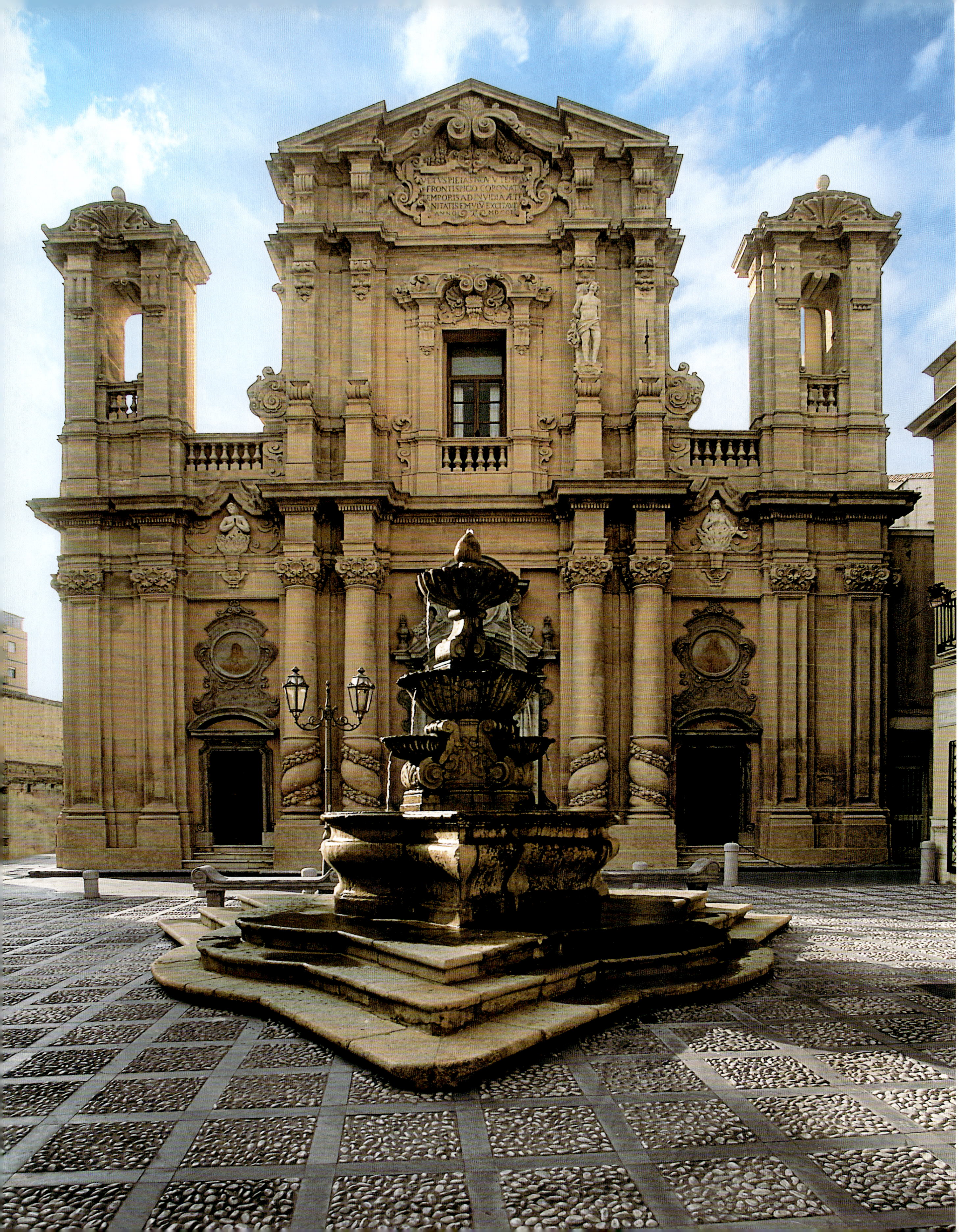

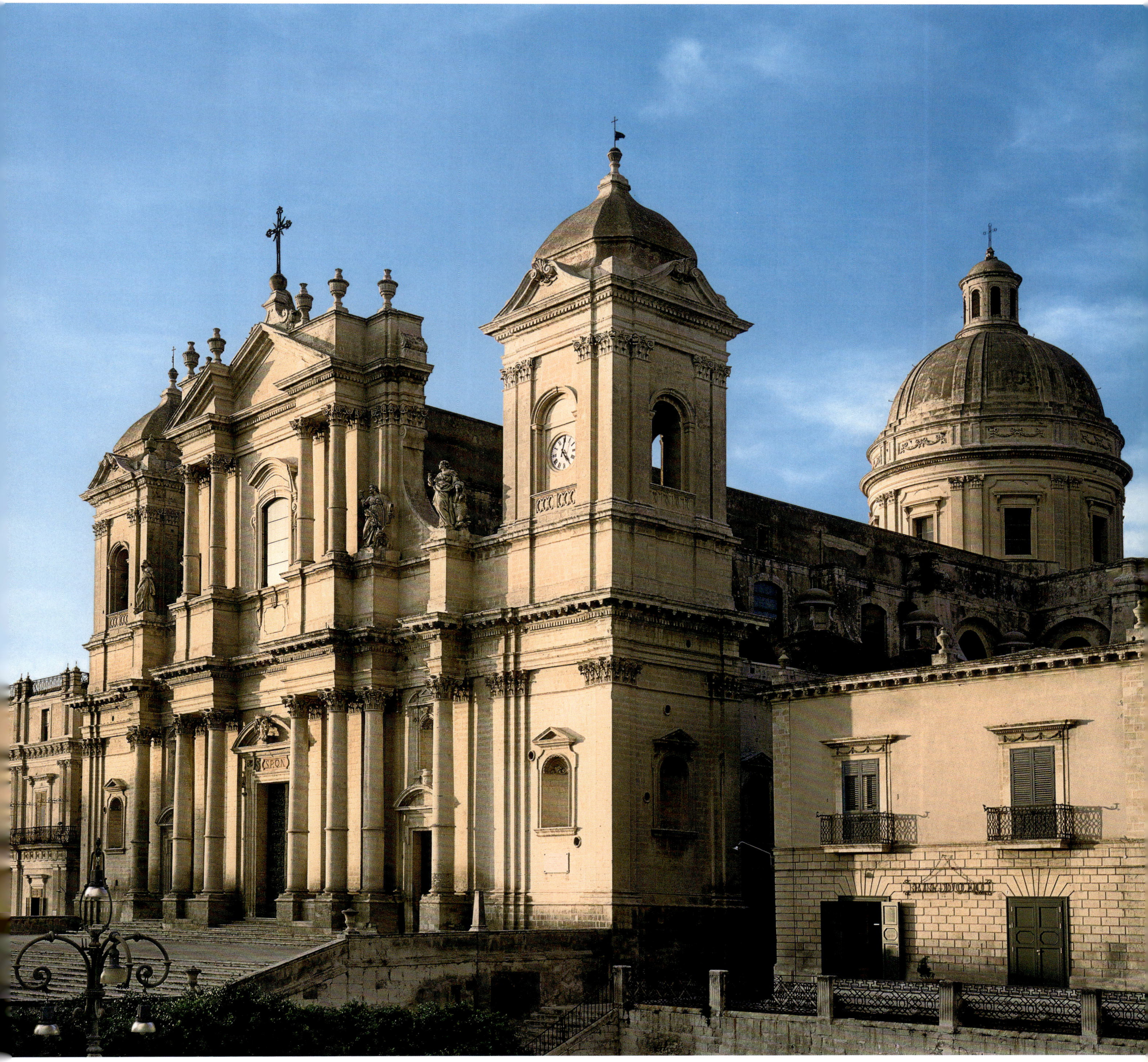

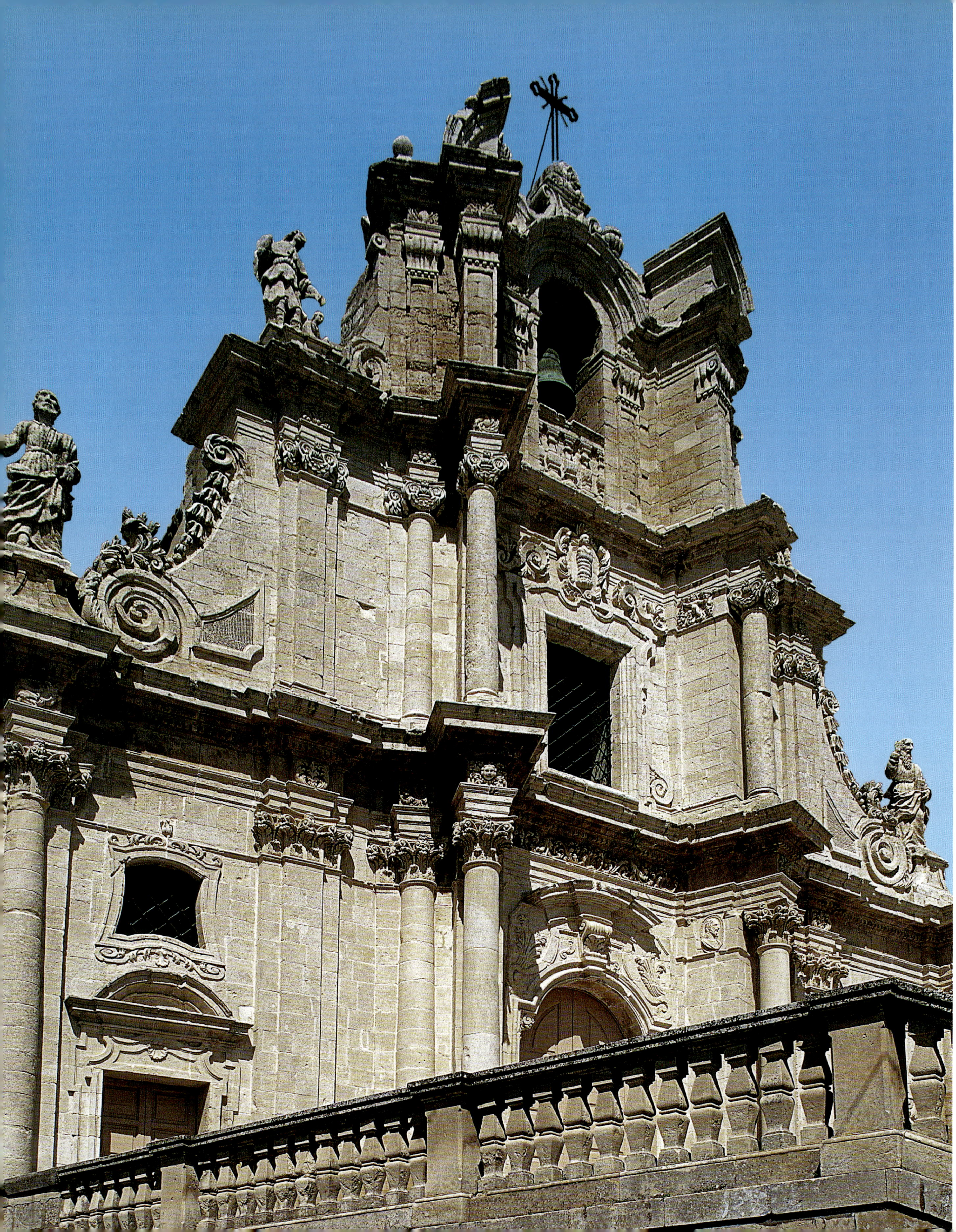

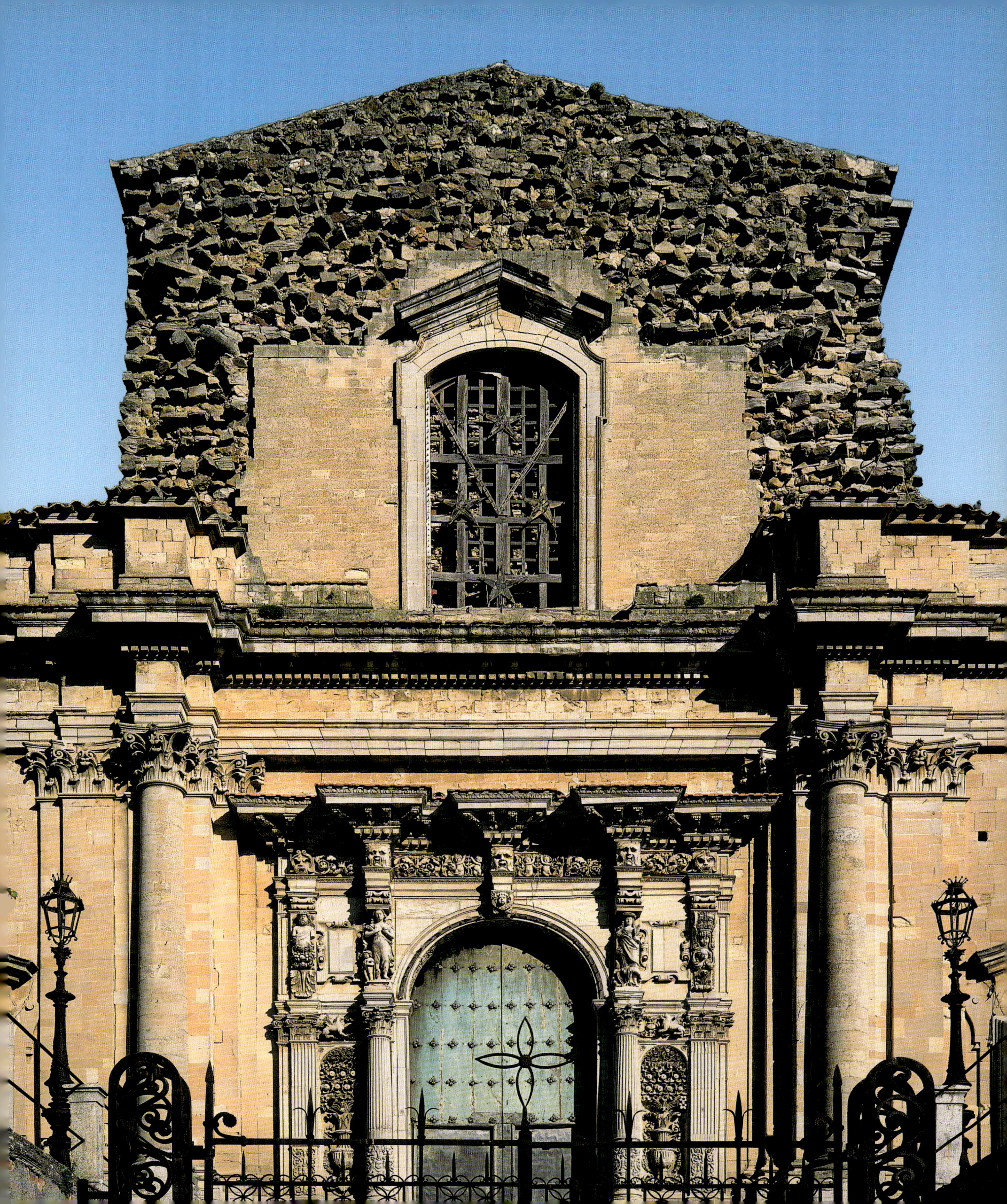

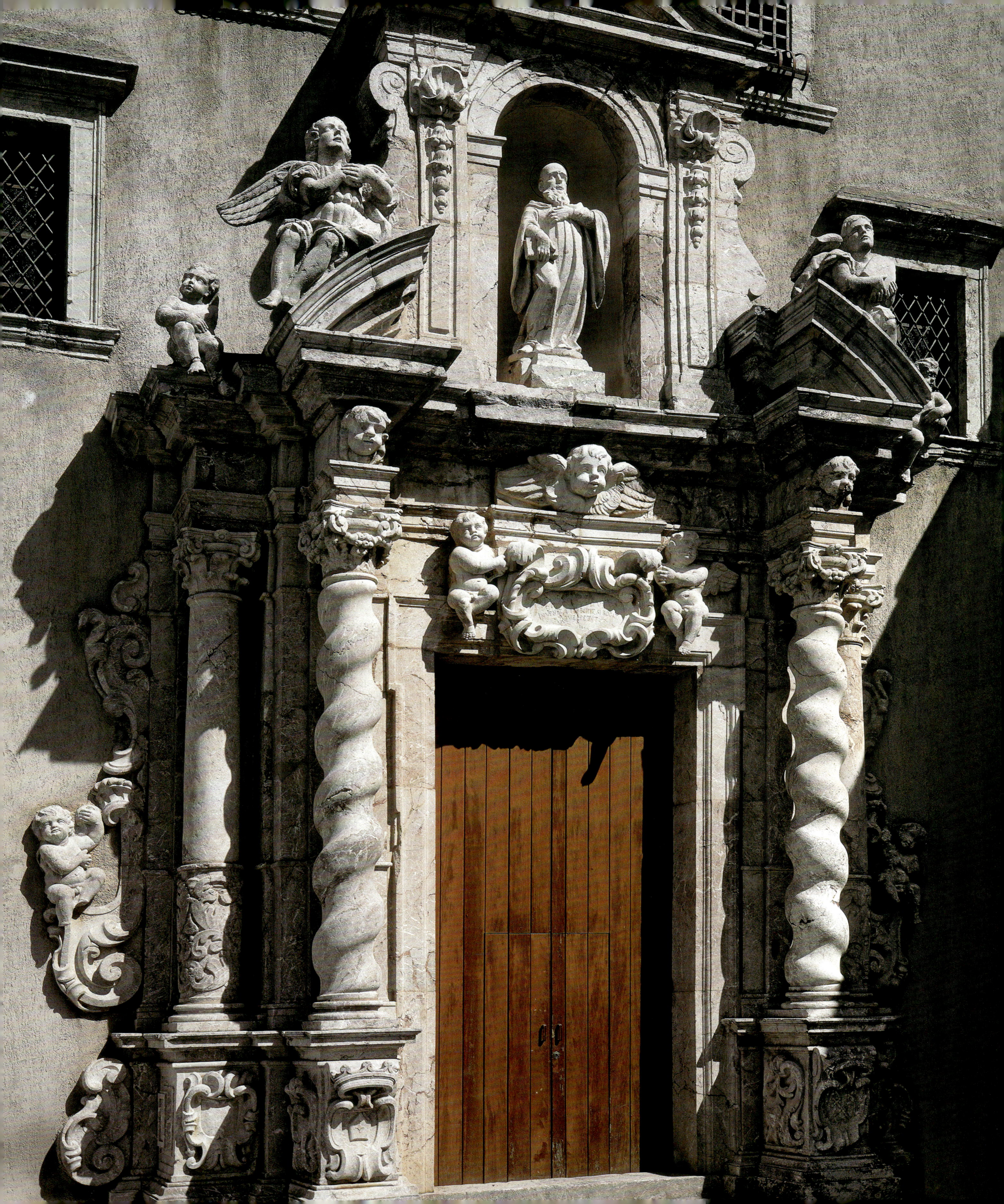

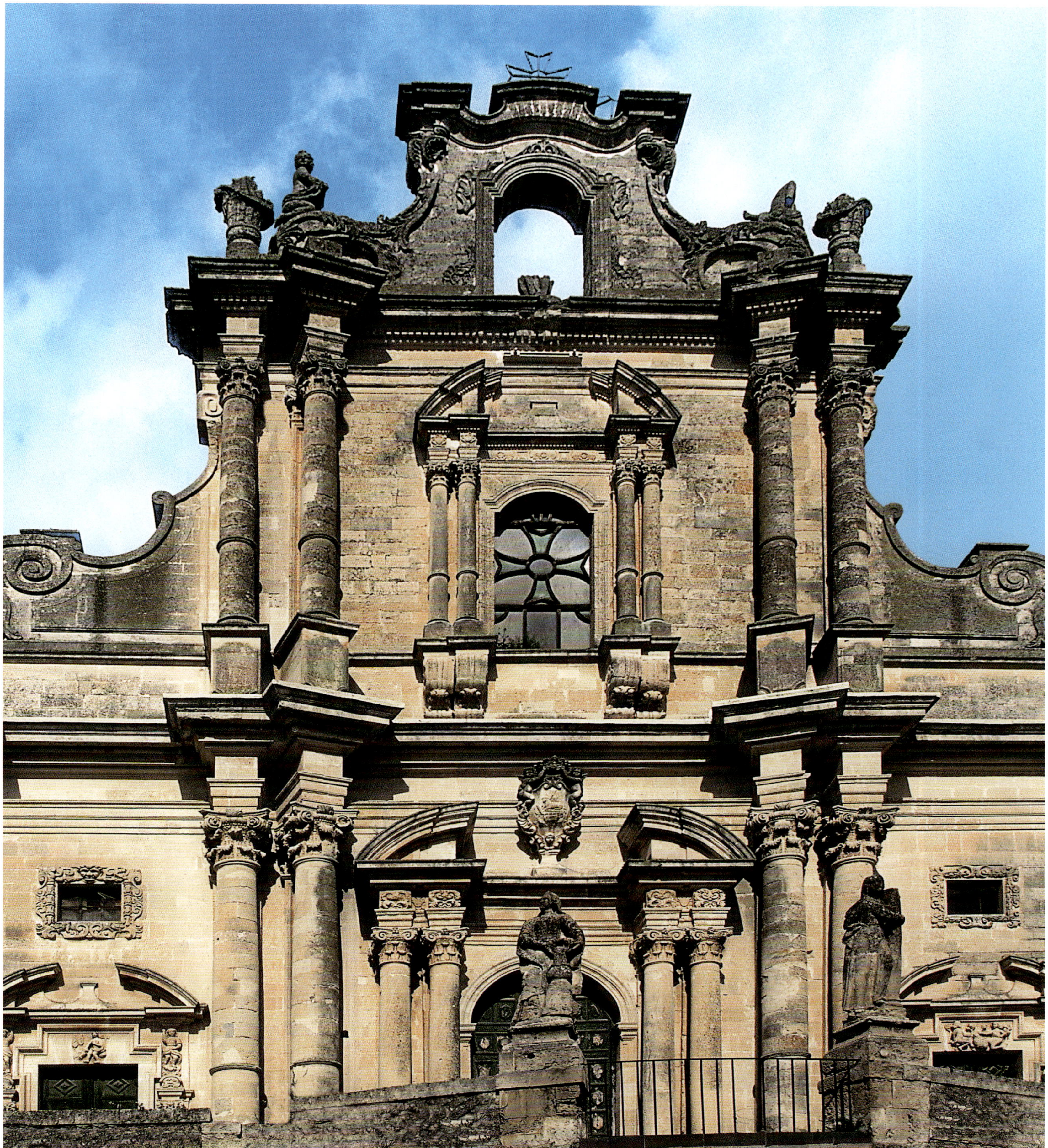

left San Martino in Randazzo goes back to the 14th century, and its medieval campanile survives. The church was remodelled in the 17th century, with a sober façade in which white plaster is contrasted with dark lava, a frequent combination in the architecture of this part of the country.

opposite The handsome façade of San Francesco d'Assisi in Caltagirone. The medieval church was destroyed in the earthquake of 1693, and it was rebuilt in a sumptuous style.

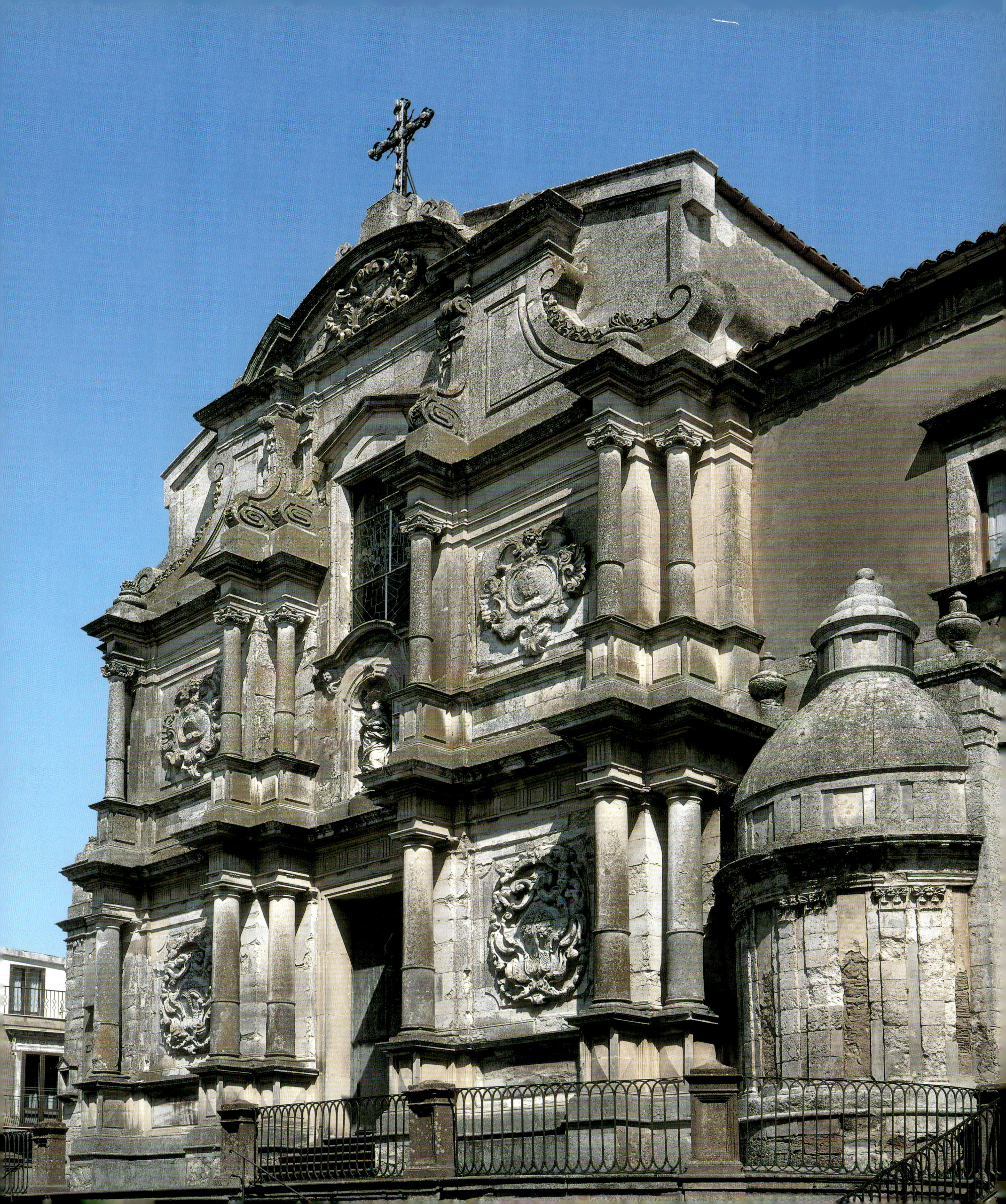

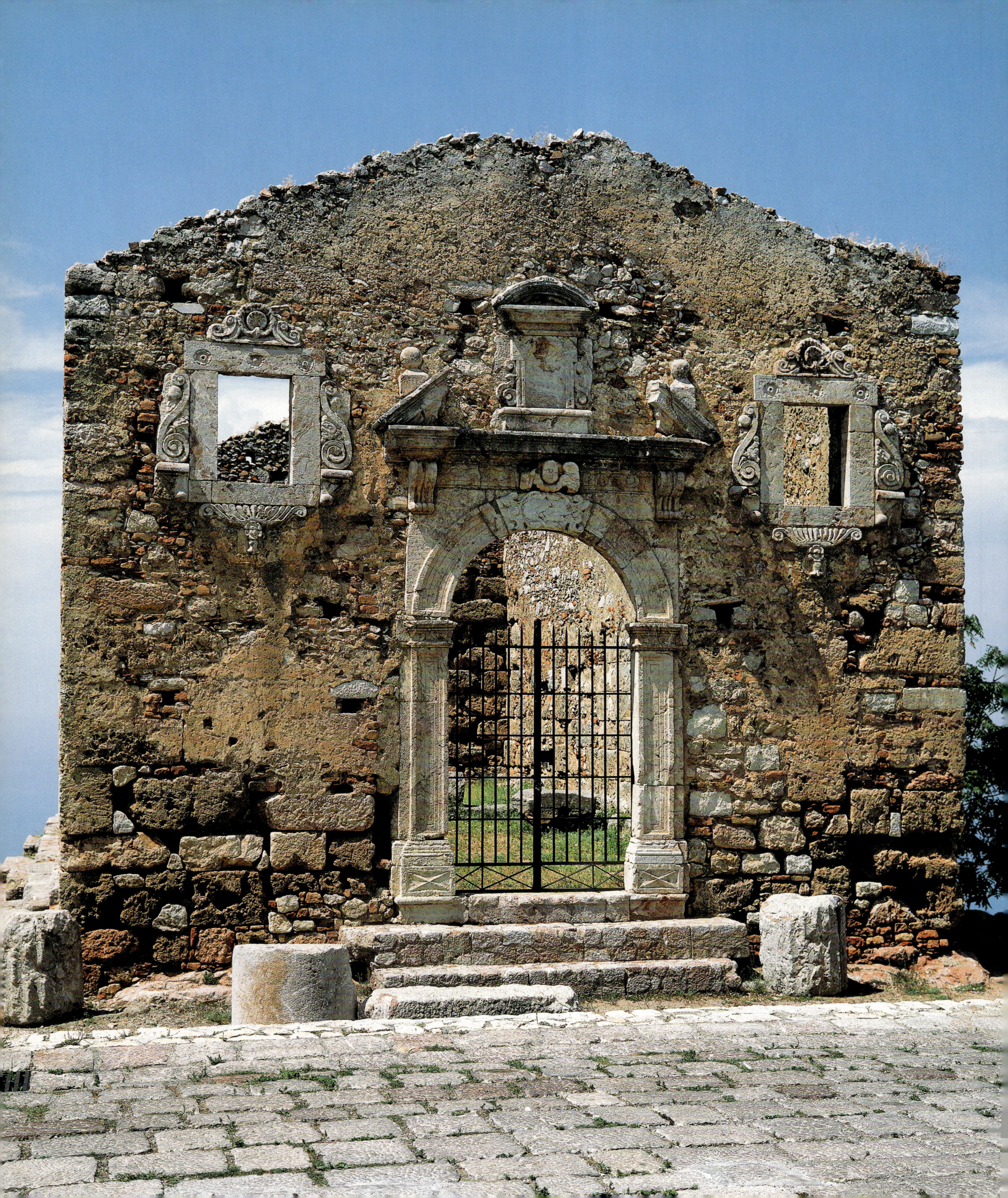

opposite The church of San Marco in San Marco d'Alunzio was built into an ancient Greek temple dedicated to Hercules. It is itself now in ruins.

right The Chiesa Madre of Belmonte Mezzagno.

overleaf left San Paolo, Palazzolo d'Acreide.

overleaf right The Chiesa Madre of Floridia, with its semicylindrical tower-façade.

The buildings: tradition and revolution

188 *The buildings: tradition and revolution*

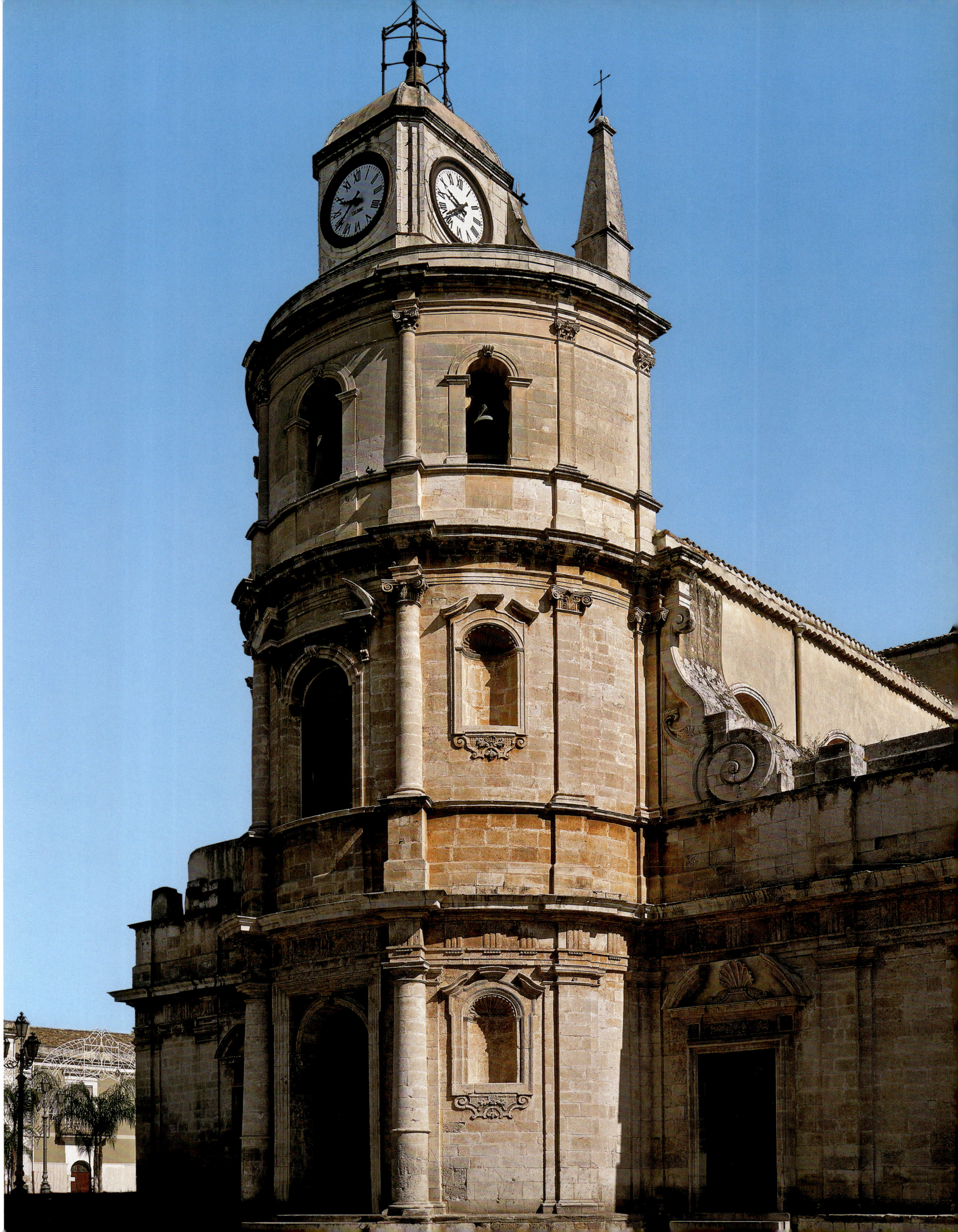

left The Carmine, Noto.

opposite San Carlo, Noto.

overleaf San Domenico in Noto, with the fountain of Hercules, which was brought from the old town.

page 194 San Giorgio, the cathedral of Ragusa, a refined example of the architecture of Rosario Gagliardi.

page 195 The unusual curved façade of the church of Sant'Anna in Piazza Armerina.

page 196 The Collegiata in Via Etnea, Catania, with its beautiful façade by Stefano Ittar.

page 197 The church of San Placido, near Palazzo Biscari in Catania, also by Stefano Ittar.

IL CAVALIER D
SALVADORE LA ROSA
INTEN DELLA PROVIN
QUESTA FONTE
RESTAURATA
RESI RIALZON
MDCCCLI

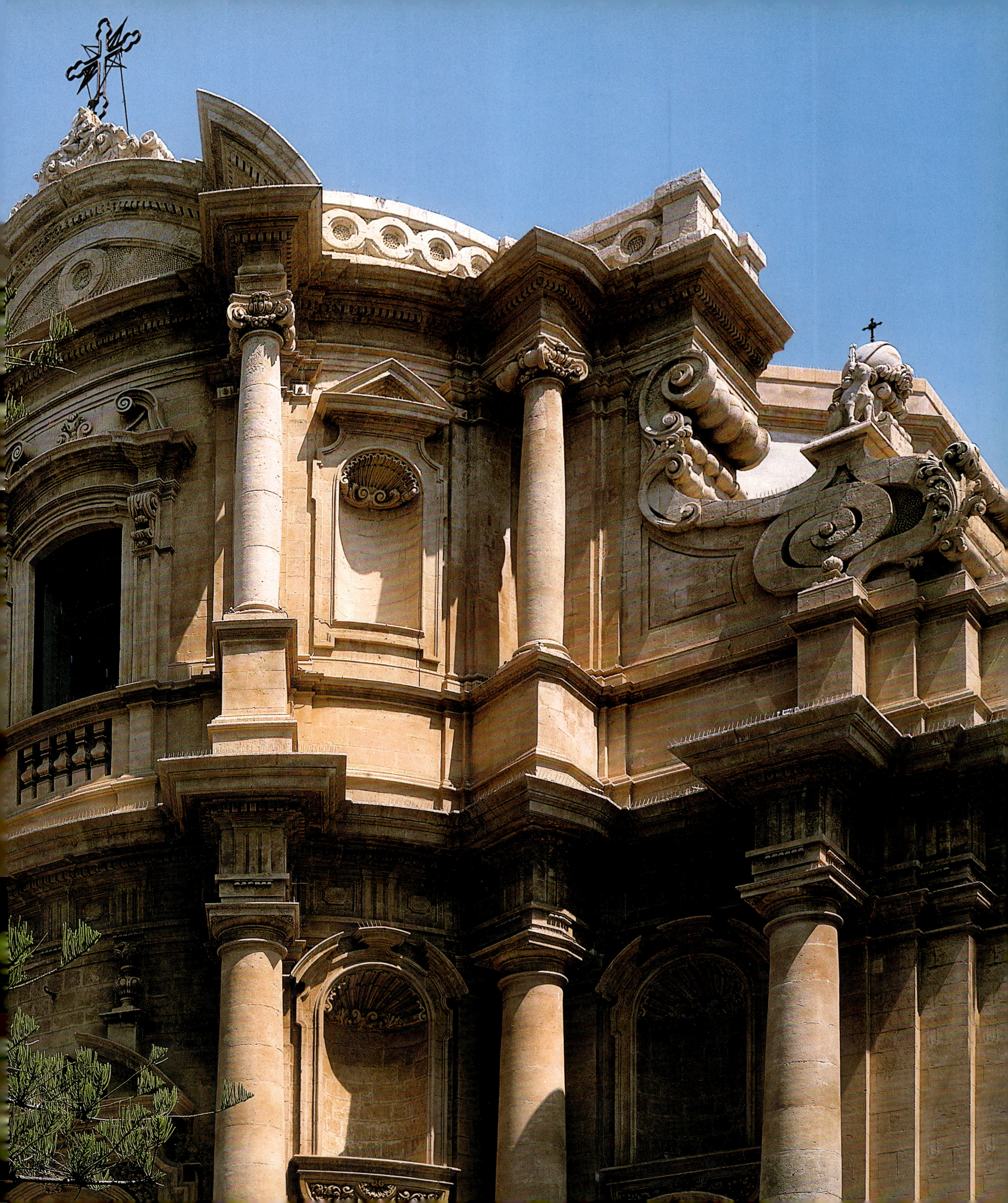

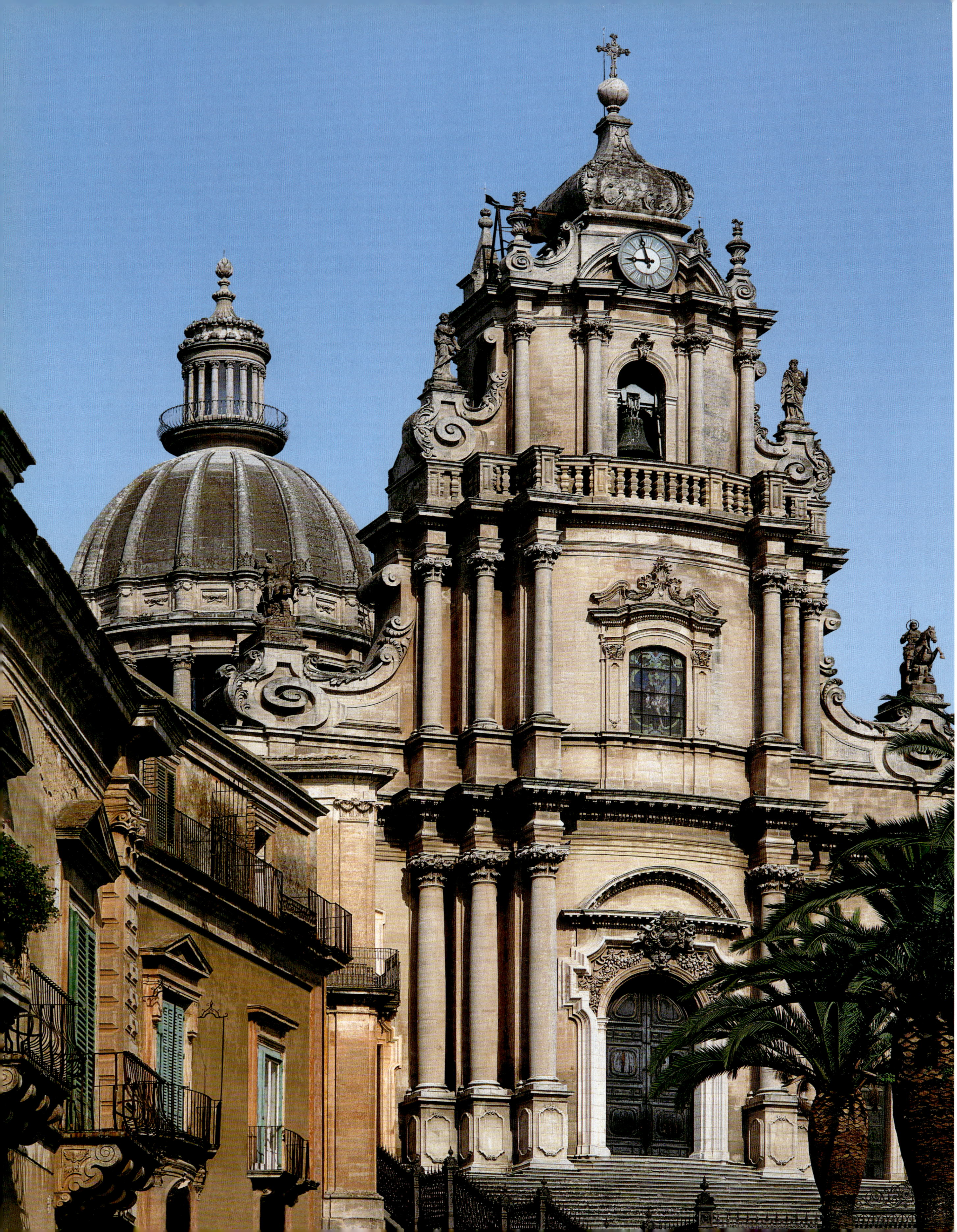

The buildings: tradition and revolution **195**

196 *The buildings: tradition and revolution*

The buildings: tradition and revolution 197

Interior of the church of the Concezione al Capo in Palermo, showing one of the altars decorated with inlaid coloured marble.

The buildings: tradition and revolution 199

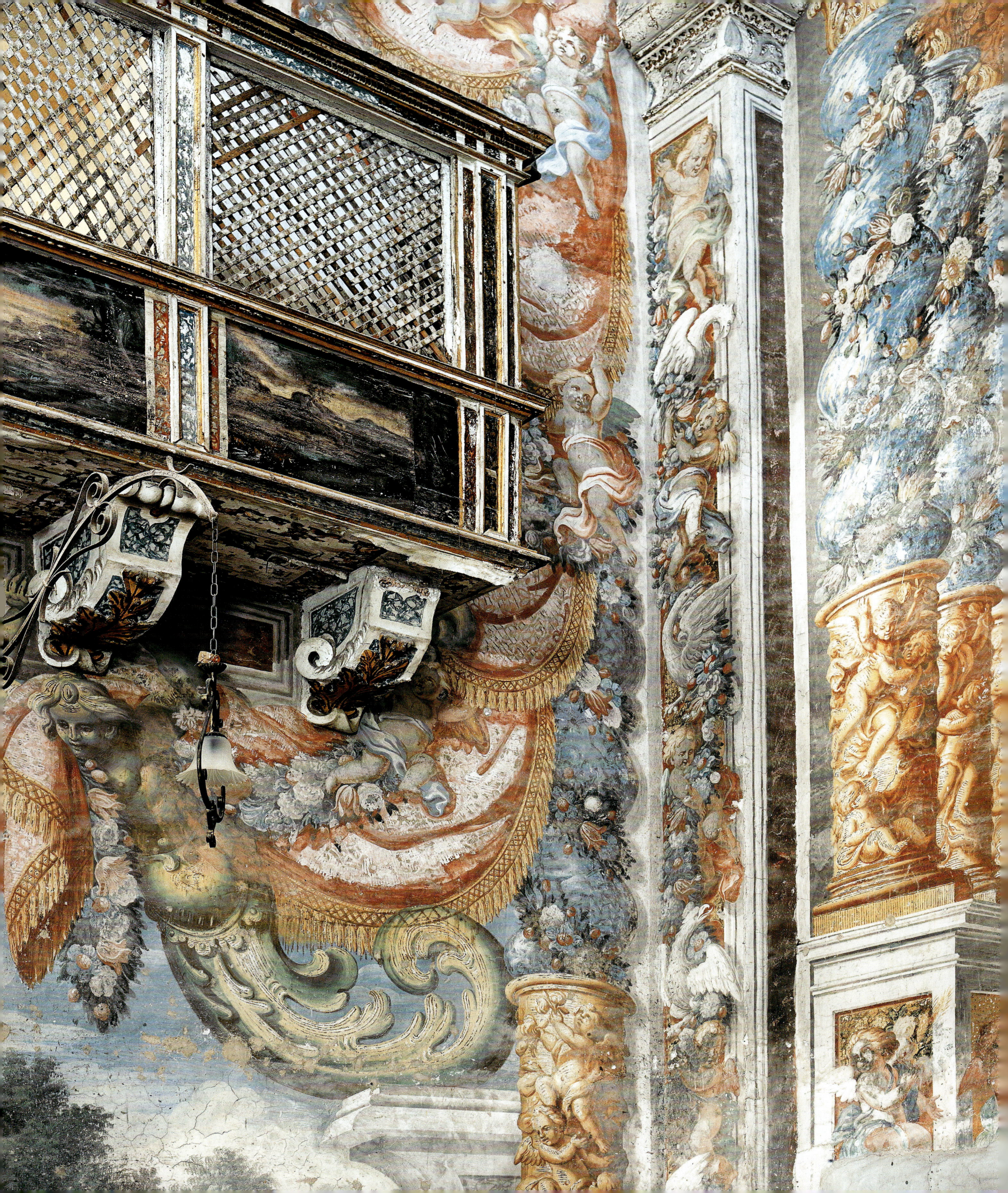

opposite A detail of the interior of the church of the Collegio in Monreale.

right Interior of the Gesù or Casa Professa in Palermo.

overleaf Detail of the interior of the church of San Francesco in Mazara del Vallo, with its remarkable stucco decoration.

S. ROSALIA
V. P.

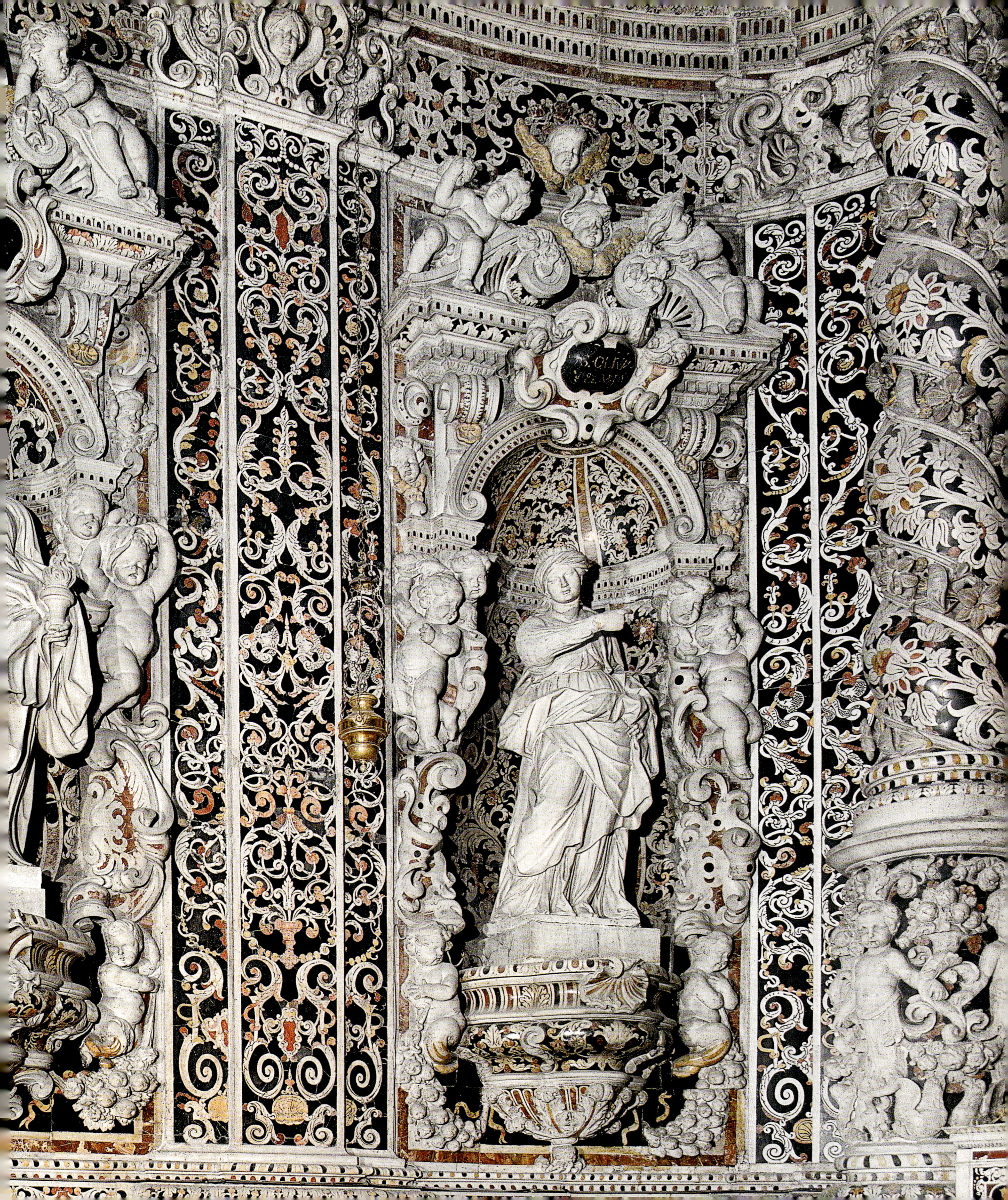

left In the apse of the church of the Gesù in Palermo sculpted figures by Gioacchino Vitaliano are set against a background of intricate marble inlay.

right San Michele, Mazara del Vallo.

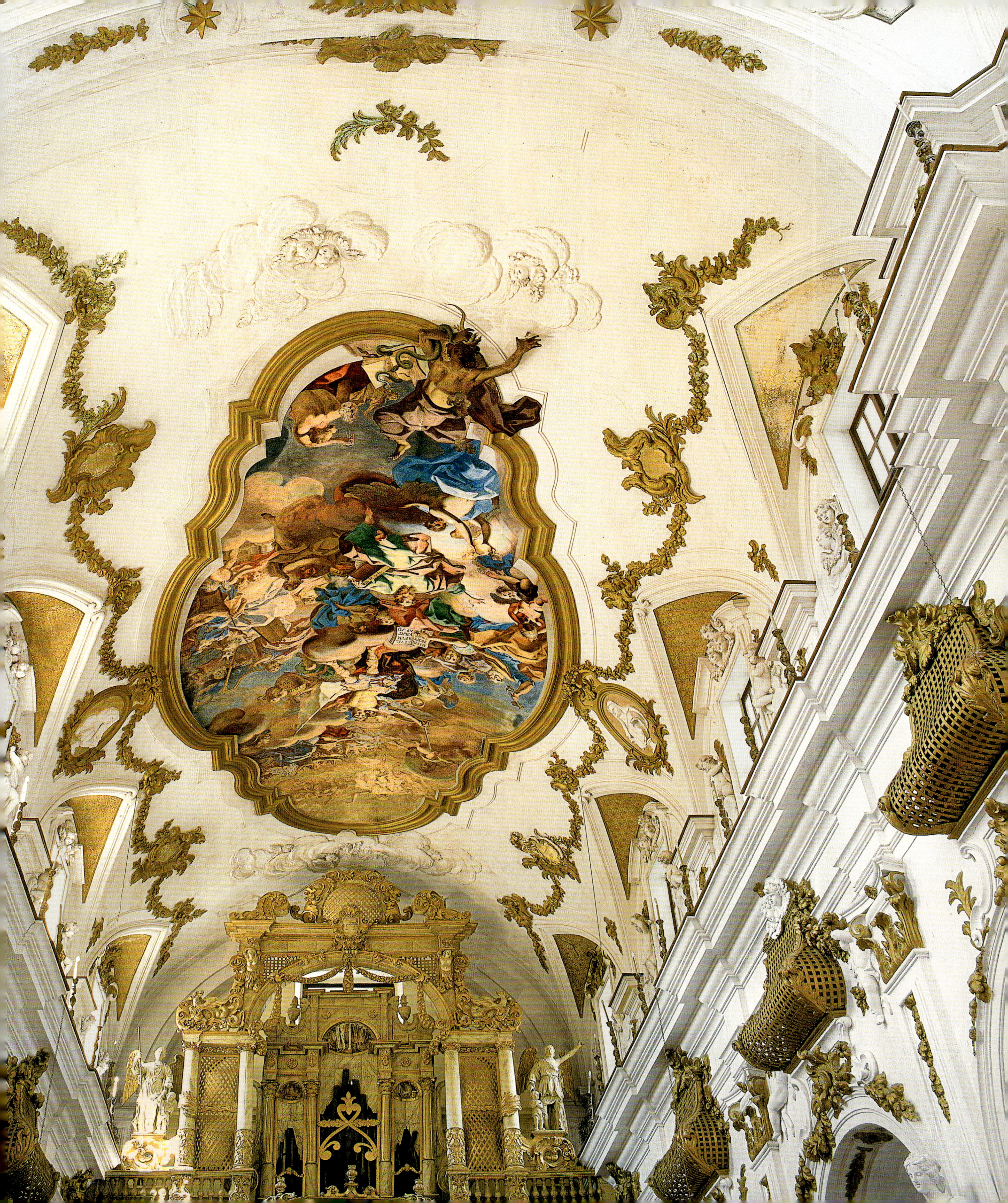

above The church and monastery of the Santissimo Rosario in Palma di Montechiaro are associated with *The Leopard* and the Lampedusa family.

right The loggias of the monastery of Santa Caterina in Mazara del Vallo are set next to the domed cathedral.

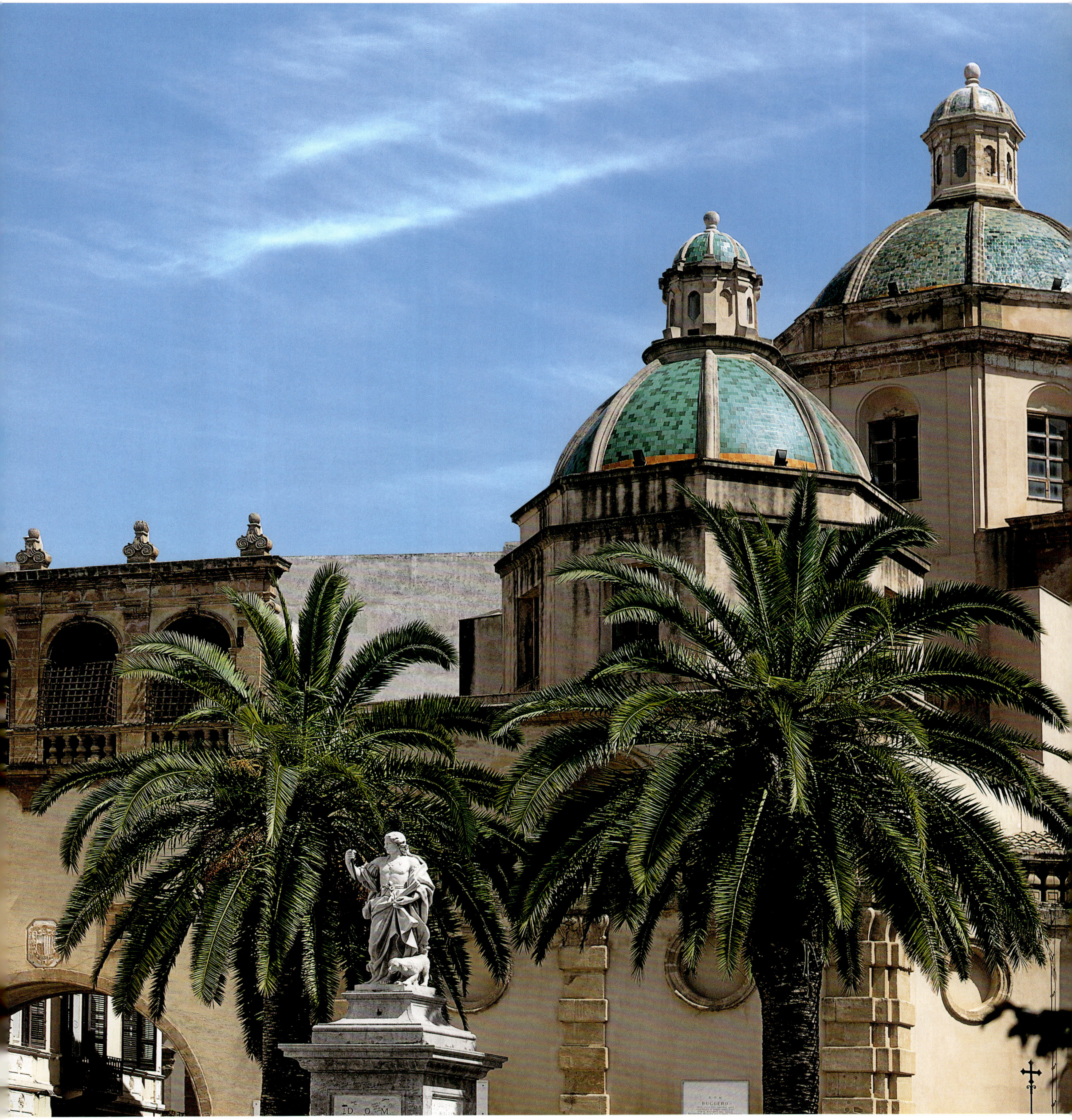

The large complex of the monastery of the Santissimo Salvatore in Noto, with its tower topped by a belvedere (see also p. 164).

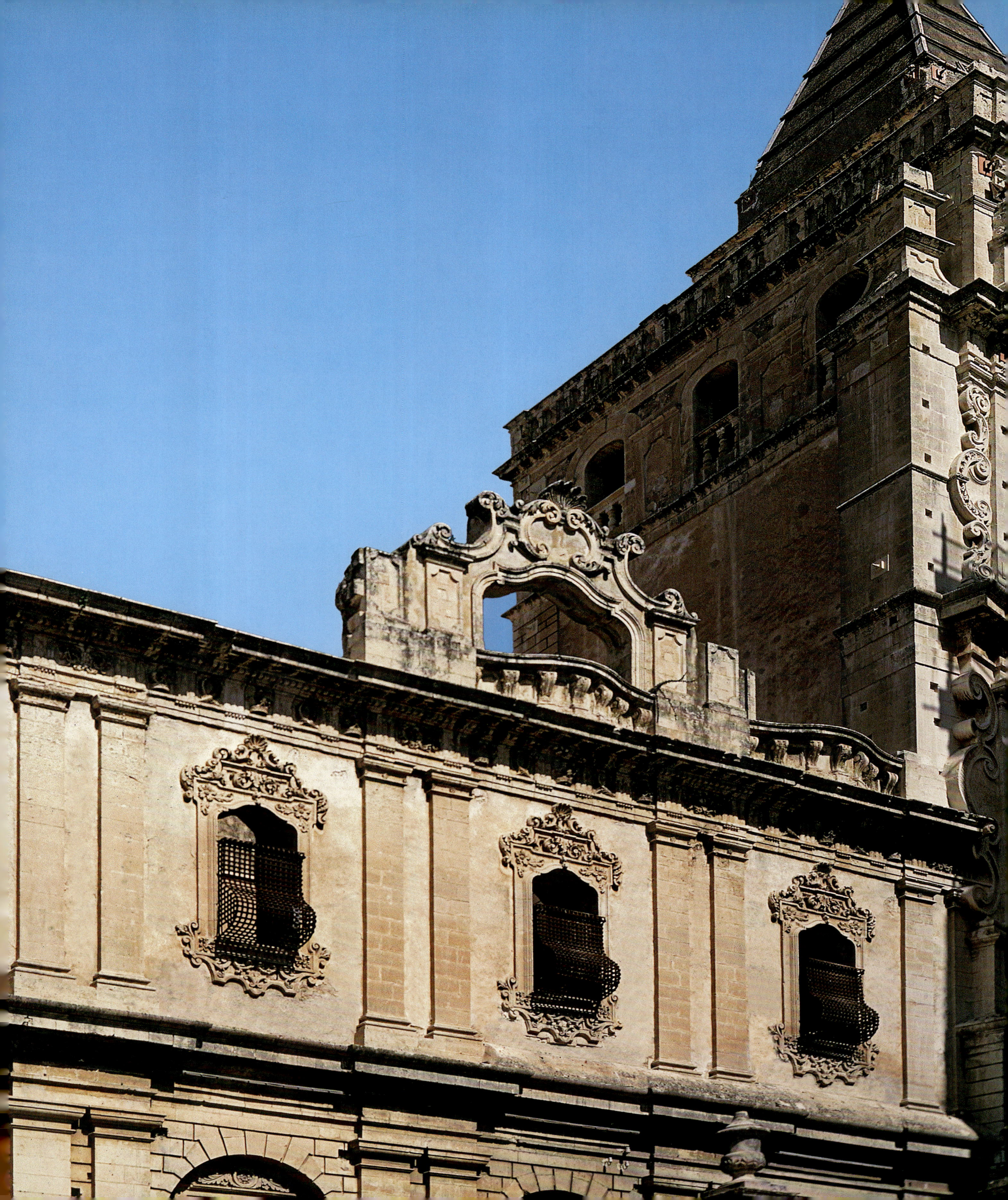

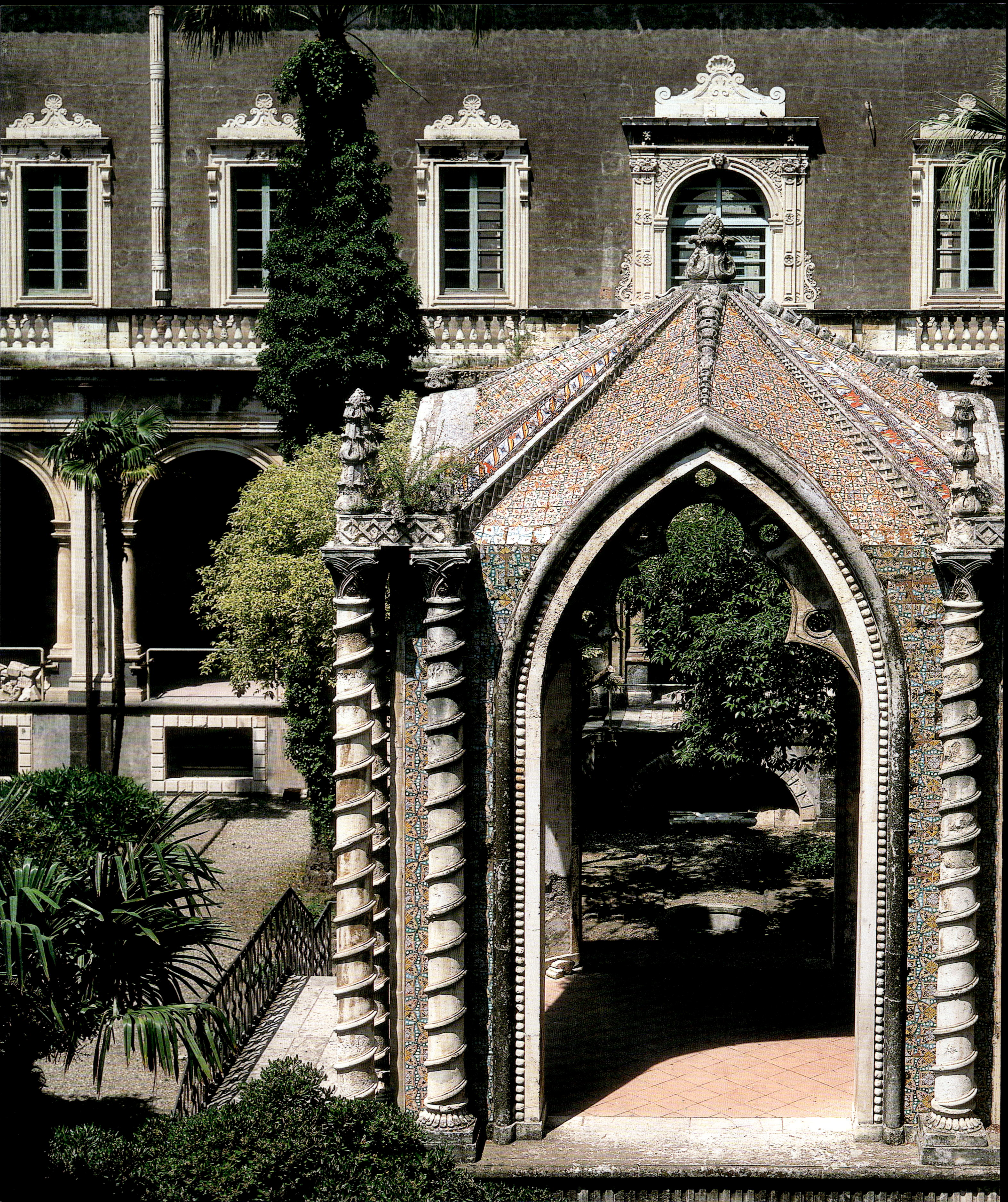

The monastery of San Nicolò l'Arena in Catania is the largest religious house in Sicily, with several cloisters (*left*), a splendid great stair (*above*), and façades with dramatic decoration (*overleaf*).

The buildings: tradition and revolution

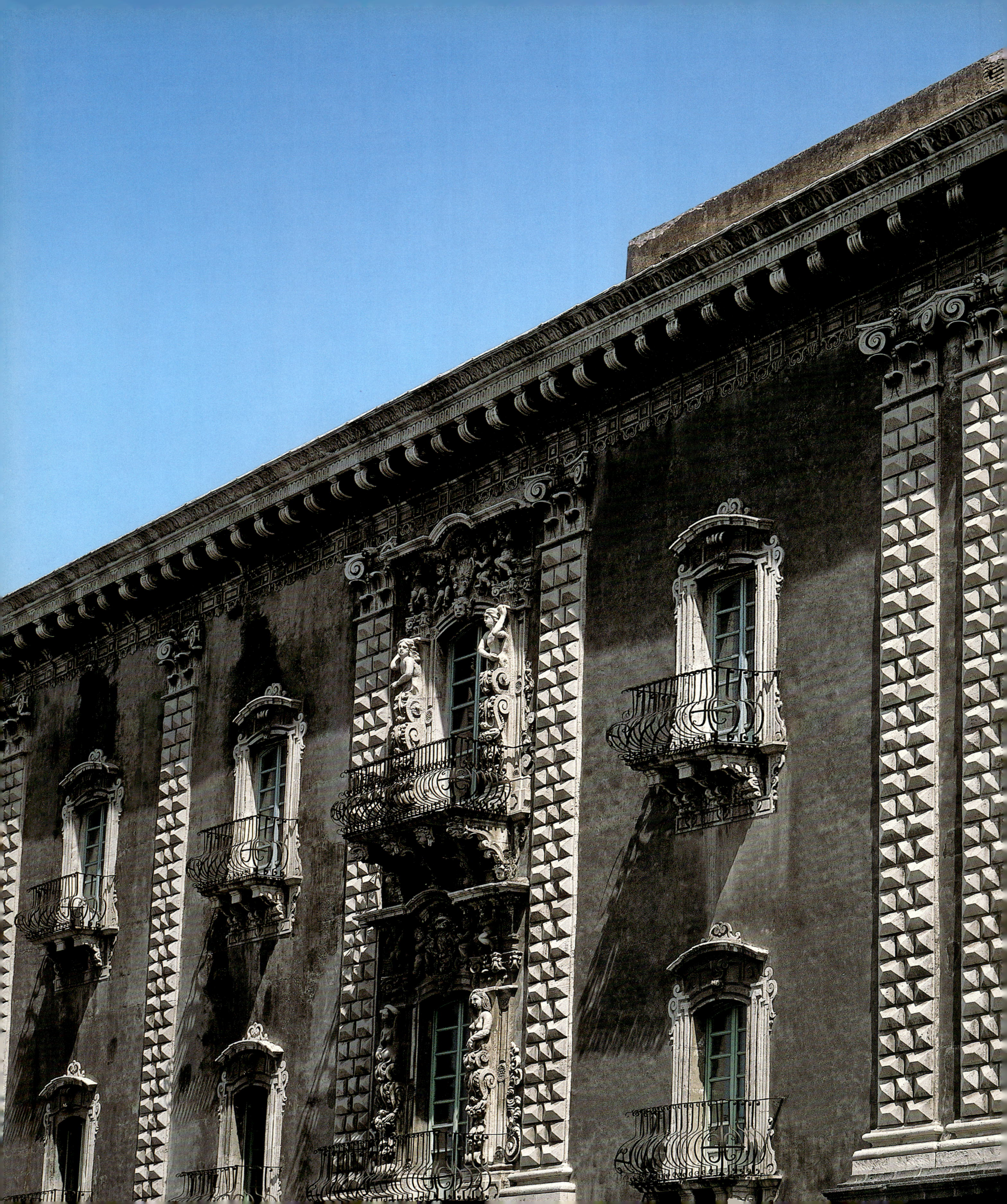

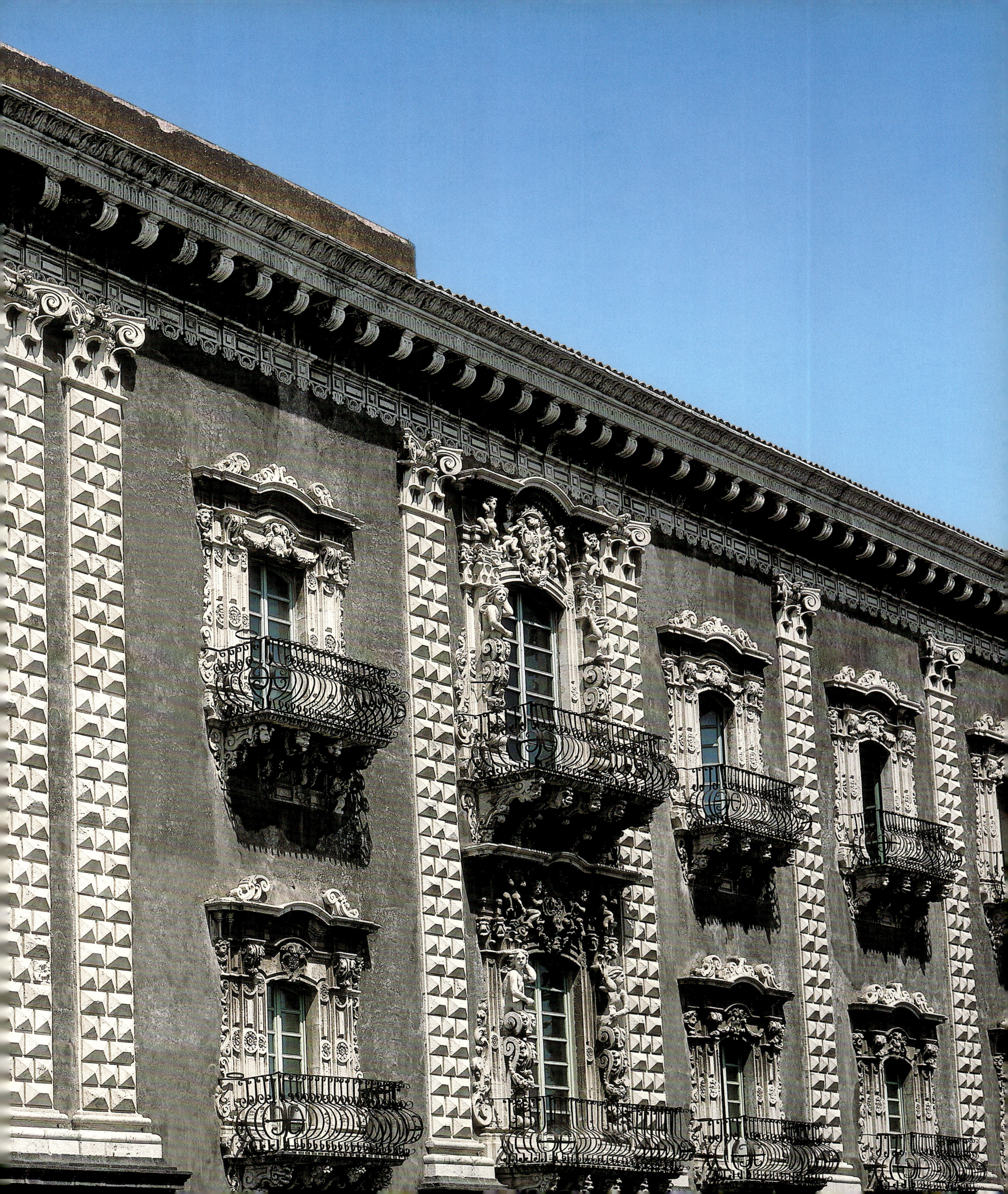

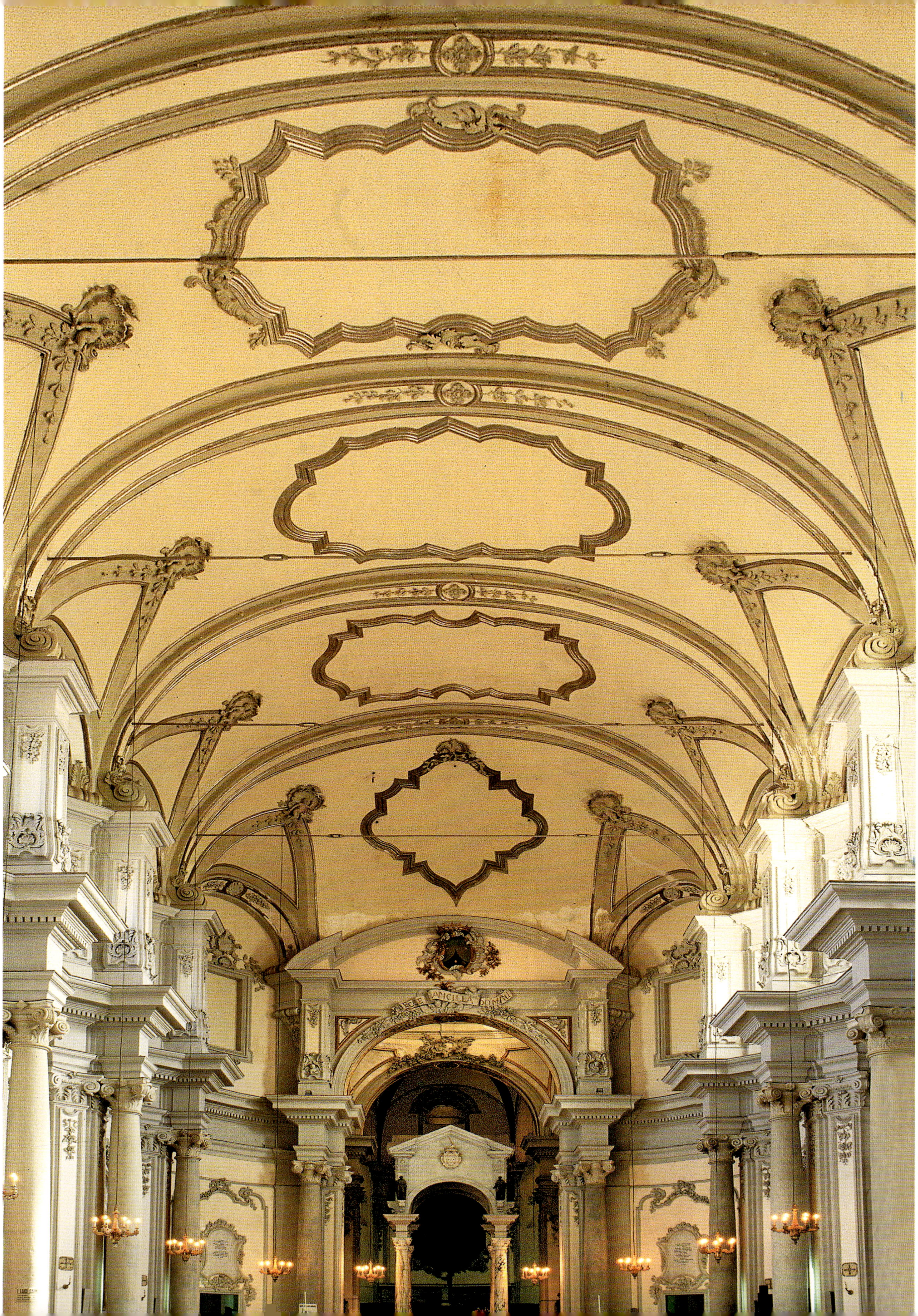
ECCE ANCILLA DOMINI

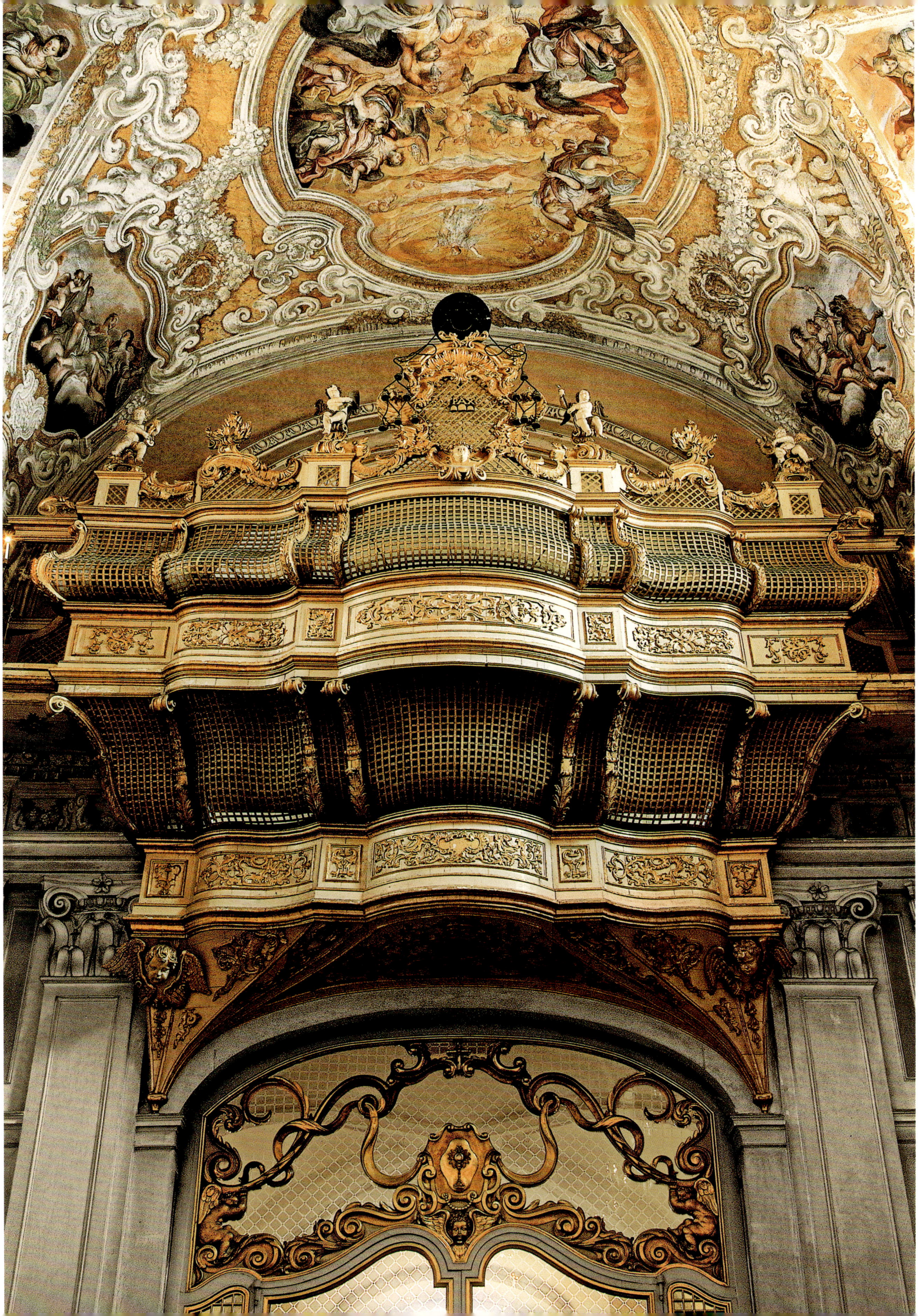

preceding pages, left Interior of the Santissima Annunziata in Trapani.

preceding pages, right The organ loft in the church of the Benedictine monastery in Catania.

left The enclosed convent of Santa Caterina is a magnificent complex in the historic centre of Palermo. The church is a riot of colourful stone inlay and frescoes.

opposite The Cappella del Crocifisso in the Norman cathedral of Monreale is a gem of Baroque art dated 1688, with its statues, twisted columns of red marble, and altar with inlaid marble decoration.

216   *The buildings: tradition and revolution*

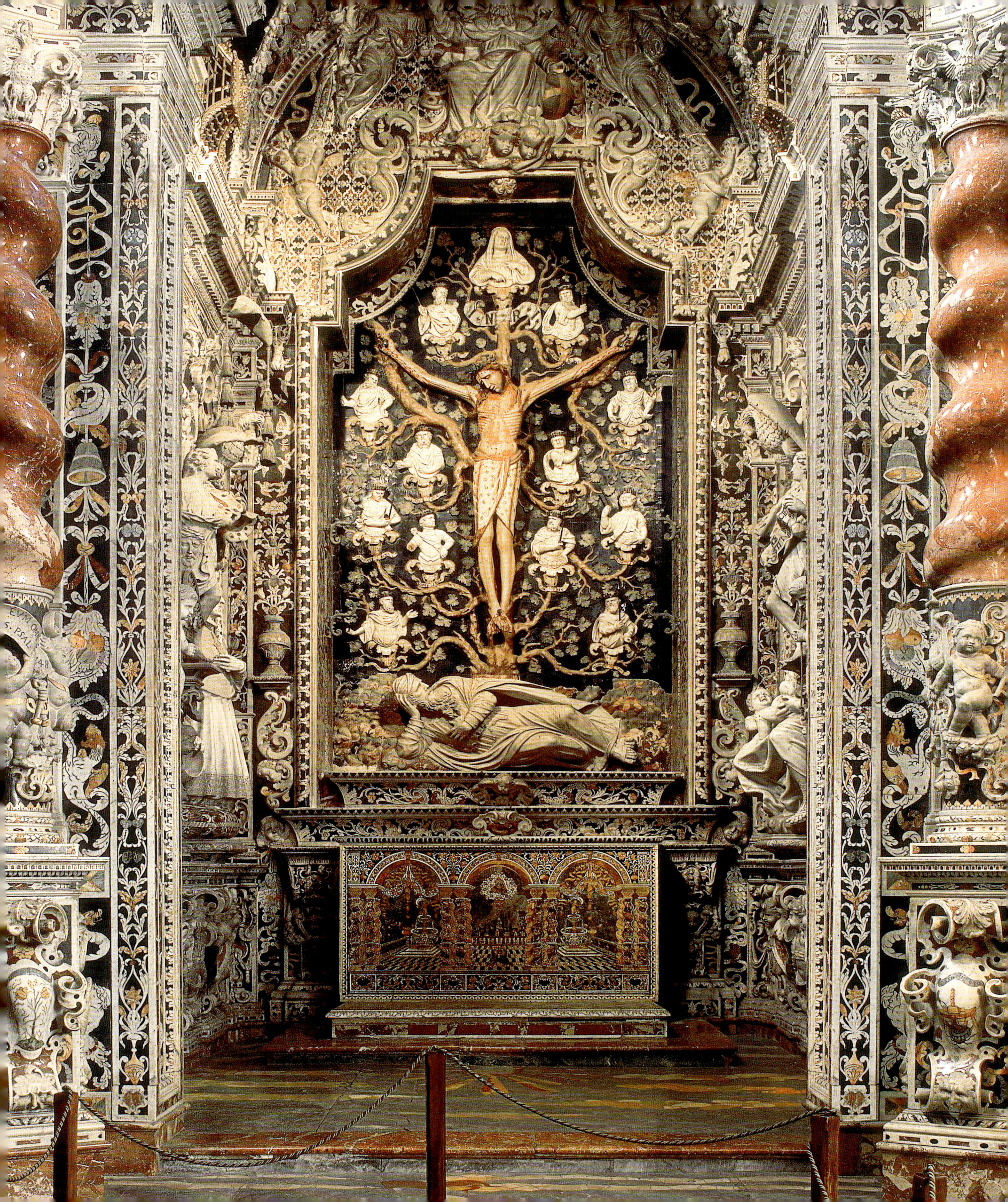

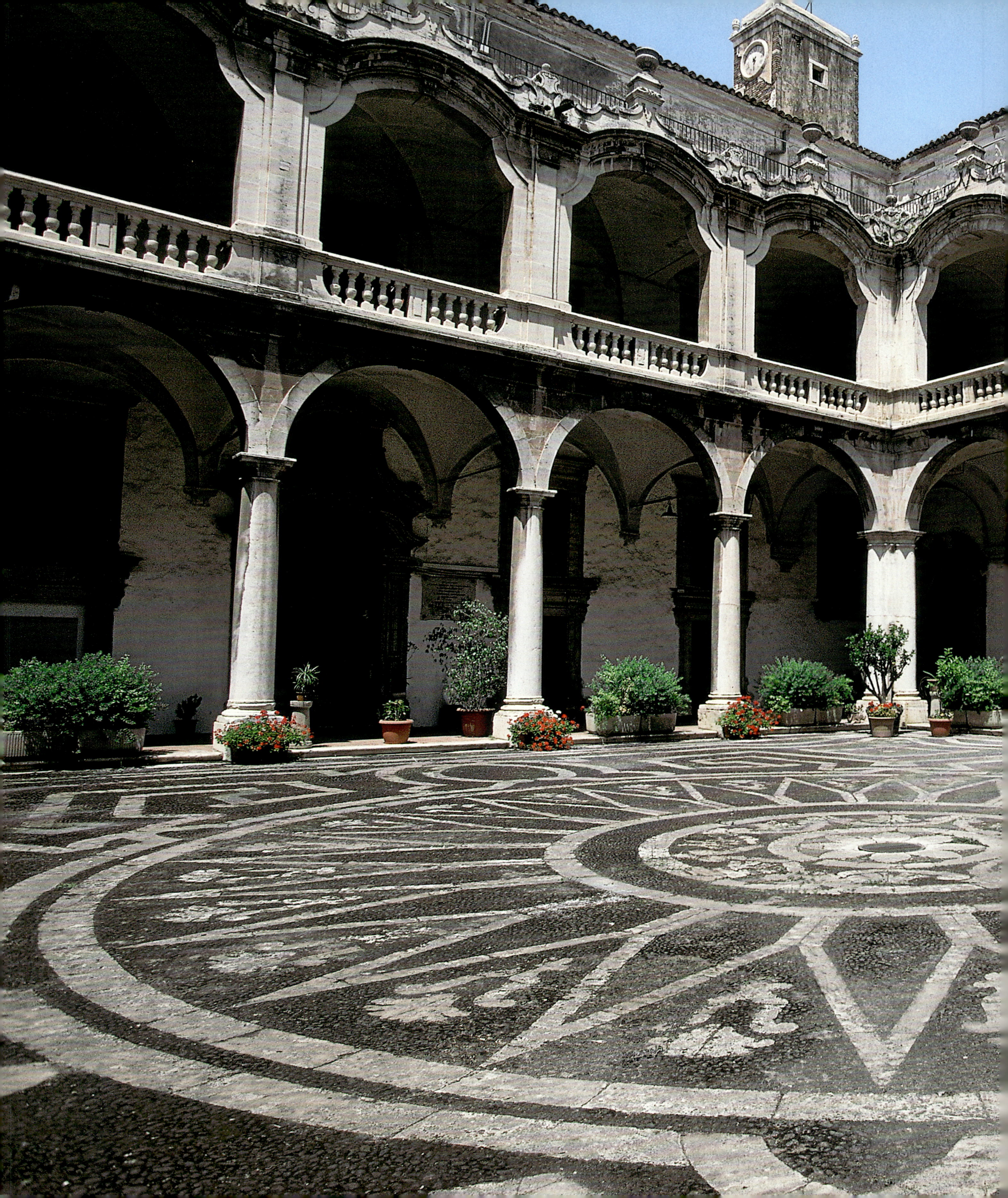

The splendid cloister of the Jesuit college in Via dei Crociferi, Palermo.

overleaf The monastery and church of San Mattia in Palermo occupy a large area between the church of Santa Teresa in the Kalsa, the Foro Italico, and the sea. They have recently been restored.

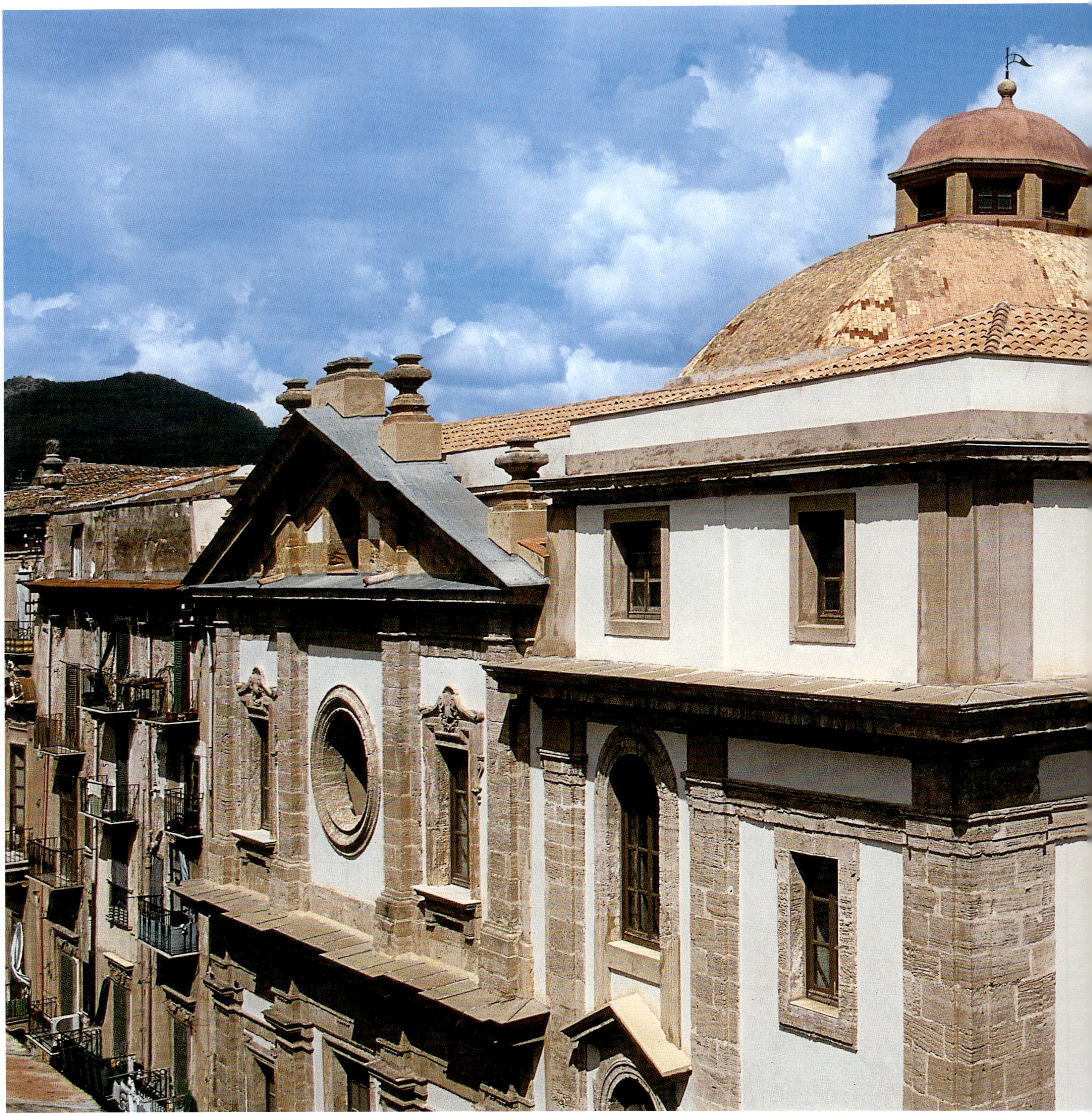

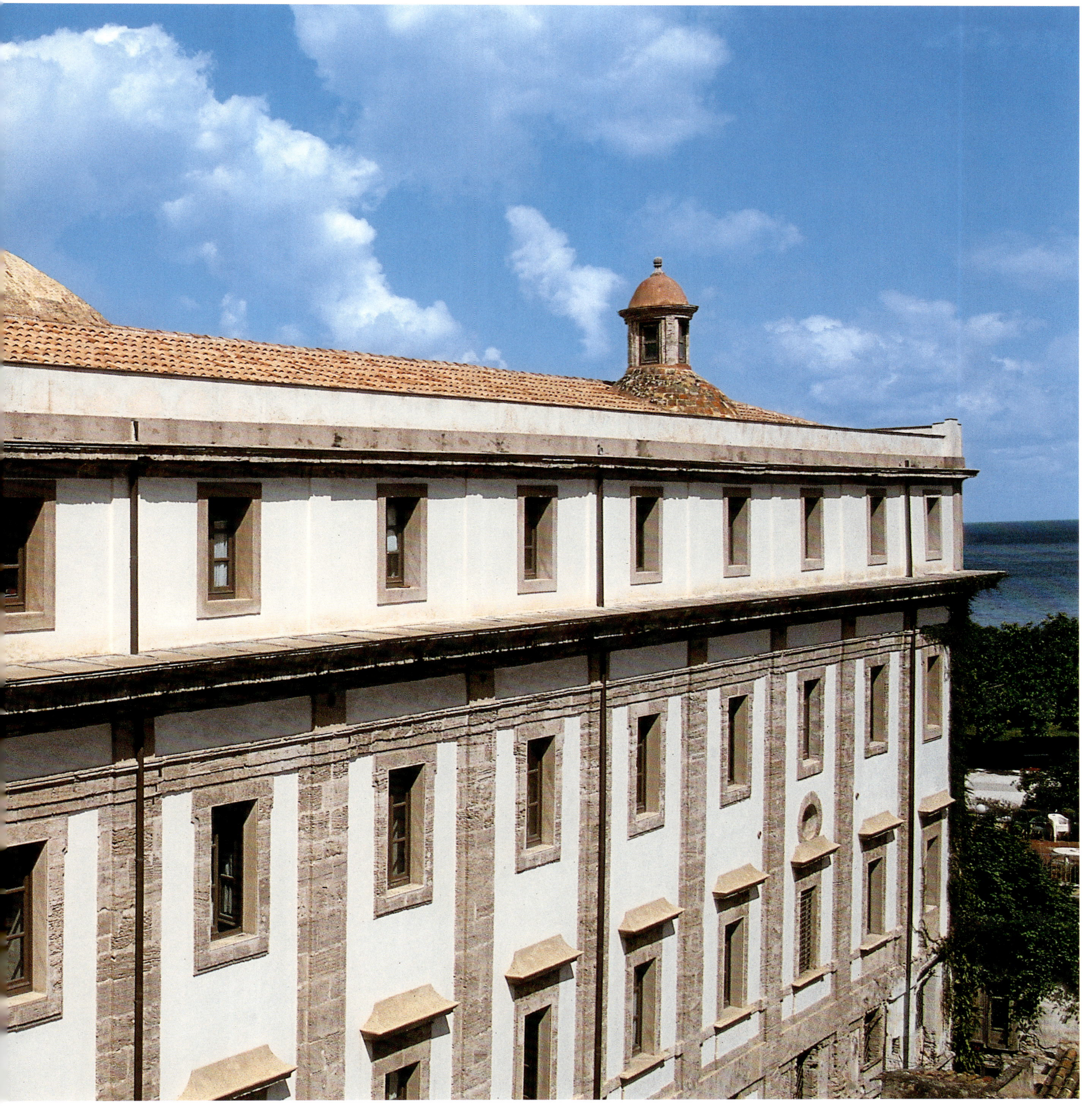

VIRGINEÆ ROSA SS. TRINI-
TATIS ROSEO TRICLINIO SEMPER
TRIVMPHATRICI AVLAM ROSEAM
ROSEI FILII D. D.

Theory and practice: from the book to the building site

The training of architects was complex, compounded of theory and practice, of tradition and of openness to foreign influences, whether acquired during an apprenticeship at home or abroad, or through the circulation of books and illustrations. It was his theoretical knowledge that distinguished the designer from the builder. Builders, however, were keen to learn as much as possible on site, so as to rise in the profession. In south-eastern Sicily, notably, after the earthquake of 1693, through the years of the late Baroque, designers with a craft background assumed a central role.

This formation was reflected in the custom of quoting sources of greater authority in the margins of drawings for a project, and also in the compiling of treatises, which were printed and circulated as much to demonstrate the status of the author as to achieve any didactic purpose with potential pupils. The possession of a good library, beyond those available in monasteries to architects who were members of religious orders, gave access to a wide range of books and illustrations, old and new, which would help in the creation of a new design. Apprenticeship to an architect on site would then complete training that had often begun in a family workshop.

The authority of the treatise

The study of treatises was common among architects and master builders before Sicily was in a position to produce its own theories. Those then tended to be concerned with practical matters of construction, although some authors – notably Giacomo Amico – could not resist demonstrating the extent of their own theoretical knowledge, in order to lay claim to a better position, or justify or consolidate an existing one. Among the early holdings of Sicilian libraries, both religious and lay, public and private, it is still possible now to find various editions of the most important treatises of the 16th and 17th centuries, as well as many foreign ones, Italian and otherwise, which would have provided a wide range of sophisticated ideas from which to work. The wide diffusion of the treatises and their increasingly didactic role, presenting ideas and forms which could easily be adapted to different times and places, was an important factor in the development of new architectural forms.

Particularly important were the treatise of Vitruvius (in many editions) and that of Serlio. Copies of Vitruvius are mentioned in two inventories, of 1484 and 1567 – the latter that of Fazio Gagini,

preceding pages The Oratorio del Rosario in San Domenico, Palermo, by Serpotta.

above The layout of the city of Palermo reflects a complex history, which this illustration from the *Descrittione del Regno di Sicilia* by Gabriele Merelli of 1677 attempts to make clear, by showing the old city between the two rivers, the Kemonia and the Papireto, and superimposing the walled city of the 16th and 17th centuries. (Biblioteca Reale, Turin)

224 Theory and practice: from the book to the building site

son of Antonello and grandson of Domenico. According to the evidence, the edition/translation of Vitruvius most commonly used in Sicily was the one published in 1521, by Cesare Cesariano, a pupil of Bramante and architect to Charles V, which was full of illustrations intended to be of practical use for construction. Cesariano's thoughts on the search for a module in the 'Gothic' cathedral of Milan, and on the reconciliation of the canon with his own interpretation of the architectural orders, reveal a freedom of thought and expression that was to be carried further by mannerist theorists such as the Bolognese Sebastiano Serlio.

These theorists had no problems in accepting variety, something that was an essential premise for the flights of fancy of the Baroque period. According to Manfred Tafuri, Serlio's treatise was in that sense the most influential 'monument of theory' of its time, in which portals and fireplaces were presented as 'a typological-figural survey based on the value of variation'. It was also one of the first books through which the classical language and forms circulated around Europe, so that they then became available to different interpretations and manipulations, all in the name of invention. Images were found particularly in Serlio's Books III and IV, first published in 1537 and 1540 respectively, and in the *Libro Extraordinario*, published in Lyons in 1551. Fulvia Scaduto has shown that Serlio fostered a common heritage in Sicilian culture as his treatise spread, not only in Palermo – where two copies were on offer from a bookseller in 1591 – but throughout the entire island, from Castelbuono to the distant region of the Iblei mountains, from the late 16th century down to the 18th.

In composition the façade of the Chiesa Madre in Chiaramonte clearly resembles Serlio's 'Corinthian Temple', while his 'Tempio bislungo' (literally, oblong temple) seems to lie behind the formula of the façade with two belltowers that was chosen around 1700 by patrons and masters for San Giovanni Battista, the Chiesa Madre of the new Ragusa. For the same building, in 1734, Paolo Nifosì has shown, the *capomastro* Carmelo Cultraro undertook for the columns of the interior to supply capitals 'with foliage, according to the design of Vignola and Serlio' – showing that by the first half of the 18th century treatises were the province not just of the architect but also of the master builder.

Treatises were, therefore, an important learning tool for Sicilian architects. An image symbolizing this appears in the first volume of *L'Architetto Pratico* by Giovanni Amico: student architects are depicted quenching their thirst with water squeezed out of the most famous treatises. Amico also included a whole array of portraits of Vitruvius, Serlio, Vignola, Palladio and Scamozzi, all authoritative experts in the practice of architecture; and as if to underline the connection between theory and practice, the architects' portraits include both their treatises and the instruments they employed.

The two volumes of Amico's treatise were published in 1726 and 1750, as we have seen. They constituted the latest and most comprehensive collection of his vast output, much of which remained in manuscript form. There were earlier theoretical works, based on experience abroad perhaps during apprenticeships, or on the gradual accumulation of knowledge acquired on building sites, constituting a body of information that could be passed on to pupils. In 1668 Tomaso Maria Napoli had published his *Utriusque Architecturae Compendium* in Rome, which took the form of two books based on Vitruvius, one devoted to civil and the other to military architecture, including geometric formulas useful in the construction of fortresses. The treatise does not appear to have enjoyed much success, but it would have been useful to its author as a demonstration of his prowess in Latin and his architectural knowledge. Military architecture proved to be significant in his career, after his work in Austria and for Prince Eugene of Savoy, and he devoted another small treatise to it, published in Palermo in 1723. Both his treatises exist in two versions, which differ only in the dedication at the beginning and in the title and date of publication. Both were published for teaching purposes, like the many theoretical works on civil and military architecture produced by his contemporary, Benedetto Maria del Castrone. Presumably also for didactic purposes Napoli bequeathed 'many architectural images' to the library of his order, but these have disappeared.

Another important figure was Agatino Daidone, an architect and mathematician from Calascibetta, who worked with Napoli on the Villa Palagonia in Bagheria. A designer of bridges and fortifications, a cartographer and an inventor of machines, known abroad through the Austrian engineer Samuel von Schmettau, Daidone published a number of books that show the wide range of his interests. The subtitle of his *Breve Ristretto delli Cinque Ordini dell'Architettura secondo le Regole di Jacopo Barozzi da Vignola, Andrea Palladio, e Vincenzo Scamozzi* (Brief Summary of the Five Orders of Architecture according to the rules of … Vignola, … Palladio, and … Scamozzi) declared that the rules were 'brought together and summarized for the convenience of beginners'. With it Daidone planted himself firmly in the tradition of theorists; but as Erik H. Neil has observed, his architectural training and education remain a mystery.

Paolo Amato continued to work on *La Nuova Pratica di Prospettiva* (The New Practice of Perspective) until his death in 1714. By then his book was already at the printers, but it was completed in 1733 by two publishers, Toscano and Gramignani, who added prefaces extolling its virtues, and a full biography of the author, including a list of his principal works. The title suggests his particular interest in perspective, which he could indulge in his work as architect to the Senate in Palermo, involving temporary architecture and decorations for special occasions, But the subtitle indicates the book's didactic purpose: it was to 'set forth new ideas, and the universal rule for drawing in whatever medium and whatever subject', and to be 'a useful and necessary tool for painters, architects, sculptors and teachers of drawing'.

Giacomo Amato does not seem to have produced a treatise, other than the six volumes of drawings recorded in Catania in the late 18th century, together with many books from his own private library, in the palace of the Paternò family, princes of Biscari. He probably collected them together as a kind of *curriculum vitae* for potential patrons, so that he might aspire to the most prestigious architectural commissions, as well as for teaching purposes. The collection included two volumes of studies made during his time in Rome, together with sketches and designs for buildings, furnishings and decoration. Taken together they demonstrated the breadth and variety of the skills he had acquired – skills that also came from reading numerous treatises, especially that of Vignola, which were present in his extensive library.

Like Giacomo Amato, Rosario Gagliardi left many drawings, now scattered among different collections in Noto and Syracuse. The drawings vary greatly in character, from theoretical studies in black and white to elaborate presentation watercolours. Perhaps the black-and-white studies, which are of religious architecture and include a frontispiece recording the author's apprenticeship with the Jesuits and the date 1726, were intended to act as a kind of treatise, offering models that would be useful for the major rebuilding that was under way in the Val di Noto. Basic to the work as a whole,

The map of Syracuse published by Leanti was drawn by Count Cesare Gaetani, Prince of Cassaro. The Latin key with forty entries proclaims the quantity of important buildings in the city. From *Lo stato presente della Sicilia*, 1761.

opposite Comiso, with the late domes of the Santissima Annunziata and Santa Maria delle Stelle, two of the most protracted and complicated reconstruction projects. The former was inspired by the Neoclassical dome of San Giorgio in Ragusa Ibla (p. 34). Of the latter, with its Gothic features, a detailed drawing exists (see p. 228).

however, were the exercises on the orders of architecture which Gagliardi, who was self-taught, had diligently copied from books, and which he inserted at the beginning of the drawings, arranged in a logical sequence.

Sources were expressly quoted in the margins of the drawings. In a design for a tower-façade for Santa Maria delle Stelle in Comiso – made *c.* 1735 but never realized – Gagliardi includes a note in the left-hand margin indicating the orders of architecture to be used, and quoting Vignola, Michelangelo and Scamozzi. It may have been intended to highlight his own role, but it would also have provided instructions for the workmen, in view of the complexity of the project, with which other architects were later to be involved. Gagliardi repeated the instruction in his drawing for the façade of San Giorgio in Ragusa, there enclosing the orders to be used within elegant cartouches.

In 1755, defending his proposed design for Catania Cathedral, Giovan Battista Vaccarini answered the criticisms of the Senate point by point, citing various authorities including Juvarra (for his works in Turin), Giacomo della Porta, Vignola, Scamozzi and Guarini, and referring to ecclesiastical buildings in Rome, Palermo, Catania itself, and even the Piazza San Marco in Venice. Thus he demonstrated his familiarity with an international body of thought that knew its sources but was absolutely up to date, and his awareness of his own professional role.

But even an unassuming *capomastro,* Giovanni Martinez, in an agreement undertaking to

Drawing by Giovanni Galeoto of the dome of Santa Maria delle Stelle, Comiso, 1894. (Archivo Parrocchiale, Comiso)

build the church of Santa Maria la Nuova in Scicli to the designs of the architect Giuseppe Fama, refers to the authority of Vignola for the architectural orders to be employed in the construction.

The treatise of Giacomo Amico, written in the first half of the 18th century, was the most comprehensive and authoritative in Sicily at the time. Covering as it did both the theory and the practice of building, it became indispensable for training architects. Its teaching involved a process of problem-solving through successive phases, starting with the first book, which taught the theoretical basics with constant reference to 16th- and 17th-century treatises both Italian and foreign (among the latter, particularly those of the Spanish Jesuit architect Juan Bautista Villalpando, and Juan Caramuel y Lobkowitz), all of which he had in his own library.

A whole chapter was devoted to twisted columns, understood as an architectural ornament and called '*torcellate*' or 'Solomonic', following Caramuel, who had used a picture of the Temple of Solomon with twisted columns as the frontispiece of his *Architettura civil recta y oblique*, published in 1678; authorities cited include Vignola (as usual) and the Jesuit architect Andrea Pozzo. The second chapter concerned the putting of theory into practice, specifically in the context of Sicily, taking into account its own traditions, practices, materials and units of measurement, where buildings needed to be resistant to earthquakes. It is in this part of the treatise that Amico makes his most significant contribution, through his practical experience of building. He suggests the best site for a church, for example, in an urban or rural context, and gives guidelines for the construction of a façade or a campanile – a contemporary issue in his time, though with roots in the 16th century. He suggests appropriate models for secular and religious buildings. Staircases of country villas, he writes, should be 'of various forms, allowing for plenty of eccentricity within the art, but always considering their function as an ornament of the façade of the house'; of grand staircases in town palaces, he writes: 'the staircase is perhaps the most important part of the whole building, and as such the architect must give it his fullest consideration, for the magnificence of the palace may depend on it'. These observations are borne out in the reality of Sicilian architecture, and show how new ideas left their mark on the culture of the time.

To help realize these ambitious aims, the large libraries of the religious orders, to which many Sicilian Baroque architects belonged, gave ample opportunity for the study of architecture.

In general architects had their own libraries as well: details have sometimes been found by happy chance in wills. Giacomo Amato had a library of three hundred volumes, including various editions of treatises by Vitruvius, Alberti, Leonardo, Vignola, Palladio, Scamozzi and others, a 'selection of various small temples' by Giovan

228 Theory and practice: from the book to the building site

Battista Montano, the *Vite* of Bellori, the *Perspectiva* of Andrea Pozzo, prints by Domenico De Rossi and books by Carlo Fontana, as well as religious, literary, historical, philosophical and medical texts, works on geometry, and collections of illustrations of 'ornaments on ancient and modern buildings in Rome'. Naturally the collection also included his own drawings.

After Amato's death, the drawings were sold, together with some of his books, by Ferdinando Lombardo, one of his pupils and possibly a beneficiary of his will, to a certain 'Rev. D. Giovanni Gerardi, commander of the Holy Inquisition in the town of Regalbuto', as recorded on the parchment binding of the drawings. From there, perhaps through Francesco Battaglia, who came up against Ferdinando Lombardo in the matter of designs for the Chiesa Madre, the drawings came into the hands of the princes of Paternò in Catania, for whom Battaglia had designed the Palazzo Biscari. Other books were purchased by an English architect working in Palermo, Charles Miller.

The library of Carlo Infantolino, a pupil of Paolo Amato active in Palermo between 1710 and 1731, numbered over eighty volumes at the time of his death. That of Giovanni Amico was much larger, numbering more than four hundred books contained in four bookcases, including treatises, works on civil and military architecture, books about mathematics, and above all religious works; among the architectural works in the 'second chest' was 'a small paper-bound volume of the architecture of Fontana', perhaps indicating a closer connection with Rome, its architects and its major building sites. Various drawings are listed in the inventories of Amato and Amico; in the case of the latter they are classified under the headings of architecture and painting, in separate files.

The library of Francesco Paolo Labisi (now in the Biblioteca Comunale in Noto) contained a translation of the Latin treatise of the German philosopher and mathematician Christian Wolff made in 1746 by Francesco Maria Sortino, who styled himself 'professor of philosophy, mathematics and the fine arts'. The study of mathematics and geometry was indispensable for the invention and construction of complex churches with central plans – oval, elongated octagon, Greek cross, and many variations on these – of the kind built especially in the Val di Noto by Rosario Gagliardi and his school.

In the second volume of his treatise, published in 1750, Giovanni Amico writes about the intended interior arrangement of a palace which was to be 'in the traditional Sicilian style' and about the owner of the palace, who was a lover of books: 'Seeing as he owns many books, the library could also be on the *piano nobile*, or perhaps it might be on a mezzanine level, with a secret staircase leading to it from a room close to the bedchamber of the owner. The library should be somewhere dry, and far away from any noise, which might disturb the quiet that is essential for study.' A small unsigned oil painting in the Civica Galleria d'Arte Moderna 'Empedocle Restivo' in Palermo shows the interior of a library in a private palace. It dates from the early 19th century, so it is post-Baroque, but it is interesting because it shows a space divided into two rooms. The first room is a study. Here the owner of the palace, who has been identified as the poet Giovanni Meli (1740–1815), is shown seated at his desk, intently leafing through a book; there is also a marble bust of him nearby on a pedestal. On the walls, which are covered with striped wallpaper or fabric, various objects are displayed – a large painting with figures, a barometer, and a clock with a pendulum – while paintings of well-known parts of Palermo, such as the seafront and the Royal Palace adorn the area above the doorways leading into the second area. This is the real library, where the valuable books are stacked in rows on shelves. A staircase visible in the background may be a 'secret' one as Amico suggested, linking this part of the house with the private apartment of the owner. The painting recalls the detailed and charming description of the study of the Roman architect Matthia De Rossi who worked with Carlo Fontana, to which attention was drawn by Giovanna Curcio.

Illustrated books stimulated an interest in drawing, a skill which was indispensable to the architect. After copying, he would experiment with variations on the theme, and from there go on new inventions, ready for submission to clients and workshops. Andrea Gigante had a vast collection of books and prints from which he drew ideas; we know this from the French Neoclassical painter Léon Dufourny, who bought some works from the collection in 1789, but who thought that the process led Gigante to design 'confused compositions'. With a solid foundation of cultural theory an architect could reach the heights of his profession and stand out among his many competitors; and the publication of one's own treatise greatly enhanced one's professional prestige.

The circulation of images

From the inventories of public and private libraries – so far only partly explored – it is possible to discover the sources behind projects, especially behind decorative schemes, even if only one book of drawings is listed, or a few loose sheets of drawings, perhaps straight from the studio. The fact that they were so useful is one of the reasons for the disappearance of so many of the relevant books, engravings and drawings from workshops the moment the job was finished. Perhaps this was the prerogative of the favoured few, who could thereby keep themselves ahead of the fierce competition.

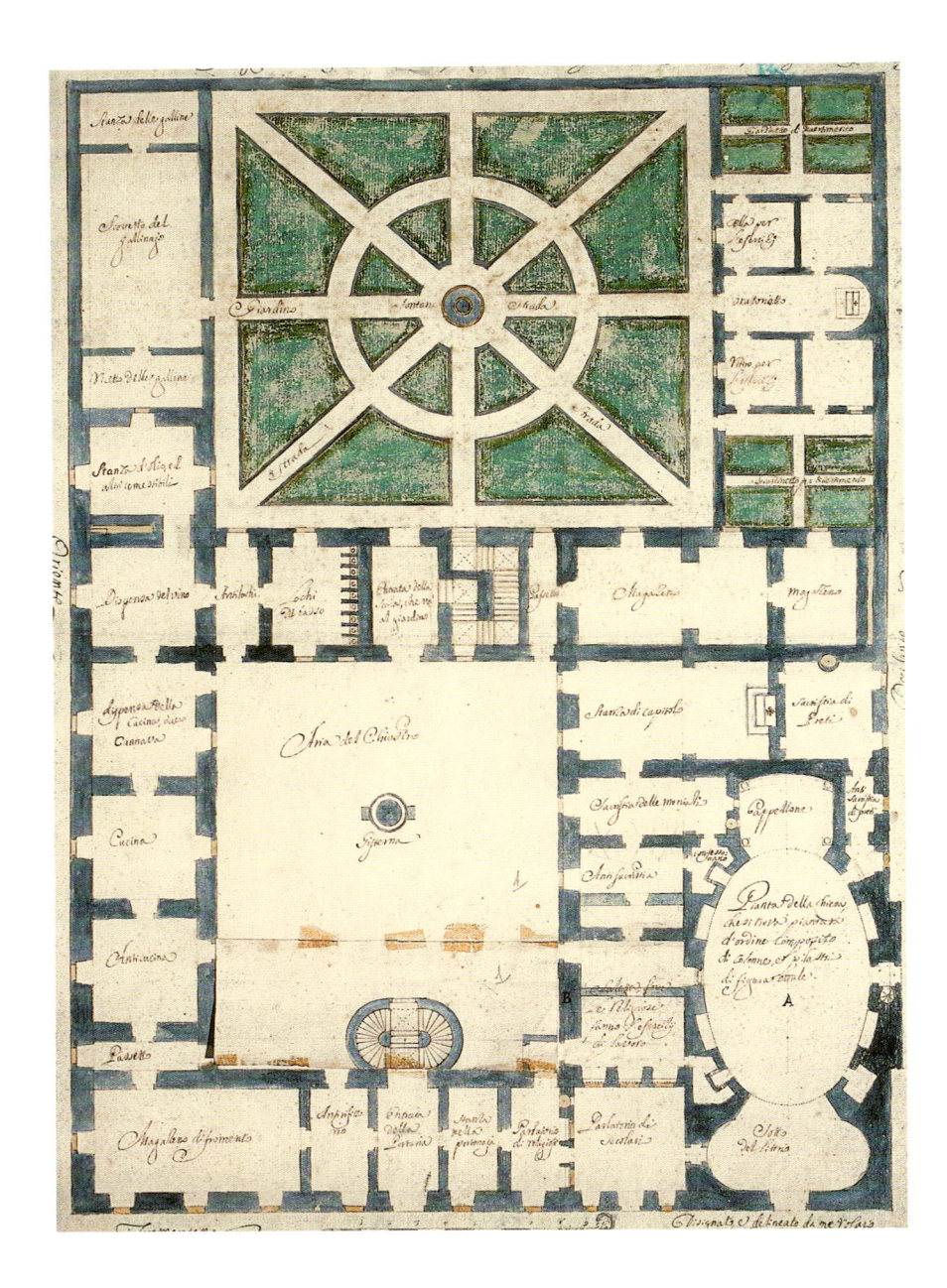

In places that 'books' had not yet reached, people would look to their own past experience for inspiration. An instance of this is recorded in a document concerning Cattolica Eraclea, which was a new town, founded by *licentia populandi* in 1610 on the estates of Don Biagio Isfar e Corilles, Baron of Siculiana. In 1668 it was suggested that a building in Palermo, the church of Sant'Antonino 'outside the gates', should be used as the model for the town's Chiese Madre, the Spirito Santo. The choice of that particular model was made for both typological and planimetric reasons, as it suited the needs of the church and the site. This is a good example of the ripple effect by which ideas spread from the major cities to outlying areas, often transmitted by masters working on several sites. An agreement was drawn up between the contractors – Antonio Battaglia of Palermo and Scipione Magni of Cattolica – and representatives of the church, under the terms of which the design was to be submitted for approval to the latter, who would be responsible for supplying the materials required. Technical supervision, and measurement of the work, was entrusted to one Carlo 'manusanta' (a nickname meaning 'holy hand', indicative of his reputation), who was in charge of the buildings of Palermo; alternatively, according to other documents, if he was too busy on other projects, responsibility would pass to another master chosen by the clients.

The use of existing buildings as models seems to have been common practice at least from the end of the 15th century, whether in verbal agreements or in contracts drawn up by notaries; there is certainly evidence of this in documents relating to the works of Matteo Carnilivari. The use of models based on architectural theory naturally came later, and coincided with the availability of printed works with illustrations, which came into circulation in the 16th century. Both types of model were only used as a point of departure: they were always modified in new ways, with different emphases, by architects who could contribute their own knowledge and experience, or

left Plan of the complex of Santa Chiara in Noto, with its oval church, by Rosario Gagliardi, first half of the 18th century. Gagliardi's signature appears at the bottom right edge. The generic character of this drawing did not allow him to show the columns along the inner walls of the church, which appear in a plan he drew of the church alone, in the Di Blasi collection. (Biblioteca Comunale, Noto)

opposite Section and elevation of the house and church of the Crociferi in Noto, including a detail of the cornice, by Francesco Paolo Labisi, 1750 (see also p. 165). (Biblioteca Comunale, Noto)

230 *Theory and practice: from the book to the building site*

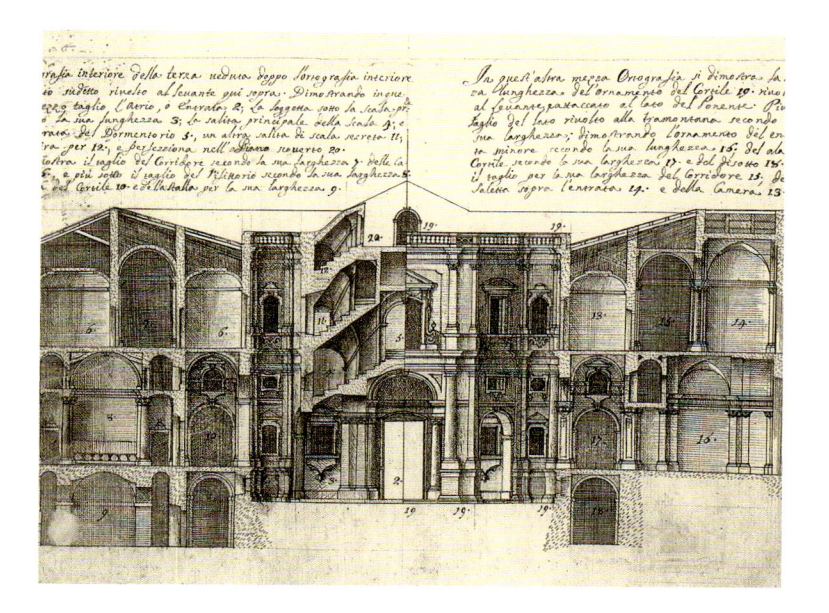

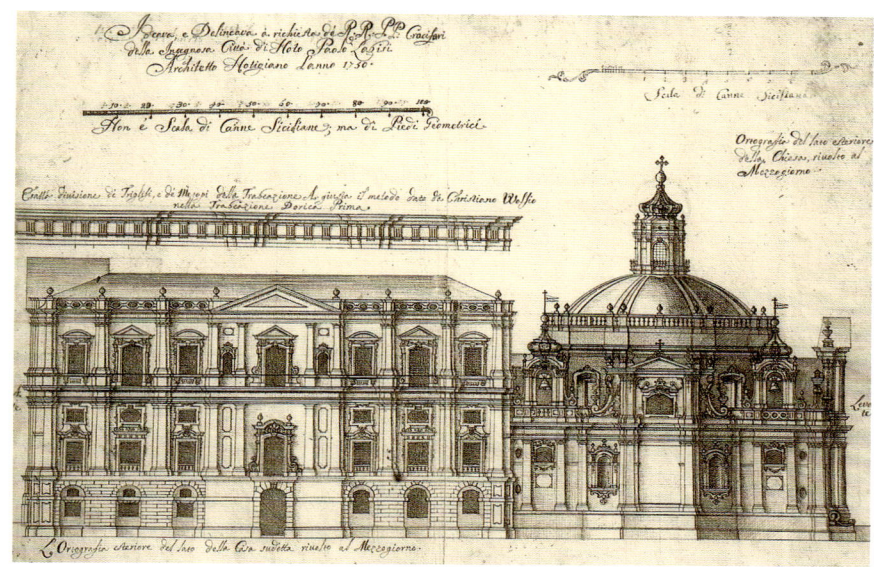

in response to the specific character of the local stone. Echoes and variations on a theme, a dialogue between architecture and decoration and between 'order' and 'dis-order', created a rich and varied panorama, characterized by the continual reinvention of the image, with results that were carried all over the world, as far as the vast territories of Latin America.

All of the above holds true for the whole of the island, an extensive geographical area, but studies on the circulation of architectural models conducted to date have concentrated on the Val di Noto in the 18th century, where both the quantity and the quality of the rebuilding offer a rich field for investigation. The purpose of using a model was not to make a slavish copy, but to use it as a guideline for a process of unmaking and remaking, of adapting the various available images in a form of *ars combinatoria*. It was only logical that decoration should play a major role in this process, since it could quickly update a traditional design.

The roots of the theoretical knowledge available at the time lay in the 16th century, chiefly in the many editions of the volumes of the treatise of Sebastiano Serlio, which circulated widely throughout Italy and was liked by master builders for its encouragement of free composition, as opposed to the rules set down by orthodox classicism. The portal of the Palazzo Trimarchi in Castelbuono in the province of Palermo, of 1554, is an early example of Serlian influence, to which Eugenio Magnano has drawn attention: the patron had his own copy of Serlio's *Libro Extraordinario*.

There are models for portals, windows, altars and architectural features in the writings of Domenico Fontana, of 1589, in 17th-century editions of Vignola's *Regola*, and in specialized works by Bernardino Radi, Giovan Battista Montano, Hans Vredeman de Vries, Wenzel Dietterlin, Jean Bérain, Jean Le Pautre and, later, Giovan Battista Falda and Domenico De Rossi (thanks to whom images of Roman Baroque spread throughout Europe), Andrea Pozzo, Gaetano Chiaveri, Giuseppe Galli Bibiena, Filippo Passarini, Paulus Decker, Jörg Herz, Charles-Augustin d'Aviler, Jean-François Blondel, Jean-François de Neufforge, Juste Aurèle Meissonier, Franz Xaver Habermann, and Johann Wolfgang Baumgartner. These and many others have been found in libraries in Sicily, where they would have been used for reference not only by architects but also by craftsmen, especially carpenters and joiners.

Illustrations of famous buildings such as the Escorial, the Belvedere and other famous palaces in Vienna, the Zwinger and the Court Church in Dresden, the Palazzo Ducale of Colorno near Parma, Sant'Ivo alla Sapienza in Rome, and Vaccarini's façade for Catania Cathedral, along with various perspective compositions by Bibiena, all generated repercussions far and wide. Other books that played significant roles are the *Opus architectonicum* of Francesco Borromini, and among works in German, Johann Fischer von Erlach's *Entwurff einer Historischen Architektur*, published in Vienna in 1721, which could be regarded as the first comprehensive history of architecture.

For books and illustrations from distant Europe to have found their way to Sicily, and influenced architectural design there, there must have been people through whom they came. In the absence of much evidence of journeys or contacts, in what direction might we look? In addition to patrons and architects, can we surmise that there were other places and other individuals responsible for the introduction of these materials, produced and published so far from Sicily, and for their rapid diffusion among the many workshops and studios?

We know that the Prince of Villadorata, who commissioned the Palazzo Nicolaci in Noto, went on journeys to Italy and France between 1728 and 1733 from which he brought back books and drawings to furnish a library full of rare editions. On the central bracket of the principal balcony of his palace he placed his own figure, consigning to darkness the architect, who remains unknown to this day.

Masons and decorators, who could not aspire to travel, had to imitate the international style in order to retain their professional credibility. Hence connections were not always made by means of direct contact, but through access to the same sources. There are many unanswered questions in this area, so our interpretation must be largely hypothetical. For example, we may look at the illustrations in Pozzo's *Perspectiva* and compare them to the fictive domes painted in Sicilian churches – in Sant' Andrea degli Aromatari and Santa Ninfa dei Crociferi in Palermo, the Chiesa Madre in Tusa, the Jesuit church in Sciacca, the quatrefoil dome of San Marco in Enna (which recent research has attributed to Agatino Daidone and/or Paolo Amato, who were working there on commission between 1705 and 1708), and the dome crowning the elongated rectangle flanked by chapels of San Giacomo in Ragusa, designed by Simone Ventura from Chiaramonte Gulfi in 1734–36. Similarly, Alexandra Krämer has highlighted the connection between the engravings of the Court Church in Dresden published by Lorenzo Zucchi in 1739 and Paolo Labisi's design for the cathedral of San Giorgio in Modica.

Marco Rosario Nobile has compiled a 'catalogue' of the connections between the compositional and decorative features of buildings in Ragusa and specific motifs in books or engravings. As rare mentions in documents confirm, these models served as references to justify modifications made in the course of building.

What examples can be quoted from this 'catalogue'? If we confine ourselves to doors, windows, columns and decorative motifs in Ragusa, there are definite connections between an engraving by Montano of a door by Michelangelo in the Campidoglio and a window in the cathedral of San Giovanni; between doors and windows by Pozzo and doors of the convent of the Carmine and a small palazzo in the Via Santo Stefano; between bases in a palace interior by Giuseppe Galli Bibiena and details of doors and balusters in the Palazzo Lupis; between decorative details of supports by Baumgartner and the capitals of a portal in the *casino* of the Schininà family; between capitals by Herz and the 'flowing' capitals on the altar of San Biagio in the Madonna dell'Itria; and between doors and windows by Habermann and the carved and painted frames of altars in the churches of the Santissima Annunziata and San Francesco all'Immacolata.

Even in the absence of more precise documentation, the establishment of a fuller and carefully chronological genealogy might identify similarities indicating that the same masters had been at work, while jealously guarding their sources. A building was the product of a master's knowledge, but also of a mingling of that knowledge with traditional ideas and motifs that were full of vitality and constituted a huge cultural network. With geography no longer a boundary, the field was wide open to every innovation and adaptation, and Sicily was like a continent in itself, and an equal to the rest of Europe.

An 18th-century map of the area around Palermo. (Archive, Servicio Geografico del Ejercito, Madrid)

opposite Noto, seen from the terrace of the church of San Carlo.

232 *Theory and practice: from the book to the building site*

Apprenticeship and learning on the job

Theoretical knowledge was all very well, but practical experience was also essential. A solid training in a workshop, usually belonging to a particular family, was the logical first step on the professional ladder. An outstanding example is Filippo Juvarra, who served his first apprenticeship in Messina as a goldsmith and silversmith alongside his father Pietro and his brothers Sebastiano, Eutichio and Francesco before his conversion to the international style of the courts during his stay in Rome. The attention to detail which characterized his work was certainly the fruit of that early training, fuelled by an exuberant imagination and an insatiable intellectual curiosity. To that were added the lessons of discipline and methodology acquired by reading treatises, and by first-hand experience of drawing great contemporary and earlier classical buildings of Rome according to the methods of Carlo Fontana's school. More is known of Juvarra's early apprenticeship than of many others: his youthful activity in Messina produced an array of religious objects in silver, or silver-gilt, in the years 1695–1701: chalices, monstrances surrounded by rays of light, altar frontals, candelabra, all rich with decoration learned in the family workshop, Baroque in style, yet reinvented with a sensitivity to movement and the play of light. The angels hovering around these objects inspired later designs in which angels are poised beside altars, about to fly off into space, liberating the inert material, as in his drawings for the altar of the church of Sant'Ignazio in Palermo, made in Rome in 1715. The sketches were only partially realized, and not until 1722, in the form of a marble tabernacle by the architect Francesco Ferrigno, a member of a family of builders from Trapani.

In 1703 Juvarra took religious orders, which gave him access to great monastic libraries and the possibility in 1704 of realizing his dream of going to Rome. During those years his knowledge of architecture was deepened through the reading of treatises, particularly that of Vignola, and we know that he studied the syntax and dimensions of the different orders from the evidence of a notebook dated 1709 now in the Biblioteca Reale in Turin. His work was characterized by the ability to reconcile apparently irreconcilable themes, drawing on his experiences in Messina and in Rome, in what his contemporaries saw as a synthesis of intricacy and complexity. Juvarra labelled many of his more than two thousand drawings 'thoughts' – mere sketches, as opposed to designs drawn to scale, sometimes they were just fragments of ideas.

Little is known of the training of other famous architects of the 17th and early 18th century, apart from the profession of their fathers and the odd report of an apprenticeship or period of study under a master, generally connected to their place of origin. The activities of goldsmiths and silversmiths must have been highly regarded in early 18th-century Palermo, if the Consulate was prepared to finance the erection of an enormous solid silver fountain in the Piazza della Loggia on the occasion of the marriage of Charles of Bourbon and Maria Amalia of Saxony.

Paolo Amato, a painter and engraver as well as an architect, had a brother who was choral director in Palermo Cathedral, and uncle of the composer Domenico Scarlatti. He tells us in his treatise entitled *Prospettiva* that he had as pupils Gaetano Lazzara and Carlo Infantolino.

Tomaso Maria Napoli may have been the son of a goldsmith, as some have suggested; whether he was or not, he was well connected professionally in society, and his godfather was a member of the nobility. In 1676 he joined the Dominican order, and benefited from an apprenticeship in Rome, during which time he worked on his treatise, which was dedicated to Carlo Fontana. In Palermo he may have been a pupil of the architects Andrea Cirrincione (1607–83) and Giuseppe Paglia (1616–83). Cirrincione's *ex libris* appears in several 17th-century treatises on architecture now in the Biblioteca Regionale in Palermo; some of them, such as the *Dieci Libri d'Architettura* (Ten Books on Architecture) of Giovanni Antonio Rusconi, had passed to Napoli, whose *ex libris* appears alongside his master's. Paglia was a Dominican friar. In 1682 he returned to Palermo from Rome, where he had been working mainly for the Orsini family, under the watchful eye of Carlo Fontana. Napoli's training, before his major commissions in Palermo and Bagheria, seems to have included a spell in Naples in 1679–80, as well as in Rome, and also, after 1688, various periods in Vienna, Dubrovnik and Hungary.

Giacomo Amato, Erik Neil has suggested, may have been the son of Giuseppe Amato, who was *capomastro* to the illustrious

above and left The towering façade of the cathedral of San Giorgio in Modica dominates the view of the city, proclaiming itself as the most important monument. Its architecture was inspired by the Court Church in Dresden; its sophisticated decorative details probably came from books and prints, but relied on the consummate skill of local masters for their execution.

At the Carmelite complex of the Santissima Annunziata in Trapani, Giovanni Amico's 18th-century design was overlaid on existing medieval structures. (The monastery now houses the Museo Pepoli, with many important holdings.) Engraving from Leanti, *Lo stato presente della Sicilia*, 1761.

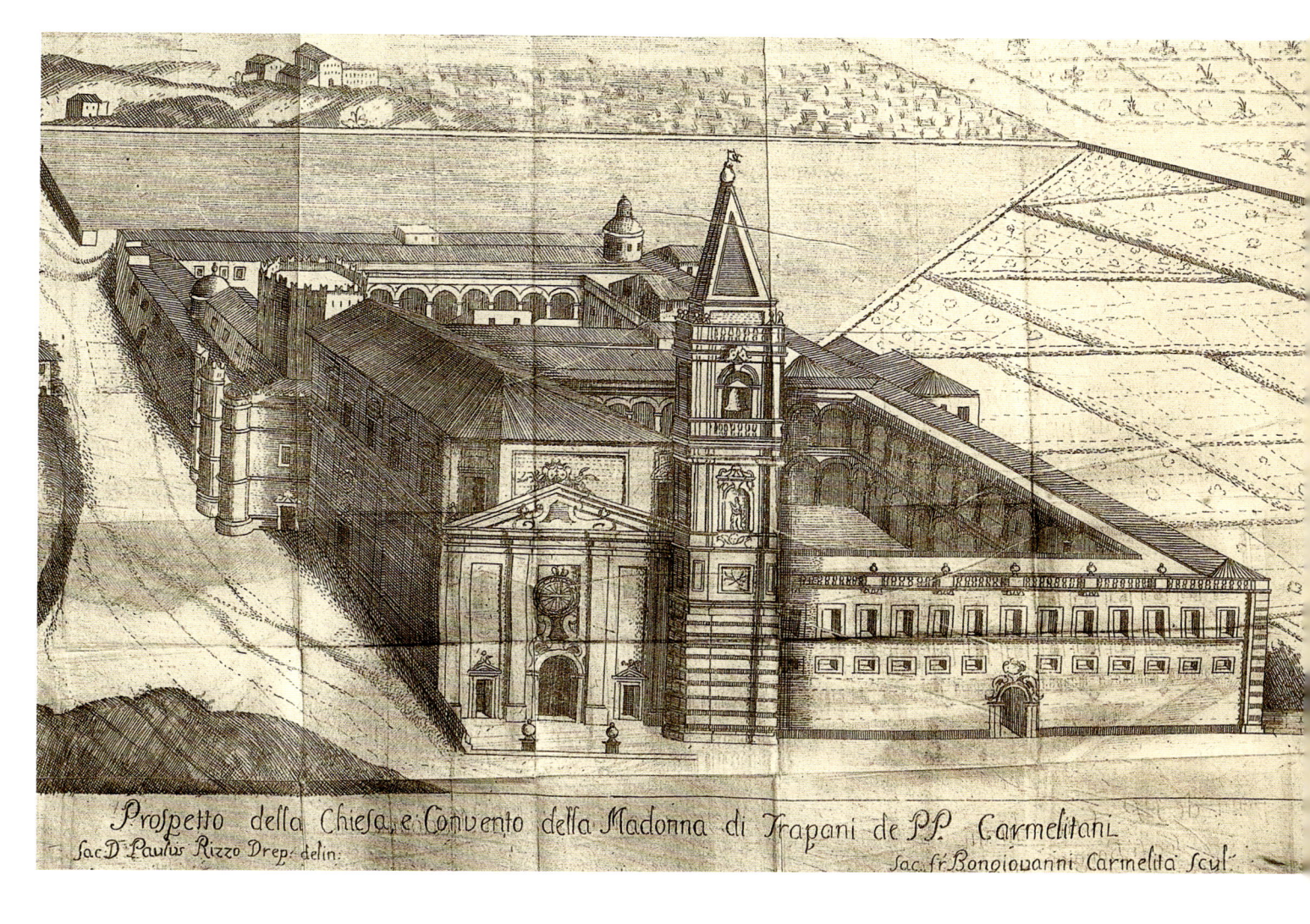

Prospetto della Chiesa e Convento della Madonna di Trapani de PP. Carmelitani
Sac. D. Paulus Rizzo Drep. delin.   Sac. fr. Bongiovanni Carmelita Scul.

Deputazione del Regno in Palermo, and was involved in many projects in Palermo and Bagheria during the second half of the 17th century. Giuseppe oversaw work on the palace of the princes of Cattolica in Palermo, and perhaps because of that the design of the palace has been attributed to Giacomo, but there is no written evidence.

Giovan Battista Vaccarini and Rosario Gagliardi were both sons of *fabri lignarii* (workers in wood) and presumably they began their training in these family workshops. The ability to work with a flexible material like wood and to create models of structures designed by architects would have given them a natural predisposition for a profession where inventiveness had to go hand in hand with technical skill. Vaccarini's family included several different types of artist: a brother-in-law and nephew were architects, while other nephews, a cousin and another brother-in-law were painters, all of them highly regarded in Sicilian society at that time.

Giuseppe Mariani from Pistoia, who arrived in Palermo in the early 18th century after a spell in Rome, came from a family of craftsmen and first worked as a carpenter. He became a follower of Giacomo Amato, as was Ferdinando Lombardo, who came from a family of stonemasons in Palermo – perhaps because they were all members of the order of the Crociferi. Giovanni Amico came from a humble background, and from childhood he served as a sacristan in the church of the Congregazione delle Anime Sante del Purgatorio in Trapani. Judging from the designs in his treatise, which make reference to various buildings in the province of Trapani, he at least had the opportunity to visit and study the surrounding area.

In the case of Napoli, Vaccarini, and above all Amico, their religious connections allowed them to study not only theology but also mathematics, and gave them access to the extensive libraries in the monasteries and colleges (especially those of the Jesuits and Theatines) and to aristocratic palaces in the cities where they lived.

Other architects were associated with Amico for different reasons. Orazio Furetto from Palermo, who is known to have spent two or three years in Naples around 1748, would have met Amico during the competition for the Albergo dei Poveri in Palermo. Andrea Gigante had a Jesuit education; but because like Amico he came from Trapani, his first experience of building, in the 1750s, was on the church of the Santissima Annunziata in Trapani.

Some architects were able to complete their theoretical and practical training with a period in

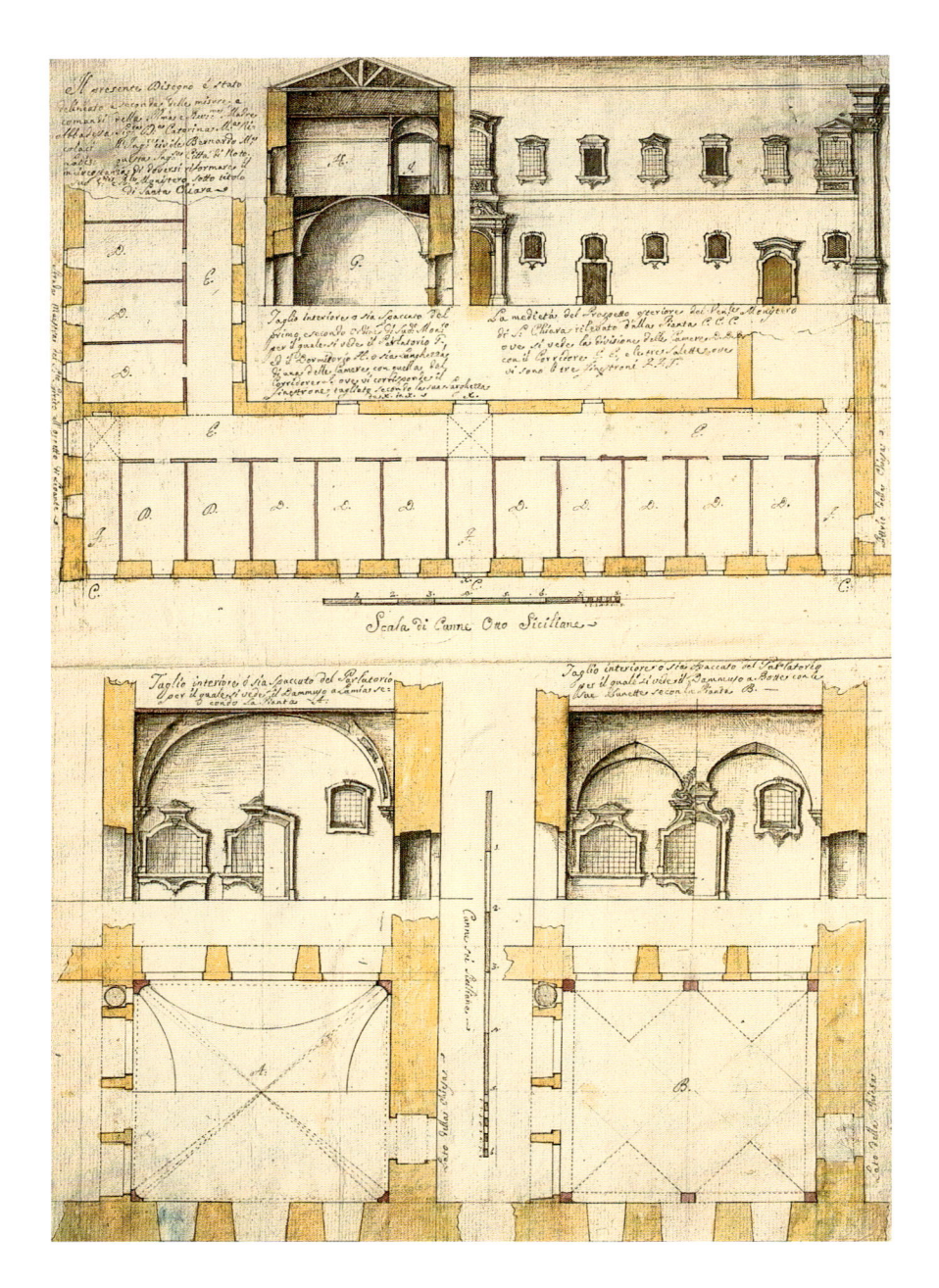

Rome (and, to a lesser extent, in Naples under the Bourbons); however, only two such journeys during the Baroque period are well documented: those of Giacomo Amato and Filippo Juvarra. Natale Masuccio seems to have served an apprenticeship on Jesuit building sites, and Tomaso Maria Napoli is thought to have been a pupil in the studio of Carlo Fontana. It seems certain, though there is no documentary evidence, that Mariani had first-hand knowledge of Roman Baroque buildings and of the publications devoted to them: his most important works – the Villa Aragona and Villa Cutò at Bagheria, and Santi Cosma e Damiano at Alcamo – show clear references to Borromini. In the case of Vaccarini, his most authoritative biographer, Salvatore Boscarino, has suggested a direct connection with the court in Rome of Cardinal Ottoboni, who was a great collector and antiquary, and a great patron of artists, particularly Sicilian ones, many of whom studied at the Accademia di San Luca. Among these was Juvarra. He won first prize in 1705 in the Concorso Clementino, and designed many other projects on a large scale which demonstrate his ability to master great themes and great spaces, while at the same time he was designing scenery for Cardinal Ottoboni's private theatre.

Amato's stay in Rome involved direct experience of the building projects of the Crociferi – primarily in the convent of the Maddalena, where Carlo Fontana and Carlo Francesco Bizzaccheri alternated as directors of the work. Fontana seems to have been responsible for the design of the façade of the church (which was never executed): its classical composition, with a giant order of pilasters and a deep cornice, recalls Michelangelo's designs for the Palazzo dei Conservatori in Rome. Amato kept the project meticulously among his drawings, and may have used it as a model for his entry in the competition for the façade of San Giovanni in Laterano in 1732.

Apprenticeship in Rome made it possible, indeed essential, to study major new buildings there. Amato's drawings include Bernini's Sant'Andrea al Quirinale and Borromini's San Carlo alla Quattro Fontane. Neither would have appealed to his classical taste, and it may be that they formed part of the curriculum of the prestigious

Few detailed working drawings have made their way into archives, because rather than being submitted to the clients they circulated in workshops, and were easily lost. Of those that have survived, two are for the complex of Santa Chiara in Noto. (Biblioteca Comunale, Noto)

left Drawings relating to the monks' dormitory and parlour, by Bernardo Maria Labisi (the son of Francesco Paolo Labisi), second half of the 18th century.

opposite Drawings of the roof of the church, by Rosario Gagliardi, 1740–50.

Accademia di San Luca, founded in 1673, around the time when Amato arrived in Rome. What is certain is that his drawings were made in total ignorance of the sophisticated geometric systems that underlay the buildings, particularly Borromini's San Carlo. Perhaps Amato's two volumes of Roman studies represent the first, as yet unexplored, result of his academic apprenticeship in the 1670s and 1680s under the guidance of Fontana, who was professor of architecture at the Accademia di San Luca from 1675. A direct reference to Fontana in the collection is a drawing of the Palazzo Altieri in Rome.

Amato's drawing instruments were kept in a walnut case, according to the inventory made after his death. As was usual for 17th- and 18th-century architects, they consisted of various types of compasses (including a three-point one), set-squares, rulers and pens.

A close examination of archival documents – not possible in the scope of this book – would shed a great deal of light on the whole process involved in a project, under the guidance of the architect in charge, who would have been an expert in both the theory and practice of construction. He would have drafted the design, supervised the execution of the work, made alterations where necessary, always with the aim of producing a finished product that would be pleasing to everyone, and he would have had authority over all aspects of the work, both construction and decoration. He would have been concerned with constructional details, and would have used the project to experiment with techniques in cases where caution was necessary after an earthquake, as in the Val di Noto. Rosario Gagliardi stressed this in his account of the vaulting of San Michele in Scicli: 'false' domes and domical vaults made of cane and plaster, and therefore light, seemed preferable for reasons of safety, and not just economy. Gagliardi used the same solution for the oval church of Santa Chiara in Noto: two drawings for the plan and transverse and longitudinal sections show the dome to be structurally independent of the roof above it. An unsigned mid-18th-century drawing shows one eighth of the dome of Santissima Annunziata in Ispica.

In his treatise Giovanni Amico says that the architect must have a good knowledge of local building materials, of all the stones and marbles in Sicily, especially those from Trapani, and that they should be used in preference to materials that Sicily could not provide, since those would entail high costs of transportation. The architect should also be an expert in innovative techniques, and should be able to apply them with the help of a good *capomastro*. The presence of Gagliardi and Amico in Palermo at the time of the earthquake in 1726 may have helped both to consolidate their practical experience by repairing the extensive damage to buildings.

Daring solutions in temporary architecture

Temporary architecture, erected on the occasion of a celebration or a funeral, was largely the prerogative of the two main cities of the island, Palermo and Messina. Such celebrations became more and more frequent in the course of the 18th century due to the many royal visits brought about by political events after the Treaty of Utrecht and the rule of Piedmont. Streets were transformed by the use of imagery drawn from books. In Palermo, the decorations of Pietro Vitale and Pietro La Placa on the occasion of the coronations of Victor Amadeus of Savoy and of Charles of Bourbon manifest a desire to renew the city through architecture. Images also survive of events in the 17th century involving towers of fire, street theatres, decorated carts for the festival of Santa Rosalia, and all sorts of ornamental confections, not only in Palermo but also in Messina, which up until the restoration of Spanish rule after the revolt in 1678 had regarded itself as a rival to the political capital, certainly in economic and cultural terms.

The sites chosen were always the most important in the city: in Palermo it was the space in front of the Royal Palace, seat of the viceroys, that in front of the Marina, seat of the Inquisition, the Stradone Colonna, and long streets like the ancient Cassaro, which could accommodate the processions of illustrious royal visitors and the vast crowds that followed the spectacle.

The task of producing ever newer and more varied forms of temporary architecture generally fell to the Senate of the town and to its own architects. In Palermo during the 17th and 18th centuries Paolo Amato, Andrea Palma and Nicolò Palma excelled in both the quality and the quantity of their output in this genre. Other institutions and well-known architects, such as Giacomo Amato and Filippo Juvarra, were also involved in such projects, which not only brought together artists, sculptors and painters (their presence is explicitly noted in the margins of Giacomo Amato's drawings), but also made possible a freedom of composition not readily applicable in permanent architecture, which had to stay firmly in place.

The promoters, be they the municipal senate or the representatives of the viceroy, would use the occasion to celebrate the particular event, but also to induce a collective amnesia with respect to all the problems afflicting the island.

Notable occasions in Palermo were the celebrations surrounding the marriage of Charles II to Maria Luisa of Bourbon (1680), the coronations of Victor Amadeus of Savoy (1713) and Charles III of Bourbon (1735), the marriage of the latter to Maria Amalia of Saxony (1738), the annual festivals of Santa Rosalia with its decorated carts and towers of artificial flames, occasions when architects could let their imaginations run wild, and funeral ceremonies involving magnificent catafalques, such as that for Philip V (1747). All were intended to promote the image of Palermo as 'most happy' – the epithet on its coat of arms – by transforming the existing architecture through drapery and fictive structures and positioning temporary structures around the city.

The interior of the Cathedral was transformed on several occasions for weddings or funerals, as were the façades of many palaces. On the occasion of the coronation of Victor Amadeus of Savoy, Pietro Vitale used ornate and expensive decoration to draw all eyes to the façade of the palace of Baron Tarallo, in the old Cassaro (now the Albergo Centrale).

In 17th-century Messina, on the occasion of the festival of the Madonna della Sacra Lettera the road down which the procession passed would be transformed, a process that involved the best-known architect-painters and architect-sculptors of the city. Nicolò Francesco Maffei, Giovan Battista Quagliata, Leonardo Patè and Giovanni Rizzo were particularly involved in devising ephemeral architecture for the festival in 1657, shortly before Guarino Guarini's arrival in Messina, and their up-to-the-minute designs stood in stark contrast to the real architecture of the city, which was still being built in a late Mannerist style. The festival was recorded by the Dominican friar Alberto Guazzi from Vicenza. Later, in 1701, Filippo Juvarra was in charge of the overall design of the temporary structures erected in honour of Philip V of Bourbon, recorded in engravings by Sclavo.

The ephemeral nature of the constructions allowed even the most traditional architects and the strictest classicists to experiment with daring. They did not need to worry about winning a serious commission, something that characterized the fiercely competitive climate of the Baroque period. They were

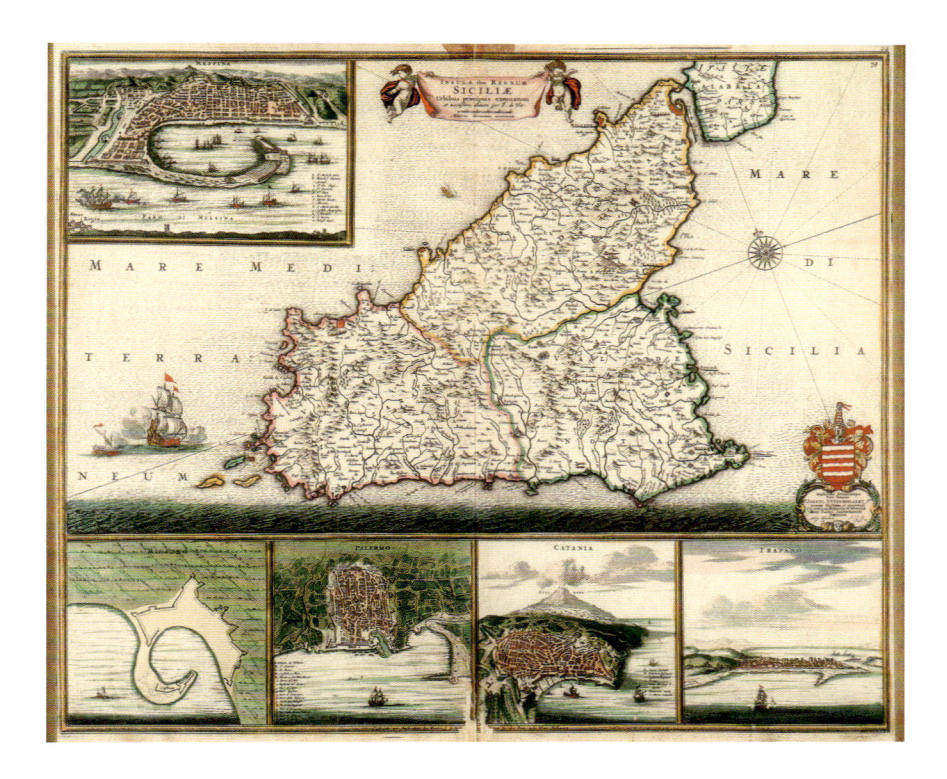

A map of Sicily published by Federico de Wit in Amsterdam, probably at the end of the 17th century. To the map are added images of the most important towns: Messina (two pictures, one mistakenly called Milazzo), Palermo, Catania and Trapani.

liberated from any preconceived ideas and open to any influences from home or abroad. The projects were transitory and reversible, and their audience came from very different cultural and social levels.

The opportunity to use languages other than those firmly rooted in the traditions and experiences of the architects in their normal professional work had some magnificent results: such were the ephemeral confections produced by the classicist Giacomo Amato in the courtyard of the Royal Palace for the Viceroy Juan Francisco Pacheco, Duke of Uzeda, in the 1690s for the festivals of Corpus Domini, which were characterized by an abundance of garlanded twisted columns, perhaps echoes of Spanish models. In his choice of designs Giacomo Amato must have been influenced by his collaboration with the sculptor Pietro Aquila, and also by his knowledge of contemporary works by Paolo Amato and Giacomo Serpotta.

In his design of 1713 for a new triumphal arch on the Strada Colonna in Palermo, Paolo Amato reworked and elaborated the twisted columns and exuberant decoration seen in his built works. Other designs for triumphal arches, however, such as the one devised by Andrea Palma in 1713 for the 'foreign nations' (the Milanese and Genoese) and that of 1735 by Nicolò Palma, explored new ideas involving detached columns and broken pediments, and the relationship between structure and space.

The insertion of trophies, reliefs, statues, tablets with medallions, emblems, paintings, and portraits of the ruler, and the possible extension of an existing structure by the addition of concave wings (as Nicolò Palma did in 1681 to Paolo Amato's marble theatre in the Stradone Colonna, to make it look modern and festive) – all are expressions of the uniquely Sicilian tendency to transform architecture through decoration. Two good examples of this, both at crucial junctions in Palermo, are the Porta Felice and the Quattro Canti, both realized by architects working for the Senate.

Nicolò Palma's designs for temporary architecture on the occasion of festivities in 1735 and 1738 are surprising both in their modernity and in the variety of typological and compositional elements, which differ from what is known of his professional work (admittedly little): there we find imposing temples using the five orders and surmounted by domes, amphitheatres with loggias, and catafalques in the form of circular temples. The character of those projects, taken together with that of his temporary constructions, and the documentary evidence that is beginning to emerge of his presence on various building sites, make Nicolò Palma someone who is definitely waiting to be discovered.

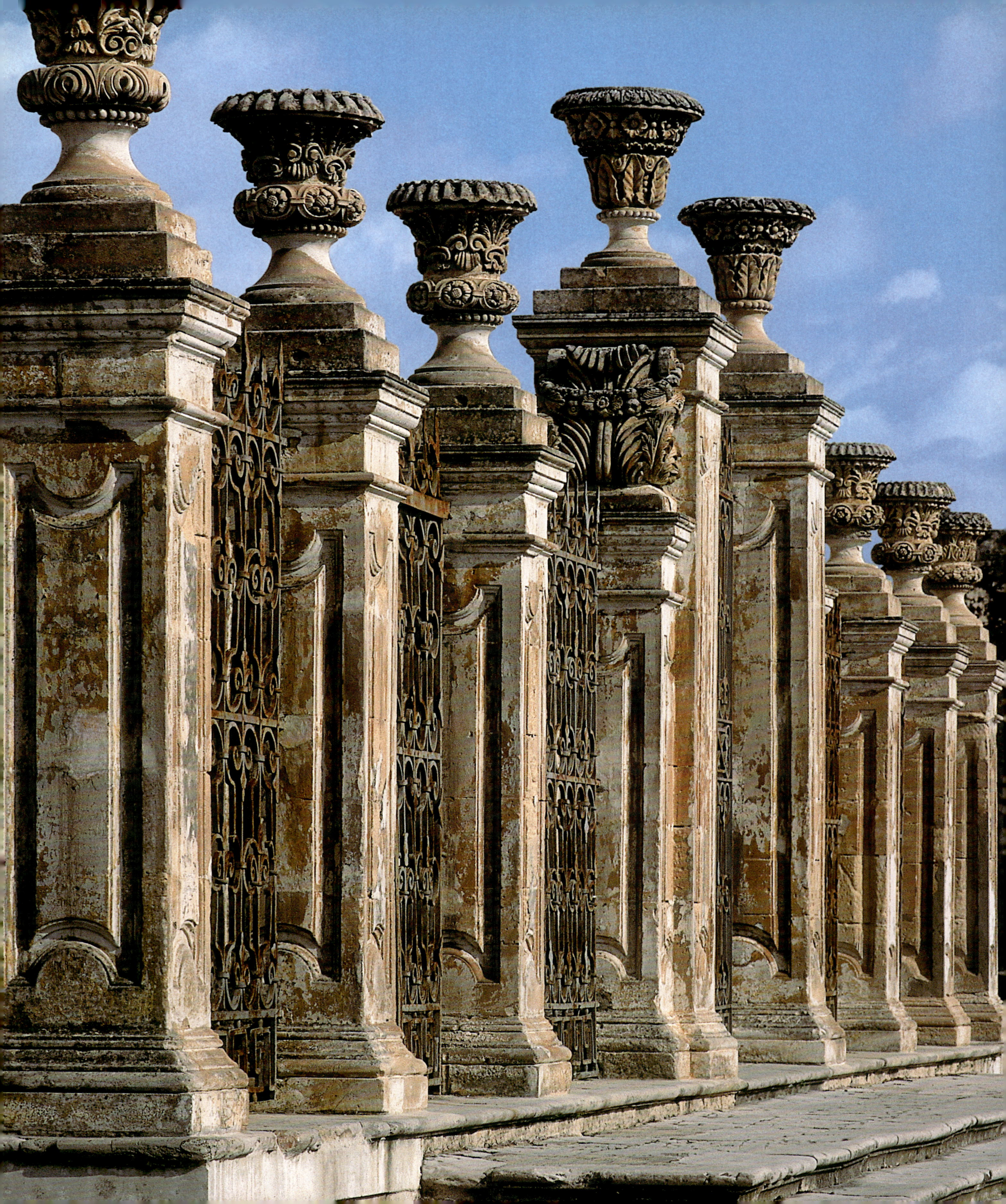

opposite The semicircular forecourt of the church of Santa Maria Maggiore in Ispica has impressive gates set between piers topped by vases.

right San Sebastiano in Palazzolo Acreide vies with San Paolo for supremacy in the town. Lions are positioned in front of the richly decorated columns of the portal.

left the church of the Concezione al Capo in Palermo is decorated with a riot of coloured marbles, even in the twisted columns.

opposite detail of the twisted columns of the portal of the church of the Annunziata in Palazzolo Acreide.

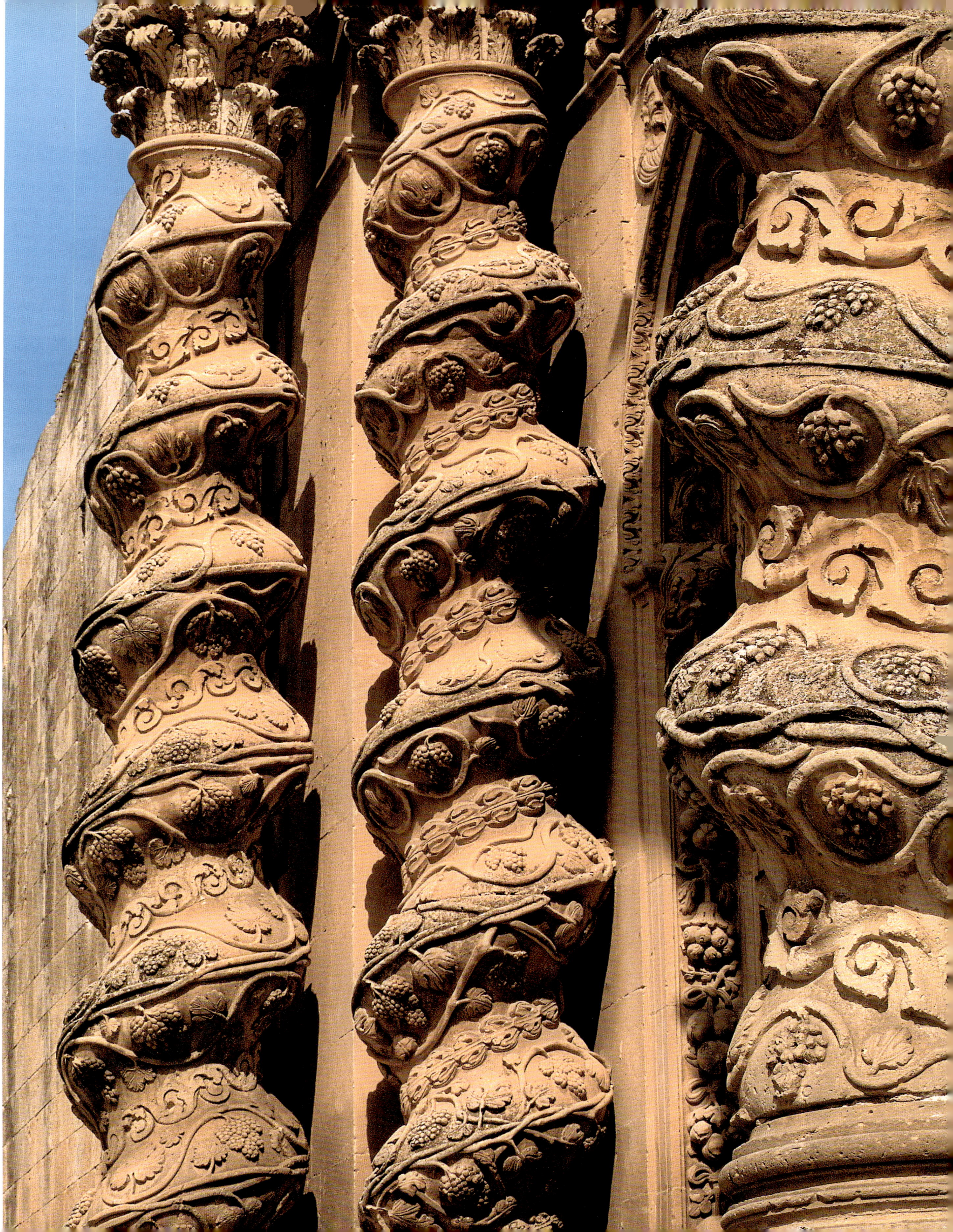

Detail of the twisted columns decorating the portal of the Jesuit church at Salemi, in the province of Trapani.

opposite The campanile of the church of San Giuseppe dei Teatini in Palermo, by Paolo Amato, was left unfinished. The dome beyond is by Giuseppe Mariani, of 1725.

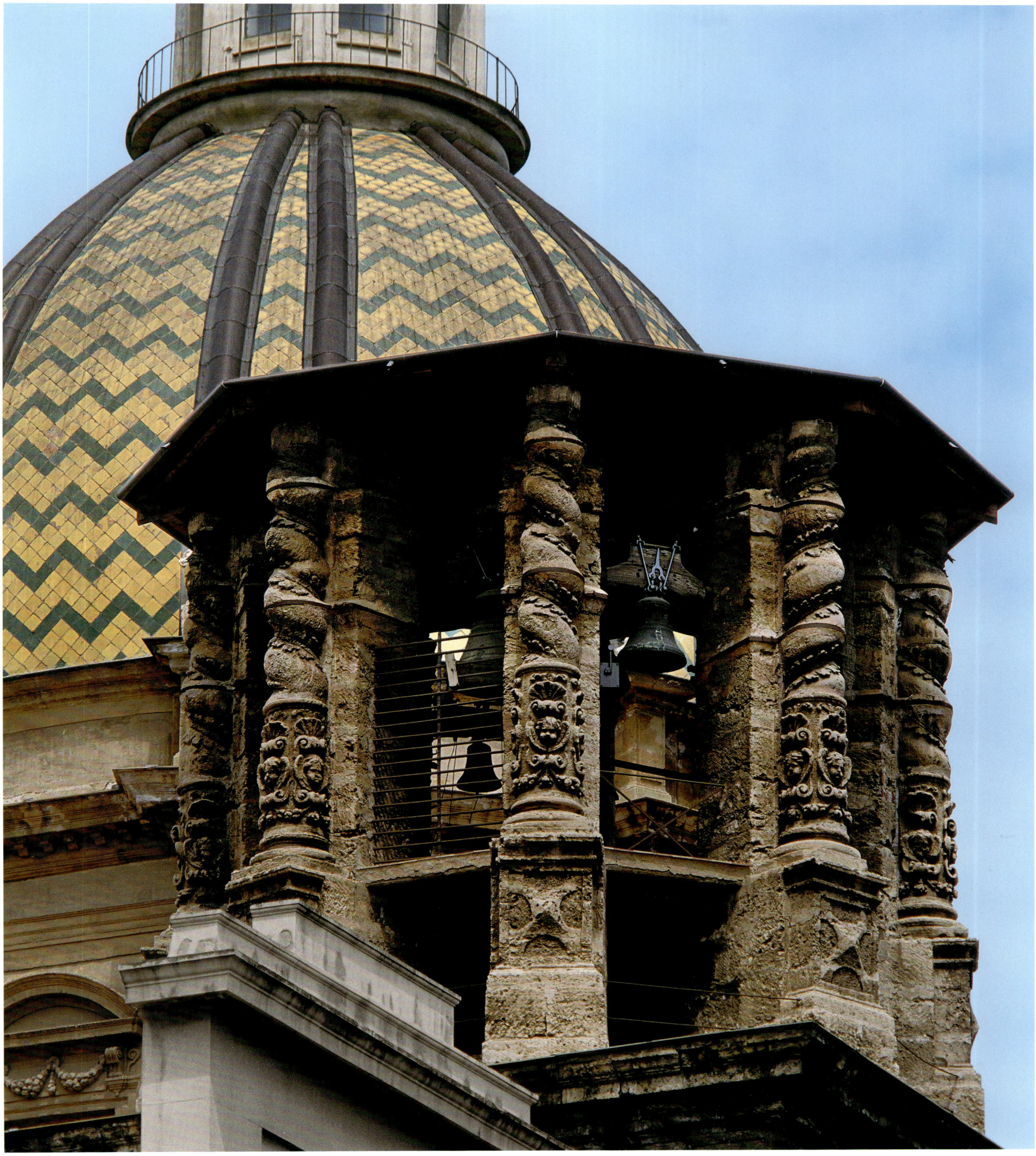

left The façade of Syracuse Cathedral, with its imposing columns, is attributed to the architect Andrea Palma from Trapani.

opposite The sculptural but unfinished façade of the church of Sant'Antonio Abate, Buscemi.

overleaf, left The lantern of the dome of the church of the Annunziata, Comiso.

overleaf, right Detail of the portal of San Sebastiano, Ferla.

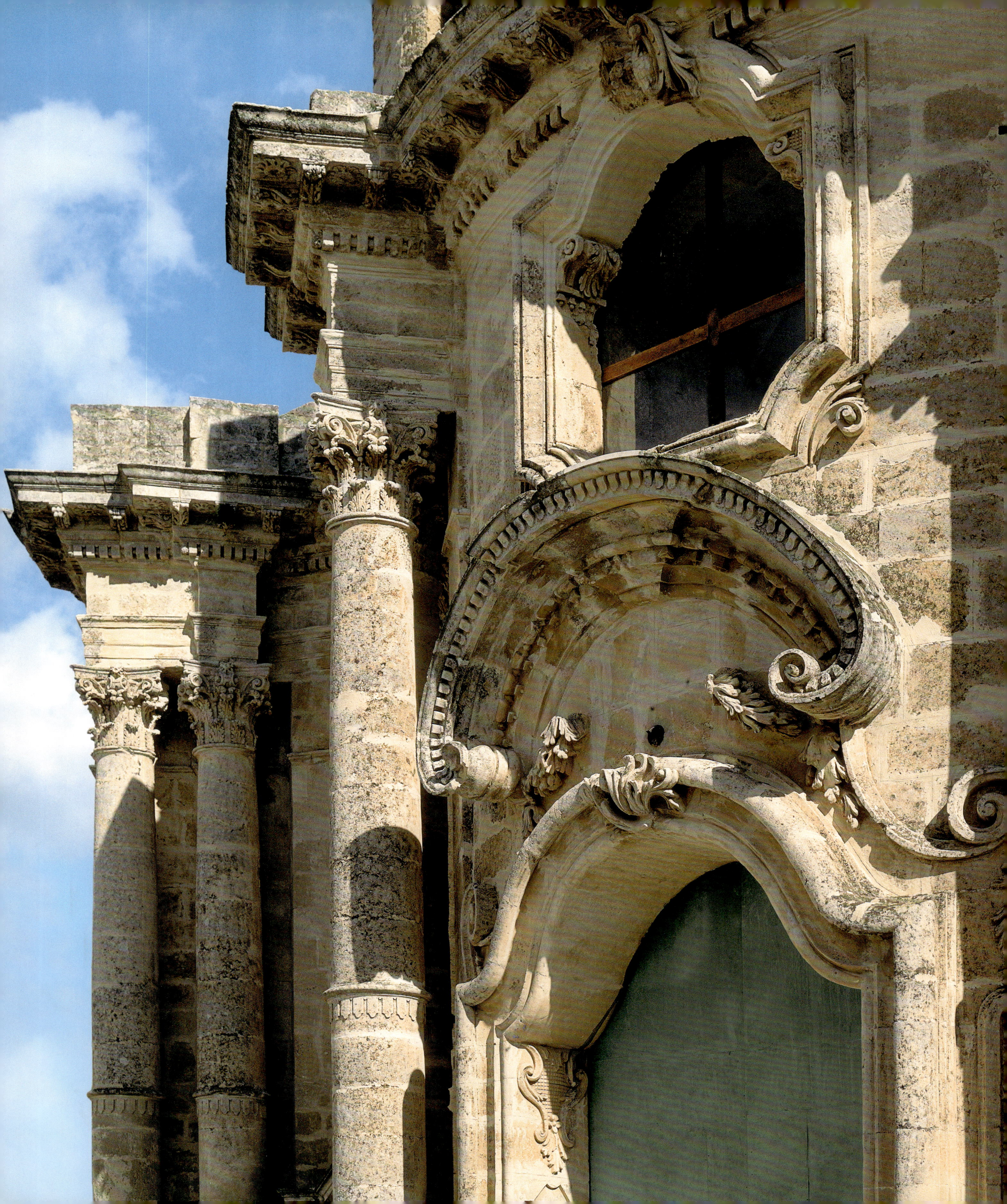

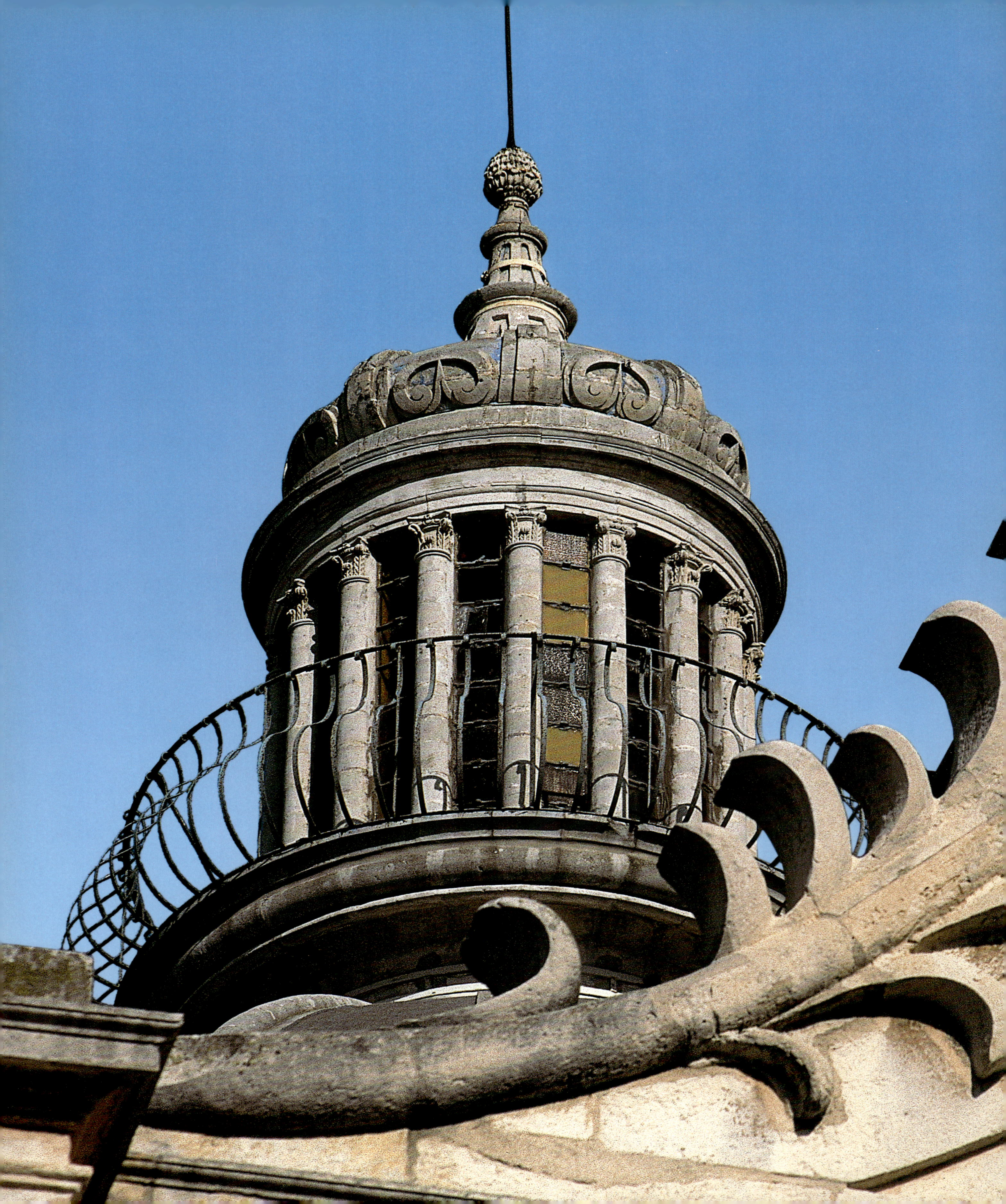

Theory and practice: from the book to the building site   249

left Detail of the highly decorated portal of Santa Maria Maggiore at Nicosia.

opposite Decoration above the portal of the cathedral at Mazara del Vallo.

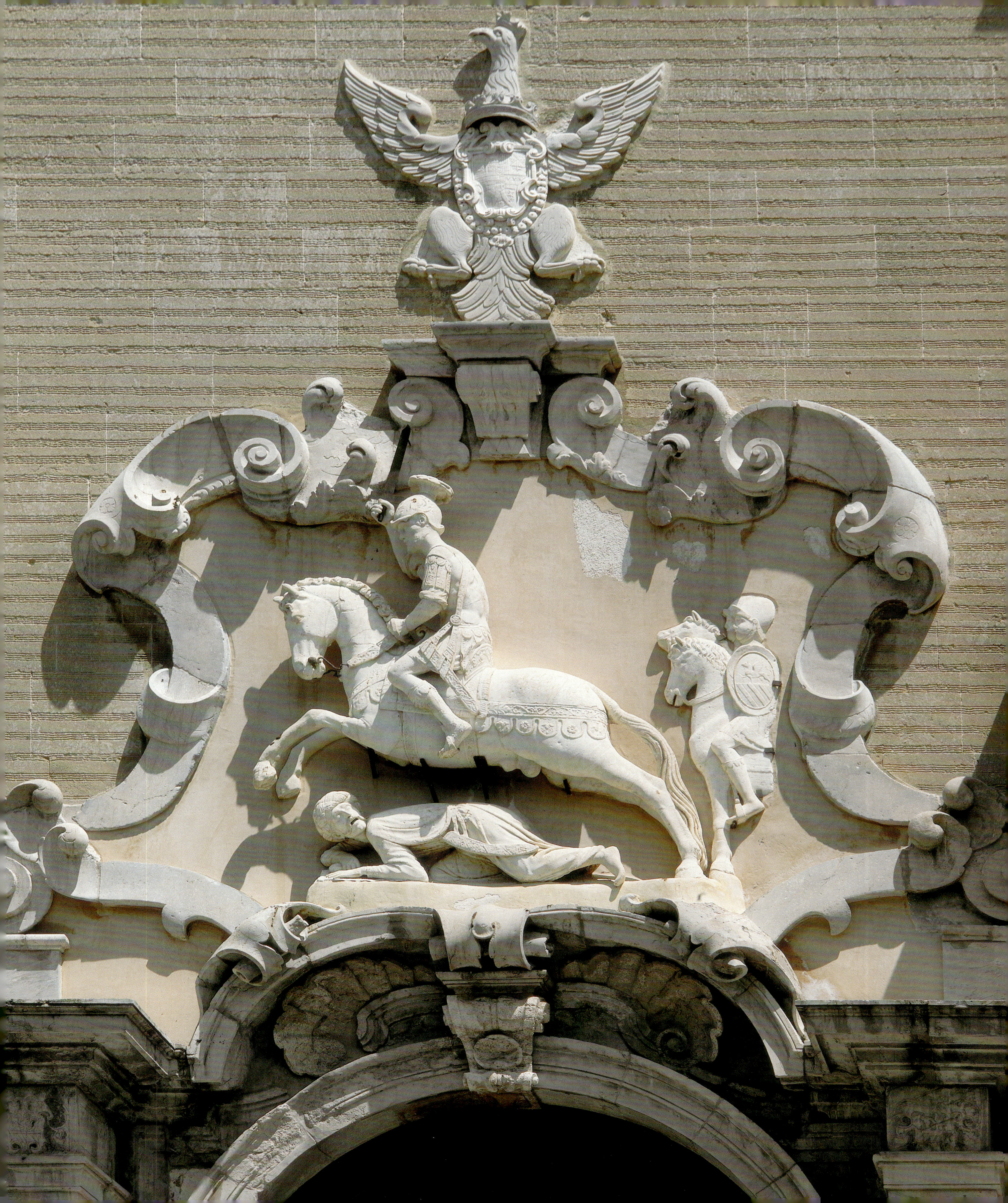

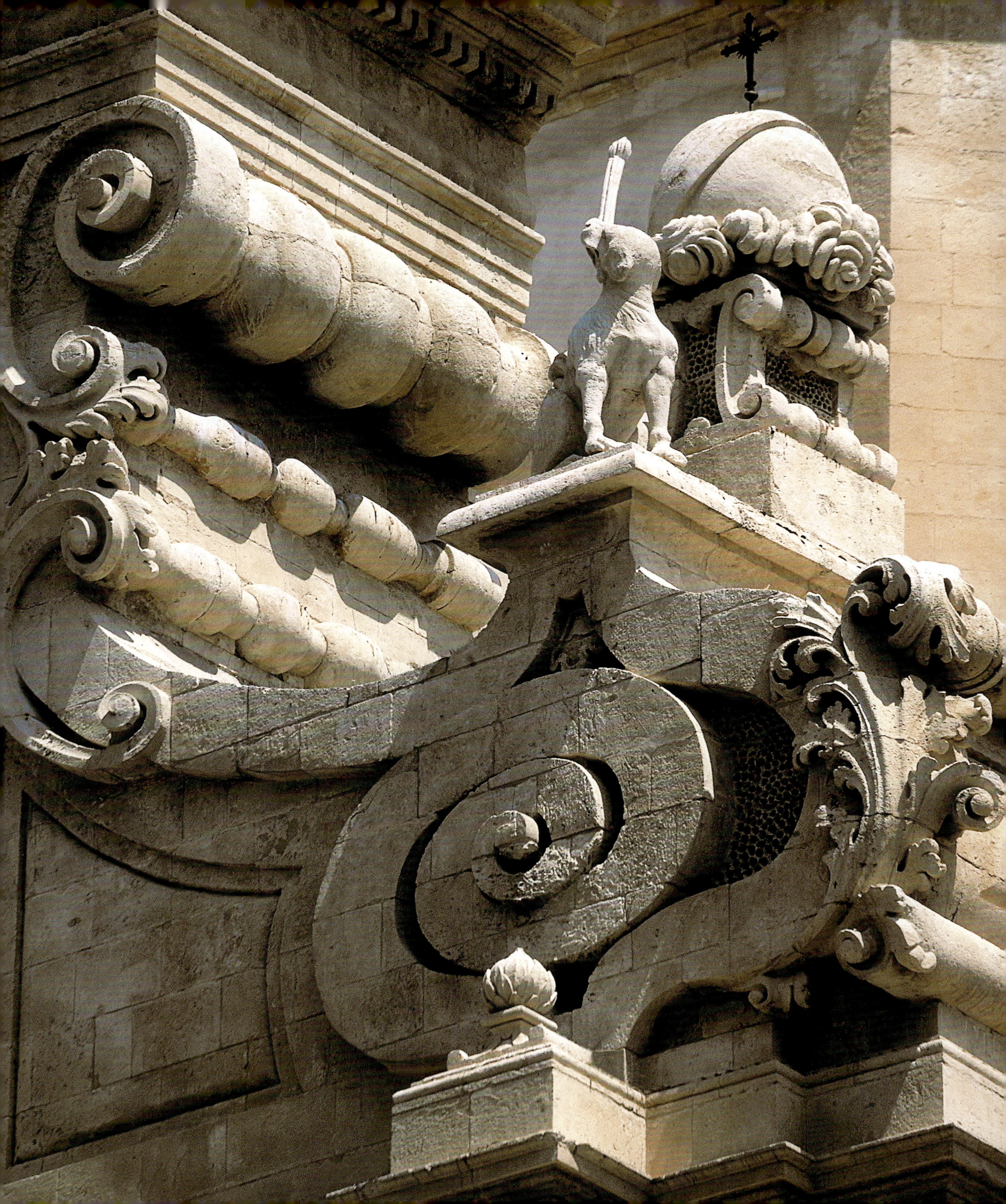

opposite Decoration on the upper part of the façade of San Domenico, Noto.

right Detail of the façade of the Chiesa Madre, Leonforte.

Theory and practice: from the book to the building site 253

below An angel offers holy water to the faithful in San Giuseppe dei Teatini, Palermo.

right Marble putti support the chancel rail in the church of the Gesù in Monreale.

overleaf, left Marble bust of St Colomba in a chapel in Santa Caterina, Palermo.

overleaf, right Detail of the stucco portal of the church of the monastery of Santa Caterina, Mazara del Vallo.

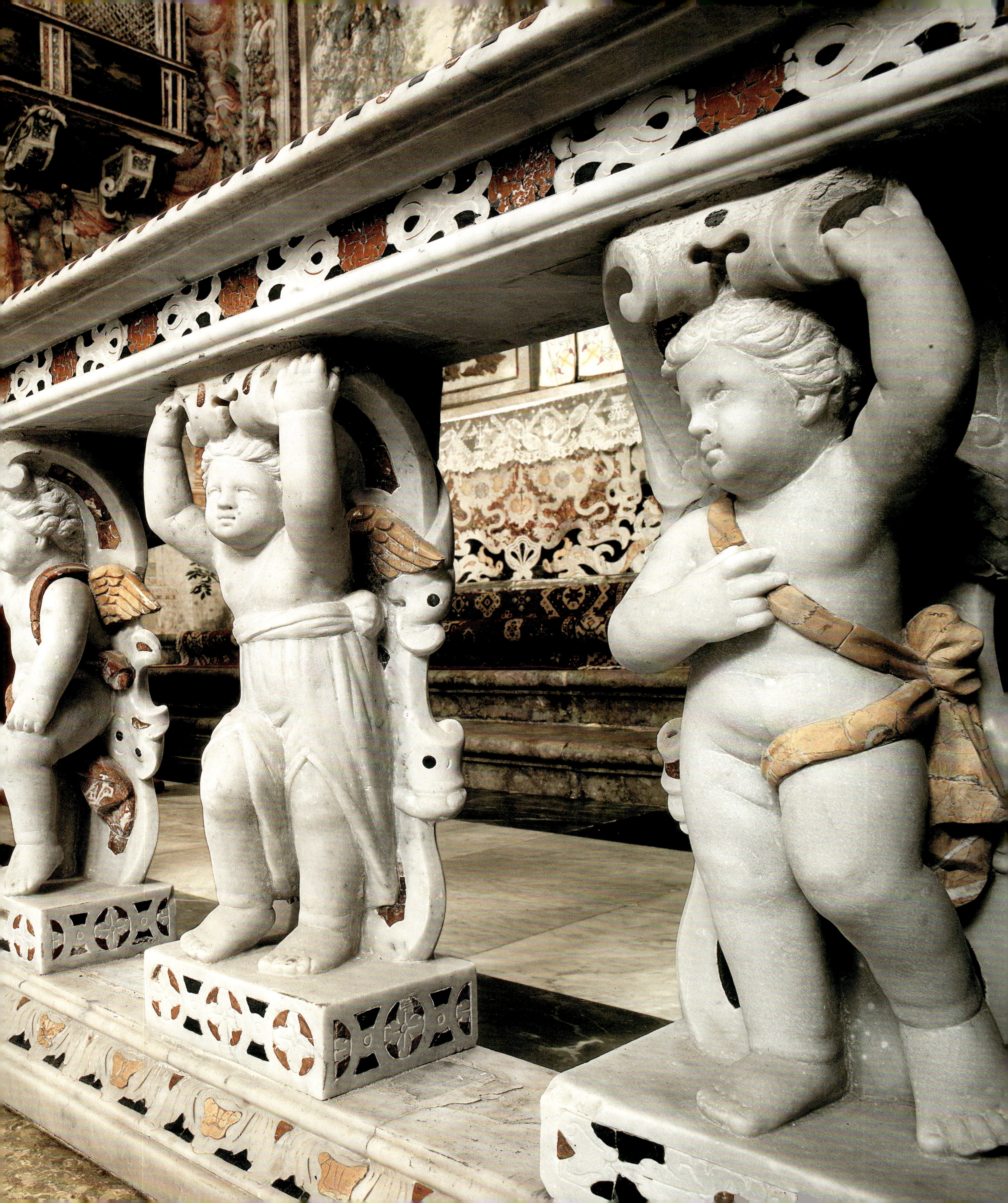

B. COLOMBA DI RIETI

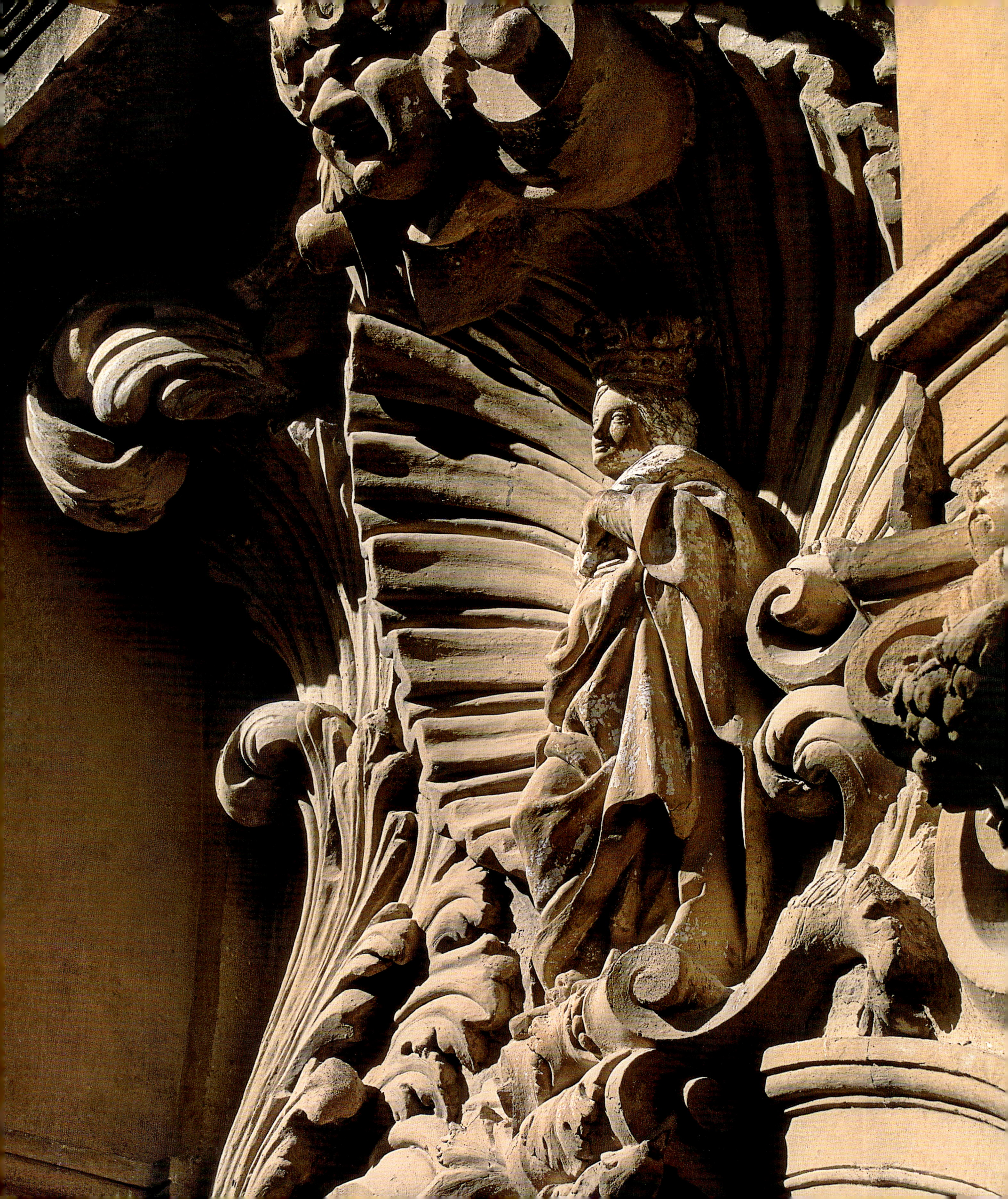

S. BARTOLOMEO

opposite Steps bearing statues of the twelve apostles lead up to the church of San Pietro in Modica.

right The façade of the church of San Giuseppe in Ragusa Ibla is decorated with statues on both sides.

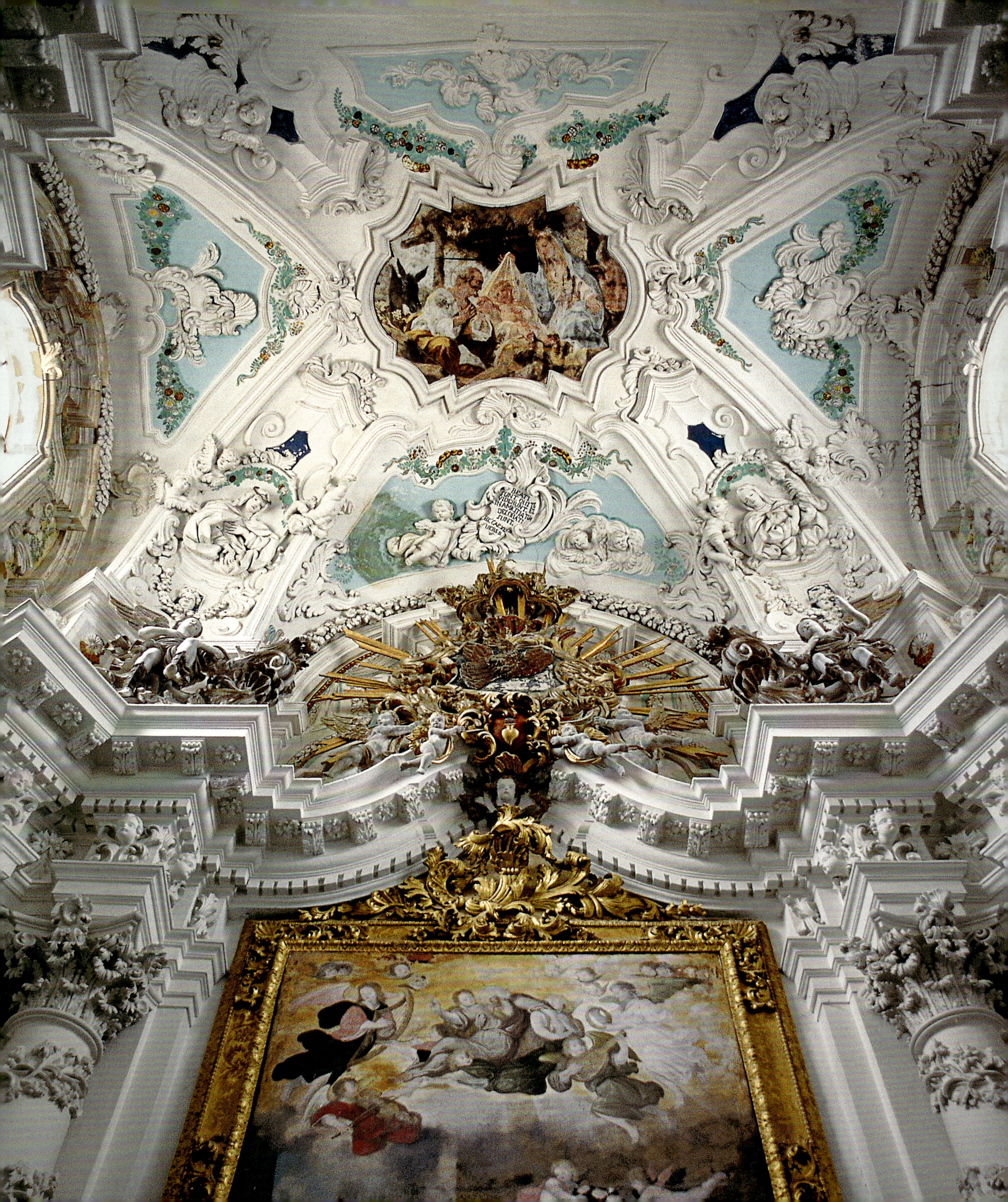

opposite Stucco decoration in Sant'Antonio, Ferla.

above Some of the 'monsters' carved from tufa which adorn the outer courtyard of the Villa Palagonia, Bagheria.

Detail of the extraordinary stucco decoration of the Oratorio del Rosario in Santa Zita, Palermo, a masterpiece by Giacomo Serpotta. The scene here commemorates the naval victory of Lepanto in 1571.

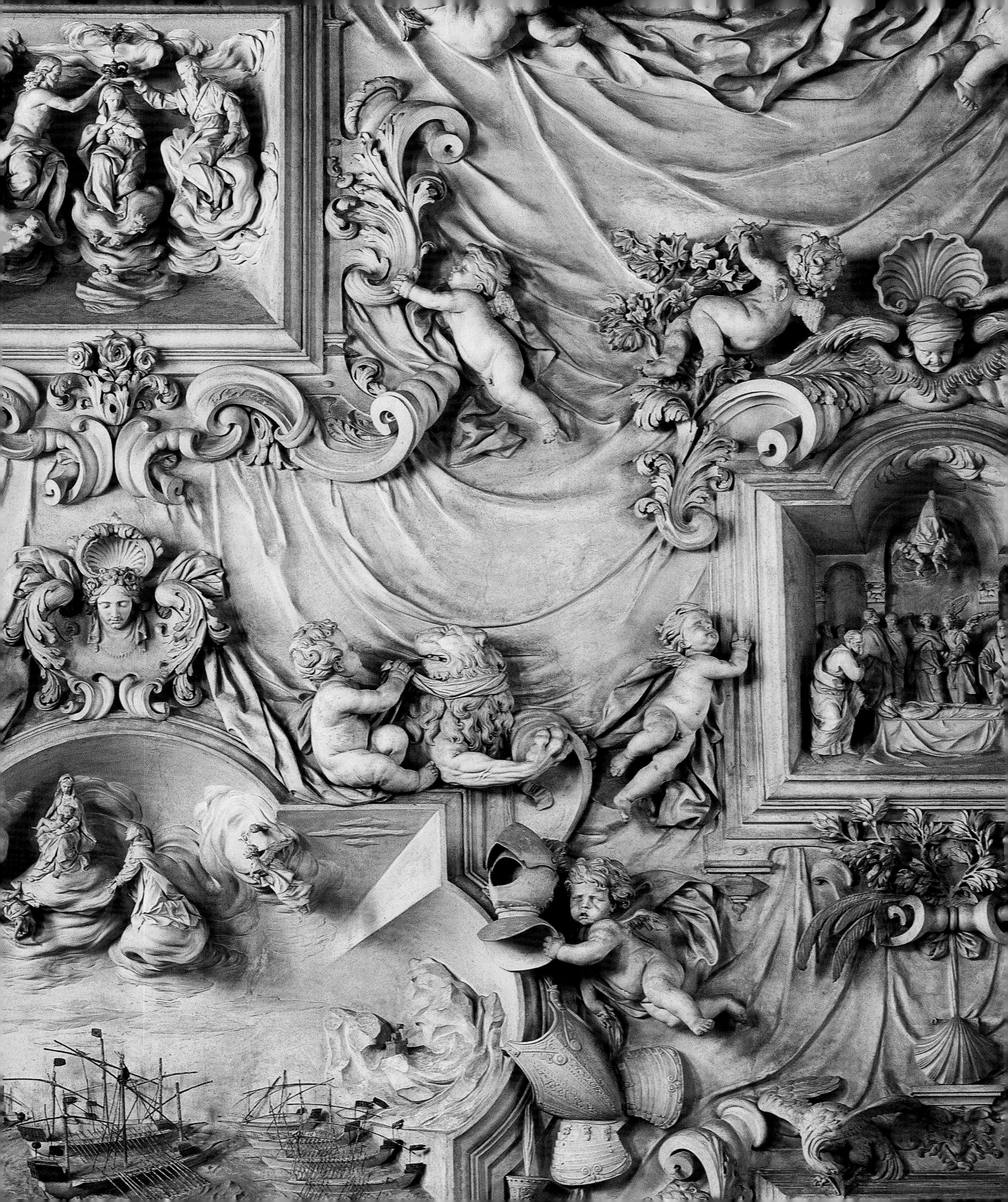

Detail of the magnificent decoration in the sacristy of the cathedral at Enna.

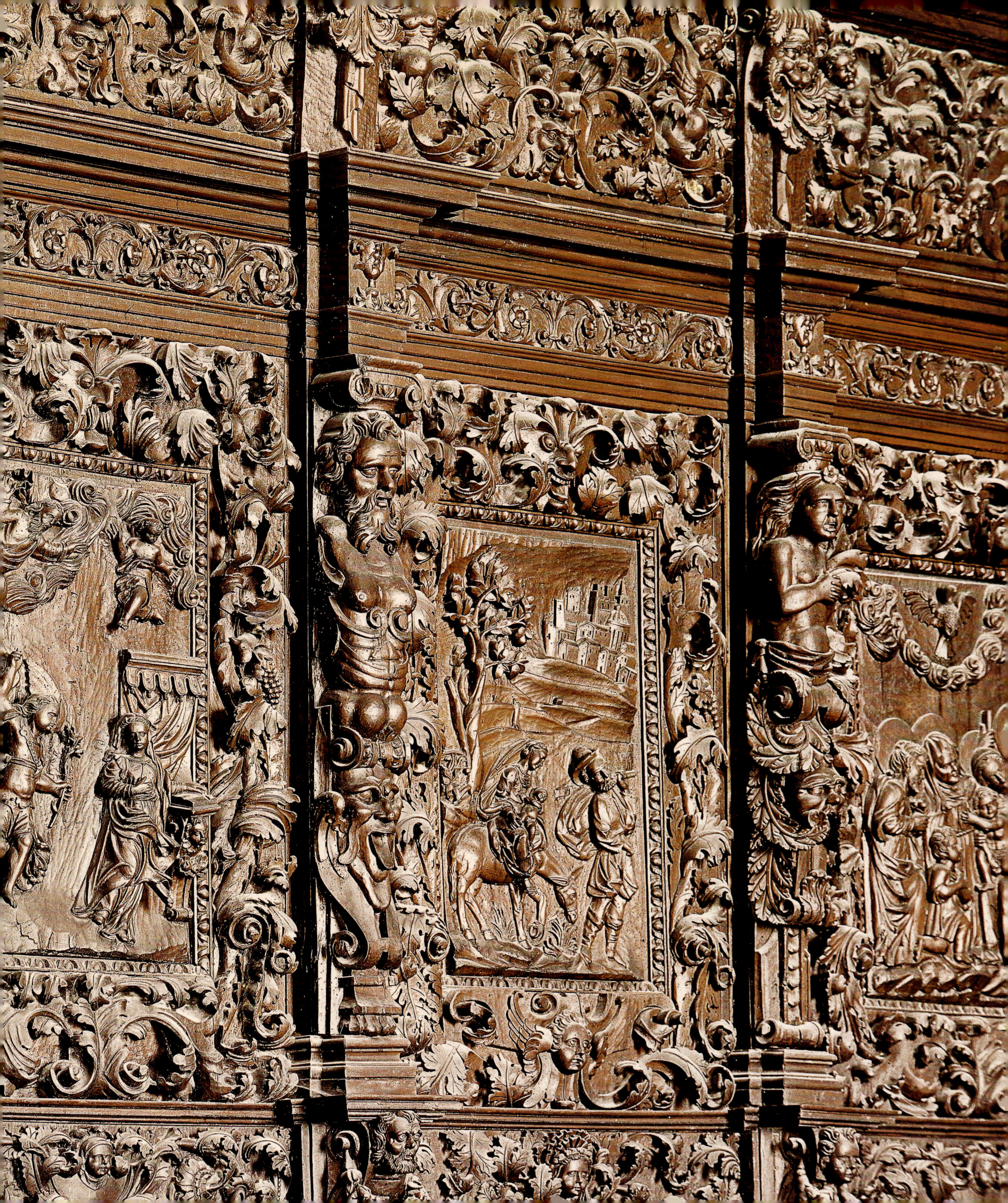

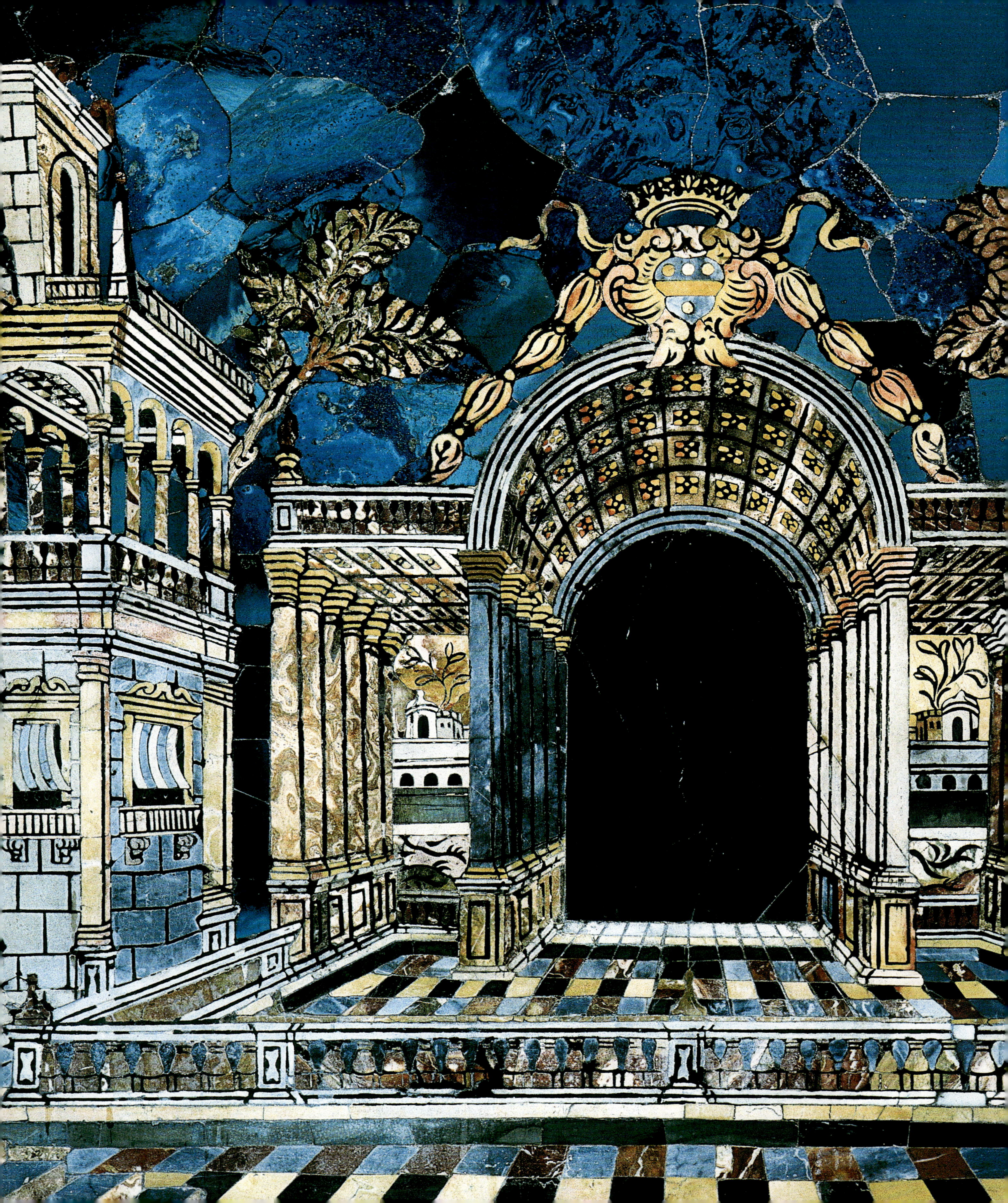

left Detail of the front of an altar in the church of the Gesù or Casa Professa, Palermo.

overleaf, left A coloured marble balustrade in the church of Santa Caterina, Palermo.

overleaf, right The prophet Jeremiah: detail of the decoration in two- and three-dimensional coloured stone of the Cappella del Crocifisso in Monreale Cathedral, commissioned by Archbishop Giovanni Roano and built between 1686 and 1700.

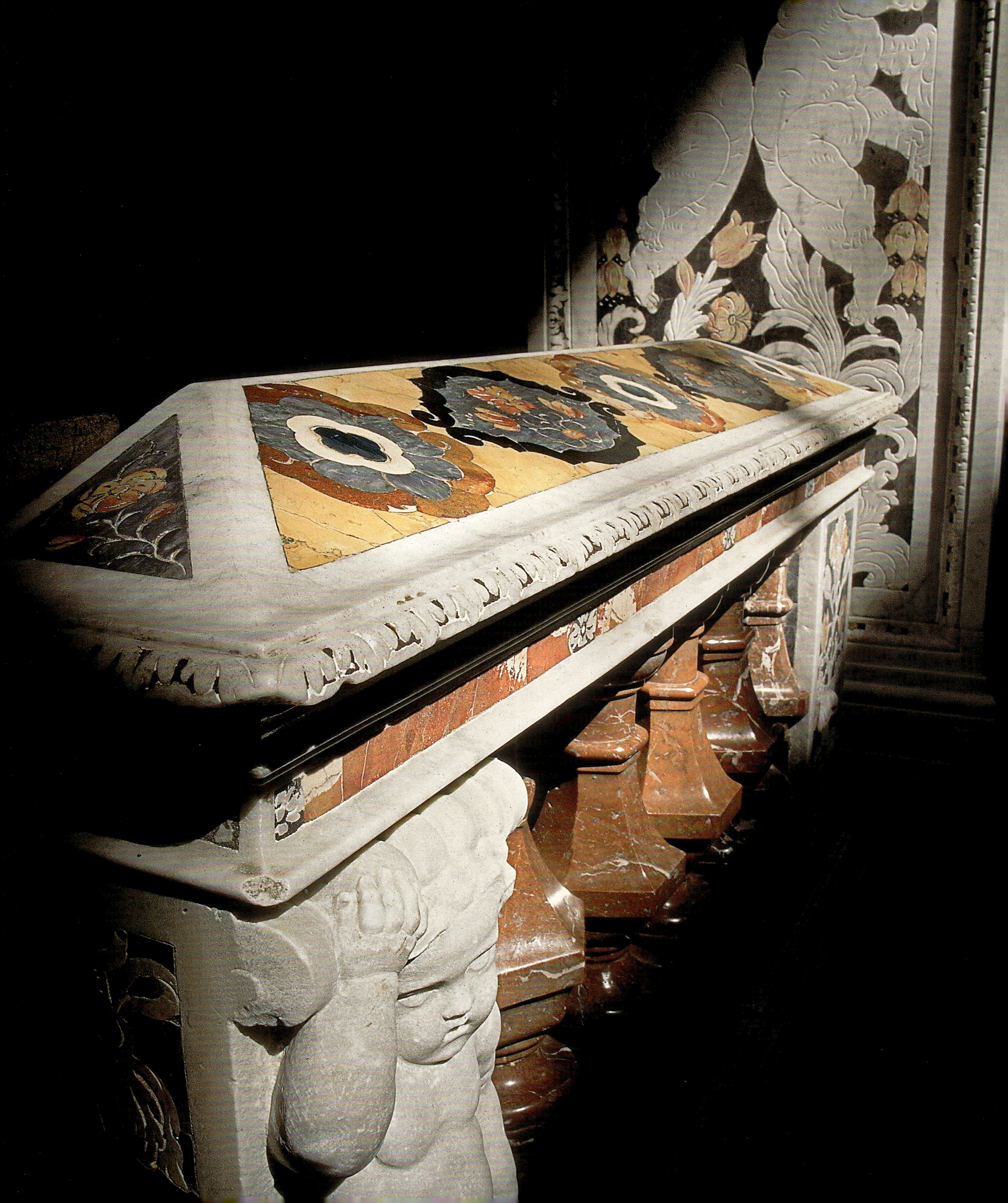

IEREMIAS

The marble floor of a room in the Palazzo Biscari, Catania.

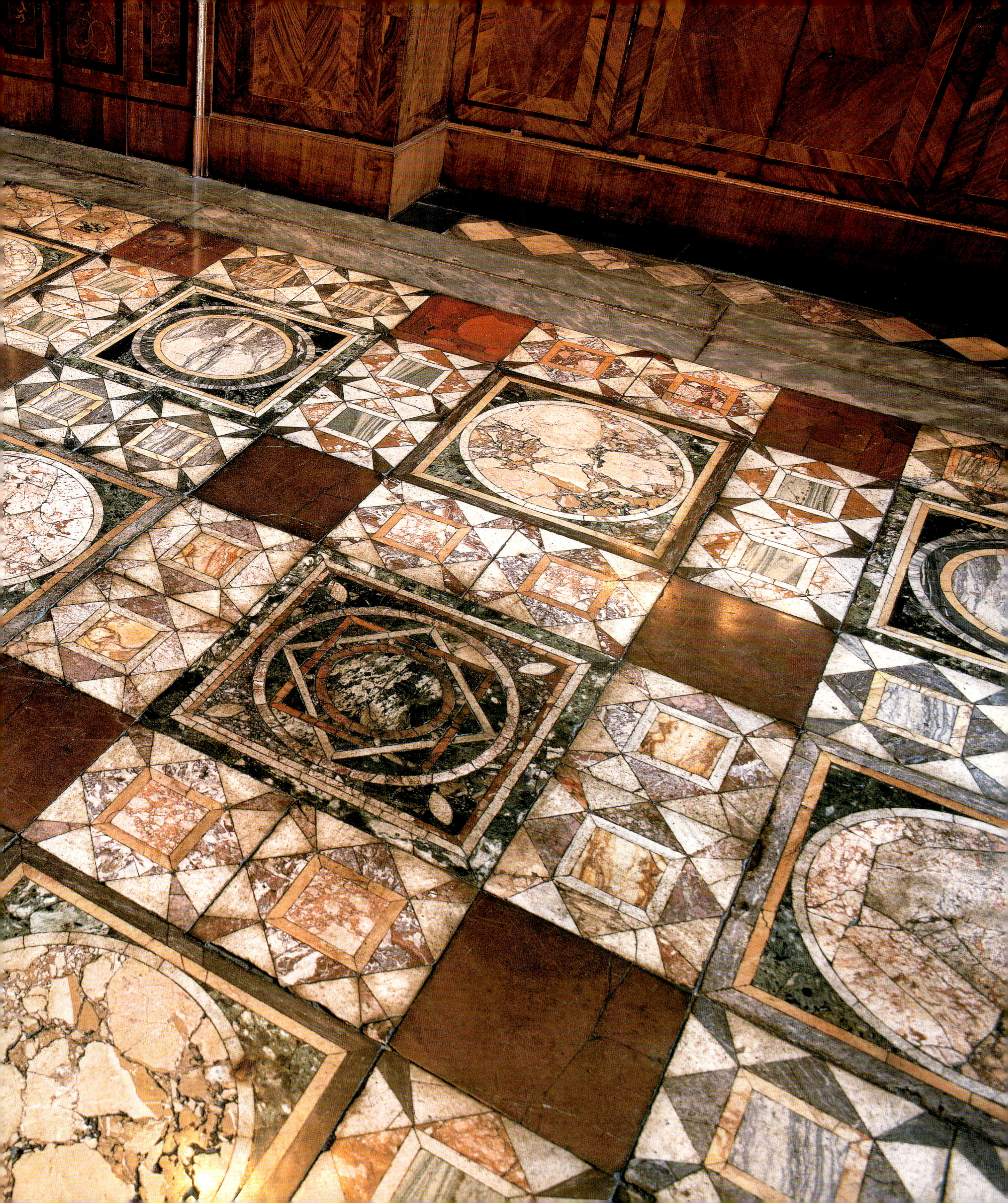

left Detail of the frescoed decoration of a room in the Palazzo Santa Croce, one of the finest Baroque residences in Palermo.

opposite detail of a fresco in the *salone* of the Villa Camastra-Tasca, Palermo.

overleaf, left Fresco on the end wall of the cloister of the Chiesa della Gancia, Palermo.

overleaf, right Detail of the Cappella del Santissimo Sacramento in Syracuse Cathedral, decorated with frescoes by Agostino Scilla, 1657.

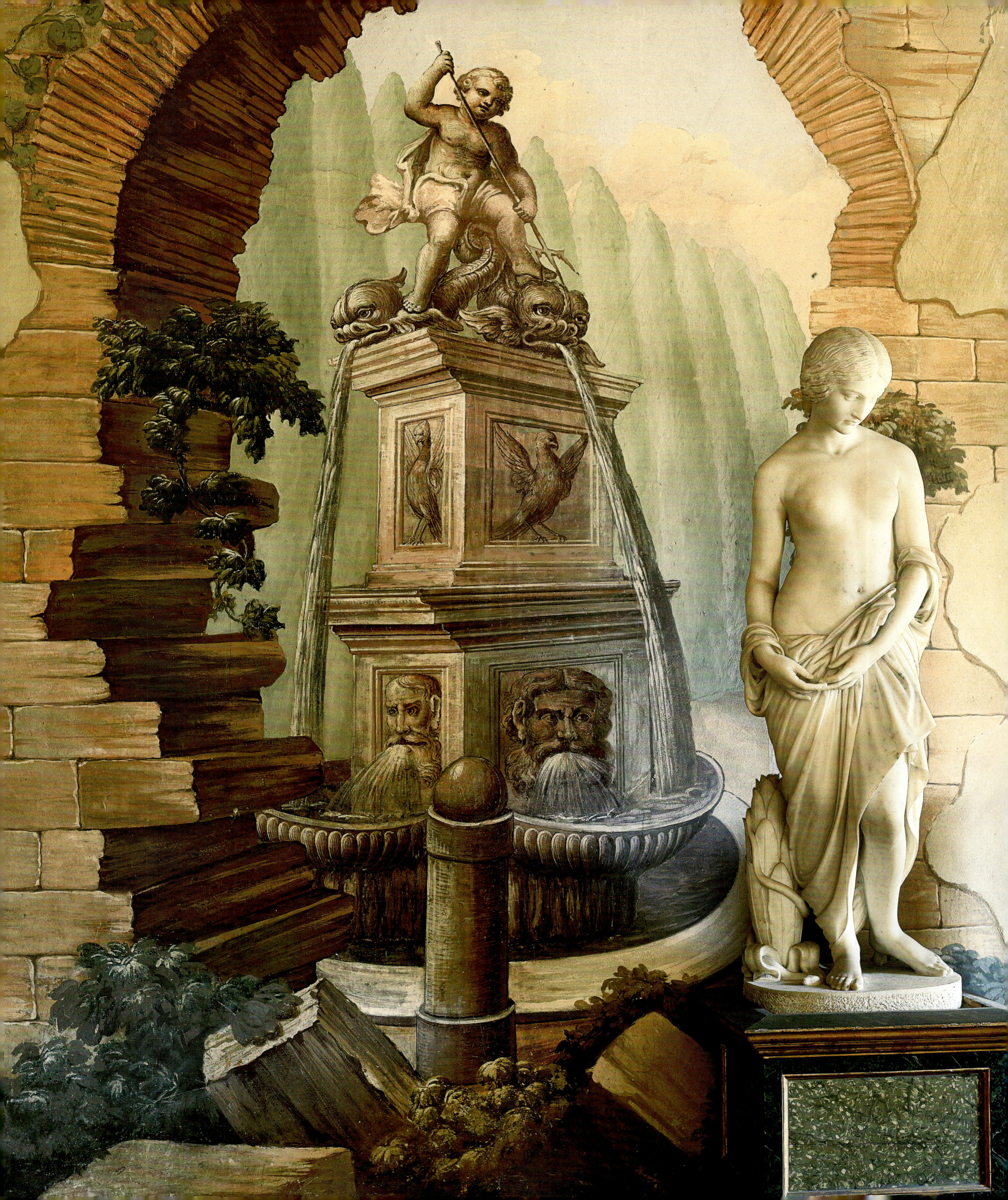

274 *Theory and practice: from the book to the building site*

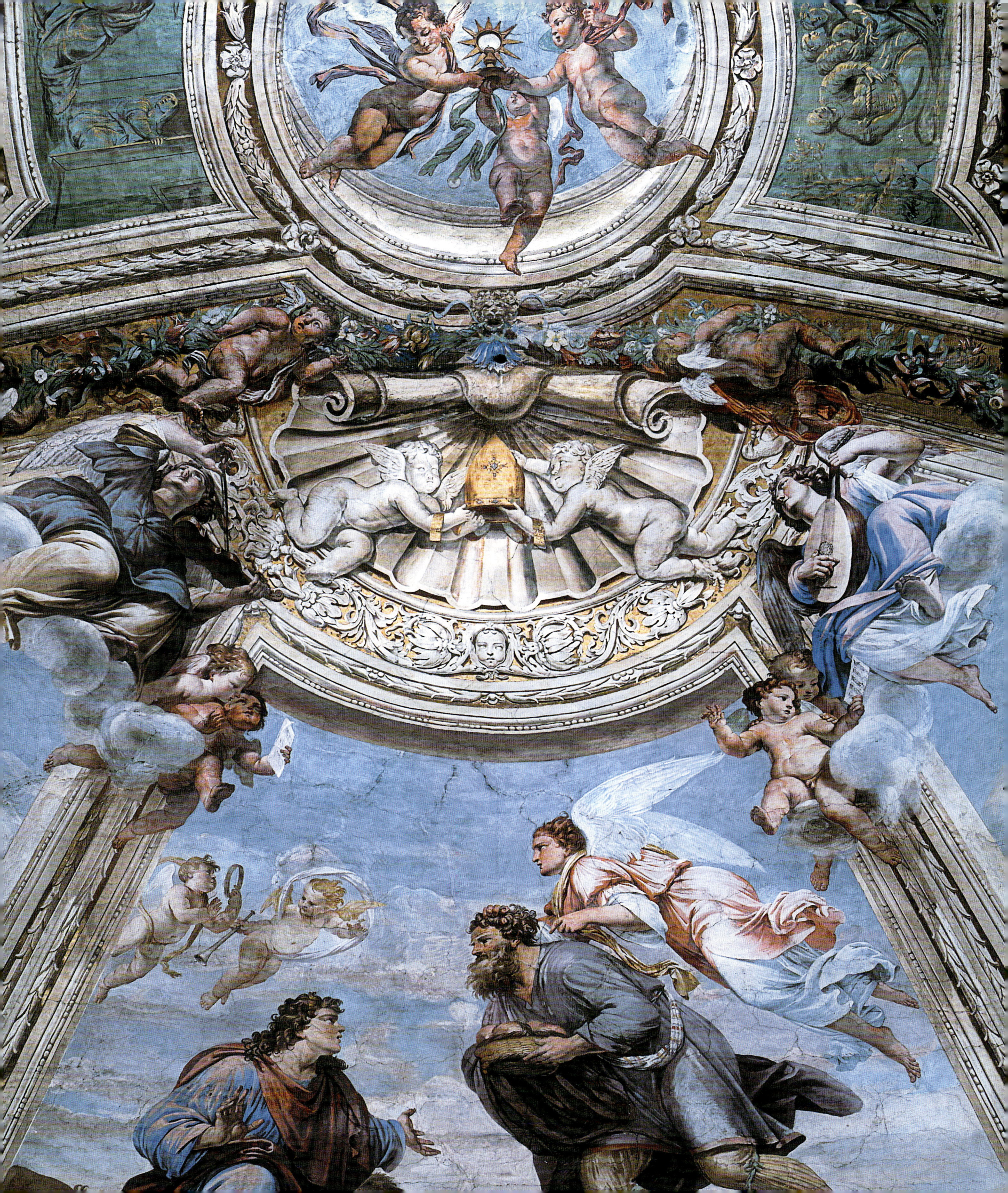

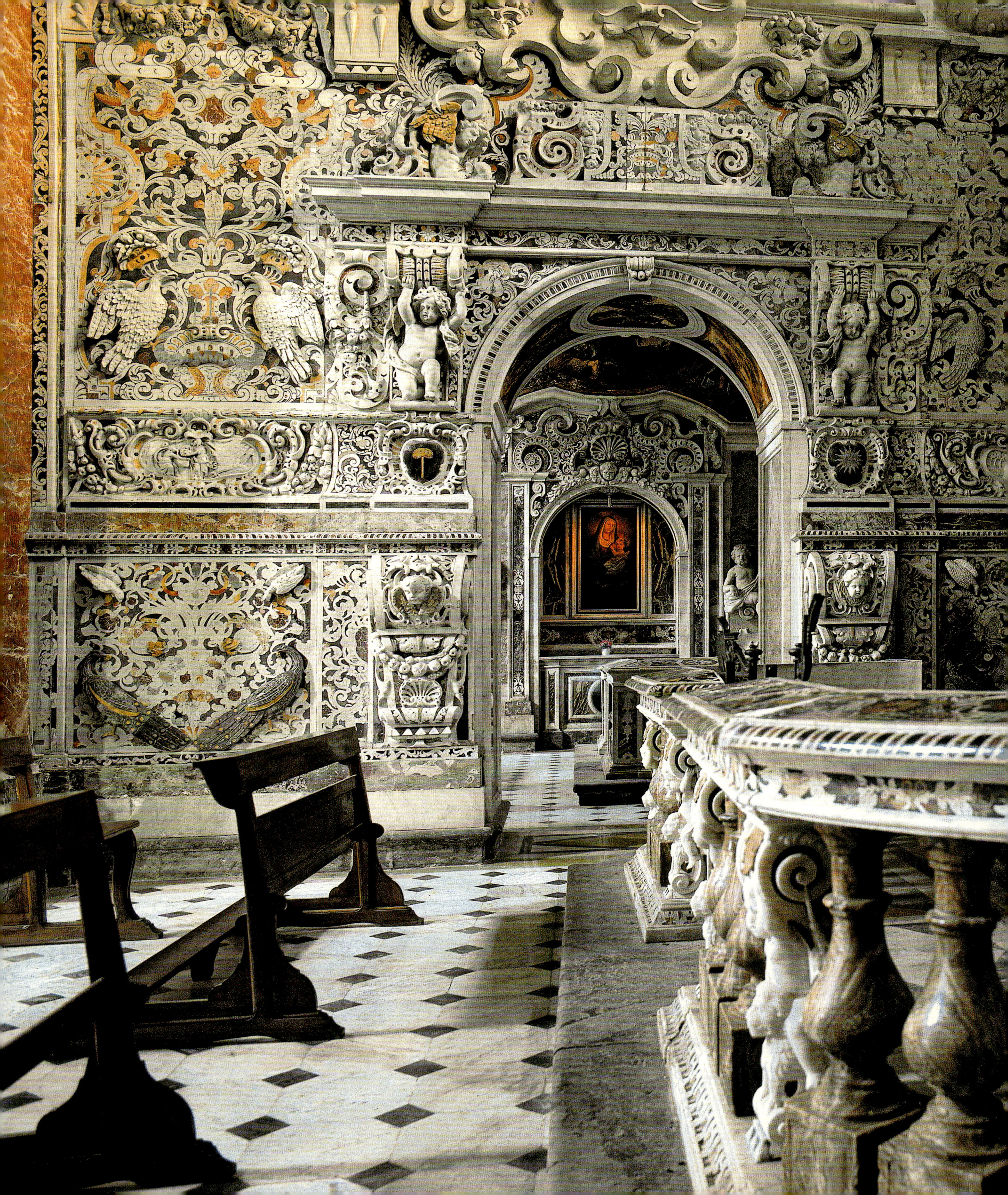

One history or many histories: the thousand faces of the Baroque

pages 276–77 The magnificent Baroque decoration, in two- and three-dimensional coloured stone inlay, in the church of the Gesù or Casa Professa in Palermo.

At the end of a journey such as this there is always a temptation to go back to the beginning and start all over again. What buildings have we forgotten? What other forms of decoration? What meanings have we ignored or glazed over? All histories of architecture must be to some extent provisional.

If it is true that every civilization has a thousand faces, perhaps Baroque was the most complex and original of them all. Can we in the 21st century really know how men and women in the 17th or 18th century experienced these works? To rely on imagination alone cannot be enough. Therefore, if this book stimulates curiosity and the desire to undertake further and more in-depth research; if some of the hypotheses put forward in its pages are elaborated upon, verified or even contradicted; if the 'virtual journey' becomes a real one, in which first-hand experience replaces imagination, then it will have succeeded in its aims.

Some immediate questions may arise: does Sicily count as 'Baroque' only because of the importance of the architecture in the south-east during the reconstruction phase after the earthquake in 1693? Can Palermo be classified as a Baroque city when it incorporates so many traces of ancient civilizations?

The 20th-century author Gesualdo Bufalino wrote, provocatively: 'With the cynicism of hindsight, one might almost bless the earthquake of 1693, for it acted as a catalyst for so much construction, ushering in such an admirable and creative period on the island.'

As a resident of Comiso, in the Iblei mountains, he could experience at first hand the remarkable results of the rebuilding. In a sense Bufalino accorded to the entire island the prestige earned by the Val di Noto: it went from being a place of cultural receptivity to being a place of cultural innovation, assisted by the involvement of many 17th-century protagonists, especially Rosario Gagliardi. Like a mirror reflecting the light and transmitting it in all directions, so it reflected and diffused new ideas. As another great Sicilian writer, Vincenzo Consolo, put it, it was a case of 'destruction turned into construction, ... chaos into logos, in short – which is always the path of history and civilization'.

One of the 'magical' destinations in the Val di Noto has always been Scicli, perhaps rendered such by the Syracusan writer Elio Vittorini's *Le città del mondo* (The Cities of the World), in which the shepherd Nardo and his son Rosario set off on a journey to the town, which they compare to the mythical Jerusalem: 'It's the most beautiful city we have ever seen ... perhaps it is the most beautiful city in the world.' It is like a mirage which they want to fix in their vision and in their minds before it disappears: 'It rises up at the junction of three deep valleys, its houses covering the surrounding slopes, with a large piazza at the bottom, on the old riverbed, and churches dotted over the hillsides, like a Baroque acropolis in the shape of an elevated semicircle.'

Palermo also gave and received, reinvented itself, and brought forth order out of chaos. In the security achieved by the victory of the

Battle of Lepanto (which later served as the inspiration for one of Giacomo Serpotta's scenes in the Oratorio del Rosario in Santa Zita) it constructed its own Baroque theatres: the Teatro del Sole or 'Theatre of the Sun', as the Quattro Canti was known, with its statues of Spanish kings and patron saints of the city; the grand streets which were festooned with decorations on festive occasions; the piazzas spread out around royal statues; the sumptuous interiors of churches, oratories and palaces, where decoration reigned supreme over all the arts; and the villas which appeared to welcome the outside world with long avenues and large staircases leading up to the *piano nobile*, yet were surrounded by high walls like fortresses. The term 'theatre' was also used in the titles of two of the 17th-century manuscripts written in the time of the Viceroy Benavides: the *Teatro delle Città Reali di Sicilia* and the *Teatro Geografico Antiguo y Moderno del Reyno de Sicilia*. These works (preserved in Madrid, with a copy of the first one in Palermo as well) – the first by an author whose identity is unknown and the second by the little-known Carlos Castilla – described the 'spectacle' of a rich and happy land through words and illustrations.

Neither the Val di Noto nor Palermo is representative of the whole island, however. Everywhere there was the desire to embrace international languages, which stimulated ideas, events and encounters, and cultural horizons widened to incorporate new aims. A *reductio ad unum* would therefore not reflect the complexity of all the different aspects of the Baroque found on the island, and any definition of a cultural identity must also encompass its 'otherness'. History is not just a heritage to be received and transmitted. It is in a constant state of evolution. Therefore there is no one history to be told about the Baroque in Sicily, but a thousand different stories.

Concise bibliography

The bibliography on the Baroque is enormous – almost all of it, naturally, in Italian – and it is impossible to include it all in these pages. What follows concentrates on sources drawn on in the text, on the more recent publications, on those providing new information, and on those putting forward new interpretations and pointing to new avenues of thought. It has been impossible to include every significant contribution, such as those in the *Annali del Barocco in Sicilia* published by the Centro Internazionale di Studi sul Barocco, based in Syracuse, which was founded by Marcello Fagiolo and is now directed by Lucia Triglia; or monographs on architects or individual buildings; or the academic theses presented at the University of Palermo, which have sometimes prompted, or substantiated, suggestions put forward in this book. The list is given in chronological order, in order to show the advances made in research into 17th- and 18th-century architecture in Sicily. For more detail, see the bibliographies in the third edition of Salvatore Boscarino's *Sicilia Barocca* (1997), and *Il Seicento* (2003) and *Il Settecento* (2000) in the 'Storia dell'architettura italiana' series published by Electa.

A. Blunt, *Sicilian Baroque*, London 1968

S. Boscarino, *Sicilia barocca. Architettura e città 1610-1760*, Rome 1981; new edn, rev. and with notes by M. R. Nobile, Rome 1997

S. Tobriner, *The Genesis of Noto. An Eighteenth-Century Sicilian City*, Berkeley and Los Angeles 1982

P. Nifosì, *Mastri e maestri nell'architettura iblea*, Ragusa 1985

V. Consolo and C. De Seta, *Sicilia teatro del mondo*, Turin 1990

F. Negro and C. M. Ventimiglia, *Atlante di città e fortezze del Regno di Sicilia, 1640*, ed. N. Aricò, Messina 1992

P. Nifosì and G. Morana, *La chiesa di S. Giorgio a Modica*, Modica 1993

I Lombardi e la Sicilia. Ricerche su architettura e arti minori tra il XVI e il XVIII secolo, ed. R. Bossaglia, Pavia 1995

E. H. Neil, *Architecture in Context: The Villas of Bagheria, Sicily*, PhD Dissertation, Fine Arts, Harvard University, Cambridge, Mass., supervised by Professor H. Burns and Professor J. Shearman, September 1995

M. Giuffrè, 'Architettura e decorazione negli oratori serpottiani', in *Giacomo Serpotta. Architettura e apparati decorativi settecenteschi a Palermo*, Palermo 1996

L'architettura del Settecento in Sicilia, ed. M. Giuffrè, Palermo 1997

Barocco e tardobarocco negli Iblei occidentali, ed. M. R. Nobile, Ragusa 1997

M. Giuffrè, E. H. Neil and M. R. Nobile, 'Dal viceregno al regno. La Sicilia', in *Storia dell'architettura italiana. Il Settecento*, ed. G. Curcio and E. Kieven, vol. I, Milan 2000, pp. 312–47

M. R. Nobile, *I volti della 'Sposa'. Le facciate delle Chiese Madri nella Sicilia del Settecento*, Palermo 2000

A. I. Lima, *Architettura e urbanistica della Compagnia di Gesù in Sicilia. Fonti e documenti inediti, secoli XVI-XVIII*, Palermo 2001

M. Giuffrè, 'La Sicilia', in *Storia dell'architettura italiana. Il Seicento*, ed. A. Scotti Tosini, Milan 2003, vol. II, pp. 560–73

M. R. Nobile, *Palermo 1703: ritratto di una città. Plano de la Ciudad de Palermo di D. Caetanus Lazzara Panormitanus*, Palermo 2003

Disegni di Architettura nella Diocesi di Siracusa (XVIII secolo), ed. M. R. Nobile, Palermo 2005

S. Piazza, *Architettura e nobiltà. I palazzi del Settecento a Palermo*, Palermo 2005

Index

Numbers in *italic* type indicate pages on which illustrations appear.

Abatellis family 13
Acireale: Chiesa Madre 57, *63*
Agrigento 13, 18, *18*, *19*, 25
Aidone: San Domenico 156
Aiutamicristo family 13
Alcamo
   Santi Cosma e Damiano 165, 173
   Sant'Oliva 165–66
Alessandria della Rocca 163
Alfano bridge, Canicattini Bagni *45*
Alì, Luciano 113, 167
Altavilla Milicia 26
Amato, Giacomo *102*, 103, *104*, 104–5, 106, 107–8, 109, 155, *158*, 159, 160, 161, 163, 226, 228, 234, 236, 237, 238, 239
Amato, Paolo 17, 103, 104, 107–8, 158, 162, 226, 234, 238, 239, *245*
Amico, Giacomo 224, 228
Amico, Giovanni 20, 99, 108–9, 110, 112, 113, 165–66, 225, 228, *235*
Anito, Nicolò 110
Aquila, Pietro 105
Aragona, Donna Francesca 157
Aragona: Palazzo Naselli 25, *126*
Attinelli, Salvatore 106
Augusta 20, 21, 22, 23
Aviler, Charles-Auguste d' 231
Avola 28, 29, 103
   Annunziata 29

Bagheria
   Villa Aragona 236
   Villa Butera *94–95*, 98, *105*, *122*, 156
   Villa Cutò 236
   Villa Larderia 109, 169

Villa Palagonia 108, *120–21*, *144*, 168–69, *168*, *225*, *261*
   Villa Valguarnera *107*, 108, *118–19*, 168, 169
Basile G. B. F. 60
Battaglia, Antonio 230
Battaglia, Francesco 21, 107, 111, 112, 160–61, 163, 170
Baumgartner, Johann Wolfgang 231, 232
Belmonte Mezzagno: Chiesa Madre 187
Belpasso 29
Benavides, Francisco de, Count of Santo Stefano 15, 22, 97
Bérain, Jean 231
Bernini, Gianlorenzo 21, 104, 236
Besio, Giacomo 100
Bibiena, Giuseppe Galli 231, 232
Blandino, Tommaso 19
Blasco, Michele 19, *126*
Blondel, Jean-François 231
Blunt, Anthony 8, 170
Bonifazio, Natale 17
Borromeo, Charles 159
Borromini, Francesco 14, 104, 108, 164, 165, 231, 236, 237
Bourbon family 96, 99, 161, 236, (Charles III) 97, 99, *104*, 234, 238, (Ferdinand IV) 100
Branciforte family 26, 28, 88, 155, 162, (Carlo Maria Carafa, Prince of Butera) 28, *29*
Buonamici, Francesco 101
Buscemi
   Chiesa Madre 163, *180*
   Sant'Antonio *147*, 164

Caccamo: San Giorgio *70*
Calamecca, Andrea 18, *114*
Calatafimi: Santa Caterina 166
Calatamauro: Santa Maria del Bosco 112
Caltagirone 22, 111
   Chiesa Madre 111, 160

   Palazzo Ventimiglia *150*
   San Francesco d'Assisi 110, *185*
   Santa Maria del Monte 22
Caltanissetta: Palazzo Moncada 155
Caltavuturo 24
Camastra, Giuseppe Lanza, Duke of, Viceroy of Sicily 13, 20, 26
Camiliani, Camillo 17, 156
Campanella, Tommaso 28
Canicattini Bagni: Alfano bridge *45*
Cannepa, Michelangelo 155
Capaci: Sant'Erasmo 26
Carlentini 23
Carnilivari, Matteo 13, 20, 230
Cascione Vaccarini, Giovan Battista 109, 164, 165, 168
Castelbuono: Palazzo Trimarchi 231
Castellammare 24, 25
Castello, Ignazio Paternò 111
Casteltermini 159; San Giuseppe 164
Castelvetrano: Fontana della Ninfa *89*
Castiglione di Sicilia: Chiesa Madre *62*
Catania 20, 161, *161*
   Badia di Sant'Agata 21, *56*, 164
   Badia di Sant'Anna 111, 165
   Benedictine monastery *215*
   Cathedral 90, 110–11, 164
   Collegiata 108, 164, 196
   Collegio dei Nobili 111
   Elephant Fountain 21, *90*, 111
   Palazzo Biscari 16, *138*, *167*, 170, *270–71*
   Palazzo Senatorio 21, 111
   Piazza del Duomo *21*, 111
   Porta Ferdinandea 20
   San Giuliano 164
   San Nicolò d'Arena *210–13*
   San Placido 164, *197*
   Via San Filippo (Garibaldi) 20
Cattolica Eraclea: Chiesa Madre

(Spirito Santo) 160, 230
Centuripe *10–11*
Cerda 159
Cesariano, Cesare 225
Charles III of Bourbon *97*, 99, *104*, 234, 238
Chiaramonte: Chiesa Madre 225
Chiaveri, Gaetano 231
Cirrincione, Andrea 234
Colonna, Marcantonio 17, 67
Comiso
   Santissima Annunziata *227*, *248*
   Santa Maria dell Stelle *227*, *228*
Comitini: Santa Caterina Villarmosa 160
Consolo, Vicenzo 105
Corso, Paolo 169
Cresti, Carlo 166
Crociferi Order and buildings 101, 103, 104,
   108, 112, 155, 157, 159, 160, 161, *165*,
   218–19, *231*, 232, 235, 236
Cultraro, Pietro and Constantino 113

Daidone, Agatino 112, 169, 225
D'Aprile, Carlo 100
Decker, Paulus 231
De Rossi, Domenico 229, 231
Di Bona, Geronimo 22
Dietterlin, Wenzel 231
Dresden 112, 231, 232, 234

Earthquakes (1693) *12*, 13, 20, 27, 113,
   (1726) 16, 106, (1751) 16, (1908) 67
Enna 22; Cathedral *264–65*
Erice: San Giuliano *64*
Etna, Mount *10–11*, 21, *33*
Eugene, Prince of Savoy 225

Falda, Giovan Battista 231
Fama, Giuseppe 228
Fanzago, Cosimo 101, 103

Ferdinand IV of Bourbon 100
Ferla
   Sant'Antonio 113, 164, 165, *176*, *260*
   San Sebastiano 162, *249*
Ferla, Michele da 28
Ferrigno, Francesco 233
Fichera, Francesco 169
Filocamo, Paolo 108
Fischer von Erlach, Johann Bernhard 108,
   170, 231
Floridia: Chiesa Madre 112, *189*
Frago, Giovanni del 109–10, 169
Fuga, Ferdinando 100, 106, 111, 112
Fumagalli, Gaspare *135*
Furetto, Orazio 111, 112, 235

Gaetani, Cesare *226*
Gagini family of sculptors 154
Gagliardi, Rosario 22, 28, 109, 110, *111*,
   111–12, 164, 169, *194*, *226*, *227*, *230*, *237*
Gallo, Agostino 106
Gangi: Palazzo Bongiorno *135*
Gela 23
Gibellina *13*
Gigante, Andrea 109, 110, 111, 168,
   229, 235
Goethe, Johann Wolfgang von 169
Grammichele 28
Grano, Antonio 105
Grunenbergh, Carlos de 15, 20, 22, *22*,
   67, 100, 160
Guarini, Guarino 14, 18, 22, 102, 103, 109,
   157, 158, 164, 165, 170
Guglielmelli, Arcangelo 103
Gugliotta, Antonino 164

Habermann, Franz Xaver 231
Hittorff, Jacob Ignaz 21, 155, 167
Herz, Jörg 231

Ibla 27
Infantolino, Carlo 169, 229, 234
Inveges, Agostino 15
Ispica 27
   Santa Maria Maggiore 74–75, 240
   Santissima Annunziata 237
Italia, Angelo 27, 28, 29, 101, 103–4, 109, 158,
   164, 165
Ittar, Stefano 20, 108, *196*, *197*

Jesuit Order 19, 27, 100, *154*
John of Austria, Don 14, *15*, *114*
Juan de Vega 23
Juvarra, Filippo 18, 98–99, 108, 169, 170,
   233, 236, 238

La Barbera, Vincenzo 100
Labisi, Bernardo Maria *236*
Labisi, Francesco Paolo 27, 112, *127*,
   165, 168, 170,
   229, *231*, 232
La Duca, Rosario 107
Lampedusa, Giuseppe Tomasi,
   Prince of 168, 206
Lanza, Giuseppe, Duke of Camastra 13, 20, 26
Lanza, Ottavio 25
La Placa, Pietro 99, 104, 238
Lasso, Giulio 100
Lazzara, Gaetano 108, 112, *155*, 161, 234
Leanti, Arcangiolo 15, 16, 18, *22*, *23*, *98*, *100*,
   109, *113*, *154*, *156*, *160*, 169
Leonforte 26, 27
   Chiesa Madre *253*
   Granfonte *88*
Leopard, The 168, 206
Le Pautre, Jean 231
Licata: Sant'Angelo 165
Lipari *30–31*; Madonna delle Grazie *65*
Lombardo, Ferdinando 112, 166, 229

Macolino, Giovanni 155, 157
Maffei, Nicolò Francesco 100
Magni, Scipione 230
Majocchi, Orazio 17
Maqueda, Viceroy of Sicily 16, 18
Mariani, Giuseppe 17, 108, 112, 165, 235, 236, 245
Marsala 19
   Addolorata 51
   Purgatorio *178*
Martinez, Giovanni 227
Marvuglia, Giuseppe Venanzio 104–5, *106*, 107, 109, *113*
Marvuglia, Simone 108
Masuccio, Natale 19, 100, 156, 236
Matteis, Paolo de *16*
Mazara del Vallo
   Cathedral *50*, *61*, *251*
   Jesuit church and college 103, *146–47*, 162
   Santa Caterina *207*, *257*
   San Francesco *202–3*
   San Michele 19, *205*
   Santa Veneranda 19
   Seminario dei Chierici 19, *82–83*
Mazzarino: Cristo del Olmo *59*
Meissonier, Juste Aurèle 231
Melilli 27: San Sebastiano *78*
Merelli, Gabriele *224*
Messina 170–71
   Neptune Fountain *93*
   Orion Fountain *92*
   Padri Stomaschi 102
   Palazzata 14, *15*, 18
   Porta Grazia *68*, *69*
   Quattro Cantoni *91*
   Royal Palace 170
   Santissima Annunziata 22, 102, 111, *158*, 164

Messina, *cont.*
   San Gregorio 108
   statue of Don John of Austria *114*
   Strada Austria 18
Messina, Straits of *15*, *170*
Milazzo: Chiesa Madre 102
Militello: Benedictine monastery 162
Mistretta: Chiesa Madre *151*; Palazzo Scaduto 156
Modica 140
   San Giorgio *36*, 112, 164, *232*, *233*
   San Pietro *37*, *258*
   Jesuit church 164
Montigore 107
Monreale 17, 103
   Collegio *200*
   Cathedral 171–72, *217*, *269*
   Gesù *255*
Montano, Giovan Battista 228–29, 231
Montorsoli, Giovanni Angelo 18, *92*
Muttone, Antonio 112–13, *113*

Naples 171; Santa Maria Egiziaca 103
Napoli, Tomaso Maria 108, 168, 225, 234, 236
Naro
   San Francesco *148*, 162
   Sant'Agostino *177*
Naso
   Santissimo Salvatore 162
   San Cono *172*
Negro, Francesco *25*, *26*, 100, 156
Neufforge, Jean-François de 231
Nicosia
   Palazzo La Motta *149*
   Santa Maria Maggiore *181*, *250*
Nigrone, Orazio 90
Niscemi 29; Addolorata 164
Noto 27, *28*, 103, *233*

   Carmine 164, *190*
   Cathedral *179*
   College of the Cruciferi 112, *231*
   Palazzo Ducezio *42–43*
   Palazzo Nicolaci *232*
   Palazzo Senatorio 112, 170
   San Camillo *165*
   San Carlo 164, *191*
   Santa Chiara *230*, *236*, *237*
   San Domenico 164, *192–93*, *252*
   Santa Maria di Montevergine 27, *42*, 112, *137*, 164
   Santissimo Salvatore 164, *164*, *208–9*
   Villa Eleonora 112, *127*, 169, *169*
Noto, Val di 13, 16, 20, *161*, and *passim*

Occhiolà 28. *See also* Grammichele

Pacheco, Juan Francisco, Duke of Uzeda 13
Paglia, Giuseppe 234
Palazzolo Acreide 162
   Annunziata 103, *243*
   Palazzo Judica *166*
   San Paolo *116–17*, *188*
   San Sebastiano *241*
Palermo *14*, 16, 17, 23, 98, 99, *100*, *101*, 164, *224*, *226*, *232*
   Albergo dei Poveri 109, 111, *169*, 170
   Carmine *46*, 103–4, 165, 171, 173, *245*
   Casa Professa *see* Gesù
   Cassaro (Via Toledo) 16, 17, 18, 156, 159, 238
   Cathedral 97, 100, (Cappella di Santa Rosalia) 171
   Chiesa della Granica *274*
   Concezione al Capo 171, *198–99*, *242*
   Garraffo Fountain 106
   Gesù (Casa Professa) *54–55*, 100, 156, *157*, 171, *201*, *204*, *218–19*, *266–67*, *276–77*

Palermo, *cont.*
  Hospital of San Bartolomeo *80–81*
  Immacolata al Capo 171
  Kalsa 16, *104*, 159, *160*
  Law Courts *see* 'Steri'
  Neptune Fountain 18
  Oratorio del Rosario, San Domenico 173, 222–23
  Oratorio del Rosario, Santa Zita *104*, 105, *152–53*, 173, *262–63*
  Oratorio di San Lorenzo, San Francesco 105–6, 173
  Palazzo Bologni 168
  Palazzo Bonagia 109, 168
  Palazzo Butera (Branciforte) 29, *104*, 106, Palazzo *128–29*, 159, 161, *167*
  Palazzo Cattolica *155*, 235
  Palazzo Chiaramonte *see* 'Steri'
  Palazzo Comitini (Gravina) 167
  Palazzo Cutò 109, *130*, 167
  Palazzo Filangeri Gravina 100, 168
  Palazzo Gangi (also Valguarnera and Gravina) 109, *132*, 168
  Palazzo Lardera 168
  Palazzo Mazzarino *134*
  Palazzo Mirto *87*
  Palazzo Raccujo 155
  Palazzo Santa Croce 110, 167, 272
  Palazzo Sant'Elia *133*, *139*
  Palazzo del Senato *109*
  Palazzo Valguarnera-Gangi 109, *132*, 168
  Piazza Imperiale 108
  Piazza Marina 18
  Piazza Pretoria 17, 18, *84–85*, 96
  Porta Felice 16, *66*, *67*, *156*, *160*
  Porta Nuova *145*
  Quattro Canti (Teatro del Sole) 17, 18, *72–73*, *98–100*, 156
  Royal Palace *97*, 99, 102, 156

Palermo, *cont.*
  Sant'Anna 109, 164
  San Carlo dei Lombardi 101, 157
  Santa Caterina 156, 171, *216*, *256*, 268
  San Domenico 76; Oratorio del Rosario 173, 222–23
  San Francesco: Oratorio di San Lorenzo 105, 173
  San Francesco Saverio 28, *47–49*, *101*, 103, 158
  San Giuliano 104
  San Giuseppe dei Teatini 17, *53*, 100, 102, 156, 254
  Sant'Ignazio 233
  Santa Lucia del Borgo 102, 103, 157
  Santa Maria della Pietà 105, *159*
  Santa Maria di Valverde 171
  San Martino delle Scale 16, 112, *113*
  San Matteo 156, 157, 164
  San Mattia dei Preti 101, 157, 159, 160, 220–21
  Santa Ninfa dei Crociferi 155, 157
  Santi Pietri e Paolo 159
  Santa Rosalia 106
  Santissimo Salvatore 10, 104, 107, 158, 171
  Santa Teresa 105, *158*, 159
  Santa Zita: Oratorio del Rosario *104*, 105, *152–53*, 173, *262–63*
  statue of Philip IV, then Philip V *98*, *115*
  'Steri' 13, 18, 102, 106
  Strada Nuova/Via Maqueda 16, 17, 18, *100*, 109, 110, 156, 157, 160, 168
  Stradone Colonna *16*, 17, 99, *160*, 238, 239
  Teatro del Sole see Quattro Canti
  Via Maqueda/Strada Nuova 16, 17, 18, *100*, 109, 110, 156, 157, 160, 168
  Via Toledo *see* Cassaro
  Villa Camastra-Tasca *273*
  Villa de Cordova *131*

Palermo, *cont.*
  Villa Trabia-Campofiorito *86*, *173*
Palma, Andrea 22, 106, 108, 110, 155, 238, 239
Palma, Nicolò 108, 110, 238, 239
Palma di Montechiaro 103
  Chiesa Madre 163, *174–75*
  Santissimo Rosario *206*
Partanna, Villa 169
Paruta, Giacomo 26
Passarini, FilippoBibiena
Petralia Soprana and Sottana 22
  Santa Maria di Loreto 22, 164
  Santissimo Salvatore 22
Philip IV, monument to *98*, *115*
Philip V, statue of *115*
Piazza Armerina 32
  Cathedral 101, 162
  Chiesa Madre 71
  Sant'Anna 164, *195*
Piedmont/Savoy ruling family 18, 96, 98, 161, 170, 238
Pignatelli family 28
Polizzi Generosa: Collegio 103, 158
Portocarrero, Gioacchino Fernandez, Viceroy of Sicily 99
Porto Pisano 402
Pozzo, Andrea 231
Priolo: Villa Gargallo 169–70

Quagliata, Giovanni 100

Radi, Bernardino 231
Ragusa/Ragusa Ibla 34–35, 40–41
  Chiesa Madre 160
  Madonna dell'Itria *40*, *58*, 232
  Palazzo Cosentini *141*
  Palazzo Lupio 232
  San Giacomo 232

San Giorgio (Cathedral) 109, *111*, 112, 163, 164, *194*
San Giovanni Battista 225
San Giuseppe *259*
Randazzo: San Martino *184*
Randazzo, Francesca 163
Regalbuto *33*; Chiesa Madre (San Basilio) 112, 163, *166*
Ricchino, Francesco Maria 101
Rocca, Angelo 22
Rosso, Valerio 23

Saint-Non, Abbé de *161*
Salaparuta: Chiesa Madre 164
Salemi: Jesuit church 162, *244*
Salmon, Thomas 16, *23*, 96, *108*, *169*, *170*
San Cataldo: Chiesa Madre 159–60
Sanchez, Diego 101–2
San Marco d'Alunzio
　Sant'Antonio 162
　San Marco *186*
　Santissimo Salvatore *182*
San Martino delle Scale *16*, 112, *113*
Santa Flavia
　Villa Filangeri *124–25*
　Villa San Marco *123*
Santo Stefano, Francisco de Benavides, Count of 15, 22, 97
Santo Stefano de Camastra 26, 28
Savoy/Piedmont ruling family 18, 96, 98, 161, 170, 238
Scamozzi, Vincenzo 113, 225, 227, 228
Schinkel, Karl Friedrich 168
Schmettau, Samuel von *28*
Sciacca 19
Scicli *38*, *165*, 279
　Palazzo Beneventano *142*, 166
　San Bartolomeo *39*, *60*

San Giovanni 164
Santa Maria Nuova 228
San Michele 237
Scilla, Agostino *275*
Serenario, Gaspare 105
Serlio, Sebastiano 224, 225, 231
Serpotta, Giacomo 103, *104*, 105, 106, *152–53*, *222–24*, *262–63*
Serpotta, Giuseppe 103, *104*
Sicily: maps of *12*, *13*, *239*
Sinatra, Vincenzo 112, 165, 170
Smiriglio, Mariano 26, 100
Sortino 27
　Natività 164
　San Giovanni Battista 77
Spagnolo 101
Spannocchi, Tiburzio 17, *20*, 22, 23, 156
Syracuse 20, *22*, *23*, *162*
　Cathedral 22, *23*, *25*, 110, 163, *246*, *275*
　Palazzo Beneventano del Bosco 113, *136*, 166–67
　Palazzo Borgia 166, *168*
　Palazzo Impellizzeri *143*
　Palazzo Municipale 113
　Palazzo del Senato *157*
　San Matteo 22

Termini Imerese
　Annunziata *62*
　bridge *44–45*, 112
Tirrito, Fedele 106
Toledo, Viceroy of Sicily 16, 18
Tomasi, Giuseppe, Prince of Lampedusa 168, 206
Torriani, Orazio 101
Trabia 25, *26*
Trapani *19*, *108*, 110
　Jesuit complex *154*, (Santissima Annunziata) 109, *154*, 162, 166, *214*, 233, 235

Palazzo Senatorio *156*
Purgatorio 109, 164
Rua Grande 19
San Lorenzo (Cathedral) 19, 109, 164, 165
Trecastagni: Chiesa Madre 79

Uzeda, Juan Francisco Pacheca, Duke of, Viceroy of Sicily 13

Vaccarini, Giovan Battista 21, 91, 107, *109*, 110, *111*, 161, 163, 164, 168, 227, 231, 235, 236
Val di Noto 13, 16, 20, *161*, and *passim*
Valguarnera Ragali 26
Vanvitelli, Luigi 111
Vasi, Giuseppe 16
Velasco, Giuseppe 99
Vella, Antonio 29
Venanzio, Giuseppe 107
Ventimiglia, Carlo Maria 25, *26*, 156
Ventura, Simone 232
Vermexio, Giovanni 113
Victor Amadeus, King of Savoy 18, 98, 108, 170, 238
Vignola, Jacopo Barozzi da 225–28 *passim*, 231, 233
Villalpando, Juan Bautista 228
Vitale, Pietro 238
Vitaliano, Gioacchino *204*
Vitruvius 224, 225, 228
Vittone, Bernardo 103
Vittoria: Madonna delle Grazie 164
Vizzini: San Giovanni Battista *183*
Vredeman de Vries, Hans 231

Zanth, Ludwig 21

INFELICIS REGNI SICILIAE TABULA

in tres Valles divisa
DEMONAE, NOTAE
et MAZARAE
ex officina
DAVIDIS FUNCKE
Norunbergae

Notarum explicatio
- Urbes Munitæ celebriores.
- Urbes non munitæ.
- Oppida.
- Loca terræ motu destructa.
- Loca solo æquata, vel in abyssum præcipitata.
- Archi Episcopales sedes.
- Episcopales sedes.
- Abbatiæ.
- Arces sive Castella.

MARE SIC[ULUM]
VAL DEMONE
VAL DE MAZAR[A]
INFERUM
MEDITER[RANEUM]
AFRICI

Ustica

C. di Gallo · Golfo di Palermo · C. Bongerbino
Mondello · Monte Pelegrino · Solanto · Rumusso
Liposelli · Porto di Gallo · Carini · Ayello · Cefala · S. Nicolai
Calapo... · Murus Carinis · PALERMO Panormo · Monreale · Fabia
Palimita · Bartahin · Torco Abba · Marineus · Caccabus
C. Rama · Elymi vestigia · Carinis · Rosalaimis · Cimina
S. Casaldi · Specula · Grecorum Oppidum · C. Musulomeni · Cattam
Golfo di · Mucilla ho · Tayearum · Calatubus · Palynur
C. Ama · Segesta · Arcani · Scala Curie · Calatabisam
C. S. Vito · Scopu · emper... · C. Eyala
S.to · C. Cofunu · C. Amar... · Coriliome
Cap. Boro olim Lily · Barbara · Bayda · Tatum · Bicari
bao Promontor.in · Segesta · Buyhuto fons · Calatafimi · Strictum · Tori · Castro novo
Li Porcelli · TRAPANO · Trapani del Monte · forici · Petra Longa · Prizzi
L. Asinelli · Nuntiata · Berbhumet · Castromur · Bahiri flu · Thermini flu · Camarata
Leuenza I. · Bon siuiglie · Acilinus flu · Salem · Rabigenis fons · Calatrasi · S. Petro
Maretamo I. · Formico · Savara fons · Ramu · Entella · Busachi · Clusa · Palatium · Tlusia · Adragnum · S. Stef.
I. S.Theodoli · Marsella · Asrala · xara · Calattamar · S. Maria · Semi nium · Comi chi an · Sambu · Biuona · ano
Sauagnana I. · Danasia · Salem · Portano Sala · Donne · Mil tusio · Guter...
Rapi calidus fons · Norri bilbiana · Syr... · Moyharta · Disindini · Aiflindini · Villa franca · Burgio
C. Bern ... · C. Foeta · C. Yetera · MAZARA · C. Granifoli · di tre fonti · Xacca fimus · Mishica · Calatabellotta · Heracl ea · Plathen · Sec Juliani
Mathnus · Pulica · de li · Calatabellotta · Maghasolo · Gergen...

Pantalarea olim Cosyr I.